PERSONNEL MANAGEMENT IN IRELAND
PRACTICE, TRENDS AND DEVELOPMENTS

GW00356941

Personnel Management in Ireland

PRACTICE, TRENDS AND DEVELOPMENTS

Patrick Gunnigle
& Patrick Flood

GILL AND MACMILLAN

Published in Ireland by
Gill and Macmillan Ltd
Goldenbridge
Dublin 8
with associated companies throughout the world
© Patrick Gunnigle and Patrick Flood, 1990
0 7171 1608 5
Print origination by
Seton Music Graphics Ltd, Bantry, Co. Cork
Printed by ColourBooks Ltd, Dublin

A catalogue record is available for this book from the
British Library.

7 8

Contents

List of Figures and Tables

TABLES

To the memory of my late father; to my mother and to my wife, Theresa, for her understanding and support

P.G.

To my wife, Patricia, and to my parents, Catherine and Bartholomew Flood

P.F.

Acknowledgments

This book represents the final product of extensive research, investigation and discussion over the past three years. The views and experiences of many individuals, including those of anonymous referees, have been incorporated into the text.

In particular, we would like to record our thanks to Professor Aidan Kelly, University College, Dublin, for his initial encouragement; Donal Dineen, Head of the Department of Business Studies, University of Limerick, for his advice and support, and Hubert Mahony of Gill and Macmillan for editorial guidance.

Colleagues at the University of Limerick provided valuable comments and direction. In particular, we wish to express our appreciation to Gisela Shivanath, Tom Garavan and Joe Wallace.

Various organisations provided data and assistance. In particular, we would like to thank Teresa Brannick and Dr Bill Roche, University College, Dublin; Dr Bill Toner, National College of Industrial Relations; John Storey, University of Warwick; Dr David Guest, London School of Economics; Gerard McMahon and Brian McGillion, College of Commerce, Rathmines; Joe McLaughlin, Department of Labour and Michael McDonnell and Margaret Cutlow, Institute of Personnel Management.

Introduction

AIMS AND OBJECTIVES

Personnel management in Ireland has traditionally been taught using British and, to a lesser extent, American literature. Such literature is indeed comprehensive and provides a useful basis for analysing this complex subject area. However, its relevance becomes questionable when dealing with the distinctive characteristics of the Irish organisational context.

This book reflects an attempt to remedy this by providing a comprehensive review of personnel management in Ireland. The basic aims of this text are as follows:

1. To provide a broad overview of the nature, role and activities of personnel management in Ireland.

2. To examine the major activity areas of personnel management and review current literature in the context of personnel practice in Ireland.

3. To evaluate critically contemporary trends and developments in the field of personnel and human resource management.

This text is designed for use by students taking personnel management as either a specialist or auxiliary subject at third level. It should be particularly suitable for students studying courses leading to membership of the Institute of Personnel Management (IPM) and those taking undergraduate or professional programmes where personnel management and/or employee relations is a component subject. The text should also appeal to personnel practitioners, managers and trade unionists with an interest in current developments in personnel and human resource management.

The book draws extensively on Irish literature and research as well as on the practical experience of the authors. Examples from Irish organisations are used throughout the text. Wherever possible, the authors have tried to apply conceptual material to its practical setting and critically evaluate policy options available to those involved in the management of people at work.

CONTENTS

The basic principles and operational context of personnel management in Ireland are reviewed in chapters one and two. Chapter one examines the nature and role of personnel management both as an integral element of the management task and as a specialist management function. Some differing perspectives on, and approaches to, personnel management are considered. The chapter concludes with a review of recent research findings on personnel management in Ireland. Chapter two provides an overview of key phases in the historical development of personnel management in Ireland.

Chapter three provides a general overview of manpower planning and discusses the flow of manpower into, through and out of the organisation. It considers key factors affecting manpower flow such as the state of the labour market, absenteeism levels and corporate approaches to manpower planning.

Chapters four to eight deal with the main activity areas in personnel management, with each area considered in terms of its contribution to organisational goals. The link between organisational context, business goals, strategic decision-making and personnel activities is constantly stressed. The main activity areas examined are:

recruitment and selection;
employee motivation and job design;
reward management;
employee development;
performance appraisal.

Chapters nine and ten cover the key area of employee relations. Chapter nine considers the national employee relations framework; reviewing the role of the three main participants (trade unions, employer organisations and the State). It also considers management approaches and strategies in employee relations. Chapter ten considers some significant employee relations activities: collective bargaining and negotiations; industrial conflict; grievance and dispute handling; discipline administration; and employee participation.

The final two chapters examine contemporary trends and developments affecting personnel management. Chapter eleven considers developments in the international and Irish business environment in terms of their impact on personnel management practice here. These include the incidence of different employment forms, adoption of new technology, 'total' quality initiatives and the 'new' industrial relations. In the final chapter the debate on Human Resource Management (HRM) is explored. Various interpretations of HRM are presented. HRM is compared with more traditional models of personnel management and differences highlighted. The case for a distinctive view of HRM is presented, using case study material from Ireland and abroad. The impact of HRM on industrial relations is considered, together with an evaluation of personnel practices pursued by non-union organisations.

Irish material and sources have been used wherever possible. These are fully referenced in the text and summarised in the bibliography. This should greatly help students or practitioners wishing to pursue further the topics discussed in the text .

CONCEPTUAL FRAMEWORK

Two major themes run throughout this text: individual needs and organisational requirements for human resources. It is the firm belief of the authors that organisational effectiveness is directly influenced by the willingness of employees to contribute towards the achievement of organisational goals. Personnel policies and procedures directly affect the willingness of employees to contribute to these objectives.

There is inevitable tension inherent in the organisation-employee relationship, and personnel policies and procedures—in conjunction with the task environment within which employees operate—either heighten or diffuse this tension. It is accepted that it is extremely difficult to create a complete 'mutuality of interest' between organisation and employee. However, the authors would argue that the extent to which 'mutuality of interest' is reinforced by personnel policies and procedures is a critical element in eliciting high performance levels from employees. The extent to which the organisation focuses on individual needs and attempts to create a congruent match with organisational manpower requirements is a major factor in this process.

Contrary to the views of some commentators, the authors believe the work ethic is alive and well amongst employees and that the majority of employees at all occupational levels potentially hold work as a central life interest. However, it is also suggested that the extent to which work and organisational life is experienced as coercive and punitive affects the degree to which employees continue to hold work as a central life interest and identify with (and contribute towards) organisational goals.

The management of human behaviour within organisational systems is a complex task. It requires vision and breadth of perspective on the role which human resource utilisation has to play in all functional areas and throughout the organisation. The authors would contend that the practice of personnel management should be devolved to the lowest possible level of management within the organisation. This does not imply that the role of the personnel specialist is to be eliminated or that the personnel department is no longer necessary. Rather it is suggested that the resulting role is altered and enhanced due to the fact that wider shared accountability for management of employees must in the long run raise the importance of the personnel considerations in the minds of middle and top management.

At all stages the text considers the influence of labour market pressures on the practice of personnel management within organisations. Recognising that many of these practices are shaped by labour market forces, including the free association of organised labour, the book traces the origins of personnel management as we know it. It looks at its early welfare base and concludes by examining the current state in its life cycle in relation to Human Resource Management (HRM) approaches. The text also charts the development of the modern non-union system of industrial relations and traces its origins to comparative practices, particularly those in the United States where HRM-type approaches are prevalent.

The application of organisational psychology integrates much of the material discussed, particularly in relation to performance management, reward systems and career development. However, the institutional context has been stressed throughout the text in order that readers may appreciate the constraints and realities facing those who devise and practise personnel management.

For reasons of convenience and conciseness, masculine pronouns have been used in the majority of instances.

Chapter 1

Nature and Role of Personnel Management

INTRODUCTION

An organisation's workforce represents one of its most potent and valuable resources. Consequently, the extent to which employees are managed effectively becomes a critical factor in increasing organisational efficiency. It is widely accepted that organisations which do not possess coherent personnel policies and procedures are under-utilising the capacities of their workforce.

Personnel management is primarily concerned with the manpower element of the management process. It incorporates those aspects of the management task which involve managing employees and embraces the respective roles of corporate management, line managers and the specialist personnel function.

At corporate level personnel management involves senior management establishing the organisation's personnel management philosophy and policies. Corporate management refers to the highest decision-making authority in the organisation. This could be the owner or manager of a small joinery firm or the corporate board of directors in a multi-establishment conglomerate.

At operational level personnel management involves line managers dealing with day-to-day interactions with employees and handling most aspects of workplace personnel management. Line management incorporates all managers and supervisors responsible for running operational departments or sections in an organisation.

Personnel management also incorporates the work of the specialist personnel function embodied in the formal personnel department. The specialist personnel function is closely involved in the development of the organisation's personnel strategy and policies. It also undertakes specialist personnel tasks and acts as a source of expert advice and guidance for other functional areas.

Personnel management practice may vary depending upon the organisational and business context within which it is operated. Variables such as organisation size and structure, industrial sector, product market, technology, corporate values, etc. will influence the nature of personnel management practice within organisations. This personnel management role may be exercised exclusively through line management, a specialist personnel department or some combination of both.

This chapter outlines some varying perspectives on the role of personnel management, identifies its primary objectives and addresses some important issues affecting contemporary personnel management practice.

THE PERSONNEL MANAGEMENT ROLE

In a text such as this, one would reasonably expect an answer to the question 'What is personnel management?'. However, a quick scan of the personnel literature will yield little in the way of consensus on what personnel management is exactly about. Rather, a number of key themes emerge which permeate personnel management practice. Fowler highlights a number of these themes in defining personnel management as:

> that part of management as a whole which is concerned with people at work, with the relationship between man and job, man and man (individually and collectively) and between employer and employee institutions. As with all management, the object of personnel management must be the promotion of effectiveness of the organisation—but with the belief that this effectiveness is directly related to the physical and psychological wellbeing of employees.[1]

A central aspect of personnel management is its fundamental concern with *managing employees*. The personnel role is seen as inherent in the management process and not merely as the work of specialists.

All managers have important personnel management responsibilities. Selecting, deploying, developing and motivating employees are central components of the line management task. Where no specialist personnel department exists such work will be carried out exclusively by line management. Even where there is a specialist personnel function, line management will remain very much involved in day-to-day personnel activities (such as motivation, appraisal, training, employee relations), receiving assistance and advice from the personnel department as appropriate. In some aspects of personnel work, the personnel department will play a more executive role, taking responsibility for certain activities, such as trade union negotiations or recruitment.

Personnel management is also concerned with contributing to *organisational effectiveness*. It is based on firm business principles, operating on the premise that good workforce management should result in improved organisational performance. An important aspect of the 'organisational effectiveness' argument is the *link between organisational and employee needs*. This concept suggests that attention to workforce concerns will have long-term organisational benefits in terms of improved performance.

These themes are clearly evident in the Institute of Personnel Management's jubilee statement on the role of personnel management:

> Personnel management is the job of all those who manage people as well as being a description of the work of those who are employed as specialists. It is that part of management which is concerned with people at work and with the relationships within an enterprise. It applies not only to industry and commerce, but to all fields of employment.
>
> Personnel management aims to achieve both efficiency and justice, neither of which can be pursued successfully without the other. It seeks to bring together and develop into an effective organisation men and women who make up an enterprise, enabling each to make his own best contribution to its success, both as an individual and as a member of the working group. It seeks to provide fair terms and conditions of employ-ment and satisfying work for those employed.[2]

Again there is the suggestion that personnel management is the resposibility of all managers. While this is clearly true it raises the issue of *line/staff responsibilities* in executing the personnel role. If personnel management is the responsibility of all managers, how are those responsibilities to be divided up between line managers and personnel practitioners, and what role should the personnel practitioner play—advisory or executive? There are differing views on whether personnel management should be exercised only through line management or be more restricted to the province of the personnel specialist. The *line management approach* sees personnel management as an inherent part of the general management process. All managers have a responsibility for managing their resources effectively. Their personnel management role should be to utilise effectively their human resources for the achievement of the organisation's objectives, while at the same time ensuring that employees are treated fairly and rewarded adequately.

The departmental approach suggests that personnel management consists of a series of activities undertaken by personnel practitioners within a formalised personnel department. Such activities would typically include recruitment and selection, training and development, performance appraisal, employee relations, compensation and health and safety.

In practice the personnel management role in most larger organisations will be exercised through a combination of line management and a specialist personnel function. Much personnel work is necessarily the responsiblility of line management. They manage most day-to-day interactions with employees and have a key role in motivating and communicating with employees. Line managers may be supported in these tasks by the personnel function. It is the personnel practitioner's job to create an operational framework within which line management can successfully carry out such responsibilities.

Another aspect of the IPM statement is the issue of *organisational justice*. Thomason suggests that some personnel practitioners do not see personnel work as solely a means of achieving organisational goals.[3] For example, Miller feels that personnel's role is ' . . . different from other staff jobs in that it has to serve not only the employer, but also in the interests of employees as individual human beings, and by extension, the interests of society'.[4]

This alternative approach rejects the business perspective and sees personnel's role as inherently different from that of other managers. It suggests a type of 'middle-man' role for the personnel practitioner which is reminiscent of the paternalist approach of the industrial revolution, where welfare officers were employed to cater for employee needs, particularly in areas like health, safety and welfare.

It also raises another important issue affecting personnel practice— reconciling the desire to achieve justice and fairness in the treatment of employees with the need to contribute effectively to organisational success.

An important aspect of the personnel practitioner's role is the creation of an organisation's structure and environment where employees can contribute positively to corporate goals. These goals will be facilitated by correct strategic choices in areas like employee selection, development, promotion, communications and rewards. It involves attempts to achieve a congruence of employee and organisational needs. This entails creating a working environment whereby employees can simultaneously satisfy individual needs for satisfaction or involvement and organisational needs for productivity and commitment.

However, one cannot always assume that the needs of individual employees and the objectives of the organisation are mutually compatible.[5] For most organisations the achievement of primary business goals, as measured on criteria such as market share, cost effectiveness or profitability, will be the over-riding objective. At workplace level this may sometimes be achieved through the extensive division of labour, tight manning levels and a strong productivity ethic. Such an approach, which stresses managerial objectives and controls, may not necessarily be in the interests of employees or promote organisational justice. Where the objective of contributing to organisational effectiveness comes into conflict with that of ensuring fair and just treatment of employees, the personnel practitioner will be expected to evaluate various alternatives and choose the option which is in the best long-term interests of the organisation. In Thomason's terms the personnel practitioner will adopt a 'managerial' rather than a 'personnel' perspective.[6]

A final aspect of the IPM statement is the view that personnel management is not just confined to the commercial sector but is relevant in *all types of organisation*. The phenomenal growth in personnel management in the post-war era has resulted both from its growing significance in the industrial sector and its extension into areas which traditionally did not have formalised personnel departments, such as education and health services, hotels, etc. Again it is important to distinguish between the functional and departmental approach. The extension of personnel management mentioned by the IPM refers to the establishment of specialised personnel departments. Undoubtedly, personnel activities were carried out in various forms in many organisations prior to the establishment of a personnel department. Nevertheless, the expansion of personnel into non-traditional areas has been an important characteristic of the growth of personnel management.

PERSONNEL MANAGEMENT PHILOSOPHY, STRATEGY AND POLICIES

We have seen that personnel management embodies those elements of managerial work which involve managing people and may also be a responsibility of a separate department which undertakes certain specialist personnel tasks.

All managers are concerned with employee-related issues and involved in personnel management activities. Unlike personnel practitioners, however, line managers may not see personnel management as their primary interest. They will be mostly involved in their own functional role (such as production) and may only be concerned with personnel issues when they exert a constraint upon the achievement of production targets.

Personnel practitioners, on the other hand, will see their primary responsibility area as personnel management. While there are variations between organisations, the primary role of the specialist personnel department is to develop the organisation's personnel strategy and approach in line with overall business goals, devise appropriate personnel policies and procedures and carry out selected personnel activities.

Table 1.1. Personnel management strategy, policy and activities

Strategic level	Operational level	Action level (Personnel activities)
* Formulate corporate personnel philosoophy * Formulate personnel strategies	* Devise personnel policies & procedures on: Employment Organisation & job design Employee development Remuneration Performance management Employee participation Employee relations	*Recruitment *Selection *Induction *Training *Appraisal *Consultation *Collective bargaining *Health/safety *Welfare *Compensation

An organisation's *personnel management strategy* refers to its basic philosophy and long-term objectives in managing human resources. It involves establishing the organisation's beliefs and values about how employees should be managed. It forms the basis for the subsequent development of personnel policies in specific areas such as compensation and industrial relations. The responsibility for developing a personnel strategy rests with top management and senior personnel specialists. An organisation's beliefs and values concerning personnel management may often be expressed as general statements of corporate philosophy (see box 1.1).

Box 1.1. Sample statements of corporate personnel philosophy

'People will seek the most efficient and effective way to do their work when encouraged to do so and when recognised for their achievements.'
'Our management climate emphasises a concern for each person as an individual and places a high value on individual judgment and on commitment to achieving mutually agreed goals.'

(Large electronics firm)

'To develop an effective workforce who are committed to high standards of service and who, reciprocally, have progressive working conditions, opportunities for personal development and equitable rewards.'

(Semi-state organisation)

Every organisation possesses a corporate philosophy in relation to how it views its employees. However, this may not always be written down as in the above examples. It may simply be inferred from how employees are treated and rewarded within the organisation. In such situations the organisation's personnel philosophy is implicit rather than explicit in nature and may often reflect a lack of strategic awareness on the part of the organisation.

Statements expressing corporate beliefs and values will be ineffective if they are not implemented in the workplace, particularly at line management level. To bridge the gap between espoused beliefs and workplace practice, organisations develop *personnel policies*. These are designed to express corporate purpose and guide managers and employees in dealing with personnel management issues. Personnel policies may cover a range of personnel issues such as recruitment, employee development, employee participation and job design (see box 1.2).

Box 1.2. Sample personnel policies

Remuneration:
'Our remuneration policy is to provide terms and conditions of employment which are competitive with the top quartile of comparable firms in our industry.'
Participation:
'We require that managers at all levels consult with their employees on all matters that affect them.'

(Large engineering firm)

Employee development:
'The organisation is committed to equal opportunity for employment and advancement for all employees. Prerequisites for promotion and progress are positive and enthusiastic attitudes towards oneself, one's fellow-employees and the organisation's business goals. While committed to a policy of promotion from within, the company must select the most capable candidate for each job.'

(Large electronics firm)

Within general policy guidelines individual managers will be responsible for carrying out various *personnel activities*. They may be supported in this role through more *explicit personnel procedures* dealing with the workplace implementation of personnel policies (see box 1.3). These may cover a range of day-to-day personnel issues such as promotions, grievance handling, appraisal and communications. The personnel department may then provide support and direction through advice, guidance and administrative assistance.

Box 1.3. Sample personnel procedures

Job posting procedure:
'The purpose of the job posting procedure is to maintain the policy of offering to each employee the fullest opportunity to achieve advancement and career development.
Each vacancy will be posted on the notice board for a minimum of two weeks. Employees must notify the personnel department of their interest. The Company reserves the right to advertise the vacancy externally as deemed appropriate. In all cases the most suitable and best qualified candidate will be selected.'

(Large electronics firm)

Probationary period:
'The probationary period for a new employee shall be 6 months. Employees will be given all necessary training and assistance to satisfactorily carry out their duties. Employee performance will be continuously monitored in this period and feedback given to each employee. Employees experiencing problems with any aspect of their work are encouraged to raise this with their supervisor who will take appropriate action.
Employees deemed not to have performed to the required standards will be discharged at the end of the probationary period.
Management may alternatively extend the probationary period for a further three months. The company's decision on such matters shall be conclusive and no formal use of the grievance procedure may be made in such cases.'

(Large retail organisation)

Personnel management goals, strategy and associated activities should be developed to aid the achievement of the organisation's business objectives. They will be developed within the context of the organisation's business plan so that factors in the wider business environment will influence the nature of organisational personnel practice (see figure 1.1).

While it is difficult to generalise on personnel goals and strategies beyond a specific organisational context it is useful to consider common areas where senior management and personnel practitioners will be keen to establish corporate goals and policies. Armstrong suggests four such areas:[7]

a) *Organisation design:*   Designing an effective organisation structure which will effectively respond to change;

b) *Manpower procurement and utilisation*   Obtaining, developing, motivating and effectively deploying the organisation's manpower;

c) *Employee relations:*   Ensuring a co-operative working climate exists within the organisation;

d) *Legal/social responsibilities:* Meeting the organisation's legal and social responsibilities.

Fig. 1.1. The context of personnel management

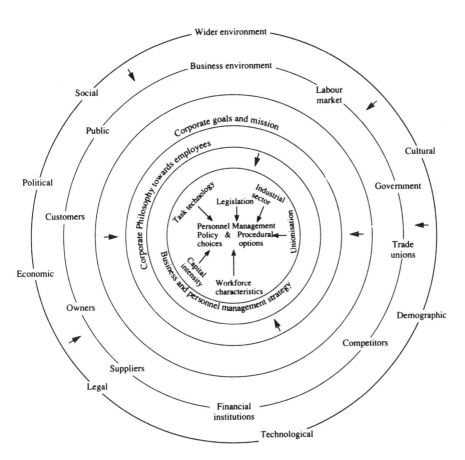

Arrows denote direction of influence upon personnel management

These objectives are general in nature but serve to give direction and purpose to personnel management at organisation level. A clear set of objectives helps to select which personnel activities should receive priority. They provide a rationale for undertaking specific activities by relating them to personnel objectives and overall corporate purpose. This avoids situations where personnel activities are undertaken without any clear evidence of their contribution to business goals. To ensure the support of both top and line management the relationship between personnel activities and business objectives must be strong and clear. Where, for example, an organisation is designing a payment system this activity should be clearly linked to a business goal like increased productivity, improved employee commitment or skill upgrading (see figure 1.2). Activities perceived as management 'fads', placing an undue administrative burden on line management, are unlikely to gain such support.

Fig. 1.2. Link between personnel activities, personnel objectives and corporate goals – payment systems as an example

Corporate goal: ⟶	*Personnel objective:* ⟶	*Personnel activity:*
Increased effectiveness through productivity; ⟵ improved employee relations	Improved morale & motivation; ⟵ reduced employee grievances	Effective payment system design ⟵

PERSONNEL MANAGEMENT ACTIVITIES

The variety of personnel activities which may be undertaken by organisations is extensive. Many are basic activities common to all types of organisation, such as recruitment. Others may be appropriate in certain organisational contexts (for example, collective bargaining in unionised firms), while still others are optional in character and their use related to managerial perspectives on personnel management (such as an emphasis on personal career development).

A useful way of reviewing both the extent and varying nature of personnel management activities is to examine how personnel practice is affected by a factor such as organisation size.

Personnel Management in Different Sizes of Organisation

The Small Firm: in smaller organisations the responsibility for all personnel matters will be in the hands of line management. Such organisations, for financial and structural reasons, would not normally employ a personnel specialist. However, good personnel management remains vital, since performance and profitability can be increased by better utilisation of the organisation's human resources. For many small firms, payroll is the largest ongoing cost [8] Poor selection, inadequate training or deteriorating employee relations can have a proportionately more serious effect in smaller organisations than in their larger counterparts.

While personnel management is equally important for small firms, the process is made potentially simpler due to the ease of communications, personal relations and the small scale of operations. Personnel management in smaller organisations will be concerned with basic personnel activities essential to the effective running of the organisation. A typical structure for such an organisation is outlined in figure 1.3.

Fig. 1.3 Personnel management in the small firm

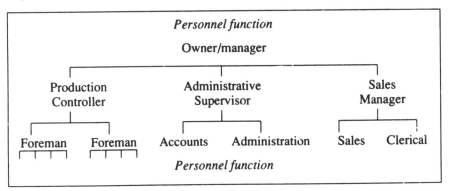

For such organisations, key personnel activities will include:

Organisation and manpower planning: establishing the objectives of the organisation and identifying its manpower needs;

Recruitment and selection: obtaining a sufficient supply of staff of the right quality to perform the work of the organisation;

Training and development: developing skills and competence among both employees and the organisation at large;

Compensation: establishing a viable remuneration system which will attract, maintain and motivate employees;

Employee relations: creating a co-operative climate of management-employee relations whereby any grievances, disputes or other issues are handled in a fair, consistent and equitable manner;

Health, safety and welfare: taking steps to ensure the health, safety and welfare of employees at work and creating an environment conducive to employee satisfaction and wellbeing.

Larger Organisations: increases in organisation size will, among other factors, impact upon the nature and role of personnel management. Complexity in the scale of workforce management, administration and employee relations often leads to the establishment of a specialist personnel department. Various policies and procedures need to be developed to deal with selected personnel activities. However, the basic purpose and objectives of personnel management remain the same.

Most larger Irish organisations have a specialist personnel department which coordinates personnel activities and carries out much of the administrative work.[9] Such specialist departments may be comprised of one or two individuals with general responsibility for personnel matters. Alternatively, the degree of task specialisation within personnel may be more pronounced, with personnel practitioners operating in specific areas of personnel management as in figure 1.4.

Fig. 1.4. Structure of personnel department (large healthcare firm)

Increases in organisation size and complexity will affect the nature and role of personnel management. Greater task specialisation allows for devolution of certain personnel activities to the specialist personnel function. However, the role of top management in deciding upon the corporate personnel approach and of line management in executing personnel tasks remains of paramount importance.

Although increases in organisation size may lead to some diversity in the personnel activities undertaken, the basic personnel activities identified as central to effective management in smaller organisations remain dominant. Changes will, however, occur in their complexity and mode of execution.

Personnel management activities should be guided by corporate policy and overall personnel strategy and objectives. These should in turn contribute to the organisation's primary business goals. Thus, the link between corporate objectives, personnel objectives and personnel activities must be firmly established. Many personnel activities require extensive research and administrative support. Such back-up research and administration will generally be provided by the specialist personnel function to help line and senior management make informed personnel management decisions. Computerised personnel record systems, where they exist, facilitate rapid information retrieval and analysis—a critical component in effectively supporting management decision-making.

Fig. 1.5. Corporate objectives, personnel objectives and personnel activities

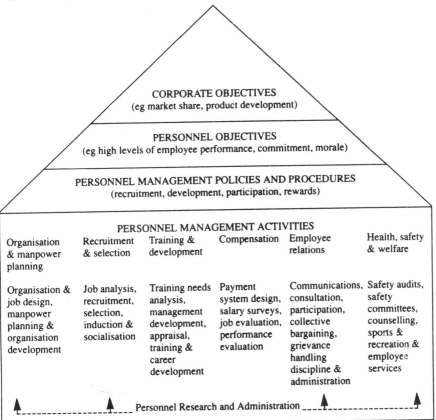

THE SPECIALIST PERSONNEL MANAGEMENT FUNCTION

The specialist personnel department essentially operates in an advisory or staff capacity. Its role is to support line and top management and provide them with a range of advice and services. The specialist personnel function may also have certain control responsibilities, such as ensuring corporate policy on promotions is adhered to.

Line management are responsible for the main operational aspects of the organisation such as production, maintenance and quality. In carrying out these various operational tasks, line managers will obviously be concerned with personnel issues. The specialist personnel department assists line management by developing personnel strategies and policies, providing expert guidance on personnel issues and undertaking certain research and administrative tasks.

A characteristic of the staff role is that decision-making on personnel matters is shared with other managers. Such joint decision-making takes place with both top management and with line management in other functional areas. It encompasses strategic planning, policy formulation and the executing of various personnel activities.

Senior personnel practitioners are well placed to influence and devise an organisation's personnel management strategy. Operating in a strategic 'architect' mode, senior personnel practitioners can influence the future direction of the organisation by anticipating trends and advising on strategic choice. They can then develop personnel strategies, policies and procedures which complement strategic purpose.

At the policy-making level personnel practitioners help to devise personnel policies and procedures which reflect the organisation's corporate approach to workforce management and provide guidelines on how this may be achieved.

In relation to personnel activities, the personnel department may act in a consultancy role, helping line management with particular problematic issues such as absenteeism or turnover and overseeing the consistent application of personnel policy. It may also exert executive authority in the implementation of certain personnel policies and procedures. For example, a personnel manager can require line managers to administer warnings in line with the agreed disciplinary procedure. Personnel practitioners may act as policy guardians with the power to approve or veto certain actions such as promotion or selection decisions. They may also have considerable authority in specialist personnel matters such as in agreeing contracts of employment or conducting negotiations with trade unions.

Armstrong identifies the main role of the specialist personnel department as providing:[10]

a) Advice: on personnel policy; dealing with top management on strategic personnel issues (e.g. approach to unionisation); on procedures and systems; liaison with senior and middle management in developing policy and procedures in areas such as recruitment, training and promotion;

b) Services: carrying out specified tasks or projects for both top and line management, e.g. salary surveys, reference checking;

c) Guidance: helping line management to interpret and apply personnel policy (e.g. approving promotions, discipline administration).

As most personnel tasks are executed in co-operation with other managers, persuasion and influence are important aspects of the personnel practitioner's role. Since many personnel practitioners report directly to the chief executive they are in a key position to influence corporate decision-making and strategic direction. It is therefore important that the specialist personnel function possesses the competence and expertise to help top and line management in their various roles.

The need to share decision-making has occasionally been perceived as a source of difficulty for the personnel department due to the fact that its staff role may restrict its influence to one of advice and assistance.[11] These potential problems can be overcome through the establishment of top management support for the specialist personnel role and by the personnel function possessing expertise in personnel affairs. Senior management must be seen to support the role and activities of the personnel department. Of course, the personnel department must ensure it warrants such management support. It must possess expert knowledge and ability on human resource issues. Its role must go beyond administrative support and 'fire-fighting' to a more strategic outlook which integrates personnel considerations into corporate decision-making, and it must develop effective personnel policies which contribute to organisational success.

To carry out effectively their organisational role, personnel practitioners should possess specialist expertise in areas such as selection, employee development, compensation systems and employee relations. As well as servicing line management in these specialist areas, personnel practitioners must also have a broad business knowledge which enables them to contribute effectively to strategic decision-making. They must assess the personnel management implications of strategic business decisions in areas like product development and technological change. They need to be aware of the interests of the various organisational stakeholders including customers, employees, trade unions, government and the community at large, in addition to shareholders, and establish mechanisms to accommodate and balance these various interests. The key role for senior personnel specialists is to establish the organisation's personnel strategy in line with its overall business strategy and to develop a network of personnel policies, procedures and activities to facilitate the achievement of business goals.

VARIATIONS IN THE ROLE OF THE
SPECIALIST PERSONNEL FUNCTION

The role of the specialist personnel function may vary between organisations. Such variations may occur due to differing management philosophies and perceptions of the 'ideal' role for the personnel department. Factors in the business environment such as competitive position or technology will also influence the organisational role of the specialist personnel function.

The role of the personnel function will also be influenced by factors relating to individual personnel practitioners such as their expertise, personality or experience.

Adopting a construction industry analogy Tyson identifies three possible role models for the specialist personnel function as summarised in box 1.4.[12] These reflect differing levels of influence, activities and representation of the personnel function.

Box 1.4. Role models of the specialist personnel function (Tyson 1987)

a) Clerk of Works: Within this role model, personnel is a low-level activity operating in a clerical support role to line management. It is responsible for basic administration and welfare provision.

b) Contracts Manager: Within this role model, personnel is a high-level function with a key role in handling industrial relations and developing policies and procedures in other core personnel areas. The role is largely reactive, dealing with the personnel implications of business decisions. This model incorporates a strong 'policing' component, where the personnel department is concerned with securing adherence to agreed systems and procedures.

c) Architect: Within this role model, personnel is a top-level management function involved in establishing and adjusting corporate objectives and developing strategic personnel policies designed to facilitate the achievement of long-term business goals. Personnel considerations are recognised as a key ingredient in corporate success with the personnel practitioner being the management specialist best placed to assess how the organisation's human resources can best contribute to this goal. Routine personnel activities are delegated, allowing senior personnel practitioners to adopt a broad strategic outlook.

In a 1987 study, Shivanath used this framework to examine the dominant role models of personnel management adopted in Irish organisations.[13] As an initial step she identified the personnel activities which presently occupied most of the time of personnel practitioners, and then ascertained which activities personnel practitioners felt should occupy most of their time (see table 1.2).

Employee relations was identified as the most important personnel activity. Respondents also reported extensive involvement in manpower planning, recruitment and selection and training activities. There was little variation in the ranking of activities on both criteria, suggesting that Irish personnel practitioners seem largely satisfied that they are devoting their time to activities considered central to the successful execution of their organisational role.

Table 1.2. Time spent /priority of personnel activities

Activity	Time spent (rank)	Score	Time priority (rank)	Score
Employee Relations	1	40	1	75
General Management & administration	2	75	3	135
Training & development	3	146	2	88
Recruitment & selection	4	209	5	294
Pay & conditions	5	210	7	406
Planning	6	294	4	196
Advice — personnel policy	7	542	9	542
Communications	8	607	6	372
Manpower planning	9	684	8	444
Organisation development	10	907	–	–
Health & safety	–	–	10	783

Source: Adopted from Gunnigle, P. and Shivanath, G. 'Role and Status of Personnel Practitioners: A Positive Picture', *Journal of Irish Business and Administrative Research* (IBAR) Vol. 9 1989.

Using Tyson's typology Shivanath felt that the personnel function in Ireland has developed beyond a basic administrative support model. Only a small minority of respondent personnel practitioners reported to a lower order manager. While personnel departments were responsible for the execution of various administrative and clerical tasks these were mostly delegated, allowing senior personnel practitioners adequate scope to become involved in more demanding work.

Employee relations was identified as the single most important personnel activity. Respondent personnel practitioners reported extensive involvement in this area: acting as the organisation's employee relations specialist, conducting major negotiations with trade unions, advising line management on labour relations matters, handling grievance and disciplinary issues and third party referral and operating a wide range of employee relations policies and procedures. Despite suggestions that the significance of employee relations has waned, the indications here are that it remains a central personnel activity in Irish organisations.

Indeed the 'contracts manager' model would seem to reflect accurately personnel management practice in many Irish organisations. Personnel practitioners were involved in constructing and implementing a range of personnel policies and procedures. For many organisations an effectively executed employee relations function, together with comprehensive systems to forecast manpower needs, recruit personnel and provide appropriate training, is seen as the optimal route through which the personnel function can contribute to corporate success.

However, Shivanath concluded that senior personnel practitioners in Irish organisations were also involved at a more strategic level. Many senior personnel practitioners operated at the top of their organisational hierarchy. They were involved in making top-level decisions and had responsibility for developing related strategies and policies. Employee relations was a priority but personnel departments were also responsible for the establishment of an integrated network of personnel systems which spanned the whole range of personnel work from manpower planning to termination of employment, and clearly impacted upon organisational outcomes such as productivity and employee commitment. These characteristics are indicative of a more strategic business-oriented approach similar to the 'architect' model.

Explaining Variations in the Personnel Role

In attempting to explain variations in the organisational role of the personnel function, Shivanath identified two particular sources:
a) personal characteristics of the personnel practitioner (age, experience, education, etc); *b)* organisational context (size, performance, ownership).

In relation to personal characteristics, Shivanath identified education as a key factor influencing the organisational role of the personnel practitioner. It was a major indicator of organisational status, with better-qualified personnel practitioners operating at a more senior level and being much more involved in strategic planning: 'If one had to single out the one personal characteristic most likely to catapult the personnel practitioner to the top of the organisational hierarchy, education would qualify as the crucial element in his curriculum vitae. . . .'[14]

In relation to organisational factors, Shivanath identified company ownership as a most influential factor affecting the personnel role. The most striking differences arose from comparisons of private sector categories: indigenous, US- and European-owned. Shivanath found that Irish and US-owned organisations presented a largely similar picture, both displaying characteristics of the business-oriented 'architect' model. However, differences were discernible in the personnel management approaches of other foreign-owned organisations. Such differences highlight both the importance of corporate philosophy and market variables in influencing the organisational role of the specialist personnel function.

PERSONNEL MANAGEMENT AS A PROFESSION

A final consideration in evaluating the nature and role of personnel management concerns the movement to establish personnel management as a recognised profession. This movement is led by the Institute of Personnel Management (IPM).

The first Irish IPM branch (then the Institute of Labour Management) was formed in 1938. Membership remained quite small up to the early 1970s but has increased significantly since then with a current membership of over 1,000.

The IPM sees itself as the vehicle for expanding the body of knowledge, establishing and preserving standards and representing members in all aspects of personnel managment (see box 1.5).[15]

Box 1.5. Strategic aim of the Institute of Personnel Management

The strategic aim of the Institute is to position the IPM firmly as the leading organisation in the United Kingdom and the Republic of Ireland responsible for the development of human resource management and the dissemination of information on this subject; which will naturally attract into membership personnel practitioners and others involved in these areas of management; and will be consulted by government and national organisations, who will heed its advice.

Areas where the IPM plays a particularly significant role are in the provision of education and training schemes and the issuance of codes of practice on various aspects of personnel management. Since its early days the IPM education scheme has become highly developed. Through this the Institute attempts to regulate entry to personnel work and maintain standards in personnel practice. Successful completion of the IPM's education scheme leads to graduate membership of the Institute and is designed to give students an understanding of the concepts, theory and activities of personnel management. After a period of practical experience graduate members may progress to full membership of the Institute (MIPM). Within this role the IPM undertakes extensive publishing and research activities. These provide an important mechanism for the dissemination and discussion of new developments and issues in personnel management.

The IPM has produced a number of codes of practice on various aspects of personnel management, such as professional practice in personnel management, recruitment and occupational testing. These encourage the adoption of professional standards in the conduct of personnel work and, although voluntary in nature, have a positive role to play in helping personnel practitioners to carry out their organisational role.

Table 1.3. IPM membership 1976–89

Year	Companion	Fellow	Member	Associate	Graduate	Affiliate	Subscriber	Student FT	Student PT	Total	Republic of Ireland
1976	153	1,619	7,534	2,676	–	1,857	421	505	4,108	18,873	(427)
1977	155	1,601	7,072	3,206	–	1,485	605	409	3,573	18,106	(426)
1978	160	1,579	6,875	3,776	–	1,406	673	638	4,045	19,152	(486)
1979	166	1,578	6,656	4,201	–	1,336	734	543	4,980	20,194	(992)
1980	166	1,592	6,507	4,989	–	1,270	839	659	5,625	21,647	(602)
1981	169	1,615	6,322	5,569	–	1,225	831	523	6,370	22,624	(672)
1982	174	1,643	6,042	6,104	271	2,717	–	607	4,621	22,179	(739)
1983	169	1,651	5,859	6,133	527	3,095	–	739	3,626	22,404	(822)
1984	184	1,779	5,996	5,780	1,361	3,328	–	501	4,403	23,332	(790)
1985	190	1,839	6,159	5,182	2,368	3,477	–	537	5,344	25,096	(869)
1986	196	2,116	6,573	4,250	3,241	3,598	–	582	5,804	27,360	(938)
1987	198	2,315	6,789	3,771	4,403	4,124	–	582	7,632	29,814	(1,012)
1988*	194	2,540	8,302	2,832	4,998	4,236	–	786	8,698	32,586	(1,035)
1989*	208	2,830	9,394	1,949	6,018	4,059	–	892	10,179	35,529	(1,081)
*1988	8	86	192	39	216	171		323		1,035	
*1989	9	95	212	26	232	152		355		1,081	

*Breakdown of membership of IPM in Ireland
Source: IPM London 1989

In relation to regulation of entry to personnel work the picture is less clear. An initial glance at the IPM's membership figures presents a very favourable picture. However, there are some areas for concern. Of particular note is the large proportion of members who are partially qualified according to the IPM's own criteria. The key membership grade, as achieved through a combination of education and experience, is corporate member (MIPM). At this level, personnel practitioners should have both the academic knowledge and the practical experience to carry out effectively their personnel role. Of the total IPM membership corporate members account for approximately one-third. At the other extreme, the largest proportion of members are either students, partially qualified ex-students or affiliates.

If we look at table 1.3 we see that while student and particularly graduate members have increased steadily the proportion progessing to corporate membership remained very low. This may be partially explained by the fact that many graduate members may not be working in specialist personnel work, thus may not have the facility or need to progress to full membership.

A related issue is the question of representativeness of the IPM of those working in personnel management. In Britain Tyson and Fell suggest that many people working in personnel are not IPM members.[16] The Irish situation would seem to be broadly similar. In a report on the IPM in Ireland (1981) the working party felt that Irish membership could 'be at least doubled' from the ranks of people then employed in personnel management.[17] A more recent survey found that just over 40 per cent of personnel practitioners were IPM members.[18] This is clearly a matter of concern for the IPM. If its membership does not comprise the vast majority of personnel practitioners it cannot claim to fully represent the personnel 'profession'. On the other hand, the Institute must encourage professionalisation by insisting that corporate members have satisfied professional examination standards as well as possessing the necessary experience.

In its role as a national pressure group the IPM has made considerable progress. Members are involved on a number of national decision-making bodies, and the Institute has been consulted on various national initiatives. The Federation of Irish Employers and the Irish Congress of Trade Unions have traditionally been viewed as the representatives of employer and worker views to government and other interested parties. The IPM has sought to adopt a unique position on major national issues, evaluating their merits and making informed responses.

Chapter 2

Historical Development of Personnel Management

INTRODUCTION
To understand adequately the current nature of personnel management it is important to examine its historical evolution. In so doing we can see how various activities were added to the personnel role, how it developed as a specialist management function, and the varying sets of beliefs and values which have led to different roles and perspectives of personnel management. This chapter reviews the key phases in the historical development of personnel management.

EARLY DAYS: THE BIRTH OF THE PERSONNEL ROLE
The origins of contemporary personnel management lie in the dramatic changes brought about by the industrial revolution which began in Britain in the eighteenth century and later spread to the rest of Europe, North America and beyond. The basis for these changes lay in technological developments, particularly in the use of steam power and improved machinery and equipment. Associated factors included the growth in consumer markets and sources of raw materials. These developments allowed for the production of goods in larger quantities for wider markets. Thus a gradual change occurred from a largely rural society based on agriculture and craft production to an industry-based society with new social divisions, where the bulk of the labour force relied on wages for their existence.

A central component of this change was the growth of the factory system where owners of capital employed large numbers of wage labourers in their factories to produce goods using, for then, technologically advanced equipment. Such changes had dramatic effects on the organisation of work. People now worked together in much larger numbers on more narrowly defined and tightly controlled jobs. From the owner's perspective the work of the new factory employees had to be directed, equipment maintained, production controlled and goods distributed and sold. Therein we have the origins of modern management: the need to plan, organise, direct and control the use of equipment, capital, materials and employees within organisations.

In the early stages of industrialisation many factory owners regarded their labour force in largely instrumental terms. Working conditions were poor and employees enjoyed few of the benefits we have now come to associate with employment, such as sick pay, pensions and basic we.fare provisions.[1] Workers could not do much about this situation since they had little economic or political power. It was not until the growth of organised labour through the trade union movement that employee concerns could command the attention and action of employers.

The Welfare Phase

The welfare phase refers to a series of voluntary initiatives undertaken in certain companies to improve the conditions of factory workers, particularly in relation to pay, working hours and health and safety provisions. This welfare phase is seen as particularly important in the development of personnel management as it was characterised by the appointment of welfare officers who are seen as the forerunners of the modern personnel practitioner. Welfare officers first emerged in the mainly Quaker-owned firms in the food and confectionery industries in Britain in the late 1890s. A major concern for the early welfare workers was the health, safety and welfare of employees.

The origins of personnel management in Ireland are closely related to developments in Britain. The welfare movement had reached Ireland by the early years of the twentieth century. Some progressive employers, influenced by religious beliefs, took various steps to improve working conditions and create a more humane working environment for employees. This often resulted in the employment of welfare officers, although this was generally restricted to a few large employers in the major cities, such as Jacobs, Wills, and Maguire & Paterson in Dublin.[2]

The need to mobilise production and output during the First World War gave added impetus to welfare work and to the employment of welfare officers in Britain.[3] Employment of women in industrial work fuelled concerns about their working conditions, particularly working hours, health and safety provisions. Emergency orders were introduced to lay down basic conditions, including a provision for the employment of welfare officers.

The welfare phase seemed to reach its height during the First World War. Full employment in the immediate post-war period in Britain soon gave way to high levels of unemployment and depression in the post-1920s. Much of the development in welfare and personnel work regressed and the welfare role was abandoned in many organisations. In 1919 the British-based Welfare Workers Association (founded in 1913) changed its name to the Welfare Workers Institute and had a membership of 700. By 1927 it had been renamed the Institute of Industrial Welfare Workers and its membership had fallen to 420.[4]

However, the impact of the welfare approach is still apparent in contemporary personnel practice. Welfare has been inextricably linked with a 'caring' approach to employees: dealing with issues such as health, working conditions and personal problems. This caring element is very much in evidence in modern personnel management practice in areas such as counselling, sickness benefits, staff loans, etc.

On a different level the welfare tradition has been a source of some confusion about the position of the personnel practitioner in the managerial hierarchy. Welfare officers occupied a semi-independent position in the factory system with employees being the main beneficiaries of their role. This led to a 'middle-man' perception of the welfare role, with employees seeing them as the representatives of worker interests. Modern personnel practitioners, on the other hand, operate as an integral part of the management team and primarily represent employer interests.

At the same time as economic depression was heralding the demise of the welfare emphasis in Britain, a number of emerging factors helped to change the direction of personnel work and to define its role in broader terms.

Scientific Management

Improved technology coupled with increases in organisation size and complexity forced employers to investigate new ways of improving industrial performance. In the US, F. W. Taylor began to apply certain scientific principles to the analysis of industrial work.[5] Based on his work at the Bethelem Steel Company (1900–11) Taylor encouraged employers to take systematic approaches to improve job design, choose and train workers, create incentive payment systems and foster good management-worker relations. With the objective of maximising efficiency, the scientific management school encouraged organisations to develop standardised work systems and methods.

Scientific management approaches were widely adopted in both the US and Britain in the inter-war years. Emphasis was placed on job analysis, time and motion studies and the creation of incentive bonus schemes, thus extending the work of the emerging personnel function. Scientific management helped to shift the emphasis in personnel away from the 'caring/do-gooding' approach of the welfare phase towards the efficiency and profitability emphasis of the work study officer. With the growing realisation that considerable improvements in both productivity and profits could be achieved as a result of innovations in work organisation, personnel became more accepted as a management function.

Despite its critics, scientific management continues to have a profound impact on management thought. The more lasting implications of scientific management have been the separation of work planning from execution. This emphasises the key role of management in establishing standards, procedures and methods. It also emphasises approaches to job design which encourage task fragmentation, the use of work study techniques and the adoption of incentive-based payment systems.

From the personnel management perspective the spread of scientific management placed greater weight on careful selection and systematic training of employees. Associated with this trend was increased attention to job design, working conditions and payment systems. Personnel also took responsibility for much of the research and administration required to facilitate these initiatives.

The Emerging Behavioural Sciences

If some developments in scientific management caused personnel practitioners to develop a more calculative approach to managing employees, this was partially redressed by growth in the behavioural sciences.

The emergence of the behavioural sciences gave a major impetus to personnel management by establishing a body of knowledge to underpin many aspects of personnel work such as selection, training, motivation, industrial relations and payment systems. It focused on problems created by work organisation in the large factories of the new industrial era, such as fatigue, monotony and low motivation.

The human relations approach is most closely associated with the Hawthorne experiments into employee productivity conducted at the Western Electric Company in Chicago by Elton Mayo and Roethlisberger and Dickson (1927–32).[6] These studies indicated that employee behaviour and performance were not solely influenced by financial incentives or working conditions. Individual employee needs and social factors influencing work-group formation and behaviour were also important. Employees established informal work-groups whose characteristics (such as group cohesiveness, team-working) influenced employee performance. Supervisory style was also an important factor influencing individual and work-group performance.

These findings gave rise to a body of literature which became known as the 'Human Relations' movement. Although the Hawthorne experiments have been criticised, they had a profound impact on management practice. The Hawthorne studies established interest in applying behavioural science principles to the study of employee motivation. They highlighted the importance of the work-group as a factor influencing employee performance. They established interest in identifying employee needs. They also highlighted the importance of supervisory style, placing particular emphasis on more participative management styles.

Research by Maslow, McGregor, Herzberg, and Argyris led to further explanations of employee behaviour and motivation. Much of this work involved investigating sources of employee motivation and attempting to match employee and management needs through appropriate organisation structures and managerial styles. The importance of intrinsic needs (needs which can only be satisfied by the job itself, such as achievement, self-fulfilment) was highlighted as a key factor in evaluating employee behaviour at work. It was suggested that management must take account of employee needs in adopting organisational structures and supervisory styles as it had been discovered that frustrated needs reduced employee morale, commitment and performance.

By the 1940s these approaches had gained significant support, particularly in the US. They challenged the scientific management premise of formal structures, simplification of tasks, work measurement, and motivation through financial incentives. The newly evolving personnel function assumed responsibility for the application of these theories at organisation level.

Labour Relations

Meanwhile, here in Ireland another strand in the personnel management tapestry was being woven. By the turn of the century, and particularly after the passing of the 1906 Trade Disputes Act, the trade union movement successfully organised many industries in Dublin, Belfast and Cork.[7]

The growth in influence and power of the 'new unionism' (large general unions catering for unskilled workers) was most obviously manifested in the leadership skills of Jim Larkin, the founder of the Irish Transport and General Workers Union (ITGWU). Much has been written of the industrial unrest in Dublin in 1913. An important effect of this turbulent period was that it served to unite employers as never before and placed increased emphasis on labour relations.

The beginning of employer organisation in Ireland can be traced to the founding of the Cork Employers Organisation in 1909 and its Dublin counterpart in 1911. Apart from trade and commercial considerations, these organisations were determined to counteract the growing power and influence of trade unions and to monitor legislative developments, reflecting the birth of a labour relations orientation among employers. By 1913 the Employers Executive Committee had been formed in Dublin to confront Larkin and the ITGWU.

After 1913, employer-labour relations moved towards a more conciliatory approach based upon negotiations and mutual agreement. The fledgling union movement was reluctantly accepted and employers began to take steps to accommodate it. This was achieved via multi-employer bargaining conducted by employer associations, and through the employment of labour relations officers to deal with personnel and industrial relations matters at establishment level. By the late 1930s a united employer front was established via the Confederation of Irish Employers later known as the Federated Union of Employers (FUE), and is now the Federation of Irish Employers (FIE), which quickly established itself as the representative employer voice in the field of labour relations.

Since the early years of this century a number of Irish organisations have employed welfare officers, very much in the British tradition. The increasing emphasis on labour relations led to greater specialisation in this area. These dual roles of welfare and labour relations became intertwined over the years. In 1937 the Irish branch of the Institute of Labour Management was founded and was the forerunner of the current Institute of Personnel Management in Ireland.

POST-WORLD WAR TWO: EXPANSION AND DEVELOPMENT

The Wage Rounds (1946–70)
During the Second World War wages in Ireland were controlled under Emergency Powers Orders which effectively prohibited any upward movement in pay. In anticipation of a flood of pay claims on removal of legislated wage restraint in 1946, the government established the Labour Court under the terms of the 1946 Industrial Relations Act.[8] Its main role was to facilitate the settlement of industrial conflict between employers and trade unions through conciliation and investigation of disputes and the issuance of recommendations. The government was also keen to improve industrial relations procedures in anticipation of increased industrial activity in the post-war period.

The removal of the Emergency Powers Orders in 1946 led to a general pay increase for unionised employees which became known as the first wage round.[9] Subsequent rounds were agreed periodically up to the twelfth wage round in 1969. A wage round was essentially a period of intensive collective bargaining between employers and trade unions occurring at regular intervals and resulting in a similar general wage increase for unionised employees.

The nature of collective bargaining in the immediate post-war period had important implications for the development of the personnel function. Growth in organisation size and complexity demanded greater specialisation and knowledge in the management of employees, particularly in industrial relations. This was often achieved through the establishment of specialist personnel departments. These developments were mostly restricted to the public sector and some of the larger private sector organisations.[10] Developments in the State sector were particularly noteworthy. The government was by far the largest employer. It needed to develop procedures to handle personnel issues, particularly in relation to pay. A comprehensive conciliation and arbitration scheme was introduced for the Civil Service in 1950 and similar schemes were later developed for other groups such as teachers and the gardai.[11] Organisations in the semi-state sector became actively involved in developing personnel structures to facilitate the increase in workplace bargaining and to deal with other personnel matters such as recruitment and training.

Centralised Pay Bargaining 1970–82

The two most important wage rounds in establishing the basis for the dramatic change in wage bargaining in the early 1970s were the eleventh and twelfth wage rounds.[12] The twelfth wage round was agreed after a prolonged strike with maintenance craftsmen in 1969 which was the worst in the history of the State.

With increasing levels of inflation the government was concerned at the prospect of further high wage increases. Discussions on a thirteenth wage round took place between employer and trade union representatives under the auspices of the Employer Labour Conference. When these discussions ran into difficulties the government introduced a Prices and Incomes Bill in 1970 to control wage increases to 7 per cent.

Faced with legislative control on prices and incomes, and an erosion of their bargaining positions, union and employer representatives returned to the Employer Labour Conference and concluded what became known as the first national wage agreement effective from 1 January 1971. There were seven such agreements up to 1979 followed by the two national understandings covering the period up to 1982. In 1982 there was a return to decentralised bargaining on a company by company basis. More recently there has been a revival of centralised negotiations under the Programme of National Recovery (1987).

An important effect of national wage agreements was to remove pay bargaining from the level of the organisation. Initially this was seen as freeing management from complex negotiations with trade unions and giving them more certainty in corporate planning. The effect on trade unions was also pronounced. At a time of relative economic prosperity and substantial growth in union membership, the key role for the trade union in the workplace, namely pay bargaining, was removed. Understandably, union representatives turned their attention to other negotiable issues at workplace level. With the expectancy that pay increases would be derived via national agreements, attention was increasingly focused on matters that could be negotiated at local level: employment conditions, pay anomalies and productivity. Far from eliminating plant bargaining, national agreements merely changed its focus. Various types of productivity deals were negotiated throughout the period. In fact productivity became an important means for work-groups to gain pay increases above the stated maxima in wage agreements and contributed to a high level of wage drift.[13]

For the personnel function industrial relations remained a priority with personnel practitioners heavily involved in workplace bargaining with trade unions. Industrial harmony was the objective and industrial relations specialists through their negotiating, inter-personal, and procedural skills had responsibility for its achievement.

Economic Growth and Industrial Unrest

The 1950s had been a disappointing period for the emerging Irish economy, with high levels of unemployment and emigration. It was against this background that the Fianna Fail government embarked on a programme of economic expansion in 1958. Foreign investment was encouraged and various incentives were given to encourage increased export production. The 1960s became the first real period of sustained economic growth. In the five-year period 1958-63 industrial exports rose by 46 per cent; output per worker rose at an average of 5 per cent per year; the population stopped declining as emigration fell and the numbers in employment grew steadily.[14] Economic growth and industrial expansion continued throughout the decade. Educational opportunities, incomes and living standards improved. It was a period of changed attitudes and increased expectation for Irish people.

This manifested itself in pressure for wage increases. Wage rounds tended to be led by relatively powerful bargaining groups, such as craftsmen in the State or building sector. These groups often secured substantial wage increases which helped to establish a high trend for the round. In addition to these general wage increases trade unions became increasingly involved in supplementary bargaining at company level on issues like overtime, working conditions and shift allowances. These factors combined to produce an inflationary climate towards the end of the 1960s.

The 1960s were also characterised by a marked increase in levels of industrial conflict. The eighth wage round (1962) was characterised by increased strike activity. This set the pattern for increased industrial unrest throughout the 1960s and into the 1970s[15] (see table 2.1).

During the 1970s the number of strikes increased by 39 per cent over the previous decade. Apart from a few temporary improvements there was a steady deterioration in our strike record in the two decades since 1960.

Table 2.1. Strike figures 1945–84

Period	Number of strikes	Mandays lost	Workers involved
1945–9	686	1,374,795	68,338
1950–4	530	1,439,507	73,625
1955–9	317	627,055	41,668
1960–4	362	1,340,638	83,811
1965–9	540	2,860,217	212,720
1970–4	799	2,246,997	170,029
1975–9	752	3,064,028	187,389
1980–4	724	1,985,786	154,263

Source: Department of Industrial Relations, University College Dublin/Irish Statistical Bulletins.

This increased unrest may be partially explained by the huge increase in the pace of industrialisation. Ireland moved in a relatively short period from being a primarily rural, agriculture-based economy to one which has experienced a rapid increase in levels of urbanisation, industrial and commercial employment, living standards and education. Inevitably, such dramatic change created difficulties for a rapidly changing economy and Ireland was to be no exception.

The industrial unrest of the 1960s and 1970s established industrial relations as a key employer concern. It gave the emerging personnel function a central management role. Personnel departments were established in many large organisations. Their major responsibility was industrial relations. The Donovan Report in Britain (1968) was also influential in encouraging collective bargaining, the adoption of comprehensive procedures and greater specialisation in industrial relations management.

Government Intervention and Employment Legislation

In many Western European countries the post-war period has been characterised by increased State involvement in commercial and industrial affairs.

In Ireland government intervention became more pronounced in the 1960s and 1970s.[16] This was particularly evident in the area of centralised pay bargaining. The early 1970s also witnessed the introduction of an unprecedented wave of employment legislation which was to impinge on the industrial scene and significantly influence the role of the personnel practitioner. Such legislation extended employee rights at work. A focus of much of this legislative change was in the areas of dismissal and equality with the passing of important acts like the Unfair Dismissals Act 1977, the Anti-Discrimination (Pay) Act 1974, the Employment Equality Act 1977, the Safety in Industry Act 1980, and the Redundancy Payments Acts 1967–84.

Organisations had to come grips with the application of such legislation. Much of this responsibility was assumed by the personnel function. Personnel practitioners had to be familiar with the new legislation and to oversee its implementation at workplace level. The personnel practitioner became a source of expert knowledge, and the importance of employment matters was recognised in organisations and industrial sectors where, hitherto, little concern had been paid to employee-related matters.[17]

Personnel Management Education

Growth in industrial output, foreign investment and semi-state activity, together with increased industrial unrest since the 1960s, contributed to the establishment of personnel as an important management function. Staffing this function required professionally competent people. Many of the newer multinational companies prioritised the appointment of qualified and experienced personnel practitioners. In the public and semi-state sector, greater weight was placed on deploying well-qualified people in key personnel posts.

While personnel management education in Ireland can be traced back to the 1940s the most significant developments have taken place since the 1960s. The establishment of AnCO in 1967 added impetus to the development of the personnel role through increased emphasis on training and development. In the 1970s the first courses leading to membership of the Institute of Personnel Management (IPM) were offered at centres in Dublin, Limerick and Galway.

In 1980 the new IPM education scheme was introduced in Britain. To cater for the Irish context a National Diploma in Personnel Management was developed under the auspices of the National Council for Educational Awards which gave exemption from the IPM's education scheme. Similar exemptions have also been awarded to degree programmes at the University of Limerick, Dublin City University, University College Dublin and the National College of Industrial Relations. Today certificate, diploma, and degree courses in personnel management are available at the variety of centres throughout the country, in addition to the vast pool of management courses which include aspects of personnel and human resource management in their curricula. These developments in personnel management education have led to increasingly better qualified and able personnel practitioners.

The Multinational Influence

Any consideration of management practice in Ireland must take account of the role of multinational organisations. The significance of multinational activity is a product of successive government strategies of attracting foreign investment since the1960s. Such investment increased in the 1970s and has continued as foreign organisations vie for position within the single European market.

A legacy of such extensive MNC activity is their impact on personnel management. Such organisations bring with them differing approaches to workforce management, some of which have been very healthy for the development of the personnel function in Ireland. Of particular significance is the emphasis on good personnel management practice in many multi-national organisations.[18] This is often manifested through the presence of a developed personnel function and high-calibre personnel practitioners.

Multinational organisations have been innovative in the development and application of new personnel approaches and techniques. This has con-tributed, not only to increased knowledge of personnel techniques, but also to highlighting the important link between strategic objectives, personnel policies and related personnel activities. Their involvement in community affairs has served to promote personnel's role in integrating the organisation into its local environment and in exercising certain social responsibilities.

The impact of multinational organisations has been particularly notice-able in employee relations.[19] Multinationals have been particularly keen to determine the parameters for employee relations interactions through the establishment of explicit policies and procedures. Where unions are recognised the relationship tends to be highly circumscribed through the agreement of comprehensive procedures. In the non-union situation emphasis is placed on effective workforce management and the develop-ment of comprehensive personnel policies.

Another characteristic of personnel management in many multinational organisations has been a sophistication in approaches to employee selection and development. To some degree this can be explained by the need to train a workforce in new skills within a tight start-up schedule. However, the emphasis on elaborate selection procedures and employee development practices, linked to particular career development and remuneration policies, would seem to have had a favourable impact in areas like morale, flexi-bility and performance.[20]

Most recent multinational investment in Ireland has been located in new purpose-built locations. These provide good working conditions and facilities. Often a strong emphasis is placed on health, safety and welfare provisions. Pay rates are usually competitive, with considerable emphasis on fringe benefits such as sick-pay schemes, health insurance and pension schemes. Communications are also a high priority. Briefings, news-letters and other mechanisms are used to facilitate management-employee communications.

THE 1980s: RETRENCHMENT AND RE-EVALUATION

The 1980s have been a decade of reappraisal for personnel management. A depressed economic climate since the early 1980s, together with increased competitive pressures, led to a slump in business activity. These changes in turn helped to change both the focus of personnel management and the nature of personnel activities.

In relation to personnel activities the emphasis switched in a relatively short period from recruiting to exiting employees. Redundancy, retirement and redeployment became the focus of personnel management. Organisations reduced numbers of permanent employees and cut indirect expenditure on areas such as catering and cleaning.[21] Tasks were contracted out and more flexible employment patterns adopted, with greater reliance on temporary and part-time staff. High unemployment and the reduced bargaining power of trade unions lessened the emphasis on traditional personnel activities such as industrial relations, employee selection and training.

The recession also facilitated a more general re-evaluation of personnel management. By the early 1980s the personnel management role was firmly established in most larger organisations. Personnel departments operated as a distinct management function with responsibility for a well-defined range of personnel activities.

The onset of recession lessened the need for some of these core activities, such as selection and recruit training. At the same time, organisations were looking for ways of establishing competitive advantage through improvements in quality, service and performance. One source of such improvements lay in the better utilisation of human resources. Some organisations began to investigate different approaches to workforce management. These led to changes in personnel management, particularly in areas such as work organisation and job design, remuneration systems, management-employee relations and employee development.

A particular focus of such change was the area of management-employee relations. In Ireland management-employee relations have traditionally been based on collective bargaining between employers and representative trade unions. This 'industrial' relations emphasis reflects a traditional reliance on collectivist dealings with employees via trade unions and has been the predominant model of management-employee relations in most public sector and larger private indigenous organisations.

The changed business climate lessened the industrial relations emphasis: trade union membership fell; unions lost much of their bargaining power; unemployment increased and industrial unrest declined significantly. Many organisations began to review their approach to management-employee relations.

Some employers adopted a more hard-line approach to industrial relations. Using established traditional collective bargaining mechanisms, trade unions were forced to concede ground and to conclude agreements effectively giving back concessions won in better days. Such a managerial approach was facilitated by the recessionary business climate and reflected a degree of opportunism in attempting to redefine management-union relations. At the same time, some organisations adopted a management philosophy which rejected that traditional approach to industrial relations.[22] Such organisations placed the accent on individual interaction with employees, emphasising company loyalty, career development and good remuneration. In turn the organisation demanded flexibility, high levels of performance and motivation. Organisations such as IBM and Digital caught the corporate eye. The term 'employee' relations gradually gained acceptance in the management vocabulary, signifying the subtle but significant change from management-union to management-employee interaction.

CONTEMPORARY DEVELOPMENTS

Although organisational practice varies it would seem that recession and subsequent recovery has led to a change in traditional approaches to personnel management, a greater devolution of personnel activities to line management and the emergence of a greater strategic role for personnel management in contributing to the achievement of business goals.

Competitive pressures, reduced trade union power and new models of management practice have encouraged organisations to investigate more innovative modes of personnel management. A significant aspect of contemporary developments in personnel management has been the emergence of Human Resource Management (HRM).

Human Resource Management (HRM) refers to the development of a strategic corporate approach to workforce management.[23] It has its roots in developments in the US which have relied on the application of behavioural science principles and related personnel techniques as a means of improving employee commitment, employee relations and overall corporate performance. While different HRM variants exist, a central contention is that organisations incorporate human resource considerations into strategic decision-making, establish a corporate human resource philosophy and develop complementary personnel strategies and policies to improve human resource utilisation.

In the Irish context, increasing attention has been focused on the human resource management approaches of non-union organisations in the high technology sector.[24] Many are subsidiaries of US organisations which espouse a particular philosophy towards workforce management, emphasising employee commitment and loyalty and high levels of quality and performance. A significant aspect of this approach is an emphasis on 'employee' rather than 'industrial' relations, incorporating a corporate preference for dealing with employees directly rather than through representative trade unions. It may also be associated with the development of various policies to promote increased levels of employee commitment, quality consciousness and performance.

An important component of human resource management approaches is a high-powered personnel department with a major strategic input and a key responsibility for ensuring that the organisation's core values permeate throughout the organisation. The responsibility for establishing competitive advantage through better modes of workforce management can only be undertaken by top management with advice and assistance provided by personnel specialists. The new-style personnel director, while responsible for the execution of a range of personnel activities, is primarily involved at a strategic level, establishing a corporate human resource culture and related personnel strategies and policies to facilitate the achievement of business goals.

These contemporary developments indicate a new and exciting strategic role for personnel management. The emergence of human resource management approaches has served to underline the central position of personnel considerations in corporate decision-making. The implications of these developments, particularly those relating to human resource management, are considered in greater depth in chapter 12.

Chapter 3

Manpower Planning and the Manpower Flow Process

INTRODUCTION

The purpose of planning is to reduce uncertainty and to enable strategies to be developed to cope with future potential changes. Studies of 'excellent' companies in the US and Britain demonstrate that organisations which invest heavily in the planning process regularly out-perform their competitors.[1] Change confronts every organisation, although the extent to which an organisation faces 'turbulence' in its internal and external environment may vary. Technological, social, political and economic developments regularly occur, and an organisation must plan to accommodate these changes.

One of the major benefits of planning is the actual *creation* of objectives both for an organisation and for its management. Once objectives are identified, an organisation can marshal its resources (material, technical, financial and human) towards goal accomplishment. As a result, the organisation develops a clear understanding of its core purpose and its central activity areas. Consequently, some organisations divest themselves of what come to be seen as ancillary or peripheral activity areas. An organisation which has a clear idea of its purpose and direction will create more focused objectives for its management team and employees. Indeed, it has been argued that job satisfaction improves when one has a clear idea of one's job purpose and adequate resources are provided.

Cascio defines strategic planning as 'the process of setting objectives and deciding upon the action to achieve them'.[2] Strategic planning includes an examination of the organisation's philosophy and purpose, formulating statements of identity, purpose and objectives (often embodied in a 'mission' statement), SWOT analysis (evaluating the strengths and weaknesses of an organisation in relation to perceived and real threats and opportunities in the external environment), creating an appropriate organisation design, developing strategies to achieve stated objectives and devising programmes of action to implement strategic plans.

Three main levels of planning may be identified, differing in terms of focus and time horizon. These levels are strategic, tactical/operational and action/budgetary planning. *Strategic planning* is concerned with the fundamental thrust of the organisation and is long term (3–5 years) in orientation. It guides acquisitions, investments and divestiture decisions (expanding existing product lines, investment portfolios and shedding particular business areas which may have become unprofitable or unsuitable). It involves considerable resource allocation in the planning process itself and requires considerable amounts of information to support analysis and decision-making. *Operational planning* deals with the normal growth of current operations and with any impediments which may block projected growth patterns. *Action planning* is short term in focus, includes budgetary development and additionally encompasses guidelines for immediate action.

There is a direct link between the business planning process and the manpower planning process. In fact it can be said that one parallels the other. The business plan will have major repercussions upon manpower planning, particularly in terms of the quantity and quality of manpower required. The relationship between business planning and manpower planning is illustrated in figure 3.1 which also indicates some associated time horizons for each level of planning.

Fig 3.1. Business planning and manpower planning

	Business planning	Manpower planning
Strategic (Long-term)	Objectives: • Decide corporate philosophy/mission • Assess environmental opportunities/threats • Establish corporate goals • Develop strategic business plans	Objectives: • Assess manpower implications of business plans • Analyse internal/external labour market • Assess manpower implications of changes in product, technology & market • Develop broad picture of future manpower requirements
Operational (Medium-term)	• Develop operational plans to achieve strategic goals • Specify functional roles and responsibilities (production, sales, etc.) • Develop tactical responses to business problems (e.g. loss of competitiveness, fall in consumer demand)	• Specify manpower needs (profile, timing, etc.) • Identify sources of manpower supply (internal/external) • Establish appropriate personnel policies (e.g. job design, career development)
Action (Short-term)	• Establish short-term unit/department objectives/targets • Develop related budgets • Establish specific schedules	Develop schedules, plans, and budgets for: • Recruitment and selection • Training/development • Redeployment • Remuneration • Employee relations

Manpower planning has been defined as 'an effort to anticipate future business and environmental demands upon an organisation and to provide the personnel to fulfil that business and satisfy those demands'.[3]

Manpower planning at the strategic level focuses upon the broad implications of the business plan in terms of the organisation's requirements for manpower. Tactical or operational manpower planning is concerned with detailed forecasts of manpower supply (internally and externally) while action-level manpower planning is concerned with the actual process of recruitment, outplacement (or redundancy), promotions, training, etc.

Manpower planning within an organisation may include all or some of the above levels of planning, since some organisations will have well-developed approaches while others will not. In many cases, the size of organisation will determine how extensively manpower planning is carried out. Many multinational corporations and their subsidiaries regularly review their 'headcount' in relation to projected business forecasts in order that they can anticipate potential problems (for example, avoidance of layoffs by restructuring future hiring plans). However, many indigenous (Irish) small- and medium-sized companies are not exemplars of well-developed planning—business or otherwise.

THE INTERNAL AND EXTERNAL LABOUR MARKET

Manpower planning is closely linked to trends in the internal and external labour market. The internal labour market refers to the current stock of manpower which an organisation possesses. Indeed, the internal labour market is regulated by custom and practice in relation to seniority provisions (how one progresses within an organisation on the basis of service tenure), trade union agreements in relation to manning levels and job boundaries, procedures in relation to screening internal applicants for promotion and transfer, and in relation to selection methods. In an 'open' internal labour market, everyone within the organisation can apply for vacant posts. Preference is given to internal candidates and the post may not be advertised externally unless there is no suitable candidate internally. Every candidate receives an interview and may well be counselled afterwards in relation to their future career paths should they be unsuccessful. 'Open' internal labour markets would not seem to be common in Irish enterprises although such practices exist within the 'hi-tech' electronics sector.

An organisation also needs to profile its workforce regularly in terms of age, service, qualifications, retirement patterns, etc. in order to establish a reliable data base for manpower decisions. Some detailed examples are discussed in a later section of this chapter.

The external labour market refers to the geographic area from which the organisation will normally expect to recruit its workforce. The external labour market may be 'tight' or 'loose' depending on whether there is an excess supply of suitable candidates for the posts to be filled or whether there is a deficit of suitable candidates. An oversupply situation (which characterises the Irish labour market at the moment) can be expected to produce high levels of competition for posts with a consequent increase in qualifications and downward pressure on wages (by the introduction of new low-paid recruitment grades, for example). Tight labour markets place qualified applicants in a stronger position where the organisation may have to develop 'designer/custom-built' remuneration packages to secure candidates. External labour markets are not geographically restricted in the sense that an organisation may recruit locally or internationally as the case demands. However, one can loosely describe regional labour markets (such as the South East, the Mid-West of Ireland), national labour markets (nationwide) and international labour markets (countrywide).

The interaction of demand and supply factors in the internal and external labour market will determine (in conjunction with legislation and collective bargaining) such factors as pay levels, occupational and differential wage rates.

THE MANPOWER FLOW PROCESS

The essential objective of manpower planning is the creation of a match between the organisation's demand for manpower and the supply which it has internally. Manpower planning is concerned with establishing plans, policies and procedures for the management of people in, through and out of an organisation. One can conceive of this as a manpower flow process whereby employees enter the organisation, are deployed within it and leave it via retirement, redundancy, resignation or dismissal (see figure 3.2).

Fig. 3.2. The manpower flow process

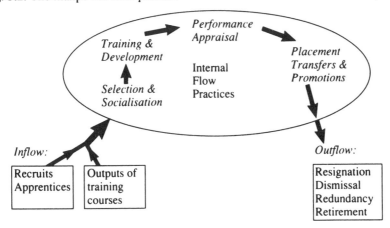

FACTORS AFFECTING MANPOWER PLANNING

The acquisition ability of an organisation affects the level of manpower which it can attract. However, the retention ability of the organisation determines how long these recruits remain with the company.

Business or product market changes affect the demand for an organisation's product or services, technological change affects the organisation's ability to produce new products while internal changes (such as productivity) affects the organisation's ability to compete effectively. All of these factors affect the organisation's future expected requirements for labour. The retention ability of a company is affected by its internal flow policies and practices and the extent to which other companies develop more attractive systems (for example in their rewards and promotions structures). Two key processes affect the manpower retention ability of an organisation: labour wastage/turnover, and absenteeism.

Labour Turnover

Labour wastage/turnover refers to the number of persons who leave an organisation within a specified time period. Reasons for leaving may include resignations, redundancy, retirement, dismissal and death. Bowey classifies the factors generating wastage into 'pull' and 'push' factors.[4] 'Pull' factors are those factors which attract employees to another organisation while 'push' factors cause employees to leave involuntarily. 'Pull' factors identified include moving for higher earnings, moving to further one's career and the attraction of alternative job opportunities. 'Push' factors identified include leaving to avoid strains arising from interpersonal conflict, 'running down' (reducing headcount) of an organisation and the induction crisis. Another factor identified which does not fit in easily with this classification is the loss of unstable recruits which is classified by Bowey as a neutral factor.

Fig. 3.3 Leaving rates

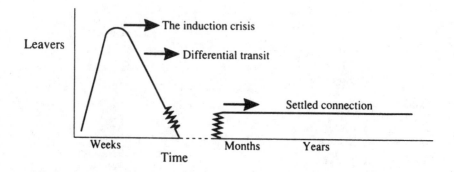

Leaving rates typically follow an established pattern (see figure 3.3). Bramham identifies three distinct phases:[5]

a) the induction crisis where new employees do not settle into their new roles and leave within a matter of weeks;

b) differential transit where employees give their job a chance but find it unacceptable and leave;

c) settled connection where employees settle down to a long period of service.

Absenteeism

Absenteeism has been defined by the Federation of Irish Employers (FIE) as 'all absences from work other than paid holidays'.[6] It affects the internal supply of manpower to the firm in the sense that an organisation which has an absenteeism problem finds itself understaffed and unable to cope with demands made upon it. It is a serious cost factor in Irish industry. Data from the Irish Management Institute (IMI) estimates that average absenteeism rates range from 7 to 13 per cent across industry sectors and its cost in terms of money lost is higher than for total time lost due to official and unofficial strikes.[7]

Absenteeism derives from a range of factors which include *a)* ability to attend work (affected by illness, sex role responsibilities, age and transportation difficulties) and *b)* the motivation to attend. The motivation to attend is a function of satisfaction with the job situation (job content, variety, autonomy and discretion inherent in the tasks performed), internal and external pressures to attend. Internal pressures to attend include a 'sense of duty' to always attend whenever possible (despite sickness in some cases). External pressures to attend include the organisation's incentive system, the extent to which discipline or dismissal is likely to follow repeated absences and the extent to which there are other job opportunities available in the local labour market. It has been noted that aggregate level absences fall in a period of recession and rise in periods of business prosperity.

THE MANPOWER PLANNING PROCESS

The key stages of the manpower planning process may be represented as in figure 3.4.

Stage 1: Analyse Current Manpower Resources

An information system must be established to support decision-making on manpower planning issues. Such a system requires a detailed inventory on employee characteristics. These include details on age, sex, marital status, tenure, skill level, qualifications, promotion potential, performance, etc. of employees. Such systems may be manual or computerised (common in large establishments). This individual or item-based information can be collated or

Fig. 3.4. The manpower planning process

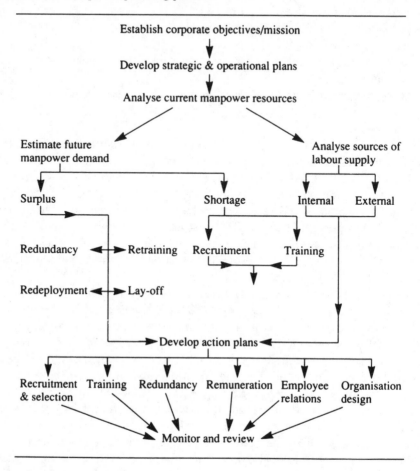

aggregated to generate a profile of the complete work-force in terms of some specified characteristics.

The existing manpower inventory facilitates the compilation of a further skills inventory which is a similar exercise concentrating on an analysis of the skills available within the workforce, (how many van drivers have a heavy goods licence or how many managerial staff a continental language).

An accurate evaluation of current manpower resources (in both quantitative and qualitative terms) is an essential source of information in determining future manpower needs. It provides information on manpower capabilities and potential which helps in both succession planning and scheduling training and development programmes. It also helps to assess the strengths and weaknesses of the current workforce according to criteria such as age, sex, experience, skills and qualifications and potential.[8] Such information is useful when new posts are created or vacancies arise.

One of the first steps will be to examine the *age distribution* of each category of employees to determine future retirement patterns, identify succession paths for younger employees and plan recruitment policies. The following diagrams illustrate some different types of age distribution:

Fig. 3.5.A Ageing workforce

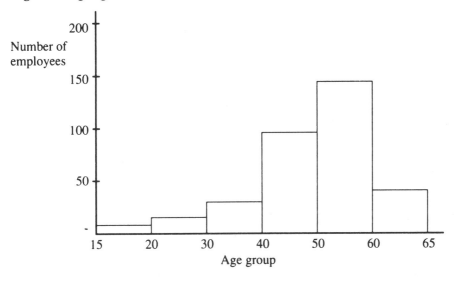

Fig. 3.5.B Young workforce

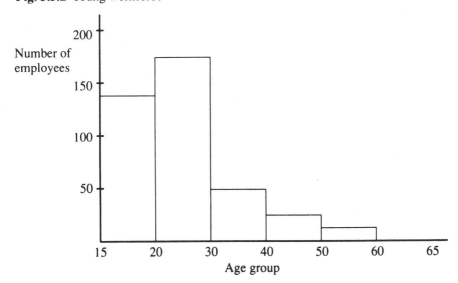

Fig. 3.5.C Middle-aged workforce

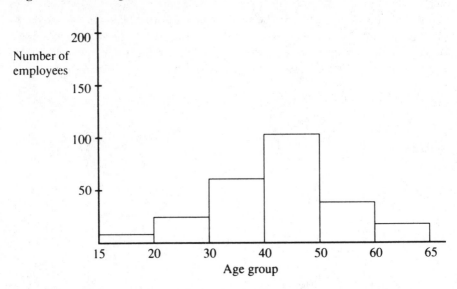

Fig. 3.5.D Young/old distribution

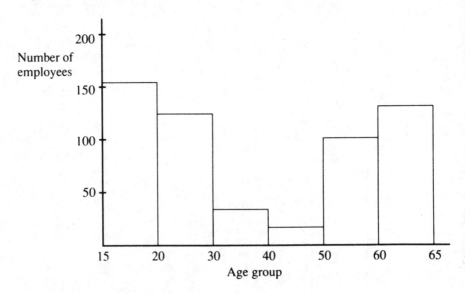

Figure 3.5A: the implications of an ageing workforce for an organisation are considerable. The firm must plan for a significant loss of staff through

retirement and ensure adequate pension funding arrangements. It may also find that older workers become ill. It has been observed that younger workers go absent more frequently than older workers. However, the duration of absence for older workers (45+) is significantly longer (probably indicating illness or disability).

Figure 3.5B highlights the potential lack of experienced and qualified staff to fill higher level posts as they become vacant. This may necessitate recruiting from outside the organisation or developing intensive training programmes to develop such staff internally.

In *Figure 3.5C* this latter problem is avoided but in fifteen years' time, should the company recruit replacement staff from younger age groups, the age distribution will change to that shown in figure 3.5A: an ageing workforce with high labour turnover.

Figure 3.5D illustrates in a more profound way the problem of finding replacements for older employees from within the organisation. Of course, a lot depends on the level of skills necessary for the job. For example, age and experience might be important for senior management posts but less significant at operator level.

Calculating age distribution assists in *forecasting promotion opportunities* for existing staff and is particularly necessary for an organisation which wishes to promote from within. Promotion from within has certain benefits, increasing the morale of employees who can clearly see career paths for their future progression. However, on the negative side it can promote 'nepotism' and a 'tunnel vision' syndrome. Recruitment policies should take into account the current and future age profiles of the organisation's workforce. Every attempt should be made to maintain a balanced workforce in terms of age. This avoids the creation of promotion blockages which occur in situations where all employees are of a similar age.

In planning future staff development, one simple but effective technique is the staff succession chart which identifies possible replacement candidates over the short and long term. An example is given below (figure 3.6), showing possible movements within the production department of a private sector organisation. As mentioned earlier, the calculation of labour turnover and absence rates is useful in establishing an organisation's ability to maintain a steady internal manpower supply. Table 3.1 identifies a number of useful measures of turnover and absenteeism.

While some level of *absenteeism* will be present in all organisations, most critical attention has focused on unauthorised absenteeism where staff are unavailable for work although scheduled to be present. Many commentators have pointed to the detrimental affects of such absenteeism on productivity and competitiveness, highlighting the large proportion of working days lost through absenteeism as opposed to industrial action.[9]

Fig. 3.6. Staff succession chart – production department

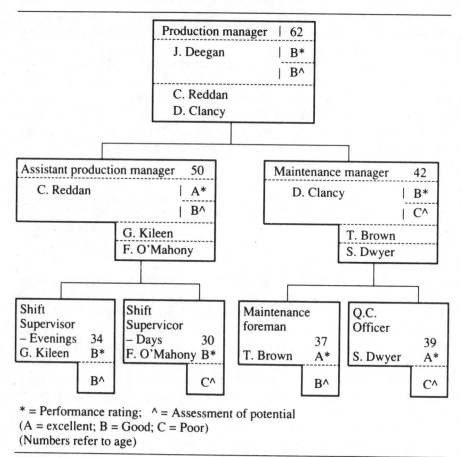

Production manager		62
J. Deegan		B*
		B^
C. Reddan		
D. Clancy		

Assistant production manager 50
C. Reddan | A*
| B^
G. Kileen
F. O'Mahony

Maintenance manager 42
D. Clancy | B*
| C^
T. Brown
S. Dwyer

Shift Supervisor – Evenings 34
G. Kileen B*
B^

Shift Supervicor – Days 30
F. O'Mahony B*
C^

Maintenance foreman 37
T. Brown A*
B^

Q.C. Officer 39
S. Dwyer A*
C^

* = Performance rating; ^ = Assessment of potential
(A = excellent; B = Good; C = Poor)
(Numbers refer to age)

Table 3.1. Useful indices in manpower planning

Separation Rate (Crude rate of labour turnover)	$=$	$\dfrac{\text{Number leaving in period}}{\text{Average number employed in period}} \times 100$
Stability index (Extent to which experienced employees are being retained)	$=$	$\dfrac{\text{Number of employees with more than one year's service}}{\text{Total number of employees one year ago}} \times 100$
Overall absence rate	$=$	$\dfrac{\text{Number of manhours lost in period}}{\text{Total number of manhours in period}} \times 100$

In a major public service study Blennerhassett and Gorman suggest that certain categories of employees are particularly 'absence prone'.[10] They feel that absenteeism levels are strongly affected by social and economic factors as well as by factors associated with the individual and organisational context. They identify unskilled employees, married women with dependent children, and employees working non-standard hours or in large work groups as more likely to have high levels of absenteeism. In tackling absenteeism, management should firstly establish the nature and extent of the problem (for example, absenteeism levels measured by department, shift, employee category). They may then identify the reason for absenteeism and take appropriate steps to reduce or eliminate unjustified absenteeism. These may involve punitive and motivational measures as appropriate (see figure 3.7). Important considerations include the effectiveness of the recruitment procedure, the nature and context of the work carried out by employees and line management attitudes. The personnel department will have an important role in establishing an effective absenteeism policy while line management will be responsible for initially dealing with individual cases, particularly in interviewing employees upon return to work as to the nature and validity of their absence.

Fig. 3.7. Absenteeism: measurement and control

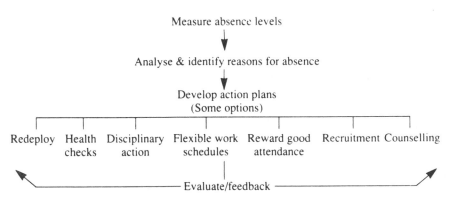

Management need to pay equal attention to *labour turnover*. Once the organisation has selected employees and made appropriate training and development provision it is important that they retain suitable employees who can contribute positively to the organisation. In analysing labour turnover, management must not only establish the extent of turnover but also identify in what areas and categories of employees turnover is greatest, the profile of leavers, (length of service, skills, etc.) and any trends in turnover patterns. They may then examine reasons for turnover through discussion with line management, exit interviews or investigation of other factors which affect the organisation's ability to retain employees. This latter category may include career development opportunities, job satisfaction and rewards. While a small amount of turnover is inevitable, and indeed beneficial, it is essential that organisations take appropriate steps to retain those employees vital to satisfying the future manpower requirements of the organisation.

An important element in evaluating current manpower resources will be an assessment of the nature and demands of the various jobs in the organisation. This process is known as *job analysis*. It involves the systematic collection, evaluation and organisation of information about jobs. It attempts to identify the key elements of jobs, the demands made upon the job-holder in terms of knowledge, skills and experience and is one of the basic information requirements of a personnel information system.

Stage 2: Forecasting Manpower Demand

Having forecast demand for the company's products, developed strategic plans for future operations and evaluated current human resource capabilities, management can estimate the organisation's future demand for manpower. This will be based on an analysis of current and future manpower needs.

Forecasting manpower demand involves the calculation of the number and quality of employees needed for a specified period into the future. The initial base for such projections will be the organisation's corporate objectives and strategic plans which chart the direction of the organisation over a medium time period of, say, 3-5 years. These would incorporate sales forecasts and budget information which allow financial plans to be developed.

Estimating future demand patterns and relating these to manpower requirements is a key corporate activity which requires senior management to estimate the future demand for the organisation's products or services and the direction the organisation should pursue over a reasonable future time period. While this is probably the most important stage in effective manpower planning it is an uncertain process since forecasting is essentially speculative. It uses past experience (current manpower information, sales volume, product capacity, etc.) and certain hypotheses about the future as a basis for projecting future demand. Key factors to be considered in estimating the organisation's manpower requirements include the corporate goals, new product development plans, future output expectations, technological change, consumption patterns, manpower and financial resources, personnel and employee relations policies and agreements.

One of the more widely used methods in estimating demand is the analysis of trends in sales and manpower requirements over time.[11] This involves the identification of the *long-run trend* in sales volume and related manpower implications (see figure 3.8). This will have an obvious impact on areas like recruitment and training. Once the long-run trend is established any *cyclical variations* should then be identified. These will occur within a medium time period (1–5 years) and are influenced by factors like changes in consumer buying patterns or temporary recession (see figure 3.8). Cyclical changes will affect manpower demand in the medium term and may lead to temporary manpower lay-offs or expansion. In the shorter term account many need to be taken of *seasonal variations*. These will account for changes covering a shorter time period (say 1 year) and may be caused by highs and lows in buying patterns due to seasonal factors such as Christmas, summer wear, etc. (see figure 3.8). These need to be planned for to avoid manpower shortages while ensuring stability among the core workforce (part-time and temporary workers may be used to cope with peak demand patterns).

Fig. 3.8. Estimating sales trend

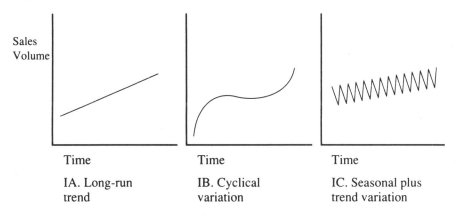

Sales Volume

| Time | Time | Time |

IA. Long-run trend   IB. Cyclical variation   IC. Seasonal plus trend variation

Once such trends have been identified they can be used to forecast manpower needs. This involves estimating manpower requirements at different levels of demand or production, possibly in terms of person/hour requirements. Again various approaches may be adopted. Work study and ratio analysis are two of the more common methods; these and some other techniques are discussed below.

Work study: where the work process of each employee is easy to measure, the ideal technique to aid manpower forecasting is one based on the number of manhours required to carry out a specific number of operations. The simplified example below shows the calculation of manpower required to meet a sales forecast of 130,000 units.

Changes in future production plans can be estimated using this information. In practice, however, the rate of technological change, and consequent productivity increases, will affect calculations and need to be taken into account.

Box 3.1. Manpower requirements

Time to construct complete product is 5 hours.
Sales forecast over next year is 130,000 product units.
Total manhours required to meet sales forecast = 130,000 x 5 = 650,000 hours.

Employees work for 47 weeks x 5 days = 235 days per year.
Employees work 8 hour day: 8 x 235 = 1,880 hours per year.

$$\frac{\text{Total manhours}}{\text{Maximum hours per employee}} = \frac{650,000}{1,880} = 346 \text{ employees}$$

Ratio analysis: where work cannot be measured directly, it may be possible to use ratios to calculate future manpower demand. For example, a secretarial recruitment agency may employ thirty staff and handle 1500 vacancies a year. In planning the opening of a new branch in a nearby town it is anticipated that 1,000 vacancies per year will have to be handled. Using simple ratio analysis (based on previous experience) a 1:50 ratio between agency staff and vacancies per year has been established. Therefore the new branch will require twenty staff to handle the 1,000 vacancies. Another common use for ratio analysis is the calculation of supervisory ratios. If the supervisory/operator ratio is 1:10 and the organisation plans to take on another 100 operators the resultant demand for extra supervisors will be ten, assuming that the same span of control is to be maintained.

Line management: the managers of each specialist activity, given the general guidelines of the organisation's corporate plan and estimates of future demand, should be ideally placed to forecast the manpower implications of the plan on their area of responsibility. To avoid 'empire building' it is important that line managers justify any expansion plans to top management and that the latter encourage line management to seek ways of improving manpower utilisation. As with other areas, the involvement of line management at the early planning stages helps in achieving accurate information and securing subsequent commitment to the plans developed.

Internal constraints: in making any manpower forecast it is essential to take into account the internal environment of the organisation. Attitudes to new technology, staff flexibility and availability, overtime working, and the employee relations climate will all have an influence on labour utilisation and the degree to which management can make effective manpower forecasts.

Stage 3: Analysis of Sources of Labour Supply

Once the organisation has calculated future manpower demands and analysed current resources it will know whether it is going to have a shortage or surplus of manpower. Should it foresee a surplus of manpower, plans need to be developed to cater for this through redundancy, retirement or redeployment programmes. Should a shortage of manpower be indicated, management attention will focus on where staff of the appropriate quality can be found and what steps the organisation can take to ensure their availability when required. These extra staff may come from within the organisation or via external recruitment.

a) Internal supply: indications of current capabilities and future potential should be available from preceding analyses of the organisation's manpower resources. This may be disaggregated into specific manpower categories and take account of previous rates of staff retention, absenteeism levels, promotion patterns and transfers. The availability of detailed manpower and skills inventories should provide composite information on manpower strengths and weakness, skills and qualifications, work history and potential. These will enable management identify employees with the particular skills and abilities to meet future company needs.

b) External supply: unless the organisation is experiencing a decreasing demand for its products/services or has an exceptional pool of qualified employees internally, it will have to look outside the organisation for some of its workforce.

The analysis of wastage, absenteeism and productivity levels, together with forecasts of the organisation's future activity levels, will provide the basic information on manpower needs. Detailed job analysis will identify the skills, experience and responsibilities required to fill vacant posts which arise. Armed with such information the organisation can assess the labour market and identify the people best suited to meet the organisation's needs. In assessing sources of supply, management should be *au fait* with developments affecting the external labour market. Particular attention should be paid to developments in the political, social and technological spheres. Examples of considerations which might be taken into account are:

(i) political: manpower policies—education and training, employment creation; legislation—working hours, holidays, etc.; *(ii) economic:* levels of present and projected economic activity, employment, inflation, exchange rates and impact on consumption/demand; *(iii) technological:* developments in technology—implications for employment, redundancy, work organisation, etc.

Apart from these broad macro-level issues, management need to take account of developments in the local environment which impact upon the manpower planning process. These might include trends and developments in population density and structure, unemployment levels and categories, availability of housing and transport, social trends, competition for labour, local economic activity (expansion or contraction), supply of specific skills from education and training facilities.

Stage 4: Development of Action Plans

While the need for and utilisation of information derived through manpower planning will differ between organisations the following may be considered as indicative of some common benefits:

i) improved utilisation of manpower resources;

ii) reduction of labour costs;

iii) identification of training and development needs;

iv) anticipation of future potential redundancy problems and the development of alternative strategies such as short-time working, redeployment, retraining.

The final product of the manpower planning process is the development of specific plans to ensure that the day-to-day manpower needs of the organisation are satisfied effectively. These plans will cover procedures and practices in relation to recruitment, selection, assessment, development, promotions, training, etc. Action plans, thus developed, should answer a series of questions posed at earlier stages in the manpower planning process: what skills should the organisation be training for; where can it find future managerial staff; where can it get high quality electronic engineers? These plans should also cater for broader policy issues such as employee relations approaches, organisation design and development, etc.

Stage 5: Feedback and Monitoring

Manpower planning is an ongoing process, both receiving and providing management with information central to the organisation's personnel management strategies. Information on issues like recruitment patterns, training, etc. should be fed back into the various stages of the manpower planning process so that corrective action can be taken. Such feedback will be in the form of reports, trends and forecasts covering areas like successful or unsuccessful recruitment trends, reasons for labour turnover, adoption to new technology, etc. Only through constant assessment of the manpower planning process can personnel practitioners provide senior management with the correct forecasts and information to develop adequately their overall human resources strategy and to cope with change.

THE MANPOWER PLANNING ENVIRONMENT AND
THE IRISH EMPLOYMENT STRUCTURE

The features of the Irish labour market are central to any analysis of manpower planning practice. The sectoral distribution of employment illustrates the progressive decline of agricultural and industrial employment and the dramatic rise in the service sector as an employer (see table 3.2). The services sector now accounts for 58 per cent of all employment in the Irish economy. Within the industrial sector, manufacturing employment suffered dramatic losses in numbers employed in the post-1980 recessionary period (see table 3.3).

Other important developments in employment structure over the past decade have been the growth in long-term unemployment, a lowering of the retirement age and the return of widespread emigration.

Within this overall pattern it is interesting that female participation rates have increased. The sectoral shifts in employment are favourably biased towards greater female employment, with women proportionately over-represented in the expanding service sectors. These increasing participation rates of women are illustrated vividly in table 3.3. Retail distribution, insurance, financial, business, professional and personal services are the areas which have the highest concentration of female employment.

Manpower planners need to be aware of such broad trends in employment and education so that sources of labour supply can be accurately analysed. One aspect of the shifts in employment structure and the depressed economic environment has been greater variation in forms of employment with a trend away from traditional employment arrangements to more 'atypical' forms of employment. Dineen highlights four major areas of growth:[12]

a) Part-time employment: substantial increases in numbers working part-time, particularly among women;

b) temporary and casual work: growth of employee numbers in temporary jobs—again most pronounced among female employees;

c) self-employment: the emphasis on self-employment and entrepreneurial activity has shifted away from the agricultural sector to the business and commercial services sector;

d) government and community schemes: greater State involvement in subsidising employment and particularly in encouraging self-employment.[13]

These trends have important implications for the options available to manpower planners and personnel practitioners. A decreasing emphasis on full-time employment and an increase in part-time and temporary working has facilitated the growth of 'core-periphery' based organisations (core representing full-time staff; periphery representing temporary and part-time staff, see chapter 11). In addition, the availability of trainees from bodies such as FÁS has perhaps encouraged some employers to substitute part-time

Table 3.2. Employment by sector 1961-88

	1961 '000	%	1971 '000	%	1977 '000	%	1980 '000	%	1982 '000	%	1984 '000	%	1986 '000	%	1988 '000	%
Agriculture	380	36	273	26	228	21	220	19	193	17	181	16.5	168	16	162	15
Industry	257	24.5	323	30.5	326	30	360	31	355	31	319	29	305	28	299	27.5
Services	415	39.5	450	43.5	529	49	583	50	598	52	603	54.5	606	56	626	57.5

Source: CSO/Labour Force Survey.

Table 3.3 Sectoral employment distribution and female participation levels 1975-87

Sector	1975 ('000s)	% Female	1979 ('000s)	% Female	1987 ('000s)	% Female	Change 1975/87 Total employment %	Female employment %
Agriculture, forestry, fishing, mining, turf, etc.	247.0	8.7	234.0	8.7	171.0	7.4	-30.8	-40.9
Manufacturing	222.0	29.5	242.3	27.4	207.9	30.3	-6.4	-3.8
Electricity, gas & water	14.6	12.3	14.0	12.9	14.0	12.1	-4.1	-5.3
Building & construction	89.2	2.2	101.1	3.2	71.3	3.8	-20.1	+37.6
Commerce & transport	223.8	28.8	229.7	28.3	232.2	30.1	+3.8	+8.3
Financial & business services	27.6	46.4	36.6	46.4	46.7	46.7	+69.2	+70.2
Professional services*	126.8	62.0	148.5	59.2	191.8	59.4	+51.3	+45.0
Public administration & defence	60.0	24.2	70.1	26.1	70.3	28.9	+17.2	+39.8
Personal services*	46.8	66.9	57.1	62.5	63.6	63.2	35.9	+28.4
Other industries	13.2	35.6	16.8	3.8	18.9	32.8	43.2	31.9
Totals	1071.0	27.8	1150.3	28.0	1087.6	32.4	+1.5	+18.4

Source: Labour Force Surveys 1975, 1979, 1987.

* Sectors with highest concentration of female employment

for full-time employment.

MANPOWER PLANNING IN IRELAND

It is difficult to assess accurately the degree to which manpower planning is carried out in Irish organisations and how much consideration is given to external trends in employment, training, education and economic activity. The major work in the area was carried out by AnCO in 1979.[14] This survey sought to establish the extent of utilisation of manpower planning in Irish organisations. It found that most organisations claimed to be involved in manpower planning (see table 3.4). This finding is substantiated in more recent research undertaken by Shivanath, and Cairns and Thompson[15] (see table 3.4).

Table 3.4. Utilisation of manpower planning in Irish organisations

Activity	Degree utilised (%)	
	AnCO (1979)	Shivanath (1987)
1. Analysing current workforce	92	87.5
2. Forecasting future demand	88	86.0
3. Forecasting future supply		
– internal	87	n/a
– external	28	n/a
4. Matching supply and demand	72	n/a

In the AnCO survey external supply forecasting was the only area not widely practised. This may place a question mark over the effectiveness of manpower planning at organisation level but more likely reflects the fact that the slackness of the labour market ensures a ready supply of potential employees. An interesting finding was that just 20 per cent of respondent organisations carried out all four manpower planning activities as an integrated exercise. This may indicate a lack of a clear understanding of the nature and ultimate purpose of manpower planning. A particularly worrying finding was that a substantial number of organisations did not engage in any formal corporate planning. Cairns and Thompson, too, found some discrepancies in their analysis. While most organisations claimed to forecast manpower demand, not all of these organisations carried out activities to facilitate the development of accurate manpower forecasts such as developing replacement policies.[16]

The Planning Horizon and Manpower Planning

Taking a closer look at the AnCO survey, the time scale for demand forecasts was short, with most concentrating on forecasts for a maximum of one year ahead. Most manufacturing companies calculated their manpower needs on the basis of production targets, taking into account past production levels and any expected changes in product mix or technology. Some also relied on managerial opinion or estimates.

Looking at forecasts of manpower supply, the lack of emphasis on external supply forecasting has already been noted. In attempting to estimate future supply most firms (64 per cent) calculated wastage rates. However, these forecasts of labour supply were established for relatively short time horizons (generally one year or less). Just over 40 per cent of the companies surveyed assessed employee potential and estimated levels of transfers, promotions or changes in working conditions.

On the issue of utilisation of manpower planning information, the AnCo survey identified three key areas in which manpower planning contributes

Table 3.5 Degree to which manpower planning aids corporate decision-making

	Number of firms answering (N = 138)		
	A lot	A little	Not at all
Recruitment	101	30	2
Training	100	31	2
Expansion	96	23	12
Contraction	80	26	17
Promotion	74	46	10
Succession	74	42	7
Redundancy	58	39	30
Payroll costs	56	50	24
Effective skills use	55	57	17
Staff turnover	45	56	28
Absenteeism	40	49	39
Location	34	37	49

Source: Fox, R. and O'Reilly, A.P., *Corporate Manpower Planning in Ireland*, AnCO 1979.

to organisational decision-making: recruitment, training and expansion: Substantially fewer companies saw manpower contraction as an important area where manpower planning can help. Cairns and Thompson found that the most important use of manpower planning was in the effective utilisation of human resources; controlling labour costs and estimating recruitment needs were other important uses identified.

Looking at managerial attitudes, most respondents to the AnCO survey believed manpower planning worthwhile for all types of organisation (see table 3.6). While most thought long-term manpower planning was both feasible and useful, only 15 per cent of the firms surveyed produced long-term forecasts of labour demand and supply. The other significant finding was that manpower planning suffered from a lack of integration with corporate planning, the absence of a clear understanding of what is involved and a lack of appropriate data. Cairns and Thompson expressed similar concern

Table 3.6. Attitudes to manpower planning among Irish organisations

Statement	% Agreed	% Undecided	% Disagreed
1. Manpower planning is not for small and medium-sized companies	17	8	77
2. Manpower planning is seen as an interference by line manager	16	11	74
3. The costs of manpower planning outweigh the likely benefits	8	16	76
4. Manpower planning suffers from lack of data in forecasting manpower demand & supply	60	19	21
5. Manpower planning suffers from a lack of readily applicable planning techniques	46	22	32
6. Manpower planning suffers from a lack of personnel qualified for planning	46	16	38
7. Manpower planning suffers from lack of involvement by top management	40	9	51
8. Manpower planning suffers from lack of understanding of what manpower planning is	67	10	23
9. Manpower planning suffers from non-existence of a corporate plan	64	12	24
10. The future is too uncertain to justify manpower planning for anything but the short-term	36	9	45

Source: Fox, R. and O'Reilly, A.P., *Corporate Manpower Planning in Ireland,* AnCO 1979.

about the 'lack of completeness' of organisational manpower planning.
The interest and involvement of top management is a vital factor in determining the significance of manpower planning in the organisation. As can be seen from table 3.6. most companies felt that top management only became actively involved in manpower planning where there was significant concern over the cost and/or availability of manpower. Technological change or productivity issues were also significant. Concern over wastage rates or redundancy problems were not seen as particularly important. More recently Downes has argued that uncertainty about the future led organisations to reject long-term forecasting.[17] She also identified the lack of external supply

forecasting which is probably due to the large labour surplus. As with the AnCO survey, the data collected through personnel record systems appeared to be under-utilised, particularly in relation to the analysis of employee performance.

Manpower planning appears to be most useful in training, recruitment and promotion/succession planning. Top management involvement would seem to be spurred on when technological change issues affect the organisation, when highly skilled or qualified employees are scarce or when labour costs are high. Cairns and Thompson suggest that personnel priorities are moving away from reactive areas like recruitment towards a more proactive role, where manpower planning is integrated with an overall human resources and business strategy.

MANPOWER PLANNING AND THE PERSONNEL PRACTITIONER

Manpower planning provides an opportunity for personnel department involvement in strategic decision-making. Adopting a long-term strategic perspective, personnel practitioners can, through the preparation of accurate manpower and skills inventories, forecast the organisation's demand for and supply of labour. By identifying and anticipating obsolescence, changes in technology, production and market trends, the personnel practitioner is ideally placed to influence the direction of the organisation.

The personnel manager who is linked by a professional network of contacts to government agencies, FÁS, etc., becomes a source of expert knowledge on national and local manpower trends and can impart these to line management colleagues. Thus, the senior personnel specialist should be ideally placed to develop a long-term strategic outlook on the role of human resources in contributing to long-term survival and growth. In Shivanath's study of personnel practice in Ireland she found extensive evidence of senior personnel practitioners operating in such an 'architect' mode.[18] Involvement at strategic level was greatest in relation to 'specialist' personnel issues such as promotions and organisation development. However, a substantial proportion of personnel practitioners also reported extensive involvement on more general strategic matters such as relocation or changes in product or technology. The only areas where personnel's involvement was considerably lower were in the key strategic issues of acquisitions and mergers. It seems that the manpower planning implications of such decisions are not fully appreciated in some organisations. Manpower planning is a vital aspect in managing organisational change, and senior personnel practitioners acting as human resources strategists should have a key role in advising on the manpower implications of such corporate decisions.

At operational level manpower planning requires extensive involvement and co-operation between line management and personnel practitioners. Personnel practitioners provide line managers with information which assists them in executing their particular areas of responsibility.

Manpower planning offers a tremendous opportunity for senior, line and personnel managers to work closely together.[19] It requires that corporate goals be clearly outlined and that manpower plans and related activities are explicitly linked to corporate goals. For manpower planning to be most effective, the personnel manager should be part of the senior management team which is responsible for developing the organisation's corporate plans. Most, if not all, strategic business decisions will have human resource implications, and the senior personnel specialist is ideally placed to provide a corporate level input on personnel issues. Manpower planning is the starting point upon which policy decisions in other areas of personnel work are based. Effective manpower planning is a prerequisite to the successful execution of related personnel activities discussed in subsequent chapters.

Chapter 4

Recruitment and Selection

INTRODUCTION

If employees are one of the organisation's most vital resources then securing that resource is a crucial step in contributing to corporate success. Selecting the right calibre and numbers of employees and having them in position at the right time is a central personnel management concern and possibly its most important activity area. If the employment process is conducted in an effective and efficient manner the groundwork for a successful organisation will have been established. An effective and systematic employment process can have numerous advantages for the organisation as outlined in box 4.1.

Box 4.1. Advantages of an effective employment process

* Clarification of organisational and job needs
* Employment of high-quality employees
* Increased productivity from a motivated and committed workforce
* Vacancies filled quickly and performance maintained
* Improved cost-effectiveness through monitoring and revision of the employment process
* Enhanced corporate profile and image through conducting the employment process in a professional manner
* More effective training and development through reduced labour turnover and selection of high calibre employees
* Favourable organisational climate which may be reflected in reduced absenteeism, better morale and employee relations
* Reduced possibility of personal failures due to selection of unsuitable employees

---

THE RECRUITMENT AND SELECTION PROCESS

On initial consideration, recruitment and selection may seem a fairly straightforward process where the organisation seeks to place the right people in the right jobs to achieve the goals of the organisation. While this general objective is indeed appropriate it should be appreciated that the recruitment and selection process is composed of a series of related activities, each crucial in its own right. These activities should be conducted in a systematic and thorough manner to ensure that the organisation has adequate manpower resources to meet its needs.

Employing people is a major undertaking for any organisation. A decision to recruit employees should be taken in response to an identifiable organisational need. Management must be able to answer the question 'do we need to place somebody in this job?' A particularly important consideration for organisations entering the labour market is to differentiate between recruitment and selection. Although often thought of as synonymous, recruitment and selection refer to different stages in the employment process.[1] *Recruitment* involves attracting a group of potentially employable candidates to apply for the vacancy identified. *Selection*, on the other hand, is the process of choosing from that group the right employee(s) to fill the vacancy. Good recruitment is a prerequisite for effective selection; if the wrong people are attracted to apply for the job there is little the company can do by way of selection to remedy the situation.[2]

Once employees have been selected, their initial placement in jobs should be closely monitored. This particularly refers to good induction and orientation and subsequent evaluation of employee performance. An outline of the recruitment and selection process is given in figure 4.1.

Fig. 4.1. The recruitment and selection process

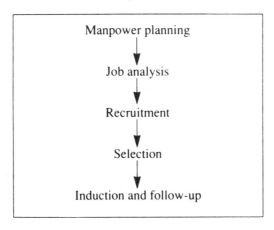

Manpower planning was considered earlier and is central to effective recruitment and selection. It helps to anticipate future manpower demands and to plan how these will be satisfied. Job analysis provides basic information on job requirements and candidate profile.

Job Analysis

Job analysis is one of the most basic personnel activities. It helps to clarify the duties, responsibilities and other job demands, and helps to identify the ideal employee profile to satisfy organisational needs. Properly conducted, job analysis establishes the groundwork for numerous other personnel activities. Some of the potential applications of job analysis are outlined in box 4.2.

Box 4.2. Applications of job analysis

a) *Manpower planning*: Helps to identify job requirements and assists in effective workforce utilisation by facilitating the optimal deployment of human resources.

b) *Recruitment and selection:* Clarifies duties and responsibilities of jobs and indicates the knowledge, skill and experience required to adequately undertake the job.

c) *Job evaluation:* Provides accurate job descriptions on which to base decisions on the grading and remuneration of jobs.

d) *Job design:* Identifies the best way of organising work and highlights opportunities for increasing job satisfaction.

e) *Training and development:* Provides details on the job skills, knowledge and standards which help to identify training needs and to facilitate the design of training/development programmes.

f) *Performance appraisal:* Identification of job standards provides a basis for the assessment of employee performance.

g) *Career planning*: Provides a basis for orienting new recruits on job and organisation demands and helps to select jobs/tasks which best suit individual employee capabilities.

h) *Health and safety*: Helps to identify job hazards and dangerous working conditions and to assist in accident prevention.

Job analysis provides some specific information, particularly job descriptions, job specifications, personnel specifications and outline terms and conditions of employment, which may then be applied in any of the above areas (see table 4.1).

Table 4.1. Products of job analysis

Outcome	Focus	Content
1. Job description	Jobs	Broad statement of the purpose, scope, duties & responsibilities of a job
2. Job specification	Tasks	Detailed specification of the knowledge and skills required to carry out the tasks/duties of the job
3. Personnel specification	Person	Describes the types of person required to do the job, including qualifications, knowledge, specific skills and aptitudes, experience, physical & personal attributes.
4. Terms and conditions of	Rewards	Statement outlining the main terms & conditions of employment associated with the job, including pay, working hours, overtime & shift arrangements, holidays, job location, hazards, etc.

The job description: job analysis involves the collection of information on jobs. A preliminary step is the preparation of a job description. This can be done in a various ways as summarised in Box 4.3. The method chosen may vary depending on organisational needs and should incorporate employee participation.

Box 4.3. Methods of preparing job descriptions

Postholders: Employees prepare their own job descriptions; possible disadvantages are variations in employee approach, related inconsistencies and risk of under/over-stated job demands.

Management: superiors prepare job descriptions; disadvantages include possibly inadequate job knowledge and absence of employee participation.

Interviews: superior or trained job analyst interviews postholders and agrees job description; advantage of participative approach but is time-consuming and costly.

Questionnaire: employees complete standardised questionnaire which forms basis for a subsequent interview with superior or job analyst to agree job description; comprehensive and participative but time-consuming, expensive and questionnaires may be difficult to develop.

Observation: job analyst or other technical specialist gathers information by observing employees and questioning employees and supervisors; can be source of resentment among employees.

In many organisations the job description and job specification are viewed as being synonymous as the difference is largely one of detail. Here the term job description is used to encompass a statement of the tasks, duties and responsibilities of a job. Whatever data collection method is used, the objective is to produce a comprehensive job description and this task should be completed with two guiding factors in mind: simplicity and accuracy. Ungerson suggests five key content areas:[3] job title; overall job purpose; reports to (superior's title); key result areas; responsible for (supervisory responsibility).

Box 4.4. Sample job description — social worker

Title: Social worker
Department: Welfare care (West)
Job purpose: To provide a professional, comprehensive welfare service to specified elderly clients in the . . . . region and to direct, advise and support home-help staff in their day-to-day duties.
Responsible to: Social services supervisor (West)
Responsible for: Six full-time and two part-time home-help staff
Key tasks:
1. To visit and promote the welfare of clients in their homes.
2. To supervise and report on the work of home helps.
3. To review and make recommendations on care of clients whose circumstances warrant special care.
4. To support families of clients in terms of advice, guidance and emotional adjustment.
5. To manage the regional elderly care welfare budget; check invoices and expenses and make quarterly returns to regional accounts.

The key result areas may be further broken down into sub-tasks. The degree of detail will vary, depending on factors such as the nature of the job and type of organisation. An equally important factor is the use to which the job description is being put. For manpower planning a general job description outlining the main characteristics of jobs will suffice. For other applications the job description may emphasise other relevant aspects; for example, a job description used for training purposes will need to be more specific on job knowledge, skills and performance standards.
The personnel specification: a personnel specification is an outline of the skills, knowledge, experience and other requirements necessary to carry out the job satisfactorily. It should indicate the requirements which are deemed essential to carry out the job effectively and those that are desirable in an ideal candidate. Personnel specifications are often prepared using

some assessment framework such as Munro-Fraser's five-point plan (see later section on employee selection).

Box 4.5. Sample personnel specification — training officer

Job title: Training officer (management development)
Department: Personnel
Job purpose: To identify management training needs, design management development programmes, organise and coordinate in-service management training, review and approve applications to attend external management training courses, lecture on in-service programmes as appropriate and evaluate and report on both in-service and external management courses.
Responsible to: Training manager

Job requirements	Essential	Desirable
Physical characteristics	Good health, good verbal ability	Good appearance; tidy dress & good first impression
Education	Degree/Diploma in Business studies or related discipline	Specialisation in personnel/ training; IPM member
Experience	5 years work experience; at least 3 in middle management with some knowledge of personnel/ training	3 years in management training; previous teaching/ lecturing experience
Skills	Computer applications in training (CBT, CAT); good interpersonal skills	Negotiating skills; organisation & methods
Motivation	Ambitious to succeed in training and to expand into other personnel areas	Ability to motivate others and to gain confidence and support of line management
Disposition/ circumstances	Ability to influence others; acceptability to different occupational groupings; adaptable	Friendly/outgoing personality; flexibility in working patterns
Interests	Variety of sporting/social interests; organisational ability	Analytical skills as might be demonstrated through interests in chess, bridge, etc.

THE RECRUITMENT PHASE
Initial Considerations
Alternatives to recruitment: even where the organisation has identified a need for additional tasks it may be useful to consider alternatives to recruiting employees. Perhaps the additional burden can be handled without taking on additional staff? Some such alternatives are outlined in figure 4.2.

Fig. 4.2. Alternatives to recruitment

Sub-contracting	Automation	Overtime	Casual/temporary staff
Redeployment	Homeworking	Productivity bargaining	Increased flexibility/ remove demarcation

Sub-contracting is becoming an increasingly important option. This is especially so for non-repetitive support jobs or tasks peripheral to the main work of the organisation (such as catering or cleaning). It relieves the organisation of a long-term commitment to employees and the legal and social obligations involved. With rising labour costs and the increasing attractiveness of new technology it may be feasible to mechanise jobs and reduce the need for additional employees. This alternative now applies to both production-type jobs and white collar employment. The options of overtime working or deploying additional tasks among the existing workforce have the attractions of alleviating the need for new staff and, possibly, increasing productivity. Other related alternatives include homeworking, increasing flexibility and negotiated productivity improvements. Flexible work modes are becoming increasingly common, and these trends are discussed in greater depth in later chapters. The last option—casual or temporary employees—is not really an alternative to recruitment. Rather, it is a variation inferring a shorter-term commitment to employees and savings on additional employment costs (holidays, pensions, etc.) as well as the possibility of lower direct costs such as wages.

Recruitment context: factors in the external business environment impact upon the recruitment process and influence its effectiveness. Economic considerations on a national and international level affect consumer demand which is a major variable in establishing the need for recruitment. Related to this, unemployment levels will influence the nature of the labour market, wage levels and labour mobility. Even in times of high unemployment levels, certain skills may be in short supply. Education and training facilities in certain areas may be inadequate or, possibly, people with these skills may be attracted elsewhere—even abroad—by higher wages, better conditions, etc. Legislation on employment equality, conditions of employment, dismissal and redundancy will affect the recruitment decision.[4] Equally, the organisation's image and perception will influence the attitudes of candidates towards taking up employment in the organisation or, having done so, their commitment to that organisation. The organisation must ensure the recruitment and selection process is conducted in a business-like manner. (A useful indication of both the organisation's and the candidate's responsibilities is outlined in the IPM's Code of Practice on Recruitment.)[5]

Sourcing Candidates

An effective job analysis exercise will indicate job demands and identify suitable employee profiles. This helps to answer some of the fundamental questions that need to be considered when a vacancy arises (see box 4.6).

Box 4.6. Undertaking recruitment — initial considerations

Question	Information source
1. Do we need to fill the vacancy?	Manpower plan; job description and job specification
2. What kind of job is it?	Job description
3. What skills and knowledge does the job demand?	Job description/specification
4. What kind of person is required?	Personnel specification
5. What possible training and development needs may arise?	Job specification
6. What is the remuneration package?	Terms/conditions of employment
7. Have we got suitable candidates internally?	Manpower and skills inventories/succession plans
8. Where should we look for external candidates?	Manpower plan

---

In considering recruitment, an initial step is to relate back to the manpower plan and ascertain whether filling the vacancy or creating a new post is justified in the long term and, if it is, what are the possible sources of recruitment. Line management involvement in establishing human resource requirements and evaluating their current utilisation will assist in the effective deployment of manpower. As a preliminary step, line managers may complete a staff requisition form when a vacancy arises. This exercise helps managers to think carefully about manpower utilisation in their section or department.

Fig. 4.3. Staff requisition form

Job title	Department	Grade

Replacement [　　　] Temporary [　　　] Starting date

New post [　　　] Permanent [　　　]

Job description — please attach an up-dated job description
Job function — brief statement of main purpose and function

Reasons for replacement/additional post

If a replacement, complete the following:
Employee replaced:　　　　　　　Date terminated:

Reason for termination

Performance of employee:　　　　　　　　Would you re-engage
Poor ☐　　　Satisfactory ☐
Above average ☐　　Outstanding ☐　　　Yes ☐　　No ☐

Signed:　　　　　　Post:　　　　　Date:

Once a decision to recruit is made, the next step is to evaluate the various sources of candidates and related costs. A basic decision is whether to confine the recruitment trawl to internal candidates or look outside the organisation for 'new blood'. If the latter option is taken the costs and benefits of such sources must be carefully considered. Table 4.2 provides a brief summary of the main sources of recruitment and a comment on related direct costs (excluding management time, administration, etc.).

Internal sources: organisations have differing approaches to recruiting from the current workforce. Some will place a strong emphasis on employee development, succession planning and internal recruitment. Others may have a less systematic approach. There are numerous advantages in using internal sources. These include lower costs, accurate knowledge on employee performance and a positive impact on morale and motivation. Certain organisations express a clear preference for internal recruitment and will only look externally to fill lower order jobs (where no internal candidates are interested) or specialist jobs where particular skills or knowledge are required. Some may prefer to recruit young employees and develop these internally for higher level positions. Together with progressive personnel policies on rewards, job design and employee relations, this approach is seen as promoting employee loyalty and commitment.

Table 4.2. Sources of recruitment

Sources	Direct costs

Internal
    Transfer
    Promotion
    Demotion
	None

External
    Existing workforce;
    recommendations–friends, relatives, etc.
	Very low

Casual applications (unrequisited–CVs, walk-ins, etc.)	Very low
Advertising (local, national media professional/technical journals, etc.)	Expensive (dependent on media used & circulation)
Schools and colleges (contacts, careers officers, 'milk round')	Low (except for travel costs)
FÁS	None (can receive financial benefits for employing some categories of workers)
Employment agencies	Expensive (10% to 25% starting salaries)
Management consultants/ executive search agencies	Very expensive (25% + of starting salary)

There may also be some drawbacks to internal recruitment. By definition the organisation is limiting its potential range of candidates with the possibility that better candidates from the wider labour market are being overlooked. There is also a potential problem of employee frustration. Should employees feel they have been unjustly overlooked for promotion it may become a source of resentment and grievance, ultimately affecting attitudes, morale and performance. Trade union attitudes are also important. Some company-union agreements insist that all posts are first advertised internally and, only having failed to fill the vacancy from this source, may the organisation look externally. Such agreements can sometimes reach cosmetic levels with internal candidates, who clearly do not meet the job criteria, repeatedly going forward and the personnel department being required to assess them before entering the wider labour market. In contrast, other organisations may have union agreements that ensure all vacancies must be advertised externally. Such practices are particularly relevant in the public sector.

Where the organisation engages in thorough manpower planning incorporating succession planning and employee development, internal sources should provide staff who are partially trained for vacancies that arise. Nevertheless, it will not always be possible to fill vacancies from internal sources. It is often useful to advertise vacancies internally first, giving employees an opportunity to put themselves forward for promotion or transfer. Circumstances are of crucial importance. While employees should not be prevented from applying for vacancies it may be advisable that they talk over their intentions with their supervisor. This has the dual benefit of keeping the latter informed about staff expectations and development plans, while preventing unsuitable candidates going forward.

The recruitment and selection process should be conducted in a meticulously thorough and fair manner so that rejected candidates do not feel the decision was unjust or biased. Rejected candidates should be counselled on the reasons for their unsuccessful application and plans outlined for their future development. Most employees will respect and appreciate frank and honest feedback designed to aid their future development within the organisation.

A decision on whether to recruit from internal or external sources ultimately depends on the nature of the job vacancy. If the skills or knowledge required are not available from internal sources then the organisation must look externally.

External sources: all organisations, regardless of their manpower strategy, will have to enter the labour market at some stage. The sources used will depend on the type of person needed and the urgency of the situation. The main sources of external recruitment are: *a)* unsolicited applicants; *b)* recruitment agencies and consultants; *c)* schools and colleges; *d)* media advertising.

a) Unsolicited applicants: most organisations keep a file on potential employees who have submitted their CVs on a speculative basis. This will be particularly common in organisations with a good profile or in periods of high unemployment. An organisation may also have details of candidates previously rejected for other positions. Such data banks should be continuously updated and used as a source of suitable applicants when vacancies arise.

b) Schools and colleges: many organisations will have developed strong links with particular schools and use these as recruitment source. Colleges and universities are a valuable source of technical and professional staff. They will be keen to develop links with employers both through careers officers and faculty. Strong personal links are very useful in securing good graduates. The 'milk round', whereby organisations visit colleges to promote themselves as potential employers and interview students prior to graduation, is a well-established recruitment mechanism. It is popular with well-known graduate employers but is open to all organisations and costs are small. Many colleges now operate sandwich-type courses involving short periods of work placement. This can be mutually beneficial, offering the organisation a chance to employ undergraduates without a long-term employment commitment, and giving students valuable work experience. Should students, thus employed, suit the organisation's needs they may be offered full-time employment on course completion.

c) Recruitment agencies and consultants: research findings in Ireland indicate extensive utilisation of consultants in personnel management and particularly in recruitment.[6] Contracting out the recruitment task has considerable advantages for the organisation; relieving it of an administrative burden, getting expertise in a particular labour market segment and retaining anonymity until the final selection stage. Recruitment agencies fall into three main categories: government recruitment agency; commercial recruitment agencies and executive search consultants and agencies.

Regular vacancies will normally be dealt with by the organisation itself and external agencies only used for specialist positions or occupations where there is a short supply of manpower. It is always useful to notify the National Manpower Agency, FÁS, of any vacancies as they will have a number of potential candidates on their books. There are no costs involved and there may be a possibility of financial benefit. This service has the reputation of dealing largely with semi-skilled or unskilled jobs catering mostly for the unemployed. Steps are currently being undertaken to broaden this service into skilled and professional areas.

Commercial recruitment agencies encompass a whole range of organisations providing a placement service, normally in specialist areas of employment. Many concentrate on providing part-time or temporary staff in clerical and secretarial areas. Such agencies maintain registers of candidates—both in and outside employment—and fill vacancies from this data-bank. Their main advantage is speed of placement.

Managerial, executive and professional placement agencies and consultants normally cater for middle and upper managerial, professional or technical staff. These organisations may operate in one of two ways. They may take over the recruitment task: using information on the vacancy, they will do the advertising and preliminary interviewing and provide the company with a shortlist of potential applicants. Alternatively, they may keep a register of specialist candidates who have indicated their willingness to consider suitable posts as they arise. These people will generally be in high-level jobs and use the executive search agency as a confidential mechanism to make themselves available to potential employers. While such an approach has earned 'headhunting' agencies quite a deal of criticism it does tend to provide top-level candidates, often with specialist knowledge and skills. It has been suggested that over half senior management appointments are 'headhunted'.[7] These agencies provide an important service which is costly and should only be used for specialist posts. An additional drawback of the 'headhunting' agencies is that employers can never be sure if the person appointed has come off the headhunter's list!

In using all types of recruitment agencies it is imperative that the organisation has carried out thorough job analysis and is clear on the type of person it needs. This information should be carefully communicated to the particular agency.

d) Media advertising: the most widely known method of recruitment involves searching the labour market for suitable candidates via media advertising. This will normally mean the press (local, national, professional and technical) as radio and TV advertising is quite rare. This situation may change with the growth of local radio and TV but as of yet the cost of such media, particularly TV, is prohibitive. In undertaking recruitment advertising a number of key considerations need to be taken into account. These include;

i) Objective: the first key issue for the organisation to consider is what it is trying to achieve. Recruitment advertising has three main objectives: to attract suitable candidates to apply for the job; to discourage unsuitable candidates from applying; to promote organisational image. As part of the recruitment strategy, advertising must help to select the right person for the job in the most cost-effective manner. This involves choosing the correct message and medium for its communication. It is important to beware of false economies. A small advertisement in a local paper may be much cheaper than a prominent one in a national daily but if the result is no, or poor quality, candidates the effort has been wasted. Choosing the wrong medium and making a marginal saving on advertising may jeopardise that total investment.

The first function of a job advertisement is to get the right type of people to apply. This depends on where the advertisement is placed and its message. This also involves eliminating, through self-selection, unsuitable candidates. Vaguely worded advertisements can generate hundreds of replies and take up many hours of management time sifting through unsuitable applications.

Part of the investment in recruitment advertising may be used in the wider perspective of affording the organisation an opportunity to portray itself as a successful, reputable, progressive organisation. While this objective should not cloud the main purpose—to attract suitable candidates—both these approaches can be complementary. People currently in employment may seek a career move to a market leader. The portrayal of this image in a well-structured job advertisement can be very beneficial.

ii) Message: compared to product advertising, recruitment advertisements have the advantage that people actively seek them out and thus the individual organisation competes against other recruitment advertisements rather than against the sports page! However, many potential job applicants may not be actively seeking a job. Rather, it is something in the job advertisement which sparks off the desire to apply. Effective recruitment advertising must get the attention of desired applicants, communicate the correct message and motivate appropriate responses. Eye appeal is important: the advertisement needs to relate to the potential candidate so they recognise themselves as possible postholders in the organisation. One technique for creating eye appeal is to structure the main heading around one of the following topics:

Job function: stress the function of the job to be filled, e.g. production management, architect;

Job title: different from above in that level of responsibility is implied, e.g. financial controller;

Career change: used for jobs where people with other skills or experience would be suitable if they can be attracted to change career, e.g. 'Administrators—bored with routine tasks? Try a career in systems analysis'.

Special interests: focusing on general occupational interest, e.g. teaching, travel.

Other approaches might be to surround the advertisement by heavy black lines or emphasise the corporate logo.

iii) Content: here the following details should be considered:

Job: title, key tasks, responsibilities; should be taken from job description.

Person: skills, abilities, motivation, profile; should be taken from personnel specification.

Remuneration: statement of pay, benefits, etc. associated with the job, and, if appropriate, mention of career prospects.

Company: industrial sector, location, expansion plans.

Discrimination: advertisements should avoid discrimination on the basis of sex, race or marital status.

iv) Medium: deciding what to say, while important, is only part of the task. Deciding where to say it is crucial since the recruitment advertisement will be rendered impotent if it is not seen by the right target group. Press advertising is by far the most common. Here there are three main options: local press, national press and professional or technical journals and magazines.

Local press has numerous advantages. It sources people in the correct geographical area, is relatively inexpensive and keeps the company profile high in the community. However, the skills and abilities required by the job need to be available locally.

National press broadens the potential source of applicants. It is more useful than local press where specialist skills and abilities are required or where the organisation wishes to make a senior appointment and get the best possible candidate. It is considerably more expensive than local press. Fridays and Sundays are the key days for recruitment advertising. However, evening papers are useful for temporary or lower level positions.

Specialist professional or technical journals and magazines have the advantage of sourcing the appropriate target audience and are not very expensive. Disadvantages are the time lag between issues and consequent delays in getting replies.

Often the choice is not between media but rather which combination to use. This will depend on circumstances, with factors like timing, urgency, cost, type of vacancy, etc. being particularly influential. Table 4.3 presents a general summary of various sources of candidates.

Table 4.3. Recruitment–source of candidates

Type of Job/candidate	Source
Entry level jobs, school leavers unskilled	Local press, FÁS, schools (careers officers)
Skilled manual	Local/national press, FÁS
Clerical, administrative	Local press, commercial recruitment agencies, FÁS
Professional/technical staff	National press, professional/technical journals & magazines, specialist recruitment agencies/consultants
Graduates	Appropriate colleges, training institutions, national press
Senior management	National press, executive recruitment agencies/consultants, appropriate professional or business journals & magazines

Application Form or Curriculum Vitae

Once the organisation has sourced applicants, it needs details on their skills, abilities, etc. The two main mechanisms are completion of an appropriate application form or submission of a curriculum vitae (CV). Again the choice is up to the organisation. A well-designed application form seems most appropriate for the majority of instances and should elicit from candidates the information the organisation wants to know. A CV, which by definition is designed by the candidate, will contain the information the candidate wishes to convey and may gloss over, or not refer to, unfavourable points in his repertory of skills, experience, etc. An added advantage is that the application form, by virtue of having a standardised format, provides a yardstick with which to compare candidates and is thus an important tool in both shortlisting and selection. CVs will not be standardised and demand much more analysis for use as a comparative mechanism. They are widely used by unsolicited applicants and should be kept on file. Should such individuals be considered for a vacancy they should complete the appropriate application form. Such forms might provide for an appendix where candidates can give additional information as appropriate.

Shortlisting

The selection process effectively begins when application forms are received. Unless the job is of an extremely specialist or senior nature it is likely that more applicants will respond than required. It would generally be uneconomical and inappropriate to investigate further a number of these candidates. Shortlisting is the process through which a number of applicants are chosen from the total respondents for further assessment before making a final selection decision. Applicants may be divided into categories, for example, suitable; possibly suitable/marginal; unsuitable; and vetted by senior management. Several candidates may be rejected at this stage. It is important that these be corresponded with as soon as possible.

Shortlisting candidates is a crucial, though occasionally an overlooked, stage in the employment process. The shortlist will determine the final selection decision. Shortlisting normally involves the personnel department sifting through numerous applications, discarding some and choosing others for further interviews, tests, etc. Criteria for shortlisting must be developed at the outset to ensure that the process is carried out in a fair and consistent manner. These criteria may be derived from the job description and personnel specification and applied to the analysis of each application form. Such criteria might be categorised in terms of priority (factors considered essential, desirable and/or additional) and cover areas like education, skills and experience. Shortlisted candidates should be informed of the further stages in the assessment process and related arrangements. Once shortlisting is completed the selection process proper can begin (see figure 4.4).

Fig. 4.4. Link between recruitment and selection

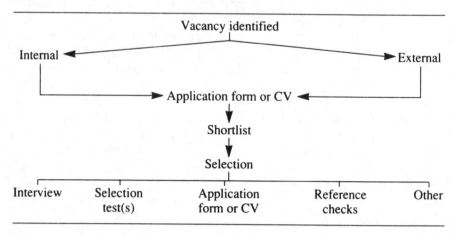

EMPLOYEE SELECTION METHODS

Since human resources are an integral component of corporate success, employee selection is one of the most vital management decisions. Choosing the correct candidate(s) from a shortlist is essentially a forecasting process with consequent risks for both the organisation and the job applicant. To reduce these risks a number of assessment methods have been developed. The interview is by far the most widely used selection method but there are several other selection tools available.[8] The choice of methods is dependent on factors such as the type of vacancy, urgency of appointment, skills and abilities of assessors, size of candidate pool, etc. The main selection methods available to organisations are discussed below.

Application Form

We earlier noted the importance of the application form or, possibly, the CV in pre-selection stage shortlisting. It is equally useful in helping to make the final selection decision. In fact, the application form and the interview have possibly the greatest impact on final selection decisions.

The application form should establish whether the person meets the basic requirements of the post. A well-designed application form should elicit relevant information on life and career history, qualifications, experience, and give an insight into career plans, interests and motivation. It also facilitates interview structure and conduct. Interviewers should know each candidate's profile from the application form. The interview can then be used to build on this and elicit further information as determined necessary.

Lewis notes two important issues relating to the use of application forms in selection: the reliability of information given in application forms and its consequent richness as a source of biographical data; its impact on final selection decisions, noting the high correlation between decisions made on review of the application form with final selection decisions.[9]

A well-designed application form based on thorough job analysis provides an important source of information on which selection decisions might be based and further assessment methods used.

Selection Interview
The selection interview has probably been the most closely analysed and subsequently criticised selection tool. A number of research studies have highlighted its lack of reliability and validity.[10] Despite this, it remains the most widely used and popular method of selection. While its popularity may be partially due to peripheral attributes of the interview—such as providing a mechanism for personal contact between the organisation and candidate—the fact remains that all organisations are involved in selection interviewing, and emphasis needs to be placed on how its conduct might be improved.

Preparation: there are two key issues here: the ability of the interviewer and the preparation for the interview. Interviewing competence varies enormously so that the decision on who conducts the interview is vital. Interviewing skills such as questioning, controlling, listening and probing are not possessed by all managers. They need development and practice. Selection and training of interviewers is an important step in determining the success or failure of the selection interview.

For the skilled interviewer, preparation is a systematic step in the interview process. It will focus on three aspects;

   i) knowing as much as possible about the vacancy to be filled;

   ii) knowing as much as possible about the candidates to be interviewed;

   iii) making appropriate physical and administrative arrangements.

Familiarity with the job description and job specification will provide essential information on the nature of the job. The personnel specification will clarify the experience, skills and qualifications needed to fill that post. These provide a yardstick to which candidates can be compared during the interview. Questions can be framed around these criteria and each candidate's suitability assessed.

Familiarity with the candidate is essential if the interview is to play a useful role in selection. This should begin with a close review of each candidate's application form. Interviewers should have a good knowledge of each candidate's background, skills, qualifications, etc. These should be compared to job requirements so that shortfalls or outstanding issues can be highlighted for further investigation. This has the twin advantage of ensuring that interview time is not wasted going over 'old ground' while allowing attention to be concentrated on any blanks, omissions or issues not adequately covered in the application form. Areas which might be considered here are career patterns (frequency of job moves, levels of salary increases, increased responsibilities), gaps between jobs, blanks or omissions to questions, inconsistencies, etc.

Other relevant sources of information should also be reviewed at this stage. For internal candidates, performance appraisal reports will be useful. Test results, medical reports or referees' testimonials may also be used as appropriate.

Lastly, the physical and administrative arrangements should not be overlooked. Candidates should be adequately communicated with on the timing and venue. Interviewers need to be aware of arrangements and be provided with all relevant details: timing, venue, application forms, etc. The interview room should be appropriate and arrangements for reception and waiting facilities made. Enough time should be set aside to allow for the interviews themselves, pre-interview preparation and decision-making.

Objectives: Plumbley highlights three main objectives of the selection interview:[11] to decide on candidate suitability; to give the candidate an accurate picture of the job; and to conduct the interview in a fair and professional manner.

The selection interview is a judgmental process where the organisation chooses those it deems most suitable to meet its particular needs. However, the candidate should not be overlooked. Often the best candidate needs to be attracted to both the job and the organisation. How the interview is conducted will influence the candidate's decision. The interview provides candidates with an opportunity to 'sell' themselves as the person best suited to the organisation's needs, while the organisation sells itself as being an attractive environment in which to invest one's future career.

Types of interview: there are three main categories of selection interview: biographical, stress and situational/problem-solving.

a) Biographical: this approach assumes that candidates are a product of their life to date. To predict subsequent job performance the interviewer needs to construct a picture of the candidate's development and experience. Such interviews normally follow a predictable pattern with interviewers probing aspects of the candidate's background, using a checklist to cover areas deemed relevant to the job (e.g. background, education, work experience, leisure activities, motivational pattern and personal circumstances).

The main advantages of this approach are that it follows a logical sequence and interviewers can soon master its technique while candidates also find it easy to follow.

b) Stress: here a deliberate attempt is made to put various types of pressure on the candidate by asking difficult, abrasive, personal or embarrassing questions. The objective is to assess how the candidate will respond to stress and is based on two main assumptions: that jobs give rise to stress and that people show their 'real' selves when under stress. While both assumptions may have elements of truth, the stress interview has a number of major disadvantages:

— it is discourteous to candidates:
— it may bear little resemblance to stress experienced on the job:
— it causes difficulties in evaluating candidate reaction:
— it may create a bad organisational image.

Higham, considering the usefulness of the stress interview, concludes that 'all a stress interview can reveal is how the candidate reacts to a stress interview'.[12] Indeed it would be dangerous to generalise that candidates are capable or incapable of withstanding pressure at work on the basis of stress interviews. For this, and the reasons outlined above, stress interviews are not recommended.

c) Problem-solving/situational: the basic assumption behind the problem-solving approach is that where applicants are asked to focus on work-related problems their reactions will be indicative of behaviour on the job. It involves interviewers presenting the candidate with hypothetical problems, such as, 'if you got the job of office supervisor how would you handle the persistent latecomer?'. It involves structuring the interview around work-based problems or incidents, sometimes using behavioural scales, and is seen as eliciting information which is a more valid predictor of subsequent job performance.[13]

Latham and Saari feel there is a strong case for using the situational interview.[14] They argue that the traditional biographical interview has two main weaknesses: lack of reliability because interviewers seldom ask the same questions of applicants, and disagreement on interpretation when the same questions are asked. To overcome these problems they suggest the use of systematic job analysis to develop both selection interview questions and performance appraisal criteria. They conclude that the situational or problem-solving interview can be particularly effective since interview questions are based on the actual job, and information so derived is relevant in predicting job performance.[15]

The main strengths of the problem-solving approach are in testing knowledge (such as technical information) and examining the relevance of past experience. It is less effective in testing ability or forecasting performance.[16] There are also problems of assessment, since any answers given are conjectural and do not necessarily indicate how the candidate would perform on the job. The benefit of this method is that it allows the interviewer to gain an insight into the analytical ability, judgment and maturity of the candidate. An inherent danger is that interviewers may be over-influenced by whether or not they agree with the candidate's opinion. Management must also ensure there is a strong link between the problems posed and actual job content.

Interview Conduct

Physical setting: the interview room should be of adequate size, comfortable and free from interruptions such as phone calls or casual callers. Seating arrangements may vary but should avoid intimidating candidates through the use of barriers such as large desks, etc. Only relevant documentation should be available and the physical setting should remain the same for all candidates.

Interview structure: interviews should be conducted according to a pre-planned structure. This ensures that all relevant job aspects are covered systematically. However, this should not lead to inflexibility. Within the structure adopted, interviewers should be free to ask different questions or probe differing areas depending on the candidate and the information available.

Table 4.4. Munro-Fraser and Rodger

Munro-Fraser	Rodger
1. Impact on others; first impressions, appearance, verbal ability	1. Physical make-up; physique, health, appearance, speech
2. Qualifications; education, training, work experience	2. Attainments; education, training, experience
3. Innate abilities; comprehension & conceptual ability, aptitude, intelligence	3. General intelligence; fundamental intellectual capacity
4. Motivation; objectives commitment, ambition, initiative	4. Special aptitudes; dexterity, numeracy, verbal, other
5. Emotional adjustment; coping with stress, working with others	5. Interests; leisure, intellectual, practical, physical, social, artistic
	6. Disposition; acceptability, interaction/ impact on fellow-workers/management, dependability, stability
	7. Circumstances; domestic, family, mobility, flexibility

In developing an interview structure the base point should be the job description and personnel specification. These help to organise the interview format by indicating areas to be covered with each candidate and enabling a systematic assessment to be made across the field of candidates at the end of the interview process. Two of the more popular structures are Munro-Fraser's five-fold framework and Rodger's seven-point plan (table 4.4).[17]

All relevant factors should be carefully considered with no single issue disproportionately affecting the final decision. Remember, the organisation is employing the total person, not one particular aspect of their make-up.

Encounter and opening: the initial meeting and opening of the interview will be crucial in determining the subsequent format and atmosphere. The effective interviewer will portray a pleasant personality, an ability to communicate and listen and an understanding of the candidate's needs and anxieties. Their approach will help put candidates at ease, encourage them to talk, communicate the needs of the job and the organisation and conclude the interview on a cordial note.

It is important to relax the candidate to ensure a free exchange of information. One approach is for the interviewer (or chairman of the interview panel) to escort the candidate from the waiting area, thus avoiding the feeling of being scrutinised on entry to the interview room. Rapport may be facilitated by introducing a non-controversial topic. Stereotypes should be avoided (weather, journey) and other possibilities explored, such as a common link (born in same area, attended same school) or leisure interest (sport, travel). Once a good relationship has been established the interview should progress quickly to the next stage.

It may be useful to agree the parameters of the interview with candidates at the start. This means informing candidates of the purpose, objectives and general format of the interview. It may involve explaining the nature of the job and areas to be covered, the need to fill information gaps and the timescale. It is also useful to inform candidates that they will have an opportunity to ask questions at the end. Lewis sees this stage as making a 'contract' with each candidate on the procedure to be followed and suggests it has a number of advantages: it creates a feeling among candidates that they have been consulted about the procedure and helps to put them at ease; it provides a mechanism for controlling and moving the interview along, and brings out any objections the candidate might have at the outset.[18]

While the initial stages may involve the interviewer doing an amount of talking, this should not continue. The purpose of the interview is to elicit relevant information from candidates and a general rule of thumb is that they should dominate the conversation by an absolutely minimum ratio of 2:1. The interviewer's role is to question, listen, observe and control.

Questioning: the questioning approach adopted will profoundly affect both the interview conduct and final decision. It is the questions asked which will determine the information gathered. Judgments should not be made at this stage. Rather, data is collected for subsequent use in comparing candidates and making a final assessment. Utilising information gleaned from the preparation stage and the interviewing framework, interviewers should know the areas to be discussed with each candidate. This should not prohibit spontaneity. Unforeseen issues may arise in the course of interviews which need to be discussed.

Candidates should be encouraged to talk freely, and open-ended questions which prevent a simple yes or no answer should be encouraged. Where a specific opinion or answer is required or where the candidate is 'rambling on' (or, possibly, avoiding the issue), closed questions should be used as appropriate. Candidates can be encouraged to expand on a topic or continue a particular line of discussion by encouraging gestures from the interviewer. Occasionally a silent pause may be useful if gentler methods of encouraging discussion fail. Multiple questions which are difficult to follow should be avoided. Similarly, leading questions which imply answers or make unwarranted assumptions provide little insight into the candidate's real feelings and opinions. Where personal circumstances are investigated similar questions should be asked of male and female candidates.[19]

All aspects of the candidate's application should be investigated systematically yet with sensitivity. Interviewers should always feel happy that they have gained all relevant information on each area. Where an unfavourable aspect is uncovered it should be fully explored. Should this indicate that the candidate may be unsuitable it should not be pursued relentlessly, causing embarrassment and discomfort for no good reason.

Control: related to the questioning approach is the need for interviewers to control the interview process. This means establishing the general atmosphere, dictating the pace and areas covered, adhering to the timescale and, finally, closing the interview. This involves striking a delicate balance between promoting a free exchange of information and maintaining an appropriate degree of control over the nature and content of that exchange. All relevant areas should be covered with none taking up a disproportionate amount of interview time. Areas of discussion should be terminated when the interviewer is happy that all relevant information has been investigated. This should be done firmly yet sensitively to ensure that further discussion is not inhibited. Normally candidates are informed of progress to the next area of discussion and given an opportunity to make a final input before this occurs ('I think we have covered your experience in ABC Ltd quite well; are there any other points you would like to make?). Talkative candidates may need to be curtailed by friendly references to the need to 'move on' or by using closed questions. Quieter candidates must be encouraged to expand by the use of open questions, gestures or expressions of interest, or silence pauses. Eye contact should be maintained where possible to demonstrate the interviewer's interest in what is being said.

Terminating the interview should also be done firmly. This might involve introducing the 'final' question and giving candidates an opportunity to ask questions. The interview should close on a friendly basis. Candidates should be told when they might expect interview results and this commitment should be strictly adhered to.

Listening and note-taking: the essence of effective interviewing is getting the relevant information from the candidate, retaining that information and using it to make the best selection decision possible. Effective listening is possibly the most difficult attribute to describe accurately. It is more than just hearing. In the interview context it is hearing and understanding what the candidate is saying, spotting patterns and inconsistencies in the information flow, identifying further areas to probe, noting informative non-verbal gestures and being sensitive to the candidate's feelings.

Note-taking is useful as an aid to information retention. However, it should be kept to a minimum using key points or shorthand. This is facilitated by having an interview structure prepared in advance so that points can be noted under relevant headings. Using a copy of the application form can also help. Again interviewers should be sensitive to candidate's feelings. Difficult or personal issues should be memorised and noted only after moving on to a new topic. It is a good idea to clear the idea of note-taking with the candidate at the start of the interview.

Number of Interviewers

Here practice varies widely from the one-to-one approach to large panel interviews. The one-to-one interview has the advantage of facilitating good rapport and frank exchange of information, and makes a lower demand on management time. Its drawbacks are related to its dependence on the ability of the interviewer and the related dangers of subjectivity and bias.

Interviews which involve more than one assessor are often recommended as a means of reducing bias and subjectivity. Such interviews may involve a combination of personnel specialists and line management or technical experts who can probe different areas. This approach seems particularly common with a preference for two or three interviewers.[20]

The panel interview (normally 3–7 people) is widely used in the public sector. Panel interviews are sometimes seen as offering a remedy to the problem of bias and a mechanism for improving interviewing expertise. In practice, however, they can present problems for both management and candidates. Coordination poses a particular problem. For panels to be effective a chairperson should be appointed, areas of questioning agreed in advance and timescales imposed on each area. Individual panel members must not be allowed dominate either the proceedings or the eventual decision. Because of these and other difficulties, panel interviews are not generally recommended unless small and well managed. Where they are used extensively this may occur for reasons other than effectiveness—such as the need to involve other sections, departments or interest groups for 'political' reasons.

There are many variations on these themes. Candidates may have to undergo more than one interview. The first interview may be of a preliminary nature with the final one being more in-depth and technical. Lewis recommends the sequential interview whereby candidates are interviewed by more than one person but with each interview conducted on a one-to-one basis.[21] He sees this overcoming the problem of bias and subjectivity while retaining the advantages of informality and ease of communication.

Finally, group selection techniques, while not strictly interviewing *per se*, should be touched upon. Here groups of candidates are assessed together. They are observed discussing or considering a particular topic by one or more assessor. Their various abilities in areas like communications, leadership and group interaction are evaluated. Group selection approaches are based on the assumption that behaviour displayed in such group assessments is indicative of the candidate's subsequent work behaviour and that the characteristics and abilities identified are relevant to the vacancy. Such group selection approaches are normally used in a preliminary screening of candidates for further assessment (airline stewards and hostesses, nurses).

Table 4.5 Comparison of interviewing approaches

	Number of interviewers		
	One-to-one	Panel	Group assessment
Advantages	• Facilitates rapport • Less formality • Low demand on management time • Speed & flexibility	• More objectivity • Reduced bias • Greater range of expertise	• Low demand on management time • Speed
Disadvantages	• Subjectivity & danger of interviewer bias • Dependent on interviewer ability • Lack of expertise	• More formality • Heavy demand on management time • Difficult to coordinate	• Superficial • Intimidating for candidates

Common Errors in Interviewing

We mentioned earlier the poor track record of the interview in predicting future job performance. Tyson and York note its failings in terms of reliability and validity.[22] They suggest that the interview lacks reliability because *a)* the instrument of measure is human; *b)* interviewers will differ in their interpretation and assessment; *c)* the same interviewer will change his interpretation and/or assessment over time. In terms of validity they suggest that the interview is a poor indicator of suitability because *a)* it is an artificial and stressful situation; *b)* it cannot accurately assess competence, disposition or potential; *c)* behaviour in interview conditions cannot be taken as a valid indicator of job performance in a quite different environment.

Other criticisms of the interview stem not from the technique itself but from its maladministration. Since the interview is likely to retain an important role in employee selection, management should make every effort to gain the best possible results from its use. An initial step is to avoid some common errors in interviewing as outlined in box 4.7.

Box 4.7. Common interviewing errors

Inadequate preparation: little job analysis; inadequate interview preparation; poor planning and administration.

Absence of interview structure.

Premature judgment: arriving at early decisions on candidate suitability and using interview to justify such decisions.

Interviewer dominance: talking too much, not listening, observing or analysing.

No rapport: atmosphere too intimidating; being overly critical and judgmental.

Horns/Halo effect: allowing favourable/unfavourable characteristics or reports to influence final decision.

Interviewer bias: allowing prejudices or subjective opinions to influence selection decisions (e.g. favouring particular schools, social/ethnic groups).

Structural rigidity: adhering slavishly to a pre-planned structure and not adapting to the needs of each candidate.

Interpreting the Interview

When each interview is finished all relevant details should be recorded. These should be brought together and analysed at the end of the total interview process. The structure and criteria established from the personnel specification should be used in the evaluation of each candidate (such as a 5/7–point plan). All relevant information on candidates should be utilised to provide a total picture of their suitability for the post.

Emphasis should be placed on identifying factual information in relation to each candidate which can be used to indicate suitability for the post. No one factor (such as first impressions) should be allowed to dominate the decision. Information from other sources (appraisals, test results, references, etc.) can be considered to enhance the total evaluation. Efforts should be made to identify candidate's behaviour patterns, such as reliability, attitude to responsibility, motivation and performance. Candidates can be compared to each other as well as to job criteria. The final decision should be based on the need to find the person best suited to the job. It should be remembered that chosen candidates must also make a decision. They should be contacted as soon as possible. It may be appropriate to have a reserve candidate should the first offer be rejected. Candidates who have been unsuccessful should be informed as soon as possible.

Selection Tests

A number of selection tests are available to assist in making selection decisions. These can be divided into four broad categories: attainment, aptitude, personality and intelligence tests. Debate continues about the reliability and validity of many selection tests, particularly those which attempt to measure personality and intelligence. However, selection tests, if appropriate and professionally administered, can greatly aid the selection decision and can act as an important complement to the interview. They increase its objectivity as they do not rely on subjective human decisions, thus compensating for the possibility of interviewer error. Tests should generally be used as an aid to selection and not as the only selection tool, and their administration and interpretation should be carried out by trained personnel.[23] The main advantages of selection tests are summarised in table 4.6.

Tests which measure specific knowledge or skills are particularly useful in aiding the selection decision, as such areas are difficult to judge through interview. Tests which attempt to measure intelligence and personality are more involved and should only be applied under appropriate conditions. Generally, selection tests seem most useful where the following conditions apply:

i) large numbers of candidates need to be assessed;

ii) jobs involve long and expensive training programmes;

iii) particular skills, knowledge or intelligence levels are an occupational requirement for the vacancies;

iv) their reliability and validity are established;

v) the organisation has the trained personnel to administer and interpret such tests;

vi) they are part of a total selection process and can contribute to its objectivity.

Table 4.6 Selection tests

	Attainment	Aptitude	Personality	Intelligence
Purpose	Measure specific knowledge or skills	Predict areas of special aptitude or flair	Measure temperament, disposition, ability to work with people, etc.	Measure mental capacity/ potential
Advantages	Accurate measure of specific skills/ knowledge where such is an occupational necessity	Help shortlist from large numbers; more objective than interviewer assessment	Gives measure of suitability for certain jobs where personality is a key factor	Gives insight into ability to learn, grasp new ideas; can indicate minimum intellectual capacity
Disadvantages	Cannot accurately predict subsequent performance; limited measure of total ability	Cannot accurately predict subsequent performance	Reliability and validity very suspect; needs professional expertise	Danger of social, cultural bias; cannot predict subsequent performance
Examples	Manual, clerical skills – e.g. typing	Aptitude; computing, dexterity	Traits test; leadership/ management	Graduate management admission test—GMAT

McMahon found that levels of utilisation of selection tests in Irish organisations was relatively low.[24] Attainment tests were most popular, with aptitude tests next and personality tests only used in a handful of cases. McMahon suggests that these usage levels are lower than expected given their relatively high level of predictive accuracy. Interestingly, multinational organisations were the main test users. Shivanath's research findings are more favourable with over 64 per cent of respondent organisations using some form of employment tests. She also found that—unlike interviewing—the major responsibility for their administration lay with the personnel function.[25]

Reference Checks

After interviewing, reference checking is the next most popular selection technique.[26] It is an important part of the assessment process. Reference checks help to validate information already received, get an assessment of previous performance and some indication of suitability and potential. References should be checked before making the final selection decision but only with the candidate's permission.

References have been severely criticised as a selection device. Such criticisms often stem from research findings which indicate that because most people get 'good' references they are of little benefit in differentiating between candidates. McMahon suggests they are used as a 'rubber stamp' in approving the final decision.[27] Some British evidence seems to confirm this, suggesting that reference checking is being abandoned by larger organisations and that, where used, it is as a 'contra indicator' in helping to check for factors which would disqualify a candidate.[28]

Reference checking will be most beneficial where specific information is requested from people who are familiar with the candidate's work. It is useful to give the referee a copy of the job description and personnel specification and ask questions related to previous job performance and the post being offered. This avoids vague testimonials which need to be interpreted as much for what they don't say as what they do. Written reference checks should be followed up by direct contact—normally by telephone—where any details can be clarified and further information gained.

Finally, it is important to note that while references are useful in establishing a candidate's past achievements and giving an indication of ability, they should not dominate the selection decision. Organisations will have conducted their own evaluation, and references should be used as an aid to such assessment.

Other Methods

In this category are a number of additional methods which are less commonly used in employee selection. Graphology, palmistry, phrenology and astrology have had their supporters but their application on a widespread basis is not recommended.[29] Astrology has occasionally been used to select personality types for specific jobs while graphology—the study of handwriting—seems to have gained a degree of minority acceptability in helping to shortlist people for senior positions.[30] Robertson and Makin found that graphology had been used by 8 per cent of respondent organisations in Britain, despite the lack of any research findings in their favour.[31] Interestingly, all the organisations who used graphology were subsidiaries of European firms. McMahon found no evidence of these techniques in Irish organisations.[32]

In contrast, biodata and assessment centre techniques have gained considerable recognition in terms of their validity as predictors of job performance and potential. Assessment centres involve candidates being subjected to a series of simulations and selection methods which are conducted and observed by a group of skilled assessors. They have been widely used in the US and their significance in Britain is on the increase.[33] Research findings on their validity have generally been favourable, particularly in assessing potential.[34] They are seen as more objective than some standard methods and are carried out by expert personnel. Apparent drawbacks include the high costs involved and remoteness from the job context. Despite their considerable promise McMahon only found one respondent organisation using an assessment centre in Ireland.[35]

Biodata techniques involve eliciting information on a candidate's life history from application forms or questionnaires and scoring these against objective scales. Using the answers given on areas such as past achievements, interests and behaviour candidates may be categorised into groups like 'ambitious/achievers', 'reliable/steady', etc. Studies on the validity of biodata approaches as predictors of job performance have been favourable and their use in Britain is on the increase.[36] McMahon found little evidence of their use in Irish organisations.[37] However, a recent Bank of Ireland recruitment drive adopted the biodata approach.

PLACEMENT, INDUCTION AND FOLLOW–UP
Once a selection decision is taken the job offer should be made as soon as possible. This should contain details of the job including its terms and conditions (pay, hours, holidays, pension, etc.). Where these details are not fixed or are open for discussion there may be need for a further meeting to iron out the details. Remember, both parties are entering into a legally binding contract of employment. Candidates who are clearly unsuitable should be written to immediately. Other suitable candidates might be kept on a reserve list until the post has been filled. These might be considered for other suitable posts in the organisation or future vacancies which may arise. Once all vacancies have been filled they should be told that their applications were unsuccessful.

When the job offer has been accepted the process of integrating the new employee into the organisation can begin in earnest. While the induction process has been initiated at the interview, the organisation must now ensure that the new recruit has all the relevant information and knowledge to ease their entry to the organisation and facilitate their progression to an acceptable performance level.

Effective induction is a matter of good management practice and an inherent part of the training and development process. It contributes to the

effective utilisation of the organisation's human resources. Beyond courtesy to the new employee, an effective induction programme helps to:
i) reduce labour turnover (which is highest in the first 3–6 months of employment);
ii) lessen the anxiety of new entrants;
iii) give necessary information about the job and the organisation (including its culture, management philosophy, etc.);
iv) settle new entrants into the job and improve performance as quickly as possible;
v) reduce misunderstandings, grievances and turnover;
vi) create realistic expectations of the job and the organisation;
vii) facilitate good employee relations.

These objectives are achieved by giving new employees information on the job, the department and the organisation in general. It helps to ensure familiarity with the work area, colleagues and facilities; creating a favourable attitude to the job and the organisation; giving adequate preliminary training in the job and following up and monitoring employee progress.

Induction is important for all new employees, including internal transfers and promotions. Particular categories may need special attention, such as school leavers, the handicapped, and women returning to the workforce.

The induction process begins with the first contact between employer and employee and should continue until the employee has been fully integrated into the organisation. Because new employees are subjected to a lot of new information and a new environment the induction process should be spread out over an appropriate time period (3–6 months). Essential information should be given at the outset. As this is assimilated, further areas may be covered as appropriate. Various areas within the organisation should be involved. Personnel will generally be responsible for programme design and administration as well as dealing with reception and personnel matters (holidays, pension, etc). Line management will be involved with job or department-related issues and on-the-job training. Other sections such as wages and safety will have an input. Senior management should play a significant role in employee induction. The idea of a co-employee acting as 'sponsor' in familiarising the new recruit with the job and the organisation might also be considered.

Induction must be seen as part of the overall training and development process. It should aid both the individual employee and the organisation at large and contribute to an effective employment process.

Finally, it is important to monitor adequately the employment process. If the objective of recruitment and selection is to get the right people to carry out the work of the organisation effectively, the achievement of this goal must be assessed in relation to employee performance on the job. This involves a systematic approach to managing both individual and corporate performance.

The performance of new employees should be monitored regularly during the initial employment period. Reports from supervisors should be checked and the employee visited regularly. Any problems should be quickly identified and investigated: is the training adequate? is s/he suited to the job? does s/he have the necessary skills and knowledge? Discrepancies between actual job performance and the decisions made at selection should be highlighted. In particular, trends in successful or unsuccessful selection should be identified and fed back into the total process so that changes can be initiated. Particular interviewers may have chosen poor candidates; certain test results have not produced accurate measurements of job performance; recruits from certain social or educational backgrounds may have proved particularly successful; good results may have been achieved from local newspaper advertising. Only through ongoing monitoring, testing and validating of the recruitment and selection process can effective feedback be produced which will increase its effectiveness and ensure that the organisation gets the best possible human resources to carry out its various tasks.

Chapter 5

Employee Motivation
and Work Design

INTRODUCTION
Attracting employees of the required calibre is only a first step in effectively managing the organisation's human resources. Once they have been employed, management must take appropriate steps to ensure that employees are motivated and operate at high levels of performance. Managers should be aware of the steps they might take to facilitate their work-groups in achieving high performance levels. Possibly even more important, they should know what motivates their work-group both as individuals and as a team. If such motives can be satisfied then a major step has been taken towards achieving high performance levels. This principle applies equally to the organisation at large.

The study of motivation at work has been based on analysing employee behaviour at work. People react in different ways to different stimuli, and various theories of employee motivation at work seek to identify factors which induce good or bad performance and suggest how management might apply these effectively at organisation level. Here we briefly examine some of the more influential theories on employee motivation and work design, and evaluate their application in practice.

MOTIVATING FOR HIGH PERFORMANCE
Motivation theory bases its analysis of worker performance on how work and its rewards satisfy individual employee needs. The general conclusions are that if these needs are satisfied employees will be motivated to work at high performance levels but, if not, their performance will be less than satisfactory. Of course, motivation is only one factor affecting performance. Other factors, particularly technology, training and individual ability, will have a major influence on performance levels.

A central management concern is how to get employees to perform at the height of their abilities. If this can be achieved, management will have gone a long way towards creating a successful organisation. The understanding of human needs at work and the creation of a working environment which satisfies those needs is a key task of senior management. Various theories have been developed over the years to aid management in identifying worker motives and needs. Some of these are briefly described below.

Needs Hierarchy

Maslow's hierarchy of needs is possibly the most well-known explanation of worker motivation.[1] It sees it in terms of a series of ascending drives to satisfy a particular category of needs. These range from basic instinctive needs for sustenance and security to the so called 'higher order needs' of esteem and self-actualisation.

Fig. 5.1. Maslow's hierarchy of needs

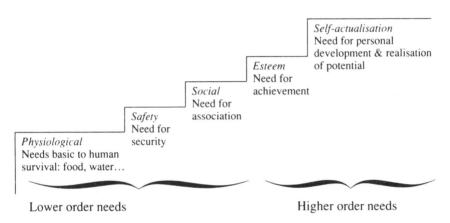

The sequential ascending order of needs is important. Firstly it implies that it is the next unachieved level which acts as the prime motivator. Thus, people without the basic necessities of life such as food, shelter, etc., will be motivated by basic physiological and, later, security needs. Only when these have been satisfied will higher order needs become important. And, then, only when all the lower order needs are satisfied, do higher level needs act as a motivator—first esteem needs and ultimately self-actualisation. This latter category is, possibly, the most abstract and is seen by Maslow as the penultimate motivator after all other needs are satisfied. Maslow describes self-actualisation as 'the desire for self-fulfilment . . . the tendency [for man] to become actualized in what he is potentially . . . the desire to become more and more what one is, to become everything that one is capable of becoming'.[2]

The second implication of the ascending order of needs is that once a particular needs category is satisfied it ceases to have major impact on motivation. Thus, any needs level only motivates while it remains unachieved. Once achieved it is the next level in the hierarchy which dominates.

The main difficulty with this approach is that, while apparently logical, it is difficult to apply or evaluate. How does one predict when a particular needs level has been fully satisfied or decide that a preceding level has ceased to motivate? It may also be overly prescriptive since people clearly react differently to different stimuli or situations, and it is difficult to apply a general framework or pattern to describe such human behaviour. Hall and Nougaim reported variations in workers' needs and motivation at different stages in their working lives, while Porter identified the increasing importance of higher order needs with managerial progression.[3] Despite such reservations, Maslow's hierarchy provides a valuable framework to analyse human motivation at work.

Existence—Relatedness—Growth (ERG) Theory

ERG theory, as developed by Alderfer, reduces Maslow's five-fold needs category into three basic groupings.[4] A second major difference, stemming from criticisms of Maslow's approach, is that less emphasis is placed on a hierarchical order of lower and higher level needs, inferring that all needs levels may be influential at the same time.

Fig. 5.2. Alderfer's ERG theory

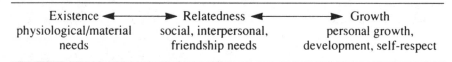

Existence ◄———►	Relatedness ◄———►	Growth
physiological/material needs	social, interpersonal, friendship needs	personal growth, development, self-respect

Another important variation is the proposition that an already satisfied lower order need may be reactivated as a motivator when a higher order need cannot be satisfied. Thus, an employee who has satisfied basic material and social needs may be concerned with his personal growth and development (promotion, for instance). If there is no scope for such development he may revert back to a preoccupation with previously satisfied needs (social or financial). The other implication, referred to above, is that more than one needs category may be important at any one time.

Acquired Needs Theory

An alternative approach, developed by McClelland, concentrated on identifying motivational differences between individuals as a means of establishing which patterns of motivation led to effective performance and success at work.[5] He distinguishes three basic needs in addition to physical drives:

a) need for achievement (nAch); consistent desire for challenging tasks demanding responsibility and application;

b) need for power (nPow); need for control over people;

c) need for affiliation (nAff); need for good social and personal relations with people.

McClelland suggested that these needs are acquired and developed over one's life. Depending on which needs are dominant, these will exert varying influences on work performance. People with a high need for achievement tend to have a strong motivation to take on challenging tasks and to do them better. This, combined with a moderate to high need for power and a lower need for affiliation, has been suggested as a good indicator of success in senior management.[6] An important implication of this approach is that, if such needs are acquired, then they may be developed through appropriate environmental conditions which facilitate the emergence of the desired needs profile.

McGregor's Theory X, Theory Y

Unlike previous approaches which concentrated on analysing the motivations of people at work, McGregor examined managerial assumptions about employees and the resultant implications of such assumptions for managerial approaches to issues like control, job design and remuneration systems.[7] He identified two very differing sets of assumptions about employee behaviour and motivation which were termed Theory X and Theory Y (see table 5.1).

Table 5.1. McGregor's Theory X, Theory Y

THEORY X	THEORY Y
Employees are inherently lazy, dislike work and will do as little as possible. Consequently workers need to be coerced, controlled and directed to exert adequate effort.	Employees like work and want to undertake challenging tasks. If the work itself and the organisational environment is appropriate, employees will work willingly without need for coercion or control.
Most employees dislike responsibility and prefer direction.	People are motivated by needs for respect, esteem, recognition and self-fulfilment.
Employees only want security and material rewards.	People at work want responsibility. The majority of workers are imaginative and creative and can exercise ingenuity at work.

Organisational approaches to workforce management differ considerably and these two contrasting frameworks are useful in helping to analyse and explain management styles. Both classifications represent extreme styles of and approaches to workforce management. In practice, organisations may adopt elements of both approaches but, often, with a particular leaning which indicates a preference for one or other approach.

Traditional autocratic management approaches were clearly based on Theory X assumptions. Despite considerable academic and practical support, it would seem that Theory Y has not got the wholehearted backing of many senior managers. Consequently its application has often been restricted to once-off initiatives designed to deal with particular problems or issues rather than reflecting a change in corporate approaches to the way employees are managed.

Dual Factor Theory

Herzberg was equally concerned about the impact of work and job design on motivation.[8] He saw the key to improving employee motivation in terms of job satisfaction. Herzberg felt that by identifying the factors at work which produced the greatest levels of satisfaction (or dissatisfaction) it would be possible to design jobs which provided job satisfaction, thereby encouraging higher levels of performance. His approach concentrated on identifying which factors contributed most to employee satisfaction at work (called 'motivator' factors). He also sought to identify those factors which influenced levels of employee dissatisfaction ('maintenance or hygiene' factors). Herzberg concluded that these two sets of factors were inherently different in terms of their impact on motivation and performance (see box 5.1).

Box 5.1. Maintenance and motivator factors

Maintenance factors: these factors influenced levels of employee dissatisfaction. By varying these factors it is possible to reduce or eliminate sources of dissatisfaction. However, they will never act as motivators to high levels of job performance. Such factors are linked to job context and include pay, working conditions, supervision and interpersonal relations.

Motivator factors: on the other hand, these factors motivated employees to high levels of job performance. Such factors were concerned with the job itself, including recognition, responsibility, achievement, etc.

A central aspect of Herzberg's dual factor theory is that only by varying motivator factors can management improve performance and motivation. Varying maintenance factors will reduce levels of dissatisfaction but will never act as a motivator (see figure 5.3).

Fig. 5.3. Herzberg's dual factor theory

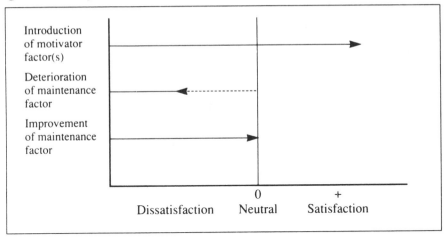

The implication here is that management can only stimulate employee motivation by designing jobs to incorporate the motivator factors (jobs which encourage and facilitate responsibility, advancement and recognition). Herzberg believed that high levels of job satisfaction could be achieved by altering job content to allow for personal growth and development while also ensuring that the job context (pay, working conditions, etc.) were appropriate. This process became known as job enrichment.

Herzberg's approach has gained considerable recognition, particularly for differentiating between the impact of intrinsic and extrinsic factors on employee motivation. Criticisms have tended to focus on its reliability of application to all types of jobs (not just professional and white collar) and the view of job satisfaction as being almost synonymous with motivation.

Expectancy Theory
Most of the approaches discussed above represent attempts to identify a general set of employee needs which cause workers to behave in a certain way. The belief is that by identifying such needs, management can provide for their ease of achievement thus facilitating improved performance. Many of these approaches rank such motives or goals in a hierarchical order with self-actualisation as the ultimate motivator.

However, most managers will probably point out that employees differ markedly in terms of motivation. One may find two employees, similar in terms of age, sex, background, etc., one of whom will strive to achieve high performance levels, undertake additional tasks, etc., while the other is content to get by doing the minimum acceptable to the organisation. How does one explain such variations? One approach which avoids attempts to find a definitive set of employee motives but seeks to explain individual differences in terms of goals, motives and behaviour is expectancy theory.[9] It is based on the concept that worker motivation is dependent on how the employer perceives the relationship between three central issues:

Fig. 5.4. Expectancy theory

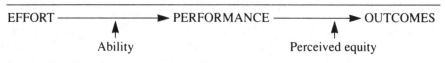

This approach suggests that employees will expend a high level of effort if they believe this will result in performance levels which will be rewarded by valued outcomes. These valued outcomes may vary between individuals. One may value money, another promotion, yet another recognition. However, it is not only outcome which is important but also the belief that valued outcomes can be achieved through improved effort and performance. The key elements of expectancy theory are discussed below.

Individual differences: expectancy theory recognises that individual goals and motives may vary. This highlights the importance of identifying what are valued outcomes for individual employees.

Instrumentality: expectancy theory suggests that employee decisions on how they perform are based upon their perception of desired outcomes, whether performance targets are achievable and whether by achieving these targets they will realise their desired outcomes.

Perception: it is how individuals view their situation which influences behaviour; for example, management may believe that individual performance targets are achievable but if this belief is not shared by employees they will not expend the necessary effort to achieve such targets.

Expectancy: this refers to the perceived probability that a particular level of effort will lead to desired performance levels. If the desired outcome (bonus pay) demands a given level of performance (production levels), the employee must believe that level is achievable or he will not expend the necessary effort. Many potential Dublin marathon runners would not consider the training and practice worthwhile if the qualification for entry was a sub-three-hour time!

Value of outcome(s)/Valency: this is a measure of the strength of attraction which a particular outcome or reward has for the individual employee.

Implications for Management: Vroom suggests that managers must seek to understand individual employee goals and motives, ensure these are clearly and positively linked to desired performance levels which in turn are achievable from the employee's perspective.[10] Nadler and Lawler go a little further and highlight specific areas for management action:[11]

i) the need to establish what are valued outcomes;

ii) the need to specify desired and achievable performance levels;

iii) the need to ensure there is a clear link between effort, performance and desired outcomes;

iv) the need to ensure adequate variation of outcomes available;

v) the need to ensure equity and fairness for the individual employee.

It is useful to look at the effort–performance–outcomes relationship in terms of a particular potential motivating factor. For example, a manager may be keen to establish the motivational impact of promotion. Expectancy theory suggests that the prospect of promotion will motivate employees to good performance if the following criteria are met:

a) Expectancy is high: the employee believes that by working hard he will achieve the necessary level of performance to put himself in line for promotion. In other words, there is a clear link between effort and performance:

Effort $\longrightarrow$ Performance

b) Instrumentality is high: the person believes that by achieving the necessary level of performance there is a strong probability of achieving promotion, a strong link between performance and (valued) outcome:

Performance $\longrightarrow$ Outcome

c) Valency is high: the employee wants promotion.

Of course, the situation is more complex. If any one of the above is unclear or lacking, the motivation to perform well may be considerably lessened. Secondly, motivation is only one factor influencing performance. Employees must have the necessary ability and training to achieve the desired performance level. They must be provided with the necessary resources, such as equipment. Finally, performance levels should be clearly specified and communicated to employees so that they know what is required. Management by objectives (MBO) can be useful here in jointly agreeing job targets, reviewing the degree to which they have been achieved and discussing any related problems or issues. The performance–outcomes relationship is particularly influential; the employee must firmly believe that the desired outcome (promotion) will be achieved as a result of good performance. If employees believe all they will get is a pat on the back— and if this is not a valued outcome—it is unlikely that they will expend the necessary effort to improve performance. Again, communication is important. Employees should be aware of the performance–outcome link, and when the required performance is achieved such outcomes should be delivered upon.

Expectancy theory does not attempt to identify a universal set of motivational factors. Rather, it highlights the importance of a range of potential motivational factors. These may be either intrinsic or extrinsic.[12] Intrinsic outcomes are those originating from doing the job (sense of achievement, satisfaction) while extrinsic outcomes are those provided by other people, particularly management, and include pay, promotion, etc.

Applying the expectancy model to executive staff in the Irish Civil Service, Blennerhassett identified four categories of basic work values which significantly influenced individual employee motivation:[13]

a) Self-development and challenge values: the value placed upon intrinsic rewards: challenge, stimulation, personal growth/development;

b) Promotion values: the value placed upon promotion and career development;

c) Social values: the value placed upon the social contribution of work, e.g. provision of community service such as public transport;

d) Easy life and money values: instrumental orientation; job viewed as a means to an end: pay, holidays, etc.

Interestingly, she found most respondents placed the highest values upon intrinsic outcomes, particularly job challenge and self-development. There was a corresponding lack of emphasis on work as facilitating an 'easy life' or pay as valued outcomes. The most important extrinsic outcome was promotion. However, promotion was valued more because of its intrinsic aspects (such as greater responsibility and job challenge) rather than extrinsic outcomes (such as higher earnings or improved status).

Traditional approaches to employee motivation have relied heavily on extrinsic factors, particularly pay. However, individual employee motivation and perceived job satisfaction will be influenced by a myriad of factors. Some will be related to individual employees and their personal characteristics. Others, such as supervisory relations or discretion, will stem either from the working environment or the job itself (see figure 5.5).

Fig. 5.5. Factors influencing employee motivation

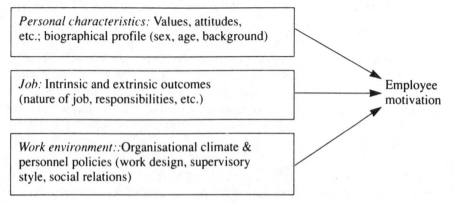

In relation to individual factors, it is important that organisations select employees whose motives and work values 'fit' the organisational environment, management approach and reward package. On the other hand, the organisational climate, management style and design of work should facilitate good performance by providing adequate opportunity for employees to satisfy their varying needs. Management must be keenly aware of the need to motivate employees through both extrinsic and intrinsic outcomes. In the next chapter extrinsic rewards, particularly pay, are considered.

Intrinsic outcomes are those which derive from the job itself. The nature of work organisation and design will significantly influence the degree to which work is intrinsically satisfying for employees and promotes high levels of motivation. Organisations should carefully consider their approach to work organisation and choose the approach which best suits their particular needs.

WORK ORGANISATION AND JOB DESIGN

In discussing organisation and manpower planning it was suggested that organisations must initially establish the overall business objectives and corporate mission. These form the basis for subsequent decisions on management strategy, organisation structure and managerial style.

Work organisation refers to the way the various tasks in the organisation are structured and carried out. It reflects the interaction of management style, the technical system, human resources and the organisation's products or services. The design of individual jobs will particularly impact upon employees since it influences job content, employee discretion, degree of task fragmentation and the role of supervision.

Fig. 5.6. Work organisation

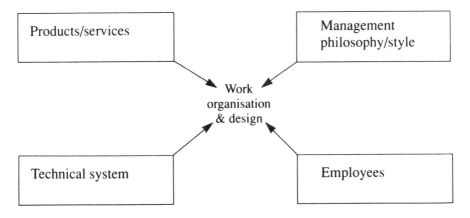

Decisions on the organisation of work are primarily a management responsibility. The particular approach chosen will be a good indicator of corporate beliefs about how employees should be managed, jobs structured and the role of supervision. It will also reflect the organisation's approach to many aspects of personnel management as manifested through attitudes to recruitment, employee development, motivation, rewards and management-employee relations.

The Traditional Model

Traditional approaches to the organisation of work have been dominated by a desire to maximise the productive efficiency of the organisation's technical resources. Choices on the organisation of work and the design of jobs were seen as determined by the technical system. Management's role was to ensure other organisational resources, including employees, were organised in such a way as to facilitate the optimal utilisation of the technical system. This efficiency approach is based on scientific management principles and has been a characteristic of employer approaches to job design since the turn of the century. Jobs were broken down into simple, repetitive, measurable tasks whose skills could be easily acquired through systematic job training.

Table 5.2. Traditional approach to job design

Characteristics	Outcomes
Bureaucratic organisation structure	Tight supervisory control
Top–down supervisory control	Minimal need for employee discretion
Work planning separated from execution	Work measurement
Task fragmentation	Reliance on rules/procedures
Fixed job definitions	Job specialisation
Individual payment by results	Reduced job flexibility
	Short training time
	Little employee influence on job/work organisation

The rationale for this approach to work and job design was based on 'technological determinism' where the organisation's technical resources were seen as a given constraint and the other inputs, including employees, had to accommodate the technical system. It also reflected managerial assumptions about people at work. Close supervision, work measurement and other types of controls indicate a belief about employees akin to McGregor's Theory X. It suggests that employees need to be coerced to work productively and that this is best achieved on routine, standardised tasks.

This traditional model of job design has undoubtedly had positive benefits for many organisations. It helped improve efficiency and promoted a systematic approach to selection, training, work measurement and payment systems. However, it has also led to numerous problems, such as high levels of labour turnover and absenteeism and low motivation.[14] Thus, short-term efficiency benefits were often superseded by long-term reductions in organisational effectiveness. Many behavioural scientists argued that organisational effectiveness could be increased by recognising employee ability and giving them challenging, meaningful jobs within a co-operative working environment.

Over the past decade the increased emphases on improving quality, service and overall competitiveness have led to work redesign initiatives aimed at restructuring work systems to increase employee motivation, commitment and performance.

Job Redesign

Much of the focus of work redesign has been the restructuring of jobs to incorporate greater scope for intrinsic motivation. This approach questioned traditional management assumptions about why employees worked. The traditional approach saw employees as essentially instrumental in their attitudes to work. Jobs were seen as means to an end and it was these extrinsic rewards which motivated employees. Consequently, employers created work systems which closely circumscribed jobs, supervised work and rewarded quantifiable performance.

The *job enrichment* approach suggested that employees gain most satisfaction from the work itself, and it was intrinsic outcomes arising from work which motivated employees to perform well in their jobs. For organisations a key problem was how to redesign jobs to provide high levels of intrinsic outcomes and job satisfaction for employees. Hackman and Oldham identified three basic conditions necessary for promoting job satisfaction and employee motivation;[15]

i) work should be *meaningful* for the doers;
ii) doers should have *responsibility* for the results;
iii) doers should get *feedback* on the results.

This approach suggested that it was the design of work and not the characteristics of the employee which had the greatest impact on employee motivation. Hackman and Oldham identified five 'core job characteristics' which needed to be incorporated into job design to increase meaningfulness, responsibility and feedback (see figure 5.7):

i) Skill variety: extent to which jobs draw on a range of different skills and abilities;

ii) Task identity: extent to which a job requires completion of a whole, identifiable piece of work;

iii) Task significance: extent to which a job substantially impacts on the work or lives of others either within or outside the organisation;

iv) Autonomy: freedom, independence and discretion afforded to the jobholder;

v) Feedback: degree to which the jobholder receives information on performance, effectiveness, etc.

Having identified the factors necessary to promote satisfaction and intrinsic motivation, the next stage is to incorporate these characteristics into jobs through various job redesign strategies. Hackman and Oldham suggest five implementation strategies to increase task variety, significance, identity, and create opportunities for greater autonomy and feedback:

a) Form natural work groups: arrange tasks together to form an identifiable, meaningful cycle of work for employees; for example, responsibility for single product rather than small components;

b) Combine tasks: group tasks together to form complete jobs;

c) Establish client relationships: establish personal contact between employees and the end user/client;

d) Vertically load jobs: many traditional approaches to job design separate planning and controlling (management functions) from executing (employee's function). Vertically loading jobs means integrating the planning, controlling and executing functions and giving most responsibility to employees (such as responsibility for materials, quality, deadlines and budgetary control);

e) Open feedback channels: ensure maximum communication of job results (service standards, faults, wastage, market performance, costs).

Hackman and Oldham suggest that such changes would have positive long-term benefits for the organisation and the individual employee. Not all employees are expected to respond favourably to such redesign initiatives. Only those with a strong desire for achievement, responsibility and autonomy will be motivated by increased intrinsic satisfaction and hence motivated to perform better. For others such change may be a source of anxiety and lead to resentment and opposition to changes in the work system.

In her study of executive officers in the public sector Blennerhassett found that respondents identified the work itself as a most important potential source of job satisfaction and motivation.[16] Interestingly, she found that respondents rated their jobs poorly on the core job characteristics of variety, significance, etc, and generally felt their jobs did little to promote satisfaction, motivation or involvement. Considering the study group were executive and higher executive officers in the Civil Service this raises serious question marks about the design of jobs in the Civil Service and possibly beyond.

Fig. 5.7. Job characteristics and employee motivation

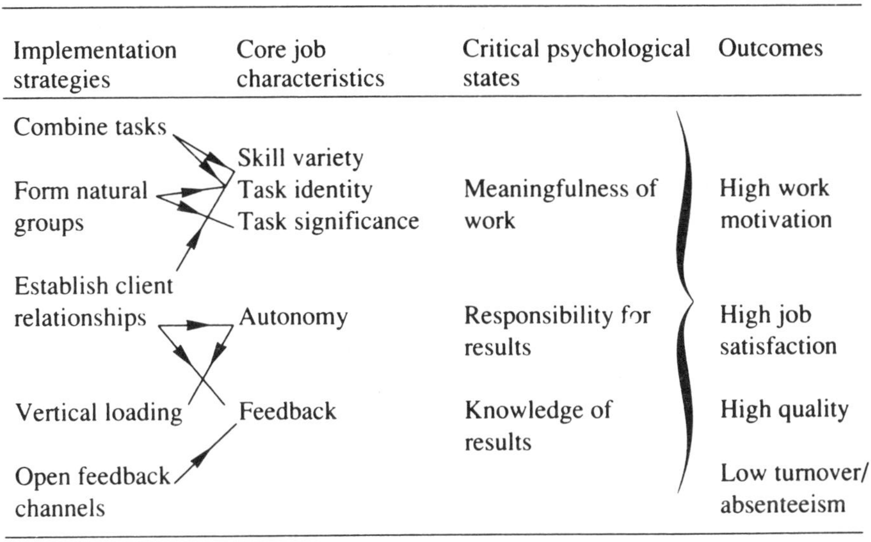

Implementation strategies	Core job characteristics	Critical psychological states	Outcomes
Combine tasks	Skill variety		
Form natural groups	Task identity	Meaningfulness of work	High work motivation
	Task significance		
Establish client relationships	Autonomy	Responsibility for results	High job satisfaction
Vertical loading	Feedback	Knowledge of results	High quality
Open feedback channels			Low turnover/ absenteeism

Source: Adapted from Hackman, J.R. "Work Design" in Hackman, J.R. & Suttle, J.L., *Improving Life at Work*. Goodyear 1977.

Employee Influence and the Quality of Work Life Movement

Concern with the nature of work organisation and its potentially adverse effects on employee motivation have caused many organisations to take steps to ensure that job design incorporates the intrinsic needs of employees. This has been manifested in the emergence of the 'quality of work life' movement aimed at eliminating many of the problems associated with traditional work systems, making work more meaningful for employees and ensuring positive benefits for employers.

Apart from the job enrichment initiatives mentioned above, the QWL movement has also been characterised by steps to increase employee influence and involvement in work organisation and job design. Again, this challenges some traditional management assumptions about employees. It involves recognising that employees can and want to make a positive input into organisational decision-making. It assumes that such involvement is valued by employees and results in increased commitment, responsibility and performance.

Increased employee influence in work system design also addresses the issue of employee supervision as an aspect of the management role. If employees are to be involved in making decisions about the organisation of work and responsible for the subsequent execution of such decisions much of the'control' aspect is removed from the supervisory role. It necessitates a change in attitude to workforce management. Supervisors become less concerned with monitoring and controlling employee performance and more involved in advising and facilitating employees in carrying out their jobs.

This approach requires high levels of commitment and trust from both management and employees. Management must feel confident that employees have the required competence and will use their greater levels of influence positively and to the benefit of the organisation. Employees must be happy that their increased commitment and sense of responsibility will not be abused or exploited by employers.

There are various mechanisms available to encourage increased levels of employee participation in the design and operation of work systems. Possibly the best-known one is *quality circles*. These are small groups of employees and managers who meet together regularly to consider means of improving quality, productivity or other aspects of work organisation. They are seen as having played an important role in the success of Japanese organisations and have been successfully applied in Western economies including Ireland. *Autonomous work-groups* are self-regulating groups of employees who operate without direct supervision, incorporate full job flexibility and encourage a participative approach to decision-making.

There are numerous other participative and consultative mechanisms which may be established and can work effectively in the appropriate organisational environment. Creating such an environment has become an important concern for organisations. Past experience in applying various techniques to improve employee motivation and involvement have demonstrated that these operate best where there is a change in the overall corporate approach. The issue for senior management is how to create a corporate culture whose values, beliefs and practices establish an organisational environment within which employees are highly committed to and work towards the achievement of business goals.

Changes in Corporate Culture: The Japanese factor

A key variable influencing the success or otherwise of changes in work organisation will be basic corporate values and beliefs about work organisation and workforce management. It has been suggested that more successful organisations develop a corporate culture which places a high value on the organisation's workforce and strives to increase trust, improve communications and participation, share information and give employees greater autonomy.[17]

Much of the impetus for such change stems from the success of Japanese organisations in creating organisational cultures which increase employee involvement, commitment and performance. Elements of the 'Japanese model' have been successfully applied in Europe and North America. Many organisations who claim to have an integrated Human Resource Management (HRM) culture incorporate characteristics of the Japanese approach. In Ireland companies such as Analog, Digital and Guinness Peat Aviation seem to be applying some such aspects successfully.

The Japanese 'humanistic' corporate system is characterised by values of sharing, participation and respect for the individual.[18] This is manifested in Japanese management approaches: mutual trust and support, co-operation, commitment, non-elitism, job security and consensual decision-making. Employees are seen as a valuable resource and are involved in organisational decision-making. Management-employee relations are seen as mutually complementary and non-adversarial. Personnel management policies are based on four key characteristics:

a) Seniority-based payment systems: wages increase with age; recognises need for family income, security; requires increased skill/knowledge levels over time;

b) Lifetime employment: (approx. 30 per cent of male workforce); promotes employee loyalty, commitment, productivity;

c) Enterprise unions: high level of management-union interaction; little class conflict; non-adversarial relations.

d) Incomes policies: element of social contract; pay guidelines.

Several reservations have been expressed about the application of Japanese approaches to differing cultures, and it would be clearly inappropriate to suggest that the 'Japanese model' presents any ready-made solutions to the quest for competitive advantage. However, the success of Japanese organisations, and western companies who have adopted elements of their management approach, suggests that employers might fruitfully consider some elements of the 'Japanese model' for incorporation with the best aspects of western managerial approaches. In the US, Ouchi contrasted Japanese approaches with those of more traditional American organisations and suggested a hybrid approach which he termed Theory Z,[19] see table 5.3.

Ouchi differentiated between Japanese and American approaches along seven dimensions.[20] Japanese organisation provide *lifetime employment* tenure. *Decision-making* is consensual rather than imposed while *responsibility* for execution is collective rather than individual. *Performance evaluation and transfer/promotion* is a much slower process as employees gain experience on a range of skills along *career paths* which are broad

Table 5.3. Characteristics of model A, J and Z organisations

Characteristics	A (American)	J (Japanese)	Z (Hybrid)
Employment tenure	Short-term/ insecure	Lifetime/secure	Long-term commitment
Decision-making	Individual/imposed	Consensual	Consensual
Responsibility	Individual	Collective	Individual
Performance evaluation	Rapid evaluation & promotion	Slow evaluation & promotion	Slow evaluation & promotion
Managerial control	Explicit/formal	Implicit/informal	Combination of both
Career paths	Specialised/narrow	Non-specialised, broad	Moderately specialised
Concern for employees	Partial (work only)	Total (family, welfare, etc.)	Total

Adopted from Ouchi, W.G. & Jaeger, A. M. 'Type Z organisations: stability in the midst of mobility' Academy of Management Review No.3 1978.

rather than specialised. *Management control* is achieved through social norms and standards rather than explicit procedures or tight supervision. *Management concern for employees* covers all aspects of the employee's life: work, family, leisure, etc.

In contrast, American organisations are characterised by Ouchi as providing less secure employment and are quicker to evaluate performance and make promotion or transfer decisions. They emphasise work measurement and reward individual performance. Imposed decision-making, individual responsibility, explicit controls and concern only with work behaviour also characterise this approach.

Ouchi proposes a hybrid management approach (Theory Z) which incorporates aspects of the Japanese approach but retains the individual emphasis of the American model. There is a long-term commitment to employment security; decision-making is consensual; employee evaluation and promotion is slower; explicit performance evaluation is retained but combined with more implicit social controls and norms; there is less specialisation in career paths and a greater concern for employee wellbeing. This approach is seen as creating a greater sense of identification with organisational goals, increasing egalitarianism, trust and participation with long-term performance benefits for the organisation.

The Choice for Organisations
The issues of employee motivation, organisation and work design are related to broader corporate choices about the nature and role of the organisation. Employee performance will be influenced by a variety of factors relating to both the individual and the work context. The work environment is seen as particularly important. As information technology becomes more flexible in its application, employers have possibly greater scope to introduce changes in work organisation. Apart from the necessity for management commitment and positive beliefs about people at work, these changes have broader implications for other personnel management policy choices. In particular it is important that any changes in work organisation complement decisions taken in other personnel areas, especially in manpower planning, selection, employee development, employee relations and remuneration.

Employee selection and development are particularly significant since corporate choices on work and job design need to dovetail with workforce needs and motives. The degree of congruence between the work system, job design and employee needs will be a major influence on employee relations. Such needs include both intrinsic and extrinsic components. Employers must assess the optimal balance of extrinsic and intrinsic rewards and ensure their availability to employees.

Some important considerations in relation to intrinsic motivation have been considered above. Management must pay equal attention to extrinsic rewards and ensure these are appropriate and 'fit' with personnel policy choices in employee selection, employee development and employee relations.

Chapter 6

Managing Rewards

INTRODUCTION

Employee motivation at work may be stimulated by intrinsic and extrinsic factors. Intrinsic rewards are valued outcomes which derive primarily from the work itself. Extrinsic rewards are those work outcomes provided by someone else in the organisation. The most important source of extrinsic rewards is management. It is the organisation which pays employees and provides other benefits such as holidays, health insurance, etc. An individual's superior is also a source of recognition, praise and feedback.

Managing rewards involves the establishment and maintenance of adequate remuneration systems which attract, retain and motivate the organisation's workforce in line with business objectives. An employee's extrinsic reward package will be comprised of a variety of components as indicated in figure 6.1.

Fig 6.1. Extrinsic rewards — examples

Pay	Job security
Promotion	Working conditions
Praise	Peer group approval
Recognition	Benefits (insurance, holidays, pension, car)
Feedback	Status symbols
Flexibility	Attractive tasks/projects

How the reward package is structured and applied will have a major impact on employee performance. Reward systems are important to the organisation because they help to attract and retain employees and influence performance and behaviour at work. They are important to employees because they provide the means to satisfy basic needs and may also allow them to satisfy less tangible desires for personal growth and satisfaction. The importance of intrinsic rewards and the steps organisations might take to increase intrinsic motivation were discussed in the previous chapter. In this chapter the role of extrinsic rewards, particularly pay, is considered.

TOWARDS EFFECTIVE REWARD SYSTEMS

As with the design of the work system, an organisation's reward system is a powerful indicator of its philosophy and approach to workforce management. High or low pay, availability of training and promotion and the range of fringe benefits provide a valuable insight into the corporate approach to human resources. Important considerations in the design of an organisation's reward system include the relative emphasis on extrinsic versus intrinsic rewards, the role of pay and whether it is contingent upon individual performance, and the compatibility of the reward system with the organisation's business goals and personnel policies. This latter issue is particularly significant since the organisation's reward system must complement overall business objectives and other personnel policy choices. Decisions on the organisation's cost structure and market strategy will influence the reward system. A high-volume low-cost strategy may constrain the organisation's ability to provide expansive rewards. On the other hand, a product innovation strategy may require a comprehensive reward system which attracts and retains high-calibre staff. The reward system must also fit other personnel decisions. Recruitment and selection will provide a particular workforce profile and the reward system must cater for their various needs. The reward system should also complement personnel practices in areas such as employee development and promotion.

The design and implementation of effective reward systems has proved a difficult problem for many organisations. Beer suggests that many employee grievances and criticisms of reward systems actually mask more fundamental employee relations problems.[1] Because extrinsic rewards are a most tangible outcome of an employee's relationship with an organisation they are an obvious target for discontent concerning the employment relationship. Dissatisfaction with elements of this relationship, such as the supervisory style or opportunities for personal development, may manifest itself in dissatisfaction with aspects of reward systems. This suggests that organisations experiencing problems with their reward system should examine decisions taken on other personnel policy issues such as selection, employee relations or work design rather than make piecemeal changes in, for example, the compensation package.

Another potential problem concerns suggestions that rewards should be contingent upon individual performance. American organisations seem particularly keen on linking the distribution of rewards to measurable performance. This approach is based on the concept that it is fair and logical to reward individual employees differentially based on some measure of performance. While this principle is rarely a source of contention, problems may arise in developing reliable and acceptable mechanisms for evaluating employee performance. These include the limited criteria used (such as work study), inconsistency of application (performance appraisal), or bias and inequity in assessing employee performance. A more basic issue may be resentment towards the exercise of managerial control via performance measurement and reward distribution which is inherent in many reward-for-performance approaches.

In attempting to develop an effective reward system the following characteristics are seen as essential:[2]

a) reward level: the award package must satisfy basic needs for survival, security and self-development;

b) individuality: apart from satisfying basic needs the reward system must be flexible enough to meet the varying individual needs of the organisation's employees;

c) internal equity: rewards must be seen as fair when compared to others in the organisation; criteria for the allocation of rewards should be equitable and clear; these should be communicated and accepted by all parties and applied consistently throughout the organisation;

d) external equity: rewards must be seen as fair when compared to those offered for comparable work outside the organisation;

e) trust: management and employees must believe in the reward system; employees accepting that certain rewards will be forthcoming when the relevant criteria are met; management trusting that employees will perform at an appropriate level in return for such rewards.

In her study of motivation and personnel practices in the Civil Service Blennerhassett found that the reward system satisfied *basic needs* for a reasonable standard of living (through adequate salaries) and security (through employment tenure guarantees and good pension plan).[3] On the issue of *individuality* the system fared less well. The range of rewards was deemed inadequate to meet staff needs. It was also felt that criteria for distributing rewards were relatively inflexible and did not adequately reflect individual performance. Incremental salary scales and other procedures militated against the use of financial or other extrinsic rewards to motivate employees. Criteria for the distribution of other rewards such as promotion or 'nicer' jobs were unclear and there was little evidence that good performers were rewarded better than poor performers. On *internal equity* the evaluation depended on whether seniority is accepted as an equitable basis for distributing rewards. Decisions on the distribution of key rewards like pay and promotion were based on seniority, with little attempt made to relate such decisions to any measure of individual performance. The system rated highly on *external equity* as measured by the ability of the Civil Service to attract and retain staff.

In the private sector one might expect greater variances in the design of reward systems and increased flexibility in the criteria applied in the distribution of rewards. Since pay is a key factor influencing both where and how people work, any discussion of extrinsic rewards must give due consideration to its important role in workforce management.

PAY AS A MOTIVATOR

Pay is important to employees. It provides the means to live, eat and achieve other personal or family goals. It is a central reason why people hold down and move between jobs. However, a key question is not the importance of financial incentives as such but whether they motivate employees to perform well in their jobs.

Once an employee has been attracted to the organisation and the job the role of money as a motivator is debatable. Clearly money—or the lack of it—can be a source of dissatisfaction. However, if the employee is reasonably happy with his income does that income induce high levels of performance? Many of the theoretical prescriptions suggest that money is important in satisfying essential lower order needs. Once these are out of the way it is factors intrinsic to the job which are the prime motivators, especially self-actualisation. Others suggest that money is important at all levels and, as expectancy theory indicates, may be a prime motivator where it is a valued outcome and where there is a strong link between effort, performance and the achievement of greater financial reward.

During the 1960s and 1970s many behavioural scientists emphasised the importance of job enrichment and organisation development and it became somewhat popular to discount the importance of money as a motivator.[4] The current emphasis on performance, productivity and cost reduction have tended to focus on primary job values like employment security, benefits and—particularly—the pay package. Most managers will agree that remuneration, especially the money element, has an important role in motivating employees. However, it is only one factor in the motivation process. Many people are not primarily motivated by money but rather by other factors such as promotion prospects, recognition or the job challenge itself. All employees do not have a generalised set of motives. Rather, an organisation's workforce will be comprised of people with varying sets of priorities relating to different situations and work contexts, resulting in differing employee motives and goals. These motives and goals will vary both between employees and among individual employees over time. For example, a young single person may prioritise basic income and free time and the job itself may not hold any great interest. Later that person, now married and with a mortgage, may be more concerned with job security and fringe benefits like health insurance and pension.

The expectancy model, discussed in the previous chapter, suggests three basic conditions which are necessary to ensure that pay acts as a motivator to high performance:

a) The reward (pay) is *valued*;
b) Instrumentality is high (employees believe that by performing well they get that financial reward);
c) Expectancy is high (employees believe that the effort expended will result in the necessary level of performance to achieve the desired reward).

These have a number of implications for management. Firstly, employees must value financial rewards. If people are paid at a very high level or simply not concerned with financial rewards higher pay will have little incentive value for employees. At this stage other factors related to the job and work environment must have the potential to motivate employees.

Secondly, if money is a valued reward, employees must believe that good performance will allow them to realise that reward. This suggests that pay should be linked to performance and differences in pay should be large enough to reward high levels of performance adequately. This approach obviously rejects remuneration systems which reward good, average and poor performance equally, such as regular pay increments based on seniority.

Fig 6.2. Financial rewards as a motivator: expectancy model

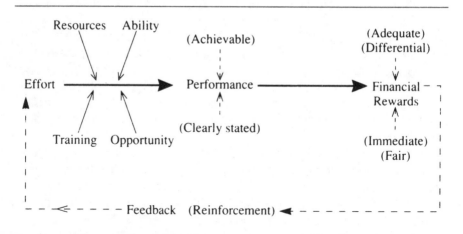

Equity is an important consideration. Employees must be fairly treated in their work situation especially in terms of the perceived equity of pay levels and comparisons with fellow-employees.[5] They will be keen that rewards (pay, benefits, etc.) adequately reflect their input (effort, skills, etc.). Should employees feel they are not being treated fairly on these criteria performance levels may fall.

Another consideration is the role of reinforcement. Reinforcement theory suggests that employee behaviour is determined by past experiences.[6] Behaviour which results in positive consequences will be encouraged and vice versa. Through operant conditioning, employee behaviour can be influenced by manipulating its consequences (rewards, punishment, etc.). In relation to financial incentives this suggests that pay can be used to positively reinforce good performance via merit awards, bonuses, etc.

Finally, employees must believe that the performance levels necessary to achieve desired financial rewards are achievable. The required performance criteria and levels should be clearly outlined and communicated to employees. Organisations must also ensure that employees have the necessary ability, training, resources and opportunity to achieve such performance levels. Otherwise employees will either not be able, or else not try, to expend the necessary effort.

Even where these factors are present, success is not guaranteed. For example, an incentive scheme based on production figures may be established to encourage employees to achieve high performance levels. However, unofficial norms established by the workgroup may dictate 'acceptable' performance levels and ensure these are not exceeded through various social pressures. Equally, such an approach may signal to employees that management are clearly in charge and may either lessen employee feelings of control and competence or encourage conflict over the standards set.

It should always be appreciated that while pay is an important source of employee motivation it is not the only one. To motivate effectively, financial incentives should be structured in such a way as to highlight the link between effort, performance and reward; to adequately reward good performance and to be equitable in the eyes of employees. The remuneration system should be viewed as part of a total motivational process which allows for individual differences and provides motivational opportunities through additional extrinsic and intrinsic factors, particularly self-fulfilment.

Remuneration systems which emphasise differential rewards based on performance are seen as motivating employees to improved performance. However, such schemes have numerous drawbacks in terms of design, operation and negative side-effects. For this and other reasons many organisations use standard pay rates which do not vary according to performance.[7] In establishing a remuneration system an organisation must weigh up the motivational aspects of a performance-related scheme against its drawbacks in terms of operational and other difficulties. It should be established in the context of the organisation's strategic needs and manpower profile and be part of the overall human resource strategy, encompassing other motivational factors appropriate to the organisation and relevant to the workforce.

COMPENSATION SYSTEMS

The choice of compensation system is an important consideration for organisations. It will partially reflect the corporate approach to workforce management and impact on areas such as employee relations, supervisory style and employee motivation. The particular package offered will be determined by a variety of factors related to the organisation, the general business environment and the workforce. As with other aspects of personnel management, the corporate approach to compensation should complement the organisation's strategic business goals, personnel philosophy and other personnel activities. Some of the major options in compensation are outlined in figure 6.3.

Fig. 6.3. Compensation — some options

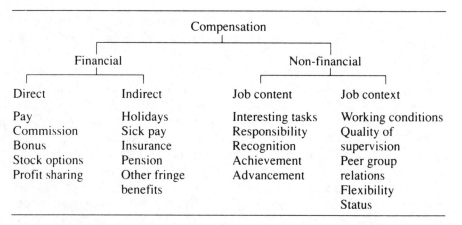

Compensation			
Financial		**Non-financial**	
Direct	Indirect	Job content	Job context
Pay	Holidays	Interesting tasks	Working conditions
Commission	Sick pay	Responsibility	Quality of
Bonus	Insurance	Recognition	supervision
Stock options	Pension	Achievement	Peer group
Profit sharing	Other fringe	Advancement	relations
	benefits		Flexibility
			Status

In relation to financial compensation the key component is the payment offered to employees. There are numerous options in the type of payment system an organisation might adopt. The more common types of payment systems are outlined in table 6.1 and discussed below.[8] From the motivational perspective effective payment systems should have the following characteristics:

i) be objectively established;

ii) clarify performance levels required and rewards available;

iii) reward the achievement of required performance levels adequately and quickly;

iv) ensure employees have the ability, training resources and opportunity to achieve required performance level(s);

v) recognise that financial incentives are only one source of motivation, and design jobs to ensure employees can satisfy other needs through their work (such as achievement, challenge);

vi) take regular steps to identify employee needs and ensure these can be satisfied within the organisation's environment.

Payment Systems

Flat rate only: flat rate schemes are popular because of their simplicity and ease of administration. They are particularly useful for managerial and administrative jobs where specific performance criteria are difficult to establish. They help to attract employees to join the organisation but their motivational potential in encouraging good performance is thought to be limited.

Flat rate plus individual, group or company-wide Payment by Results: many commentators suggest that individually rewarding performance has a strong motivational impact. Payment is related to the individual employee's contribution, required performance levels and related financial rewards are specified and these are achievable immediately after such performance criteria have been met. However, it can have potentially harmful side-effects, as mentioned in table 6.1.

Payment systems which pay a flat rate plus an incentive based on group or sectional performance may be used where it is difficult to measure individual performance or to avoid some of the harmful side-effects of individual PBR-based schemes, while still providing some incentive which is related to performance. These schemes are seen as having a more limited affect on individual motivation.

Company-based schemes are still farther removed from measures of individual performance. Consequently they are seen as having little direct impact on employee motivation but can achieve broader personnel goals such as improved employee relations, greater identification of employees with corporate performance and improved information exchange.

Piecework involves payment solely by performance. While it remains popular in some areas (such as seasonal work in agriculture, outworkers) it is unacceptable to many employees and organisations since it provides no guarantee of a minimum income to satisfy basic requirements for individual and societal well being.[9]

In Mooney's study of wage payment systems in Ireland, he found flat rate systems by far the most popular, particularly for indirect employees.[10] Individual PBR is little used for indirect staff, highlighting the difficulties in measuring performance for these categories. While the flat rate only system is the most widely used, the utilisation of approaches which combine the flat rate with payments based on some measure of performance is increasing. Mooney estimates that in 1990 over one-third of manufacturing establishments in Ireland will be operating some type of wage incentive scheme for direct manual employees. Piecework systems were little used.

Table 6.1. Payment systems

System	Characteristics	Advantages	Disadvantages	Necessary Conditions
Flat rate only	Fixed hourly, weekly or monthly rates	Simple; cheap; easy to administer; easily understood; provides stability of earnings; facilitates good employee relations	Limited incentive value; tolerates poor/average performance	Where work quantity/quality difficult to measure or where high production level is not crucial; where workflow is outside employee control
Flat rate plus individual incentive payment (individual payment by results – PBR)	Pay based on measurement of performance (e.g. piece rates, bonus schemes, commission)	Good motivator due to immediacy of reward; increased production; performance closely monitored	Difficult to establish & administer; source of conflict; possibility of emphasis on how to 'beat' scheme; work-group restrictions on output	Where money is a valued reward for employees; possible to measure work accurately; regular work-flow; work-group acceptance & commitment; easy to understand
Flat rate plus group incentive payment (PBR)	Rewards group performance (section, department)	Can be a good motivator if the link between effort, performance & pay (reward) is strong from the individual employee's viewpoint; encourages teamwork	Difficult to administer; individual performance differs & these are rewarded equally – therefore can tolerate poor performers	Where it is difficult to measure individual performance; good work-group relations/ atmosphere
Flat rate plus company-wide incentive payment (company-based PBR)	Large numbers of employees rewarded for good performance, flexibility, or participation based on specific corporate criteria (added value, etc.)	Facilitates change; encourages participation; promotes awareness of wider corporate performance among workforce	Unclear link between effort, performance & reward; rewards may be affected by factors outside employee's control; sometimes very complex	Good employee relations climate facilitating co-operation, trust & information exchange

System	Characteristics	Advantages	Disadvantages	Appropriate Conditions
Merit rating	Employees receive bonus payments based on a systematic assessment of performance generally linked to some method of performance appraisal	Rewards good performance; not just based on production factors; can facilitate participation, co-operation & feedback	Difficult to find accurate measure of overall performance; danger of subjectivity/ bias (may impair value of exercise)	Useful where production is hard to measure or where other factors need to be taken into account in evaluating performance
Gainsharing	Employees receive bonus/ rewards related to improved company performance (money, shares)	Creates employee awareness of corporate performance; encourages employee commitment & loyalty; legal/tax advantages	No clear link between individual effort & reward; rewards can vary due to factors outside employee's control; administration problems with securing tax relief	Where profit/loss figures published & where there is employee interest and commitment
Piecework	Employees only paid for work completed	Rewards directly tied to measurable performance	Source of conflict & resentment; often unacceptable as it does not guarantee any minimum income	May be appropriate on specific types of work where money is a valued reward & employees have an opportunity of satisfactory earnings

In relation to choices of payment schemes Mooney feels these are related to characteristics of the organisation and the product. In particular he identifies the significance of:

a) Company ownership: Mooney feels that a continuing influx of foreign companies will increase the utilisation of performance-related bonus schemes;

b) Size: performance-related schemes are more common in larger organisations while small firms tend to rely on flat rate only;

c) Technical system: organisations operating large batch production techniques—which are common in Ireland—are more likely to use performance-related payment systems.

d) Labour costs: Mooney feels this is the most important factor influencing the choice of payment system. Flat rate only or company-wide schemes dominate in capital-intensive organisations, while individual or group incentive schemes are popular in high labour cost organisations.

Gainsharing schemes incorporate arrangements which reward employees for improvements in corporate performance through profit sharing, share ownership or some other compensation mechanism. Gainsharing schemes differ from more traditional profit sharing arrangements insofar as they link rewards based on corporate performance to changes in managerial philosophy and style which incorporate greater employee influence and involvement.[11] The direct effects on employee motivation are believed to be poor because of their weak relationship with individual performance and lack of immediacy. However, they are seen as having important long-term benefits in increasing employee participation, awareness and commitment.

Table 6.2. Utilisation of payment systems in Ireland

Payment system	% Utilisation	Direct manual employees only	Indirect employees only*
Flat rate only	70.5	53.4	66.3
Flat rate + Individual PBR	15.3	27.4	6.2
Flat rate + Group PBR	8.6	12	15.8
Flat rate + Company PBR	2.6	3.9	6
Piecework	3	3.3	0.2

(* figures here do not add up to 100% because remaining percentage–5.5%—used some form of 'lieu bonus' for indirect employees.)
Source: Mooney, P., 'An inquiry into wage payment systems in Ireland', ESRI/European Foundation for the improvement of living and working conditions 1980.

Most gainsharing schemes involve either profit sharing or employee share ownership. Profit sharing involves the payment of a variable bonus to employees based on corporate profitability. Employee share ownership schemes involve the allocation of company shares to employees according to an agreed formula. Gainsharing arrangements incorporating either profit or equity sharing are generally linked to organisational attempts to increase employee involvement and commitment. Such schemes have become particularly popular in Britain and the US and have been linked to corporate success on such criteria as market share, profitability and quality.

Legislation passed in 1982 and 1986 provides tax benefits to employers and employees adopting 'approved' profit sharing or share-ownership schemes. Notable examples of Irish organisations with such schemes include Guinness, Analog Devices, Waterford Glass, Guinness Peat Aviation, Bank of Ireland and Allied Irish Bank. In general, however, the take-up has been low. In a 1988 study Long found that organisations expressed little interest in profit or equity sharing with only a minority of organisations having approved schemes.[12] Organisations who opposed profit or equity sharing feared a loss of privacy and control over how the organisation was run. There was also a misconception that tax concessions were only available to publicly quoted companies. Organisations who favoured the introduction of such schemes saw their benefits in increased employee commitment, productivity and improved employee relations.

An interesting aspect of the experience with equity participation in the US has been its link with concession bargaining, whereby unions give up various benefits or practices in return for share ownership for employees. In Ireland there have also been some instances of agreements on increased flexibility and changes in work practices linked to share ownership schemes, most notably in Waterford Glass.

*Merit rating:*in recent years there has been an increasing trend towards relating pay more closely to performance. Fowler suggests that a number of organisations are moving towards the evaluation of employee performance against specified objectives and using this as a basis for deciding on merit awards.[13] He also notes the extension of performance-related pay systems into the public sector, the use of performance appraisal for all grades of employees and attempts to move from regular increments to pay increases based on evaluation of individual performance. Improved performance management, use of appraisals and tying rewards to specified criteria are issues either being currently considered or applied in a number of Irish organisations.[14]

Bowey suggests there is a positive correlation between variable individual incentive payments and improvements in costs and quality.[15] However, she also points to potentially adverse affects on attitudes to work and employee relations. A continuing problem in merit-based pay is finding an acceptable mechanism to assess performance equitably and consistently. Without it, merit-based payments can lead to problems resulting from resentment to managerial control, or inequity or inconsistency in performance evaluation. A key factor seems to be the extent of employee involvement in the design of merit-based schemes with those involving extensive consultation having greater chances of success. Murlis identifies six factors which underpin successful merit-based reward systems:[16]

i) equitable mechanism for performance measurement incorporating performance appraisal;

ii) consistency of rewards among individual employees;

iii) managerial flexibility to link reward decisions to organisational needs to attract and retain employees;

iv) simple to understand and apply;

v) good basic compensation package;

vi) clearly defined employee development policy.

It is important that management clearly outline key performance criteria and reward employees accordingly. Employee acceptance of merit-based pay will depend on perceived equity in performance evaluation. It demands a climate of trust and fairness—the main responsibility for whose development lies with management.

Trade unions may sometimes oppose payments based on individual performance, preferring collective increases achieved through management-union negotiations. Grafton feels that merit-based schemes which provide for pay increases in addition to general salary awards are less likely to cause employee opposition as they operate as a discretionary element which does not cut across the collective bargaining role of the trade union.[17] In an appropriate organisational climate merit-based pay can be effectively used to augment negotiated pay and benefit increases and stimulate improved employee and organisational performance. In her study of employee motivation in the Civil Service Blennerhassett also favours the use of financial incentives as a means of rewarding good performance.[18]

ESTABLISHING AN ORGANISATION'S PAYMENT STRUCTURE

Choosing a payment system is only one aspect of managing the compensation process. A different but related issue is that of establishing basic pay levels for various jobs. Here again the organisation must be aware of the need to establish pay equity.

This initially applies to *external comparisons* with pay levels in other organisations. Comparable pay rates influence an organisation's ability to attract and retain employees. Suitable comparable organisations should be chosen to maintain pay competitiveness while keeping wage costs at reasonable levels. Pay levels will be influenced by factors in the broader business environment such as:

a) economic climate: here factors like levels of inflation, disposable income and industrial activity will exert both direct and indirect influences on payment levels by affecting employment levels, demand, consumer price indices, etc.

b) labour market: the state of the labour market will be influenced by general economic factors. It will also depend on labour supply, demand for certain skills and local factors like the level of company closures, emigration, etc. Information on local and national pay rates may be obtained through wage surveys of comparable organisations.

c) government policy: government will exert considerable influence on pay levels both indirectly (fiscal policy) and directly through what it pays its own employees (State, semi-state sector), national pay guidelines, minimum pay levels (Joint Labour Committees), and legislation (such as equal pay).

d) trade unions: through collective bargaining trade unions will seek to improve or, at least, maintain their members' earning levels. Such claims will generally be based on comparability, differentials and cost of living increases.

Pay levels also depend on factors relating to the organisation itself. Managerial philosophy and style in managing employees will impact upon approaches to the supervision, development and payment of employees. An organisation's competitive position will influence its ability to reward employees. These factors help to determine the organisation's position as a low, high or average payer, which in turn will influence the choice of comparable organisations for pay purposes, trade union approaches and employee expectations.

Organisations must also strive to maintain *internal equity* in determining differential pay rates for various jobs. The establishment of an internal pay structure involves deciding the relative value of jobs within an organisation and results in the creation of a hierarchy of job grades. The perceived equity of internal job grades will impact upon employee performance and commitment. Grading can equally be a source of grievances and conflict.

Establishing fair and consistent pay rates and differentials between jobs is an important step in developing an effective compensation system. Management will want to ensure that jobs which contribute most to the organisation are rewarded appropriately. They will also be keen to ensure that conflict over pay and job gradings is kept to a minimum. Aspirations for pay equity can be partially satisfied by ensuring that pay rates are competitive in comparison with other organisations. However, the organisation must also establish an acceptable mechanism for internally grading and evaluating jobs.

The initial stage in establishing the relative worth of jobs is an analysis of job content. This may be achieved through systematic job analysis, which should provide detailed information on the duties, demands, responsibilities and skills of the various jobs in the organisation. Such information may then be used to establish the organisation's grading structure and decide related pay levels through some method of job evaluation.

JOB EVALUATION

Job evaluation is a technique for determining the relative worth of jobs within an organisation so that differential rewards may be given to jobs of different worth. It operates by examining job content and placing jobs in a hierarchy according to their contribution to the attainment of corporate objectives.

Job evaluation is not concerned with market rates or the performance of postholders. The determination of actual pay levels is done only after the grading structure has been agreed and is usually a matter for negotiation and agreement between management and employees.

The main characteristics of job evaluation are that it attempts to establish a rank order of jobs according to agreed criteria.[19] Once jobs are evaluated they are placed into appropriate grades. Decisions on the grade awarded to particular jobs are taken on objective grounds, based on the analysis of job content and comparison to previously graded jobs. Part of this process is the selection of 'benchmark jobs' which are seen as indicative of jobs in a particular job grade and can be used for comparison purposes in the job evaluation process.

Despite some of the obvious benefits of job evaluation it is important to add a word of caution. Job evaluation is not infallible. It attempts to create a consistent and equitable system for grading jobs. However, it depends on the judgment of people with experience and training, requiring them to make decisions in a planned and systematic way, and the results do not guarantee total accuracy. A summary of the main benefits of job evaluation and some of its drawbacks are outlined in table 6.3.

In addition to some of these specific benefits, job evaluation can have a number of broader advantages for the organisation. Through encouraging systematic job analysis, better information will be available for selection, training and promotion decisions. It shifts the focus of attention away from pay parity and towards productivity, facilitating the more effective use of manpower by identifying under-capacity or wastage. The job evaluation process also facilitates the improvement of working methods and conditions and helps to spot and remove job hazards. Lastly, job evaluation can help shift the focus of management-employee relations away from negotiations and collective bargaining towards joint problem solving. It provides a

Table 6.3. Job evaluation — the pros and cons

Benefits	Possible drawbacks
Helps to rationalise existing pay structures	Rise in payroll costs (upgradings, personal allowances)
Increased equity in job grading	Installation costs (management time, consultants fee, etc.)
Reduces managerial bias (e.g. 'blue-eyed boys' syndrome)	Benefits difficult to quantify (improved morale, better IR)
Reduces grievances over job grading	May reduce flexibility (employees adhere strictly to job description)
Creates simpler and easily understandable systems	Possible employee or trade union opposition
Creates permanent mechanism for grading new jobs	Some degree of subjectivity always present
Encourages management/union and management/employee co-operation and participation	Downgradings may affect morale

common ground between management, trade unions and employees and a common language with which to discuss complex pay issues.

Job evaluation is extensively used by Irish organisations. Gorman *et al* found that over 57 per cent of large organisations used job evaluation.[20] An IPM study found that 32 per cent of organisations used job evaluation but also found that larger organisations were more likely to use job evaluation and that levels of utilisation were on the increase.[21]

Types of Job Evaluation Schemes

Job evaluation schemes may generally be classified into two main categories as follows:[22]

Analytical: jobs are broken down into a number of critical factors (such as responsibility, skills) which are then analysed and compared, using some quantitative measure of relative importance (such as point scores). The most commonly used analytical scheme is points rating, which allocates point values to different job factors and grades jobs according to their overall point scores. Factor comparison is a variation on this approach which uses money values rather than points to compare jobs factors. However, this method is not widely used.

Non-analytical: here comparisons are made between 'whole jobs'. Unlike analytical schemes, jobs are not broken down into distinct factors. The most widely used non-analytical schemes are job ranking and job classification.

Each type of job evaluation method has its own particular advantages and disadvantages. The choice of scheme must be related to the individual organisation's needs and will depend on factors like the number of jobs to be evaluated, the nature and complexity of such jobs and the views of management, employees and trade unions. It is possible to tailor and alter job evaluation schemes to meet an individual organisation's needs and there are many such hybrid schemes in existence. The main characteristics of the three most commonly used job evaluation schemes are discussed below.

Job ranking: often referred to as the simplest form of job evaluation, job ranking aims to judge each job as a whole and determine its place in a job hierarchy by comparing one job with another and arranging them in order of importance. A ranking table is then drawn up and the jobs thus ranked are arranged into grades. Pay levels may then be agreed for each grade. Sometimes a single factor such as skill is used; alternatively a list of factors such as skill, responsibility, complexity, physical demands, etc. is used.

The main advantages of job ranking are that it is simple and easy to understand. Its characteristics are easy to communicate to the parties involved and ranking schemes can be quickly implemented. Consequently it has been suggested that ranking is most useful for small organisations with a limited range of jobs to evaluate.[23] Its disadvantages are that it provides no detailed analysis of jobs and there is no clear rationale to explain why jobs have been ranked in a particular order. Thus, there remains a strong element of subjectivity in this method. Since there are no detailed standards of judgment, ranking can only indicate that one job is more difficult than another—it cannot indicate the actual degree of difference between jobs.

Job classification: this approach is a step up in complexity from job ranking. It starts, not by ranking jobs, but by agreeing a grading structure. Initially the number of job grades and particular criteria for these grades are agreed, so that for each job grade there is a broad description of its key characteristics. Benchmark jobs considered to be particularly characteristic of each job grade are chosen and, using detailed job descriptions, all other jobs are evaluated by comparison with both the benchmark jobs and the criteria for each job grade. Evaluated jobs are then placed in their appropriate grades.

Like job ranking, an advantage of job classification is that it is simple to operate and easy to understand. However, it has the added advantage of greater objectivity, in that standards and criteria for each job grade are established, and the evaluation process compares evaluated jobs with these criteria and the benchmark jobs. The main drawbacks of job classification are that it is difficult to apply with more complex jobs where duties and skills do not fit neatly into one grade but overlap with other grades. Also it may not be able to cater for a wide range of jobs or for senior jobs where grade descriptions have to be very general.

Points rating: points rating is the most commonly used job evaluation technique. This method is analytical in that, instead of comparing 'whole jobs', it breaks down each job into a number of component job factors. It then analyses these separately defined factors which are assumed to be common to all jobs. It is based on the assumption that the degree to which differences in the job factors arise will accurately reflect the actual difference between total jobs.

The procedure with points rating is as follows:

a) Determine job factors: a key step in points rating is selecting and defining the job factors considered common to all jobs to be evaluated. These may differ between organisations and can range in number dramatically. A commonly used factors list is outlined in figure 6.4.

Fig. 6.4. Sample job factors for use in job evaluation

```
*Skill
*Responsibility
*Mental requirements
*Physical effort
*Working conditions
```

Each of these job factors may then be broken down into a number of sub-factors. Taking the factor 'responsibility' above, this may be further broken down as follows;

Responsibility
{
financial
quality
equipment & materials
training
other
}

b) Agree factor levels: the importance of the various factors will vary between jobs and for this reason different factor levels are agreed which reflect the varying degree of importance attached to a particular factor when comparing jobs, see table 6.4, p. 132.

c) Allocate point values to job factors: as can be seen from table 6.4., various point values are assigned to each of the sub-factors and their level of importance. These will reflect the relative importance of each of the sub-factors and result in different weightings for some job factors and sub-factors.

In the example below, responsibility is seen as being twice as important as working conditions, while in relation to working conditions, hazardous conditions are seen as warranting greater significance than those considered unpleasant.

Table 6.4. Factor levels in job evaluation — example

| | Level | | | | |
| | 1 | 2 | 3 | 4 | Total |
Factor	Minimum	Low	Moderate	High	Points
Responsibility					
a. Financial	10	20	30	40	
b. Quality	10	20	30	40	
c. Equipment	10	20	30	40	
d. Training	10	20	30	40	
e. Other	10	20	30	40	200
Working conditions					
a. Hazardous	15	30	45	60	
b. Unpleasant	10	20	30	40	100

d) Define each job factor and level of importance: to aid the job evaluation process the characteristics of each job factor and the criteria for each level of significance may be outlined. In relation to a factor like responsibility this might read as follows (see box 6.1).

Box 6.1. Sample factor definition — responsibility

Quality: All employees are responsible for the quality of the company's products and services although the level of such responsibility will vary considerably. Such responsibility involves reporting any defects immediately, identifying any problems with materials and equipment, co-operating with quality control and maintaining equipment, materials and work station in a clean and tidy condition.

Level 1; Responsibility for simple maintenance of equipment and reporting of any defects in material, equipment and product.

Level 2; Responsibility for preliminary product inspection, reporting of defects and preventative maintenance of equipment.

Level 3; Responsibility for detection and repair of minor quality defects and equipment maintenance.

Level 4; Primary responsibility for inspection of quality. Regular liaison with quality control, maintenance and purchasing personnel to report and discuss problems or issues related to product quality, equipment or materials.

e) Evaluate jobs: using the job descriptions developed through job analysis and the factor definitions, the various jobs may then be evaluated and placed in their appropriate grades. This can be done by either taking one factor and evaluating its significance in all jobs under consideration, or taking each job and evaluating it in terms of all job factors. The former approach is recommended as it concentrates on the comparable worth of jobs in terms of a specific factor and this information can be brought together at the end to give a total picture of relative job worth. The main strength of points rating is that it is a much more systematic and objective method, relying on job data and using clearly defined standards of comparison. The main criticism levelled against points rating schemes is that they are complex and can be both time-consuming and expensive to develop and maintain. Also it could be suggested that the use of in-depth analysis and numerical ratings gives a false impression of scientific accuracy to a method which still relies heavily on subjective decision-making. Indeed, it might be suggested that it is impossible to put numerical values on different aspects of jobs, since skills are not always quantifiable in this way, particularly when comparing the skills demanded by jobs of often disparate demands and responsibilities.

Introducing a Job Evaluation Scheme

Introducing job evaluation will have a tremendous impact on company pay structure and employee relations generally. Therefore any decisions should only be taken after careful deliberation and consultation with the parties concerned. The following steps can be considered indicative of the major issues in introducing an effective job evaluation scheme.

a) Advice: as we have seen, the introduction of job evaluation can be quite a complex process. Therefore expert advice and assistance should be sought at the initial stages. In introducing a job evaluation scheme, companies often find it useful to use an agreed external consultant. This helps to give the scheme objectivity and independence. Their overall role is to ensure that a fair and effective system of job evaluation is introduced. Consultants will generally be responsible for advising on the technical aspects of the scheme and will help in *(i)* deciding on the type of scheme to be used; *(ii)* the technical aspects of the scheme; *(iii)* the composition of the various committees; *(iv)* the training of job analysts, evaluation panellists and staff representatives; *(v)* communicating the details of the scheme to management and employees.

b) Participation: a key to the success of any job evaluation scheme is that it is understood and accepted by management, workers and their trade unions.[24] At all stages in the process staff should be kept adequately informed. It is vital that those who will be most directly affected by the scheme should know its objectives, content and operational aspects to ensure there are no misunderstandings or false fears about its impact. Middle management and supervisors should not be overlooked in this process. They will play a vital role in successfully implementing the scheme so it is imperative that they understand it and appreciate their role in its operation. Employee participation is an important hallmark of many successful job evaluation schemes. The Institute of Personnel Management stated in its survey on job evaluation in Ireland (1976):

> Thus job evaluation provides the opportunity for achieving genuine participation in practice and for developing a working relationship in which unions are not simply making claims on the employers but are participating with them in a joint problem-solving and decision-making exercise which has a vital bearing on differentials and other negotiable issues.[25]

While direct employee participation is not a necessary component of job evaluation schemes, it does have numerous advantages. Co-operation and commitment of employees and their trade unions will be greater where they are directly involved in the operation of the scheme. This can be done through job evaluation committees, appeals panels, etc. Either way it is essential that management take the necessary steps to involve and communicate with all interested parties at all stages in the process so that agreement can be achieved on its introduction and operation.

c) Choice of scheme: an IPM survey found points rating the most widely used job evaluation scheme in Irish organisations, followed by ranking, job classification and factor comparison.[26]

The choice of scheme will depend on factors relating to the organisation itself (size, technology, employee relations) and the jobs to be evaluated (number, complexity, current pay structures). Every company will have to seek expert advice and get the views of management and staff on the most appropriate scheme. Armstrong suggests that the golden rule in selecting a job evaluation scheme is to choose the simplest scheme first and reject it only if the situation is too complex or circumstances demand a more sophisticated method.[27] The most important criterion to be applied is that the scheme is fair and results in a structure which is acceptable to employees and management. A summary comparison of the three major job evaluation schemes is contained in table 6.5, p. 135.

It is up to the individual organisation, having taken the appropriate steps, to decide on the method that best fits its needs. Many organisations use ready-made schemes. Possibly the best known is the HAY–MSL Guide Chart and Profile Method. This scheme is particularly appropriate for professional and managerial grades. It adopts a points system based on three key factors; know-how, problem solving, and accountability.

Table 6.5. Comparison of job evaluation methods

Criteria	Job evaluation schemes		
	Ranking	Classification	Points rating
Characteristics	Non-quantitative		Quantitative
Yardstick	Job-to-job		Predetermined category definition
Method	Whole job		Uses job factors
Pros & cons	Cheap, easy to install, lacking in rigour, limited application		Complex, costly, cater for wide range of jobs
Similarity to other job evaluation	Crude form of factor comparison	Crude form of point system	Refinement of job classification

d) Monitoring: Any job evaluation scheme must be accurately documented and the personnel adequately trained in its operation. This ensures its continuity in evaluating new jobs and dealing with appeals and jobs whose content has changed over time. Provision should be made for periodic appraisals to evaluate its effectiveness. Any problems with the scheme can be identified and appropriate adjustments made. It is important that the commitment to monitor and review the scheme be a concrete one.

Job evaluation does not provide the total answer to problems of deciding equitable financial rewards. Rather, it attempts to eliminate some of the pitfalls in job grading and pay determination. It seeks to reduce subjectivity and place the focus on the job and not the person. However, people considerations will always be present. Indeed, evaluating job demands is only one aspect of effectively managing performance. The other side of the coin involves the equally difficult task of facilitating and evaluating employee performance in the job.

Chapter 7

Performance Appraisal

INTRODUCTION

Achieving and maintaining satisfactory performance levels is a central aspect of managerial work in all types of organisations. Indeed, it might be suggested that managers can best contribute to organisational success by facilitating the achievement of high performance levels by their work teams. Effective performance management is a continuous process involving the establishment of performance standards, monitoring of actual performance and construction of action plans to review standards, deal with problem areas and take appropriate steps to improve performance (see figure 7.1).

Fig. 7.1. The performance management loop

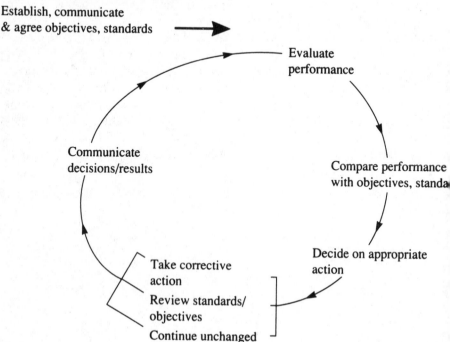

Establish, communicate
& agree objectives, standards

Evaluate
performance

Communicate
decisions/results

Compare performance
with objectives, standards

Take corrective
action

Review standards/
objectives

Continue unchanged

Decide on appropriate
action

A central component of the performance management process is the appraisal of employee performance and the provision of feedback and development opportunities for employees.

WHAT IS PERFORMANCE APPRAISAL?

Performance appraisal refers to systematic approaches to evaluating employee performance, characteristics and/or potential with a view to assisting decisions in a wide range of areas such as pay, promotion, employee development and motivation.

Many Irish organisations operate formal appraisal schemes. In 1975 Gorman *et al* found that over two-thirds of large organisations used formal appraisal systems, while in 1987 Shivanath found this had increased to 80 per cent.[1] Both these studies noted that formal appraisal schemes were often restricted to managerial, supervisory or clerical grades.

A principal instigator of performance appraisal systems is often the specialist personnel function. However, the responsibility for actually monitoring and evaluating employee performance will lie with line management. Appraisal in an area where liaison, understanding and commitment from both line management and the personnel function is essential for success.

Some form of employee appraisal takes place in all organisations. This may comprise of occasional informal discussions, counselling or evaluation which is an important aspect of the management process. Apart from day-to-day interactions it is, however, necessary that managers and employees devote some time to the objective consideration of employee performance. Such an exercise facilitates understanding and feedback, allowing management to communicate its priorities and targets to employees. It also allows employees to express their needs and concerns to management. Performance may be reviewed against standards. Issues like career development may be discussed and agreement reached on future job targets, appropriate training and the nature of further performance reviews.

OBJECTIVES OF PERFORMANCE APPRAISAL

A first and crucial step in establishing an effective appraisal system is deciding what is the primary objective of appraisal. Performance appraisal may be used to fulfil one or a number of specific objectives for the organisation. Some possible objectives for performance appraisal are outlined in figure 7.2. Management must be careful in designing performance appraisal schemes. Some of these varied objectives of performance appraisal are not necessarily complementary. Attempts to achieve multiple objectives or lack of clarity in objective setting can lead to serious problems in the operation of performance appraisal.

Fig. 7.2. Objectives of performance appraisal — examples

Provide feedback	Improve performance
Review past performance	Assess potential
Facilitate career counselling	Set performance objectives
Improve communications	Identify training needs
Assist manpower planning/ recruitment	Aid salary review

Therefore a prerequisite for effective performance appraisal is clarity of objectives and the design of an appraisal system which is appropriate to the organisational context, contributes to the achievement of business goals and complements other personnel policies such as those relating to rewards or employee development. For example, the objectives of one large engineering company's performance appraisal scheme are:

i) to review past performance against job targets;

ii) to discuss an overall assessment of employee performance;

iii) to identify training and development needs and agree plans;

iv) to agree job targets for future review period.

This example emphasises the evaluation of employee performance against job targets and the identification of training needs. This seems to reflect current trends in the application of performance appraisal. In Britain the trend has been away from assessments of potential and personality towards greater emphasis on evaluating current job performance and improving communications.[2]

This is manifested in an increased emphasis on improving current performance and more extensive use of results-oriented schemes. Associated with this trend is the decline in the use of appraisal systems which assess potential or promotability, possibly reflecting criticisms of traits-oriented approaches which attempt to measure personality factors in a subjective and somewhat arbitrary fashion.

Table 7.1. Rank order of purpose of performance appraisal schemes

Purpose	1973	1977	1985
Help to improve current performance	—	2	1
Set/review performance objectives	2	—	2
Assess training/development needs	3	1	3
Assess potential/promotability	1	3	—

(IPM Surveys 1973, 1977 & 1985: Rank 1–3).

Table 7.1 highlights this movement away from assessing potential or promotability and towards a greater role for performance appraisal as a mechanism for setting, communicating and assessing performance standards and motivating employees to improved job performance. In Ireland Gorman found a similar emphasis on assessing employee performance against jointly agreed job targets.[3]

The purpose of performance appraisal will influence appraiser and appraisee attitudes. If, for example, the objective is to assess performance in order to decide on merit increases, appraisees will be keen to show themselves in the best light. This may militate against an open discussion of weaknesses, training needs or reasons for poor performance. Thus, the nature of appraisal interaction in terms of communications and openness will depend on the purpose and consequent structure of the performance appraisal scheme. It also influences the role and approach of appraisers, particularly whether they should play the role of judge (deciding on merit increases) or facilitator (helping to improve employee performance).[4]

The purpose of performance appraisal will also influence the type of scheme chosen. There now seems to be less emphasis on using appraisal schemes which assess personality attributes (such as initiative, conceptual ability). Organisations are focusing on job performance by agreeing key objective areas, evaluating performance against targets, identifying strengths and weakness in individual performance and agreeing ways of improving current performance. This approach relies less heavily on detailed rating scales and requires a more general evaluation of performance against targets. It may also reflect a desire to increase objectivity by concentrating on job performance and facilitating open discussion on ways of improving performance.

PERFORMANCE APPRAISAL METHODS

Associated with the wide range of functions performance appraisal can carry out are an equally varied array of appraisal techniques. These are summarised in table 7.2 (p. 140) and discussed below.

a) Rating scales: appraisal methods which rate employee performance, behaviour and/or characteristics according to a predetermined scale have been one of the most widely used, and indeed widely criticised, methods of conducting employee appraisals. Many such rating scale approaches rely on the assessment of personality and behavioural characteristics according to a sequential scale ranging from poor to excellent or some similar classification (see table 7.3, p. 141).

The main advantages of rating scales are that they facilitate comparisons between employees according to predetermined criteria and encourage appraisers to adopt a systematic and analytical approach in completing the appraisal form.

Table 7.2. Summary — appraisal techniques

Method	Characteristics	Strengths	Weaknesses
Rating	Appraiser specifies on a scale to what degree relevant characteristics (normally related to job-related behaviour or personality) are possessed by appraisee	Ease of comparison, range in complexity from very simple to very involved using descriptions of behaviour/ performance	Subjective; personality/ behavioural traits difficult to measure
Ranking	Appraiser ranks workers from best to worst based on specific characteristics or overall job performance	Simple, facilitates comparisons	Little basis for decisions, degrees of difference not specified, subjective
Paired comparison	Two workers compared at a time and decisions made on which is superior resulting in a final ranking order for full group	Ease of decision-making, simple	Difficult with large numbers plus weaknesses attributed to ranking
Critical incident	Appraiser/supervisor observes incidents of good/bad performance. These are used as a basis for judging and assessing/discussing performance	Job related; more objective	Needs good observational skills; time-consuming
Free-form	General free-written evaluation by appraiser	Flexible	Subjective; difficulty of comparison
Performance/ objectives- oriented systems	Appraiser evaluates degree to which specific job targets/standards have been achieved	Job related; objective; participative	Needs measurable targets; danger of collusion
Assessment centre	Appraisees undergo a series of assessments (interviews, tests, simulations, etc.) under- taken by trained assessors	Range of dimensions examined; objective	Expensive; not necessarily job specific
Self- assessment	Appraisees evaluate themselves using a particular format/ structure	Participative; facilitates discussion; promotes self-analysis	Danger of lenient tendency; potential source of conflict between appraiser and appraisee

A problem with rating scales is that, while apparently objective, they largely rely on subjective judgments based more on personal opinions than factual evidence. This is particularly so when behavioural or personality characteristics are being assessed. These are prone to the 'halo/horns effect', whereby the appraiser's judgment is disproportionately influenced by a favourable or unfavourable appraisee attribute.

Table 7.3. Extract from performance review report — electronics firm

Performance review report

Name:	Date of review:
Job title:	Date of hire:
Division:	Date of last review
Location:	

Part 1	Individual effectiveness			(Tick as appropriate)	
Characteristic	Out-standing	Exceeds requirements	Satis-factory	Minimum acceptable	Unsatis-factory
Communications					
Developing people					
Motivating people					
Planning					
Organising					
Schedule control					

Another problem is inconsistency in appraiser ratings. Appraisers may have different approaches and values which result in different ratings and variations possibly due to appraiser bias rather than actual differences in performance. Similar problems may arise where rating techniques are used for large numbers of employees doing jobs which differ in terms of key duties, responsibilities, etc. and which are not appropriate for evaluation using the same criteria.

Lastly, there is the possibility that a majority of ratings will fall into the average or above average category, rendering the whole process of differentiation meaningless. Attempts to remedy this problem have involved the use of forced distribution and forced choice techniques. The former requires appraisers to rate employees according to quotas imposed by a normal distribution curve (only 10 per cent in excellent category, 20 per cent in satisfactory, etc.). Forced choice techniques require appraisers to choose a descriptive statement which best describes the employee's performance and characteristics while ensuring there is no middle position, thus forcing appraisers to make a significant choice. For example, on a factor like initiative the choice might be as follows:

Fig. 7.3. Initiative (tick as appropriate)

Takes responsibility & uses it well	Keen to tackle new tasks	Needs direction	No initiative

A further development on this theme is the use of behaviourally anchored rating scales (BARS). These provide narrative descriptions of job behaviour levels using critical incidents on a defined scale. This approach attempts to reduce subjectivity by relating the rating scale to specified job performance criteria helping the appraiser decide on the actual rating to be awarded.[5] A sample extract from a behaviourally anchored rating scale is shown in table 7.4:

Table 7.4. BARS example — discipline administration

Factor 1 – Legal knowledge/awareness

Good	Satisfactory	Poor
Always follows correct procedures; discusses disciplinary issues with employee & records outcome; seeks advice when unsure	Good knowledge of law; ignores some minor transgressions; aware of serious disciplinary issues	Does not know basic principles; takes disciplinary action without establishing facts or seeking advice

Such attempts at improving the reliability of rating scales are difficult and expensive to develop and the benefits are not well established.

b) Results-oriented methods: results-oriented techniques have their origins in the use of management by objectives (MBO) in many organisations since the 1960s.[6] MBO-based approaches encourage organisations to specify what they want to achieve (objectives); communicate and agree these objectives with employees at all levels (participation); evaluate to what degree these objectives have been achieved (measurement); and take corrective action or analyse reasons for good or bad performance (action and feedback). While MBO's popularity as a specific managerial technique has declined, the adoption of its principles for structuring performance appraisal systems has become increasingly widespread.[7]

The main characteristics of results-oriented systems is that appraisers are required to assess employee performance against previously agreed objectives (sometimes called key result areas). An important element of this approach is employee participation in objective setting. It is felt that such joint involvement encourages employee commitment to the achievement of objectives and goals and allows for their re-negotiation as appropriate. It is also necessary that objectives are specified in terms of measurable targets and results. These targets then become the basis for periodic reviews of employee progress and achievement in the job. An underlying assumption is that this job focus allows for a frank discussion of employee performance in a less threatening atmosphere than where employee traits are assessed. It also involves a simple administrative process with less detailed forms and an absence of elaborate rating scales. However, it is demanding on managers and supervisors; requiring their active involvement in observing performance, agreeing standards and giving feedback to employees on performance and related matters. The primary advantages of results-oriented methods are related to the focus on actual job performance. From the appraisee's perspective, goals are clearly set out and the appraisee has been involved in their selection. This should encourage greater motivation towards their achievement. The review process itself will be results-oriented and concentrate on the degree to which job targets have been achieved and finding ways to improve performance.

The drawbacks of results-oriented methods may also stem from the job focus. It is difficult to draw comparisons between employees who have been appraised on different criteria for different jobs. Additionally, the feasibility of achieving job targets may change over time (for example, a salesperson's capacity to sell may be reduced by a competitor launching a superior product).

Another potential problem is an over-emphasis on measurable and immediate job factors which ignores the importance of less tangible aspects like customer relations. There is also the danger of superior-subordinate collusion, resulting in targets which are easy to achieve and do not provide a basis for any worthwhile discussion or feedback.

c) Free-form methods: this approach requires the appraiser to write a free-form report on employees, often in an essay style. Its strengths lie in its flexibility. No restraints are placed on the appraiser, and it can be a rich source of information on employee performance and potential. Its weaknesses relate to its dependence on the competence of the writer, related problems of subjectivity and the fact that it does not facilitate comparisons between employees. Fletcher suggests that it should rarely be used alone and that it is most appropriate where the appraiser lacks detailed knowledge of the job or the individual.[8] This may apply in 'grandfather' appraisals where performance is reviewed by a manager one level above the employee's immediate superior.

d) Critical incident methods: here appraisers are required to observe employees on the job and record incidents of good or bad performance over the evaluation period. In this way a series of critical incident behaviours are established which are then used as the basis for assessing and discussing employee performance. This approach depends on the observational skills of the appraiser and the relations between appraiser and appraisee. It is a useful mechanism for facilitating discussion and feedback since it is related to actual job performance. Its drawbacks include the time and effort required in its design and its potential as a source of negative reactions among appraisees. It is of little use as a vehicle for comparison and may tend to over-emphasise particular incidents or issues rather than giving an overall view of employee performance.

e) Other methods: assessment centres have been widely used in the US to predict future job performance and to aid both selection and promotion decisions.[9] They involve the use of a series of assessment techniques such as simulations, tests and interviews to evaluate employee performance and ability. The results of these various assessments are evaluated by a panel of trained assessors. Research findings on the reliability and validity of assessment centres in accurately predicting performance and assessing potential have been favourable.[10] Despite this they are little used by Irish organisations, although it is anticipated that this will change in the future, particularly in aiding decisions on promotion and selection for senior positions.[11]

Ranking involves the appraiser placing appraisees in a rank order from best to worst. It is based on assessments of overall performance rather than specific characteristics. The main problem with this method is the danger of subjectivity and lack of criteria for assessment. *Paired comparisons* are a development of this approach. It involves comparisons between two employees at a time until every possible pair in the workgroup has been appraised. A rank order is then drawn up.

Self-appraisal involves employees evaluating their own performance, either in general terms or in relation to specified criteria. It is seen as a means of increasing employee participation and involvement in the appraisal process. Some organisations use an element of self-appraisal through requiring employees to complete a pre-interview appraisal form. However, moves towards more comprehensive forms of self-appraisal have been slow. *Peer appraisal* involves employees appraising their colleagues and may sometimes be used for managerial grades to help to develop leadership or management skills. However, it is little used in practice.

Utilisation of Performance Appraisal Methods

The utilisation of various performance appraisal techniques has been examined in a number of IPM surveys which are summarised in table 7.5.

These findings suggest the following trends in the application of performance appraisal in organisations:

a) Results-oriented methods are most popular and are mostly used for managerial and professional grades;

b) most organisations use a combination of methods—possibly reflecting the limitations of any single method;

c) rating techniques are still very much in evidence with trait rating popular for non-management jobs;

d) narrative approaches (free-form and controlled) are often used along with some form of rating scale;

e) critical incident and other methods are not widely used.

Table 7.5. Utilisation of performance appraisal methods

Method	Degree of utilisation †		
	1973	1977	1985
Result-oriented	51%	57%	63%
Job behaviour-oriented*	—	—	52%
Alphabetical/numerical rating	36%	11%	28%
Personality trait rating	18%	34%	29%
Free-form	6%	1%	2%
Controlled written	4.5%	6%	44%

* Not available for 1973 and 1977;
† Totals are greater than 100% due to multiple responses, ie organisations using more than one method.
Source: IPM Surveys 1973, 1977, 1985.

Although there is a lack of up-to-date empirical information on the Irish context, appraisal practice in Ireland seems to largely reflect these general trends. Gorman also found that results-oriented methods were the most widely used in Irish organisations.[12] Performance targets were normally agreed between employees and their manager. Appraisals involved asses-sing the extent to which jointly set job targets were achieved. Personality ratings were used in only a small minority of instances. In a study of motivation and personnel practices in the Civil Service Blennerhassett noted the absence of formal appraisal procedures.[13] She also highlighted the lack of any clear link between individual performance and promotion as a barrier to improved employee performance and motivation. Blennerhassett suggested the introduction of performance appraisal as a means of tying decisions on promotion and the distribution of other rewards to individual employee performance. She felt that formal appraisal, together with the specification of promotion criteria, would have a positive impact on employee motivation and performance.

DESIGNING AND IMPLEMENTING
A PERFORMANCE APPRAISAL SYSTEM

Performance appraisal can fulfil a number of functions for an organisation. To be successful a performance appraisal scheme's primary objectives should be clearly established. This helps to facilitate understanding and acceptance by all parties involved.It also helps to avoid goal conflict and to secure employee and management commitment by clarifying the scheme's rationale. Thus, appraisal should be seen as a systematic process which makes an important contribution to corporate objectives. Of course, organisational needs vary and so too will the role of performance appraisal. However, an effective appraisal system can play a central role in the motivational process since it has enormous potential for employee involvement and the provision of intrinsic and extrinsic rewards based on assessments of employee performance.

The appraisal process is outlined in figure 7.4. Below we consider a number of general pointers which management might consider in the design and implementation of a performance appraisal system.

Fig. 7.4. The performance appraisal process

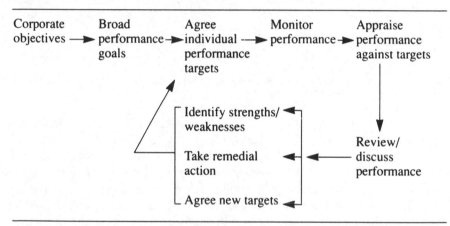

Step 1: Specify objectives: as emphasised earlier, performance appraisal cannot possibly achieve a disparate range of management goals. Management must decide what they want to achieve and then design an appropriate scheme. A central concern for all organisations will be an emphasis on performance.

Performance appraisal is an important mechanism through which management relate to employees. It assesses the degree to which specified objectives and related performance levels are being achieved. It is top management's responsibility to specify such objectives and secure commitment at all levels of the organisation to their achievement. Approached in this way, performance appraisal is more than a useful personnel technique. Rather, it becomes a powerful vehicle for establishing and achieving corporate goals through the effective management of employees.

Step 2: Outline performance standards: an effective performance appraisal system demands that desired levels of performance are clearly outlined. Ideally these performance goals will be an extension of strategic and operational plans, effectively bringing the achievement of organisational objectives to the level of the individual employee. An important benefit of specified performance standards is that employees know what is expected of them. Through job analysis and, particularly, through participative objective setting, employees will be aware of the key result areas within their job, their manager's expectations of desired performance levels and the role of performance reviews. A further benefit is that the actual appraisal process can review progress against targets and provide constructive feedback to employees. It is important that performance standards should consider all aspects of the job and not just those which are quantifiable. For example, a shop assistant will be responsible for stock control, customer relations and company image in addition to the generation of sales.

Step 3: Monitor performance: performance appraisal is an ongoing process, demanding close observation of performance and coaching as appropriate. Feedback should be given continually and not left to the appraisal interview. Feedback should be a two-way process where employees feel they can discuss work problems with superiors and influence management decisions or change performance targets as necessary.

Step 4: Evaluate performance: evaluation of actual job performance against previously established and agreed performance standards should take place at agreed time intervals. It requires careful preparation by the appraiser. This facilitates a constructive dialogue with appraisees. Actual performance is evaluated in terms of targets set, strengths and weaknesses and action plans. The communication flow should be two-way. Factors which militate against the achievement of performance targets should be outlined and the appraisee's opinions on the standards set, priority areas, resources, etc., carefully considered. The approach should be participative, with praise and criticism given as appropriate. Performance targets for the future review period should be agreed.

Step 5: Implement action plan: decisions reached through appraisal should be acted upon as soon as possible. These may range from training and development initiatives through improving resources (such as equipment) to revising standards.

THE APPRAISAL INTERVIEW

Of all the component aspects of the performance appraisal process, the appraisal interview is a central focus. Ideally the appraisal interview should be part of a continuing process of communication and feedback. It provides an opportunity to take stock, check developments, initiate remedial action and agree future targets.

Difficulties with the appraisal interview stem from the problems it poses for appraiser and appraisee. For the appraiser there is a need to be clear on the purpose of appraisals. Appraisal interviews are among the most difficult for managers. They demand skill in giving feedback (both negative and positive), handling defensive reactions, facilitating improvement in job performance and generally increasing employee motivation and satisfaction. For these reasons some writers have criticised the appraisal interview, citing the difficulties it poses for appraisers, its ritualistic nature and, consequently, its potential for detrimentally affecting the tenuous manager-employee relationship.[14]

Despite these criticisms the appraisal interview remains a vital part of the appraisal process, providing an opportunity for appraiser-appraisee interaction.

IPM surveys have found that responsibility for the conduct of appraisal interviews normally lies with the immediate supervisor (father) or, in a minority of cases, with the superior's superior (grandfather). Appraisals conducted by committee or the specialist personnel function are rare (see table 7.6). The time taken for appraisal interviews varied between managerial reviews and non-managerial reviews. For managerial reviews the average time taken was 1-2 hours, while for non-managerial reviews it was less than one hour.

Table 7.6. Who conducts appraisal interviews

	1977 %	1985 %*
Immediate superior	86	93
Superior's superior	12	12
Personnel department	—	2
Committee	2	1

Source: IPM Surveys 1977 & 1985.   * Multiple responses.

Guidelines for the Conduct of Performance Appraisal Interviews

a) Clarify objectives: appraisers should be clear on the purpose of the interview. They should know what they are evaluating and why. The emphasis should be on reviewing and improving performance. Appraisees too should be clear on the purpose of the appraisal interview so that no misunderstandings arise in the course of the interview.

b) *Time and venue:* day-to-day interaction between manger and subordinate provides an opportunity to communicate on work-related matters and give feedback on performance. However, a formal appraisal review gives both parties an opportunity to concentrate solely on performance evaluation without other distractions. The appraiser's commitment should be demonstrated by arranging an appropriate time and venue and informing the employee well in advance. The appraisee can then prepare for the interview by carrying out some form of self-appraisal, ideally using a similar format to the appraisal review form.

c) *Preparation:* both parties should be clear on required performance levels. The appraiser should have carefully observed actual performance against targets and should use such information to facilitate discussion. Appraisees should have analysed their own performance: particular strengths and the degree to which they are being utilised; weaknesses and how these might be improved; training or career development needs and any contingent factors which affect job performance.

d) *Interview:* the objectives of the interview should be re-established at the beginning of the interview. This preamble should include an outline of targets agreed at the last review. Appraisees should be put at ease and encouraged to talk about their performance, attitudes and problems in a frank and open fashion. Good performance should be acknowledged and any problem areas carefully reviewed. This can be facilitated by using open-ended questions and then listening to the appraisee. Areas of difficulty must be confronted and ways of improving performance discussed. Feedback should be given to reinforce good performance and negative feedback given in a constructive manner, focusing on the job and on ways to improve performance. Appropriate future action should be agreed, along with job targets for the next review period. The overall discussion should be summarised and agreed with the appraisee.

Interview style will depend on the particular circumstances—notably the respective approaches of appraiser and appraisee and their ongoing relationship. Meyer identifies three alternative styles as summarised in table 7.7.[15]

He advocates a joint problem-solving approach as it involves the appraisee in identifying job targets, problems and remedial action. This facilitates increased employee motivation and commitment to performance improvement. He also feels this approach will be less of a source of defensive reaction.

e) *Follow-up:* a major source of employee grievances about appraisal interviews is that issues agreed upon are not followed up by management. It

Table 7.7. Styles of appraisal interviewing

Style	Appraiser Characteristics	Appraiser Role	Approach
Tell & sell	Directive	Judge	Communicate evaluation and required steps for improvement
Tell & listen	Consultative	Judge/ counsellor	Communicate evaluation; listen to response; deal with reactions
Joint problem-solving	Participative	Facilitator	Focus on performance in the job; jointly agree targets; tackle problems and agree remedial action

is imperative that appraisers note areas for action, carry out such commitments and communicate this to appraisees.

OTHER ISSUES IN PERFORMANCE APPRAISAL
Pay and Appraisal

Linking performance appraisal with decisions on remuneration has been an issue of some debate with practice differing on both sides of the Atlantic. In the US a primary role for performance appraisal has been to assist decisions on pay, particularly merit increases.[16] In Britain and Ireland performance appraisal has generally been used to facilitate the achievement of other personnel objectives (such as identification of training needs, improving communications) with decisions on pay made through other mechanisms (such as collective bargaining). Even when individual salary reviews are carried out, this is often done at a different time from more general performance appraisals.[17] More recently there has been increased interest in developing performance-related payment schemes, particularly for managerial and professional grades.

The main objections to linking pay and appraisal arise from its impact on the appraisal process. It is felt that where pay is involved it will dominate the performance review and inhibit open discussion on job performance and employee strengths and weaknesses. Grafton also notes the reluctance of line managers to decide on differential merit pay awards for employees.[18] This raises the importance of equity and consistency in operating pay-related performance reviews. It also highlights the difficult role of appraisers within pay-related systems requiring managers to act as judge rather than coach or facilitator. This will impinge on the nature of management-subordinate relations and may prohibit greater employee involvement and participation in decision-making.[19]

Another problem in linking appraisal and pay is the potential for trade union opposition. Unions are often reluctant to accept performance-related payment systems. They may see it as a threat to the union's role in representing the collective interests of employees in securing general pay awards. They may also point to dangers of bias and inconsistency in the application of pay-related performance appraisals.

Those who favour using appraisal as a basis for decisions on remuneration refer to its motivational affect as an incentive to high performance. To be effective as a motivator, pay-related appraisals require that performance criteria and related rewards be clearly specified. These rewards should be significant, worthwhile and immediately forthcoming on achievement of specified performance standards. Decisions on merit awards should equitably reflect actual performance and be consistently applied by all managers.

Openness in Performance Appraisal

There is an increasing trend towards greater openness in performance appraisal.[20] This involves greater openness in discussing employee performance and affording employees the opportunity to view their appraisal reports.

The key advantage of greater openness is that it reduces suspicion and defensiveness on the part of appraisees. This trend possibly reflects a greater emphasis on openly discussing job performance and facilitating two-way communications and feedback. It may also indicate a move away from the more contentious area of trait rating. However, all information gathered through appraisal may not necessarily be disclosed to employees. This applies particularly to assessments of promotion and potential.

A criticism of fully open systems is that they discourage appraisers from making totally honest evaluations of employee performance. However, some mechanism for disclosing how appraisers feel an employee is performing is imperative if there is to be a worthwhile discussion of employee performance and if improvements are to be effected.

Self Appraisal

Related to the trend towards greater openness in appraisal systems is an increased emphasis on self-appraisal; encouraging employees to analyse their own performance, ambitions and potential as part of the review process. This increasingly involves appraisees completing a self-evaluation form prior to the appraisal interview. This approach is felt to be most appropriate where appraisals are based on job performance, there is a good working relationship between appraiser and appraisee and pay is not linked to appraisal.[21]

Feedback

One of the most powerful ways of motivating employees is by giving feedback on performance, encouraging their participation in determining job targets, and taking cognisance of their opinions on job-related issues. For feedback to be effective, employees must know what is required of them and have the resources, ability and training necessary to achieve these performance targets. Feedback should be given regularly and not retained for the appraisal interview. It should be constructive but must not avoid difficult issues and poor performance. This is aided by focusing on job performance and not personal attributes. Reasons for poor performance should be identified, explored and solutions agreed. Any agreed measures to improve performance should be implemented.

Performance appraisal can be an important facilitator of improved performance and motivation by specifying the performance levels required, ensuring these are achievable via adequate selection, training and resources, and clarifying the outcomes or rewards available (see figure 7.5).

Fig. 7.5. Feedback and motivation in performance appraisal; expectancy model

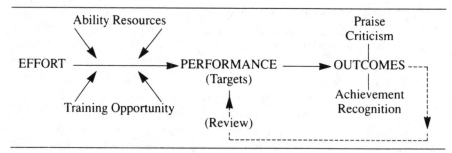

Training

Numerous studies point to the difficulties inherent in the performance appraisal process and the need for training in appraisal skills. Training is a vital part of performance appraisal. All parties involved should be able to review critically their own role with a strong emphasis on self-appraisal. Appraisers should see their role as facilitating discussion, adding perspective and ensuring agreed action plans are carried out, rather than 'playing God' and being the main source of feedback.[22]

Current trends towards greater openness and participation, together with a more results-oriented approach, demand even greater attention to appraiser training. Areas demanding consideration are observational skills (in continually assessing performance) and interviewing skills which encourage a joint problem-solving approach and facilitate constructive feedback. Such training should help to reduce or eliminate some common sources of error in performance appraisal such as:

i) unequal standards: variations between appraisers;

ii) rater bias: undue discrimination on the basis of a particular factor or characteristic;

iii) lack of management commitment;

iv) too much paperwork: resentment caused by administrative burden;

v) inadequate follow-up: action plans or commitments not implemented;

vi) false expectations: employee hopes raised of rewards or outcomes which cannot be realised;

vii) inadequate preparation: poor planning, knowledge, skills of appraisers;

viii) central tendency or positive skewing: tendency to rate employees as average or good, allowing little discrimination.

Assessing Potential

Assessing employee potential for development and promotion is possibly the most difficult aspect of appraisal. Often reviews of employee potential are combined with the performance review, although Long feels this practice has declined notably over the past decade.[23] Assessments of potential tend to be much more judgmental and subjective. They tend to rely on managerial opinion which is based on past performance, often without any specific idea of future promotion opportunities.

The usefulness of this approach is questionable, and it is interesting to note some growth in the use of assessment centres and psychological testing to aid assessment of potential. Another positive trend is the increased emphasis on employee development and career counselling, indicating a greater awareness of the resource potential of employees and encouraging greater employee participation and involvement in tapping that resource to the benefit of both the organisation and the individual employee.

Chapter 8

Employee Development

INTRODUCTION

Ensuring good performance requires that employees have the necessary knowledge, skills and abilities to carry out their current jobs effectively and to meet future organisational requirements. Employee training and development is an important facilitator of satisfactory employee performance, allowing employees to satisfy personal and organisational needs through their work. However, adequate training and development is only one of a number of factors influencing employee performance, albeit a very significant one. Employees must also have the ability to achieve required levels of performance. Equally, they must have adequate resources (such as equipment) and be given the opportunity to perform at required levels. Employees must also believe that by performing at these levels they will realise valued intrinsic and/or extrinsic rewards. These factors highlight the need for an integrated approach to workforce management which links employee development approaches with policy choices in other key personnel areas such as selection, job design and rewards.

EMPLOYEE DEVELOPMENT POLICY

An effective employee development policy represents an important organisational strategy for survival and expansion through investment in human resources. By developing a competent, motivated and committed workforce, an organisation will be well equipped to deal with future challenges and to effect appropriate changes to achieve business goals. An organisation's employee development policy is an important mechanism for ensuring that the workforce has the capacity to achieve its business goals.

However, philosophies and approaches to employee development differ. Some organisations pursue unsophisticated employee development approaches. Most attention is concentrated on basic skills training with little emphasis on employee needs for personal development and growth or on broader organisational needs to develop a workforce capable of dealing with future challenges. For such organisations, employee development is not a strategic tool. Consequently there is little coordination between employee development activities and other personnel policy choices, such as in recruitment or appraisal; nor is there any integration of employee development considerations into strategic decision-making on broader business issues (such as product diversification). For such organisations basic training represents a necessary cost which should be curtailed where possible.

On the other hand, many successful organisations are convinced of the broader corporate role and benefits of an effective employee development policy. Employee development is seen as an investment in human resources which, properly managed, will yield substantial long-term benefits for the organisation. There is considerable evidence that successful organisations invest substantially more resources in employee development than less successful ones.[1] The recent Report on Management Training documented case histories of Allied Irish Bank, Howmedica Inc., Blarney Woollen Mills, Department of Social Welfare, Electricity Supply Board and Guinness to demonstrate the relationship between investment in employee development and improved performance.[2] For such organisations employee development is an important component of corporate strategy, which is linked to other personnel policy choices to comprise an integrated personnel management strategy designed to facilitate the achievement of business goals. Training and development activities are conducted on a continuous and systematic basis to improve current employee capabilities and to help to cope with change. This approach applies to all employees, although particular groups or issues may be prioritised as the situation demands (management development, or new recruits). The potential benefits of an effective training and development policy are outlined in table 8.1.[3]

Table 8.1. Benefits of Employee Development

Improved job performance	Increased flexibility
Shorter learning time	Reduced demands on management time
Helps validate selection process	Better health and safety practices
Better morale	Improved employee potential
Improved skills	Facilitates organisational change
Facilitates career development/ succession planning	Improved employee satisfaction/motivation
Facilitates delegation	
Reduced labour turnover	
Less absenteeism	

Along with the substantial strategic and operational benefits for the organisation, an effective employee development policy also benefits employees. Organisations can help employees to realise their potential through facilitating personal development and growth through their work. This in turn significantly influences individual employee motivation.

To successfully meet organisational and employee needs an organisation's employee development policy and related activities must attempt to integrate organisational needs for improved capacities and skills with employee needs for personal growth and development. Employees should be involved in career planning and development decisions to help to achieve this congruence between organisational and individual needs.

While organisations can ensure that some basic skills training takes place, employee development is largely an organic process, requiring employee commitment and involvement to develop their skills and knowledge through a range of work experiences. The major challenge for organisations is to create an organisational climate which facilitates, supports and guides this process to achieve a fit between organisational and individual needs.

At a strategic level the development of an appropriate organisational environment involves the establishment of a corporate philosophy which recognises the resource value of employees and facilitates the development of a comprehensive employee development policy. At operational level it requires the provision of adequate training and development opportunities and a supervisory style which places a high value on, and facilitates, employee development. It also involves the establishment of appropriate communications, appraisal, guidance and reward systems. Line managers must have the motivation and ability to develop their employees. The organisation should specify desired career paths and outline the criteria on which promotion and development decisions are based. Managers who successfully develop their employees should be appropriately rewarded in order to reinforce the high corporate value placed on effective employee development.

Once these conditions have been established, various training and development activities can take place, using a wide variety of approaches and techniques.

UNDERTAKING TRAINING AND DEVELOPMENT
Learning: Training, Development and Education

In undertaking training and development, it is important to understand what is meant by terms commonly used in discussing employee development. *Learning* refers to relatively permanent behaviour changes brought about through practice and experience. Activities designed to encourage learning have been classified as either contrived or natural.[4] Contrived activities are structured in nature and designed to speed up the learning process (such as case studies). Natural learning is a slower process and arises from day-to-day experiences. Natural learning is considered more valuable in the longer term, though a combination of both approaches will generally be employed in undertaking training and development.

Training and development both involve learning. *Training* is concerned with acquiring the knowledge, skills and attitudes to perform an existing job effectively. *Development* is a broader concept incorporating the additional need to satisfy future job or organisational demands. It may refer to employee development for managerial positions (management development), the acquisition of higher level skills and qualifications (career development) or adaption or change of the organisation at large (organisation development). It may involve *education* which is seen as a more formal activity designed to develop critical faculties and understanding.

In practice, distinctions between training, development and education may be unclear, with differences arising in relation to time horizon, objectives and learning methods. In the current context *employee development* is taken to incorporate all training and development activities undertaken on a continuous basis to improve employee capabilities, to enable them to perform well in their present jobs and to cater adequately with future jobs of a different or more demanding nature.

Learning Principles

In undertaking training and development activities it is important that managers understand the learning process, so that training and development programmes can be developed to facilitate the assimilation and application of training content. Individual ability and commitment to learn vary considerably. This may result from factors related to the individual (intelligence, abilities, attitudes) and the learning context (environment, methods, etc). Careful selection, combined with a clear identification of training needs, helps to ensure that the right people undergo appropriate training and development.

In relation to the learning context, management should ensure that some key principles are considered and learning methods adopted to suit different situations (such as different employees or objectives).[5] Some conditions necessary for effective learning are outlined in figure 8.1.

These factors have important implications for the design and implementation of training and development activities. A key issue relates to employee motivation. Employees will only benefit from training and development activities if they are perceived as relevant, are interested in its content and are committed to the total process.

The issue of valued outcomes and rewards is particularly important. Employees will be motivated to learn if it helps them to achieve valued outcomes, such as personal development (increased skills, knowledge), recognition, monetary gain or promotion.

Fig. 8.1. Effective Learning — Necessary Conditions

Motivation:	Employees must want to learn & be committed to the learning process
Involvement:	Employees learn best by being involved in the learning process
Relevance:	Learners should see content as relevant to their needs
Reinforcement:	Employees need feedback & guidance on their progress
Standards:	Learning works best where specific standards are set against which progress can be measured
Time:	Employees should be given adequate time to absorb training/development content
Methods:	Training development methods should be appropriate to the audience & varied to maintain interest & involvement

If the link between training and valued outcomes is weak or unclear, individual motivation may be reduced. Where, for example, an employee values promotion but feels that particular development activities will not help to achieve it, then motivation may fall. The link between effort and performance is equally important. Even if a person sees a particular development activity as useful (such as computer skills) they may not be motivated to develop such skills if they believe they do not possess the ability to cope with the training content.

The choice of training approach and methods should be related to the training content and the learner profile. Generally a participative approach is encouraged. Training and development programmes are designed to improve current and future job performance. The emphasis should always be work-related, offering employees the opportunity to analyse, discuss and apply learning concepts in their work environment.

THE TRAINING AND DEVELOPMENT PROCESS
An organisation's training and development activities should be aimed at achieving specific results. These results or targets should originate from overall corporate objectives and be specified as performance goals at the level of the organisation, the section or department and the individual employee.

A starting point in the employee development process is the accurate identification of training and development needs. This involves an analysis of the gap between current performance and future targets and demands. These training and development needs may then be adapted into target objectives which provide the basis for the design and content of employee development activities. They will also provide a basis for subsequent evaluation of the success or otherwise of such activities.

Actual training and development activities may then be undertaken. The effectiveness of these activities in relation to target objectives should be regularly evaluated. Results of such evaluations can then provide feedback on the nature of further training and development activities. The training and development process is outlined in figure 8.2.

Fig. 8.2. The training and development process

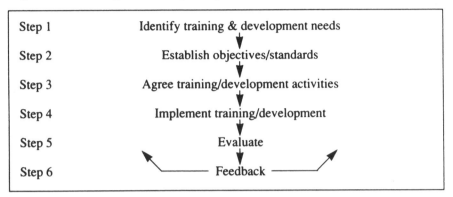

Identifying Training needs

Accurate identification of training needs is imperative for the development of effective training and development programmes.[6] As Walters comments:

> The ability to recognise learning needs is therefore the cornerstone of the trainer's art. Identifying areas in which training can make a real contribution, choosing between competing needs so as to get the maximum return for the organisation from its investment and then clarifying these needs.[7]

Training needs refer to any shortfall between current knowledge, skills, attitudes, etc., and the level required now or in the future. This is often referred to as the 'training gap' between what is and what should be, and is represented in figure 8.3.[8]

Fig. 8.3. The training gap

It is management's task to identify such gaps and construct appropriate training and development programmes to fill them. Inevitably this means prioritising certain areas and allocating resources appropriately. A guiding principle should be contribution to organisational effectiveness. The identification of training needs arises at three different but related levels: strategic, operational and individual, as outlined in table 8.2.

Table 8.2. Levels and outcomes of training needs analysis

Level	Sources	Results
Strategic	• Corporate objectives • Manpower plans	• Forecasts of future direction (products, technology, etc.) • Details of current manpower resources, anticipated needs & sources of supply
Operational	• Job analysis • Line management	• Job description • Personnel specifications etc. • Indications of work demand • Profile of required recruits
Individual	• Performance appraisals • Career development activities (counselling etc.)	• Indications of performance against required standards • Feedback on individual development needs

Strategic level analysis provides information on the future goals and objectives of the organisation. An evaluation of the manpower implications of business decisions should involve consideration of the role of training and development in helping to achieve strategic goals.

At the operational level job analysis provides information on job purpose and content; giving a detailed outline of the knowledge (product, process etc.), skills (conceptual, social, operational etc.) and attitudes (to change, flexibility, etc.) required to complete jobs satisfactorily. Such analysis should provide information on job requirements leading to a precise description of performance targets, training content and the demands imposed on employees.[9]

The establishment of performance standards provides a basis for setting training objectives and for subsequent evaluation of the effectiveness of employee development activities. Performance standards may be stated in behavioural terms, describing what the employee should be able to do (e.g. operate a forklift), the operating context (e.g. without supervision, wet or hazardous conditions), and the standard of acceptable performance (e.g. 2 percent breakages). One approach to establishing performance standards is to specify criterion and terminal behaviour:[10]

a) Criterion behaviour: what the employee should be able to do at the end of training (description of observable end-product behaviour; e.g. operate a CNC turret lathe, programme in Cobol).

b) Terminal behaviour: The employee's actual abilities or behaviour at the end of training. Criterion and terminal performance should ideally be the same.

Performance appraisal is an important source of information on individual training needs. Identification of training and development needs should be linked to performance standards and form part of an ongoing dialogue between employees and management. Together with other communications mechanisms, managers can facilitate the identification of employee strengths and weaknesses, development needs and career plans.

Establishing Training Objectives
Comprehensive job analysis provides information on duties and responsibilities of various jobs. Priority areas for training and development can then be identified. Performance standards in these areas may be specified in terms of criterion behaviour (see figure 8.4).

Fig. 8.4. Establishing training objectives

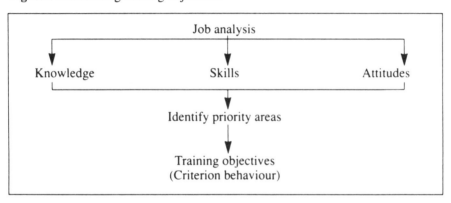

Implementation
Once the training objectives have been established and the target group identified, the actual training and development programme may be designed and put into operation (see figure 8.5).

This stage involves a number of choices, particularly in relation to training methods used (see table 8.3, pp. 163-5). In making such decisions the principles of effective learning, discussed earlier, are important. Training and development activities should focus as closely as possible on the job or task to be performed and take place as close to the job as possible. This facilitates the transfer of acquired knowledge and skills.[11] Learning on the job increases the relevance of training, facilitates its application to job performance and involves the trainee actively in the learning process. Training off the job can also play an important role but this should be related to specific objectives and support on-the-job learning.

Fig. 8.5. Designing and implementing a training and development programme

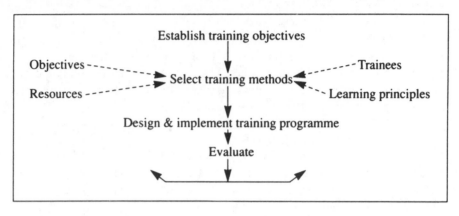

In implementing training and development activities the organisation can choose from a wide variety of methods and the major options are summarised in table 8.3. In choosing training methods the following issues merit thorough consideration:[12]

a) Training objectives & content; specifying the knowledge, skills, etc. to be acquired helps to indicate which methods or combination of methods will best achieve the desired results;

b) Resources; a key factor here is money, as reflected in the training budget. Other considerations are time (trainee/trainer), expertise (internal and external), physical and material resources (equipment, etc);

c) Employee(s): factors relating to the ability, experience, attitudes, age, numbers, etc. of trainees will be an important concern in the choice of training methods;

d) Learning principles: the key issues of motivation, relevance, involvement and feedback should be considered to enable the selection of training methods which ensure the greatest transfer of learning to behaviour on the job.

Along with deciding on training methods, it is useful to consider what media or training aids would be most appropriate. Again, the decision will be guided by the objectives, the audience, and the resources available. On this issue it is worth noting that sight is the most effective channel for communicating information. The most popular types of training aids are various types of audio and visual aids ranging from the blackboard to closed circuit television and computer-controlled simulations. As with the choice of training methods, variety is recommended as a means of reinforcing learning and maintaining trainee interest.

At this stage it should be possible to compile the detailed training plan which will answer the following questions:

What?	outline of the training/development to be undertaken;
Why?	specified training objectives ;
Who?	target training group and who conducts training;
How?	training methods and media;
Where?	location(s);
Resources required?	cost, equipment, etc.

All contingent factors should be fully considered at design stage. The programme can then be closely monitored with checks established at various points to ensure satisfactory progress or highlight any problems and undertake appropriate remedial action.

Evaluation

Evaluation of training and development activities ensures that control is maintained over the total process and allows a considered assessment of the outcomes, methods and overall impact of any particular training and development programme. Training and development activities should contribute to organisational effectiveness. This contribution may be evaluated in terms of cost-effectiveness: did the training programme justify the cost; what are the implications for further training budget allocations? Less tangible contributions should also be assessed, such as effects on employee motivation, satisfaction and morale. Evaluation provides a useful source of feedback; helping to determine future employee development activities and to choose the most effective training methods.

Table 8.3. Training Methods

Method	Nature of learning	Characteristics	Advantages	Disadvantages	Appropriate conditions
Sink or swim	Natural	Throwing new employee into job 'at the deep end', hoping they will cope and learn by experience	May be useful with some direction/ guidelines	Slow; cost of errors; no control on what is learned; risk of personal failure	Not recommended
Sitting next to Nellie	Natural	New employee assigned to experienced worker and learning by watching/ copying	Cheap; involved in actual work, guidance given	Slow, dependent on competence of Nellie; may learn wrong things; depends on work pressure	Nellie must be dependent and have adequate time; used for operative training

Coaching	Natural	Supervisor/ actively advises/ guides and develops employee through appro- priate work opportunities	Job related, good for manager/ employee relations, facilitates succession planning	Depends on work pressure and ability/ attitude of coach	Coach is good trainer; job allows for trainee involve- ment through 'doing'; appropriate for senior level training including management development
Projects	Natural	Short consul- tancy type exercises carried out on a specific topic/area resulting in an action plan	Work related, errors not crucial	Hard to find suitable projects; possibility of negative reaction from staff; needs suitable super- vision	Where there is need to develop analytical skills; complement other employee develop- ment activities
Work- shops/ group discus- sions	Contrived	Meeting of group of employees to consider particular issue	Active; participants develop analytical skills	Demands good leadership, control	Useful in gener- ating group interest in dealing with particular issues and develping possible ideas/ solutions
Computer assisted/ based training	Contrived	Trainee follows a programmed training schedule using computers	Active; feedback provided	May not be directly relevant to job; needs careful planning and develop- ment	Needs adequate resources and back- up but is useful in developing skills/ concepts through an interactive learning device
External courses a) Quali- fications based	Contrived	Longer, education oriented with broad developmental objectives	Comprehensive; facilitates knowledge accumulation & also succession planning	Expensive; may not be practical/ applied; trainees off-the-job for long period; leads to higher employee expectations	Needs a planned organisational approach incorporating a a career development policy
b) Skills, knowledge based	Contrived	Shorter; aims at giving particular knowledge, skills	Uses 'expert sources'; 'state of the art' concepts covered	May be expensive; organisation context may not be considered; seen as 'perk'; hard to transfer material to job	Useful in imparting specific know- ledge, skills; needs have to be identified and the best course chosen; transfer to workplace facilitated on return to job

Self development	Natural	Learners take responsibility to train, develop themselves (reading, courses, etc.)	Active; motivational	No direction; little feedback or control	Highly motivated trainee with strong knowledge and/or skills base
Secondment	Natural	Employees given leave to work in another company/ organisation	Greater experience; new ideas	Loss of employee for long period; little direction/ control; employee may not return	Can be useful on a limited scale to increase knowledge, skills and experience new ideas while rewardring employee performance and allowing for self-development
Groups	Contrived	Trainees put into groups to consider issues; sometimes highly trained sometimes not	Increases insight of how people behave; facilitates unfreezing of attitudes	Trainees may opt out; trainees may gain/learn things they find distasteful; changes not long lasting	Possible use in management development particularly to learn about the effect of behaviour on other people
Simulation/ vestibule	Contrived	Training carried out in simulated work environment	Reduced cost of error; recreates situations which occur infrequently in practice (e.g. accidents); reduced stress/ job pressure; relevant to job	May be expensive to develop; needs good guidance and supervision	Useful where it is difficult or risky to train 'on the job' (e.g. airline pilots)
Lecture/ discussion	Contrived	Oral delivery of prepared exposition on particular topic	Good at conveying knowledge, flexible, can access large numbers	Difficult to transfer concepts to job; no account of differences in learning ability; passive	Well prepared and presented, it can be a useful way of communicating cognitive information, should not be used alone
Case study	Contrived	Situational representation of actual or hypothetical incident or event	Participative, flexible, helpful in developing skills (role-play)	Different to work environment; needs careful organisation	Facilitates learning where case is appropriate and participants have required skills, knowledge to tackle issues; role-play exercises can helpdevelop interpersonal skills

Evaluation is possibly the most problematic aspect of employee development. The major difficulty lies in accurately assessing the degree to which training and development has facilitated improved job performance. This highlights the problems in assessing the extent of transfer of knowledge, skills, etc. covered in a training programme to behaviour on the job. Many of the key benefits of employee development are difficult to demonstrate in quantitative terms (e.g. improved morale, job satisfaction, employee relations). However, such difficulties should not deter management from evaluating training and development activities, or indeed from undertaking employee development initiatives.

The evaluative process is greatly facilitated by a clear outline of training objectives and the establishment of performance standards against which progress can be assessed. Decisions on effectiveness are then based on objective information and contribute to future employee development activities which are relevant to organisational and employee needs.

A popular approach to the evaluation of employee development activities is to focus on the contribution made at a number of different levels, ranging from short-term trainee reactions to the long-term impact on corporate performance.[13] Each level requires a different evaluation strategy and is seen as a measure of the progressive transfer and application of training content (see table 8.4). It involves some element of cost/benefit analysis to indicate the usefulness of particular training and development activities and provides feedback on training content, design and methodology.

Table 8.4. Evaluating training and development

Level	Methods	Timing
1. Reactions (Opinions of trainees)	Questionnaires	End of each stage; end of programme; after return to job
2. Learning (Measure of learning)	Test, exam, case study, project	Before start; on completion
3. Job behaviour (Impact on job performance)	Observation, measurement (e.g. output, quality)	Before start; after return to job
4. Organisation (Contribution to objectives)	General indicators (e.g. profit, turnover); specific measures (absenteeism, accidents)	Before start; periodically after completion

This approach seeks to evaluate the effectiveness of employee training and development at progressively more demanding levels. Assessing trainee reactions is the most basic level and a common approach to evaluation. At level 2 an attempt is made to measure the amount of learning that has actually taken place. This requires some form of objective test. Level 3 focuses on the degree of transfer of knowledge and skills to actual job performance. This may be straightforward where skills and output can be accurately measured (such as typing skills). However, many jobs and related performance measures are much less precise and there are considerable difficulties in assessing changes in job performance. The final level (impact on organisational effectiveness) is even more difficult to assess. General measures of performance may be used (profitability, productivity, turnover) or more specific measures such as absenteeism, labour turnover or accident rates.

Most employee development takes place in a dynamic work environment where such systematic approaches to evaluation are not always practicable.[14] Indeed, the development of control groups, before and after measurements, and in-depth questionnaires may be beyond the scope and resources of many organisations. However, without some systematic approach to evaluation it is impossible to assess the effectiveness of employee development or identify deficiencies in the current approach and make appropriate changes.

Employee development activities should be based on organisational objectives and their effectiveness should be measured against specified performance criteria. This avoids the danger of 'training for training's sake' or undertaking training activities without any clear identification of employee development needs. Investment in employee development should be justifiable along a broad range of cost/benefit criteria. This establishes employee development as an important contributor to organisational success and ensures that its activities are related to organisational and individual needs.

Evaluation is the final stage in the development process and provides information central to its continuing contribution to the organisation. While issues of practicality and resources must be considered in deciding upon evaluative measures, the fact that training without evaluation remains largely uncontrolled and, possibly, wasteful of financial and human resources should be weighed against the challenges of evaluation, and appropriate evaluative measure adopted.

RESPONSIBILITY FOR EMPLOYEE DEVELOPMENT

Employee development is essentially a line management responsibility from the managing director to the line supervisor. Top management will be responsible for developing the corporate approach to employee development;

deciding on issues such as the priority and resources accorded to employee development, interaction of training and selection, and the role of the specialist personnel or training function.

A key responsibility for the continuous development of employees rests with the immediate manager or supervisor. They are closest to actual job performance, can assess training needs and effectiveness, suggest appropriate development routes and provide the most significant advice and direction.

The specialist personnel or training function will be involved in the development of a comprehensive training policy and have an important coordinating role in the design and execution of training and development activities. It will be responsible for translating corporate directives into appropriate training strategies, developing training programmes and evaluating their effectiveness.

The Specialist Training Function

In recent years employee development has become a significant component of organisational strategies on workforce management. Kenny and Reid point to the newness of training as a distinct management function which has undergone considerable growth over the last twenty years.[15] The nature of the training function will vary in different organisational contexts. In small organisations it will be exercised through line management, while growth in size can lead to the development of a specialist training role (training officer), the structuring of training as a sub-function within the personnel department or the establishment of a separate training function.[16]

An AnCO survey on the role of training managers in Irish industry found the training function was well established in Irish organisations.[17] They identified two distinct types of senior training specialists; *a)* those with a larger occupational role but who spend a high proportion of their time in training, such as personnel managers (75 per cent of cases); *b)* those with primary involvement in training; training managers or specialists (remaining 25 per cent). The study identified the principal areas of training emphasis as operative training and management development. Interestingly, it found that training specialists were very concerned with the financial assessment of training and development in cost/benefit terms. Most training in the organisations surveyed was undertaken within companies, although many also used external trainers. The survey also looked at the attitudes of top management towards training. Again a positive picture emerges, with the vast majority recognising both the importance of employee development and the specialist training function (although most felt this should be a part-time rather than a full-time activity).

In her survey of personnel practice in Ireland Shivanath found that training and development was a high priority activity within the specialist personnel function (see table 8.5).[18] She found that most employee development activities were undertaken jointly with line management except for the more administrative task of liaising with AnCO (FÁS) which was generally the sole remit of the specialist personnel function.

Table 8.5. Training and development activities in Irish organisations

Activity	Companies Involved %	Personnel No. %	Department Involvement	
			Jointly %	Totally %
Assess training needs for:				
White collar employees	88.7	4.8	69.8	25.4
Blue collar employees	81.7	6.9	69.0	24.1
Management	83.1	6.8	67.9	25.4
Plan in-house training	85.9	4.9	55.7	39.3
Execute in-house training	88.7	9.5	50.8	39.7
Liaise with AnCo (FÁS)	77.5	7.3	21.8	70.9
Monitor effectiveness of training	85.7	8.3	51.7	40.0
Design/plan management development programmes	81.7	5.2	56.9	37.9
Authorise time off and/or financial support for employees attending company related training	81.7	8.6	48.3	43.1
Organise training re industrial relations for:				
supervisors	71.8	5.9	43.1	51.0
managers	71.8	7.8	45.1	47.1
Prepare training costs/ budgets	81.7	13.8	36.2	50.0
Conduct induction training	78.9	1.8	35.7	67.5

Source: Shivanath, G. 'Personnel Practitioners 1986: Their Role and Status in Irish Industry' unpublished MBS Dissertation NIHE Limerick 1987.

MANAGEMENT AND ORGANISATION DEVELOPMENT

The linking of initiatives in training with the need to develop managerial capacity, facilitate change and improve organisational structure and performance has resulted in the evolution of the related areas of management and organisation development.

Management development refers to initiatives to ensure an organisation has the managerial capacity to meet current and future demands.[19] It incorporates any deliberate attempt to develop the effectiveness of the current managerial pool, equip managers to deal with change and future job requirements and ensure there is a suitable body of managerial talent available as and when required.

Management development activities are based on the premise that an organisation can develop and improve its managerial talent over time through planned initiatives which facilitate self-development, learning and growth. It is based on a corporate value system which places a high value on managerial resources and views management development as an investment in these resources which can yield substantial benefits for the organisation. Management development demands the commitment of the employees involved (current or potential managers) to a long-term process which may include a variety of on- and off-the-job training and development activities such as coaching, job or work rotation, supervised project work and external courses.

Management development is often linked to performance appraisal. This facilitates the identification of present and potential levels of employee performance. It helps to assess progress over time and provides a valuable communications mechanism through which management can guide and evaluate performance, and appraisees can influence their career direction and future development activities.

Effective succession planning is an equally important component in management development. It facilitates the orderly flow of manpower through the organisation. Succession planning involves the identification and evaluation of the current managerial pool in terms of current jobs, abilities and potential and of employees with the skills and abilities to assume such positions should vacancies occur (as a result of retirements, transfer, etc.).

Management development activities often place considerable emphasis on developing leadership and supervisory skills. It may be based on some variation of Management by Objectives (MBO), whereby managers and subordinates jointly agree performance and development targets for a specified time period and subsequently review the degree to which these have been achieved, the reasons for success or failure and agree future targets and plans.

When such initiatives form part of a longer-term, corporate level effort to change the organisation's climate, decision-making processes and overall values it is often labelled *organisation development (OD)*. Organisation development refers to strategic level initiatives designed to improve organisational performance through changing the organisational culture to incorporate values such as collaboration, openness, participation and trust. It is designed to equip the organisation to cope adequately with change and instil a spirit of renewal and development.

The main characteristics of OD are that it is a planned organisation-wide initiative having the support and commitment of top management, with the overall objective of improving organisational effectiveness through group and behavioural processes. These 'processes' generally refer to situations whereby an external consultant (often called a 'change agent') facilitates various group activities in which managers and employees evaluate and discuss their own experiences with the overiding aim of changing attitudes, beliefs and values,thus altering the organisational environment.

The techniques used to facilitate OD may differ considerably between organisations. It commonly involves participative learning approaches and self-analysis, whereby groups of employees discuss various issues such as individual needs, styles and work-group relations with the objective of promoting team spirit and co-operation.

OD has been a focus of some criticism emanating from its ambiguous conceptual base, its reliance on openness of self-analysis by employees and managers and the lack of empirical support for many OD techniques.[20] On a more applied level many managers might argue that organisations should continuously be adapting to change. Indeed this is now the basis of OD activities in many organisations. As approaches have become more refined its contribution to developing commitment and team spirit, facilitating communications and improving job and organisational performance can prove valuable.[21]

CAREER DEVELOPMENT

Along with these initiatives many organisations are now placing a greater emphasis on matching the life and career aspirations of employees with the needs and challenges of the organisation through systematic career development and planning.

From the employee's perspective a career refers to the sequence of jobs which people pursue throughout their working life. Leach suggests that a person's career is influenced by three key factors: heredity (ability, potential); shaping factors (culture, parents, education, income, etc.); and life stages (explaining changes in interest, attitudes, priorities, etc.).[22]

If an organisation is to attract and retain a committed and productive workforce it needs to incorporate employee needs for security, experience and growth in designing jobs, reward systems and organisation structures.

Although organisations cannot offer unlimited advancement opportunities it is imperative that they take steps to meet the career aspirations of their workforce through job enrichment, employee development and career progression. This helps to ensure that work provides employees with valued intrinsic rewards in addition to appropriate extrinsic outcomes.

Career development involves a systematic attempt by organisations to help employees to analyse their abilities and interests and guide their placement, progression and development through various assessment, counselling and training activities. In recent years the changing business climate has given a greater impetus to career development, as organisations seek to establish competitive advantage through changes in workforce management which increase morale, facilitate good employee relations, cater for changing employee expectations and increase productivity.[23] These initiatives commonly incorporate a greater concern for career planning to facilitate organisational and personal development. Some of the potential benefits of effective career development are outlined in table 8.6, together with some potential drawbacks.[24]

Table 8.6. Career development

Benefits	Potential drawbacks
Facilitates equal employment opportunity	Creates false expectations
Creates more challenging jobs	Puts unreasonable strain on personnel resources/training & development
Avoids skill/managerial obsolescence	Increases employee anxiety
Reduces turnover, absenteeism	Administrative burden on line management
Increases motivation	
Facilitates succession planning	
Improves communications	
Improves productivity	

Life and Career Cycle
Individuals hold different priorities and views at different points in life which significantly influence career decisions. Changes in individual needs and aspirations are influenced by the different stages in a person's life cycle.

In establishing a career development policy, management need to be aware of the factors influencing career decisions. The concept of life and career cycle is important since it provides a basis on which to develop training plans, conduct career counselling and plan for succession and continuous development.

A person's life cycle may be viewed as a series of life stages through which a person passes, each involving different priorities, views, concerns and activities. A basic outline of life and career stages is outlined in table 8.7.[25]

Table 8.7. Life and career stages

Stage	Characteristics
I. Childhood	Focus on ego-identification, development of self-concept, search for values and roles; (latter stages) search for definition of interests & capabilities
II. Early adulthood — growth and exploration	Focus on achieving a sense of identity through role & occupational analysis. Attempt to more closely define needs, interests & capabilities; potential conflict between need to establish identity & feeling of losing autonomy
III. Adulthood — establishment	Focus on establishing self in work & life stations; clear career pattern; search for stability & personal security
IV. Late adulthood — maintenance	General emphasis on acceptance & consolidation of position; possibility of review & modifications of life/work role; concern with providing for & guiding next generation
V. Maturity and decline	Conclusion of career role; acceptance of life/career pattern; need to prepare for post-work challenges

This model is a useful benchmark in analysing and developing a systematic approach to career development However, an employee's career is shaped by a variety of factors such as heredity, culture, social class, parents, education and experience, as well as life stage. People are constantly changing their views and approaches and thus their career aspirations will change over time; sometimes because of the particular life stage and sometimes due to other factors.

Management must attempt to understand and cater for the different developmental needs of employees at different stages in their life and career. In early career stages employees will test different roles in an attempt to establish their preferred choice. Once this has been resolved employees may become concerned with establishing and developing themselves to achieve growth and upward expansion through their work. Later employees will develop, through analysis and experience, a clearer picture of their career goals, expectations and opportunities, and an identifiable pattern in resolving the commitment to work *vis à vis* external considerations (leisure, family, etc.) will emerge. Career planning and development activities should incorporate these considerations and cater for the varying development needs by providing work which gives employees an opportunity for growth, a sense of identification and a general source of satisfaction. It should cater for all employees, not just those in senior positions or 'high fliers' as is often the case.

An effective career development policy should facilitate both succession planning and individual development. Employees should be encouraged to evaluate continually their own achievements, skills, interests and motivation. They should improve their knowledge and skills through training and work experience. The organisation can facilitate employee development by providing well-designed and challenging jobs, appraising employee performance, providing feedback and direction, having a good reward system, and establishing a positive employee development policy, supported by a management team which is committed to employee development and which has the necessary skills and resources to carry out this role.

Career Development in Irish Organisations

In a pilot study of career development practices in Irish organisations Garavan and Gurren distinguish between the planning and management of the career development process.[26] They suggest that *career planning* is an individual-centred activity with employees making decisions on future career paths. The organisation can assist this process through career counselling, etc. *Career management* is based on corporate criteria and involves matching employee career plans with the needs and demands of the organisation and undertaking a range of initiatives to support this process (such as development and support facilities, career workshops or direction, career breaks).

Garavan and Gurren found that the organisations surveyed were involved in a range of career development activities as outlined in table 8.8. They suggest that these activities are often linked to other personnel policies and activities such as appraisal, manpower planning and rewards.

Table 8.8. Career development activities in Irish organisations

Activity	% of organisations
Career pathing	
• Planned job progression for new employees	35%
• Career pathing to help employees acquire necessary experience	60%
• Planned job moves for high potential employees	63%
• Rotation of supervisors to prepare them for upper management	37%
• Annual review of employees' strengths/weaknesses to develop a career plan	85%
Career information systems	
• Job posting of vacancies internally	100%
• Communication of job requirements to employees	73%
Training	
• Technical skills training for lower levels	88%
• On the job training	100%
• Supervisory training	95%
• Tuition reimbursement policy	93%
Management development	
• Special programmes for individuals moving into management	78%
• Formal management development programmes	86%
• Management development committee	28%
Personnel	
• Succession planning	60%
• Records of interests, education and aptitudes of individuals	73%
Career Counselling	
• Career counselling as part of performance appraisal	70%
• Informal career counselling by personnel and supervisors	83%
• Special career counselling for downward transfer	26%
• Pre-retirement counselling	29%
• Career counselling for high potential employees	50%

N=150

Source: Garavan, T.N. & Gurren, P. 'Career Development Practices in Irish Industry' in *Industrial and Commercial Training International* (forthcoming).

CONTINUOUS DEVELOPMENT

To operate effectively, an organisation's employee development policy should be integrated with the reward package so that development opportunities are part of the range of outcomes available to employees. This involves utilising employee development as a mechanism for developing employees personally and giving them outlets to achieve growth, recognition and satisfaction from their work, as well as giving them the skills and knowledge to perform particular jobs adequately. It involves a continuous process of assessment, interaction and feedback where employees have an input into their job and career progression, but where this process is facilitated and guided by the organisation in line with corporate and operational goals.

Another reason for this continuous emphasis on staff development is to ensure the workforce keeps up to date with changing and expanding knowledge and technology. In particular the thrust of modern technology represents both a challenge and a threat to individual employees and the organisation at large. The danger of skill and managerial obsolescence is ever present. A large part of the responsibility for up-dating lies with employees who must be committed to continuous development, recognise themselves as learners and develop a positive attitude to ongoing learning and training. A realistic self-concept through analysis of individual strengths, weaknesses and ambitions is important in helping the individual employee to grow and develop with change. The organisation can play an important role by providing a challenging and developmental work environment.[27]

The specialist personnel or training function plays an important role in facilitating continuous development. It should adopt a strategic perspective, spotting and anticipating change, developing a positive system of continuous development and monitoring and updating this with changing circumstances. Line management have an important role in assessing and interacting with employees and facilitating their growth and development through training. Employee development is a vital part of the manager's task, and those who can assess, develop and utilise the abilities of their employees are important contributors to corporate success.

While Kenny and Reid agree that continuous development is an ongoing process involving all employees, they suggest five particular categories requiring intensive retraining and development:[28]

i) employees needing to acquire new skills and knowledge (e.g. an accountant responsible for newly computerised financial records);

ii) retraining for promotion (e.g. technical person requiring management skills in preparation for a line management position);

iii) retraining due to job obsolescence;

iv) retraining as a result of poor performance;

v) retraining for a different job in a new organisation.

Job obsolescence is a particular concern for both management and employees. In a pilot study on managerial obsolescence in Irish organisations Dillon concluded that the job itself was the principal factor influencing employee motivation to update their skills and ability.[29] The need for challenging jobs which utilise the individual's skills and knowledge is imperative.

Continuous development is obviously a concern for both employees and management. It is possibly the most influential reason for organisations to develop a positive employee development policy which is integrated with the overall strategic approach to workforce management. The IPM Code on Continuous Development stresses these points and highlights the responsibilities of both the organisation and the employee in identifying development needs, agreeing development plans and providing adequate support and back-up facilities.[30] The organisation's primary role is to provide a supportive organisational setting which facilitates the process of continuous development.

THE NATIONAL SCENE

The State has traditionally adopted a voluntarist approach to training and development. The organisation is seen as having prime responsibility for employee development and the role of the State, through agencies such as FÁS, is to facilitate organisational initiatives through the provision of advice, expertise and financial support.

The Irish Management Institute is a leading provider of management training. It is a user-owned organisation providing a range of advanced management and specialist programmes. Regional training centres have been a later development, although the Plassey Management and Technology Centre has been providing a number of management and technical programmes since the 1970s. In the public sector the Institute of Public Administration is the central training agency.

The Irish Institute of Training and Development (IITD) is the professional body for personnel concerned with employee training and development. It provides a forum for discussion of national training and development issues, establishes standards of professional conduct and seeks to improve practice in the field. It has over 700 members and provides a range of services including a quarterly journal, seminars and workshops, and a mechanism for the representation of membership views to government and other institutions. The IITD has been particularly active in recent years and has successfully launched a three-year Diploma in Training and Development leading to graduate membership of the Institute. The Institute of Personnel Management in Ireland also caters for a large number of training specialists.

The first significant attempt to analyse the Irish system of management training and development was undertaken through a 1988 government report entitled *Managers for Ireland: A Case for the Development of Irish Managers*.[31] The report noted that economic performance is significantly influenced by the quality of management. With the onset of the single European market and greater international trade, the report highlighted the need to improve the quality of Irish management.

The report outlined a number of key strengths and weaknesses of the Irish system of management training. The main strengths identified were the quality of the key providers, the standard of general education, the wide choice of provision and experimentation with different delivery systems.

Box 8.1. Summary findings of the advisory committee on management training

Issues	Recommendations
1. There is an unacceptably low level of commitment to management development in Irish organisations	1. Increase commitment to management development as an urgent national priority; undertake a high profile promotion of management training spear-headed by an action group for management development
2. There is a lack of understanding of what management development involves & how a management development policy might be developed in organisations	2. Develop a set of national guidelines on management development which can be used as a code of practice
3. Many managers lack a common core of relevant knowledge & skills	3. Adjustment of business education to reflect business needs; providers of business education should offer a broadly common syllabus and other qualifications (e.g. engineering) should have a business education input
4. Small firms have particular problems in implementing a management development policy	4. Recognition of the special needs of the small business sector with particular emphasis on providing incentives to promote management development in small firms
5. The State's role in funding management development is unclear, inconsistent & is not linked to national objectives	5. State funding to be redirected from support for providers to support for users; closer alignment of utilisation of funds with economic policy
6. Separate training for public & private sector managers is not in the national interest	6. Merge the management training activities of the IMI and the IPA

A number of significant weaknesses were also highlighted. In particular, the report identified a low level of commitment to management development in many Irish organisations. Few organisations recognised the investment value of management development and expenditure in the area was very low: over one-fifth of the country's top thousand companies spent nothing on management development and over half spent less than £5,000; foreign-owned organisations spent on average 50 per cent more than indigenous firms; new organisations spent considerably less than established firms.

The report also identified a lack of customer focus by providers, an inadequate supply of trainers and an inability to link management development with other strategic considerations in the organisation. The report identified six key issues and made six major recommendations as summarised in box 8.1.

This report clearly acknowledges the strategic importance of employee development, particularly management development, for both the organisation and the economy at large. Its proposals represent a progressive step forward for management development in Ireland, and if effectively implemented will be of considerable benefit to Irish managers and their organisations.

Chapter 9

Employee Relations Framework and Management Role

INTRODUCTION

As noted in the report of the Commission on Industrial Relations (1981), the primary responsibility for the conduct of employee relations lies with management.[1] Studies both here and in Britain have identified employee relations as the single most important activity area within the personnel role.[2]

Employee relations encompasses the total spectrum of the employer-employee relationship, involving both its individualist and collectivist aspects. The most basic element of this relationship revolves around the contract of employment. However, there are many other issues of concern to both employer and employees. These include the establishment of pay levels, working conditions and mechanisms for resolving grievance and discipline issues.

Since the early 1980s there has been a tendency to link 'employee relations' with so-called 'employee-oriented' approaches to workforce management which incorporate a preference for non-union status. Within this approach preferential emphasis is placed upon dealing with employees as individuals as opposed to collectivities, and various policies are designed to foster employee loyalty and commitment (such as gainsharing, career development). More traditional 'industrial relations' approaches involve an extensive role for trade unions and a heavy reliance on collective bargaining, procedural agreements and management-union negotiations.

In this text 'employee relations' is broader in orientation and includes *all* employer-employee interactions incorporating both union and non-union approaches; it is not restricted to relations of a collectivist nature or to recognising trade unions as the 'natural' representative of employees.

Employee relations structures and practices are inextricably linked to their political and economic context. In Ireland two key factors have exerted a major influence upon employee relations: the close political and economic links with the United Kingdom and the enactment of the Irish Constitution in 1937.

This chapter initially considers the Irish employee relations framework, reviewing the roles of the three key parties: trade unions, the State and employer organisations. It then examines employer approaches and strategies in employee relations. In the next chapter the nature of employee relations activities at organisation level are considered.

EMPLOYEE RELATIONS IN IRELAND

The Irish employee relations system has traditionally been described as 'voluntarist' in nature. This is generally taken to indicate an approach in which employers and trade unions are largely free to regulate the substantive and procedural terms of the employment relationship without State interference. The State, however, provides auxiliary facilities to the parties involved in the employee relations process, creating a floor of individual rights and establishing agencies to resolve any conflicts which may arise between the parties.[3] Roche terms this strategy one of 'auxiliary State control' and suggest that Irish governments adopted this approach more or less consistently from the end of the Second World War up to the 1960s and in a somewhat changed format following the demise of centralised pay bargaining in 1982.[4] The major characteristic of this strategy is the abstention of the law from the conduct of collective bargaining and particularly from matters pertaining to pay determination, trade union affairs and industrial conflict. State intervention through legislation, where it does take place, tends to focus on providing various conciliation and arbitration facilities, propping up bargaining arrangements in sectors where collective bargaining is poorly established, and enacting individual employment legislation in areas where unions see little interference with their traditional bargaining freedom.[5]

While the Irish Constitution of 1937 marked an initial parting of the ways in the approaches of the British and Irish systems, differences have become considerably more marked during the past decade of Conservative rule in the UK. The Irish system too has undergone change. While the voluntarist approach persists, it has been diluted by developments over the last twenty years. Roche has argued that our system moved towards a neo-corporatist model, involving greater State control in employee relations decision-making.[6] This involved a strategy of greater integration of the social partners, particularly trade unions, in policy-making, and took place initially through joint consultative bodies and later through direct involvement in macro-level policy making, reaching a high point in the centralised pay bargaining era of 1970-82. In 1982 the trend towards State involvement reversed with the 'auxiliary' model re-emerging. However, the 1987 Programme for National Recovery has reaffirmed a strong State involvement in establishing general employee relations parameters. The essence of this programme is a social contract between employers, trade unions and government in relation to broad issues of tax reform, employment creation and pay determination. While it would seem that the scope, for the unions particularly, to revert to the traditional 'hands-off' approach of the post-war era the main tenets of our employee relations system remain rooted in the voluntarist approach, which contrasts starkly with the primacy of the law in regulating the systems of countries such as the USA and West Germany.

Collective bargaining takes place at various levels, ranging from estab-lishment-level negotiations to those which may occur at multi-establishment, industry or national level. At organisation level, negotiations may take place with more than one union and cover a variety of issues such as pay, working hours, holidays, overtime, shift premia, etc.

Below, the three main participants in the Irish employee relations system—trade unions, government and employer organisations—are reviewed. A particular emphasis is accorded to the role of employer organisations, reflecting their significant role in employee relations and the fact that this role is often neglected in analyses of employee relations in Ireland.[7]

TRADE UNIONS

The manner in which workers organise themselves in employee relations varies from dealing with employers on an individual basis (individual bargaining) to forming work-based associations to joining trade unions in order to help represent their interests through collective bargaining. Trade unions have traditionally been seen as the most effective means of countering employer power and achieving satisfactory pay and working conditions for employees. Their role is well established in the Irish context with most legislation dealing with the legal recognition of trade unions dating back to pre-independence days. The legal definition of trade unions as outlined in the Trade Union Act of 1871 and amended by subsequent legislation is very broad ranging and extends to employer organisations.[8] For our purposes, trade unions may be viewed as permanent associations of organised employees whose objectives include:

i) replacing individual bargaining by collective bargaining, thereby redressing the balance of bargaining power in favour of employees and reducing management prerogative in employment related matters;

ii) facilitating the development of a political system where workers have a greater degree of influence on political decisions, resulting in an economic and social framework which reflects the interest of wage earners and the working class;

iii) achieving satisfactory levels of pay and conditions of employment and providing members with a range of services.[9]

Types of Trade Unions[10]
Irish trade unions may be loosely grouped into four broad categories: craft, general, white collar and industrial.[11]

a) Craft unions cater for workers who possess a particular skill in a trade where entry is restricted through an apprenticeship system or otherwise. Craft unions, by controlling entry to the craft, create a situation where they have considerable negotiating power. For this reason craft unions tend to be vigilant in ensuring that only qualified people holding union cards carry out certain types of skilled work. This has often led to criticisms of restrictive and inefficient work practices and sometimes to disputes over demarcation. Increased mechanisation and consequent de-skilling of certain trades has had a detrimental impact on the membership and power of craft unions. This is reflected in the reduction of their share of union members from 17 per cent in 1940 to less than 12 per cent in 1983.[12] Examples of craft unions in Ireland are the Electrical Trade Union (ETU) and the National Union of Sheet Metal Workers of Ireland (NUSMWI).

b) General unions take workers into membership regardless of skill or industry. They have traditionally catered for semi-skilled and unskilled employees although some have been successful in organising both craft and white collar workers. General unions, because of their open recruitment policy, tend to be the largest unions and account for just less than half of all trade union members. They organise in all types of organisations and industrial sectors, and well-known examples include the Irish Transport and General Workers Union (ITGWU), the Federated Workers Union of Ireland (FWUI) and the Amalgamated Transport and General Workers Union (ATGWU). The FWUI and ITGWU have merged in 1990 to create the new Services, Industry, Professional and Technical Union (SIPTU).

c) White-collar unions normally cater for professional, supervisory, technical, clerical and managerial grades. These unions experienced significant growth in membership in recent years as reflected in their increased share of total union membership, up from 24 per cent in 1940 to 35 per cent in 1983.[13] White-collar staff represented a relatively 'greenfield' area for union membership drives as they had not been traditionally organised. An additional factor has been the structural changes in employment involving considerable increases in the number of people working in white-collar jobs. Examples include the Manufacturing, Science and Finance Union (MSF) and the Local Government and Public Service Union (LGPSU).

d) Industrial unions: pure industrial unions (those catering for all the workers in a particular industry) are not part of the Irish union structure. However, we do have some unions who only recruit workers from within certain industries, many of which are confined to the semi-state sector (such as the National Busworkers Union, Irish National Teachers Organisation), while some others with membership bases in traditional industrial sectors have been absorbed into the larger general unions, for example, the Irish Shoe and Leather Workers Union. The Irish Bank Officials Association (IBOA) which recruits members at every level within the banking sector might also be described as an industrial union.

TRADE UNION MEMBERSHIP

There are in Ireland some eighty unions catering for a total membership of over 470,000 or approximately 46 per cent of the workforce.[14] This level of union density compares favourably with many European Community countries and is considerably higher than the US, where union density as a proportion of the non-agricultural workforce is 19 per cent. However, since achieving a high of over 524,000 members in 1980 the Irish trade union movement has undergone the most severe decline in membership figures since before the war and lost over 51,000 members in the 1980-85 period.[15]

Table 9.1. Trade union membership 1945-85

Year	Overall membership	% change	Union density (% of workforce unionised)
1945	170,800	—	25
1960	310,000	81.5	45
1970	416,300	34	52.5
1975	448,100	7.5	53
1980	524,600	17	55
1985	473,700	-9.7	46.2

Source: DUES Project UCD 1987.

Table 9.2. Membership by union category (1983)

	Number of unions	Membership	% of total
General unions	5	224,650	47
White-collar	43	165,010	34
Other unions	32	89,180	19
Total — all unions	80	478,840	100
Affiliated to ICTU	67	446,950	93
Not affiliated	13	31,890	7
Head office in Ireland	65	409,060	85
Outside Ireland	15	69,780	15

Source: Irish Congress of Trade Unions 1983.

Looking more closely at the breakdown of membership it is evident that there is a notable imbalance in membership numbers with, at one extreme, a few large unions representing almost three-quarters of the total membership, while at the other extreme there are over forty unions catering for less than 7 per cent of total membership.

Table 9.3. Aggregate union membership 1983

Number of members	Number of unions	Total membership	% of total
Less than 1,000	34	14,790	3.1
1,001–2,000	11	16,300	3.4
2,001–5,000	17	55,700	11.6
5,001–10,000	6	45,350	9.5
10,001–15,000	6	76,600	16.0
Over 15,000	6	270,200	56.4
Total	80	478,840	100

Source: Irish Congress of Trade Unions 1983.

Union Structure and Government

While it is difficult to generalise about organisation structure, a number of similarities can be identified in relation to Irish trade unions. A basic characteristic is that ultimate decision-making authority is vested in the membership and executed through resolutions passed at the Annual Delegate Conference (ADC). It is then the job of the union executive to implement union policy. The union official's primary task is to carry out the operational aspects of the union's role, servicing the membership through negotiations, advice, research and information. The branch is the basic unit in the union structure and it may be organised on either a geographic (catering for members organised in several companies within a specific area) or establishment basis.[16] A typical union structure is outlined in figure 9.1.

At workplace level the shop steward is the key union representative. They are elected by fellow-employees and represent different sections within an organisation. Their role is to represent employee interests on shop floor issues, liaise with union officials and generally keep members *au fait* with union affairs. In practice, shop stewards may become involved in much workplace bargaining involving shopfloor grievances or disputes. On major issues such as pay negotiations their role is to support union officials and give feedback to the membership.

Fig. 9.1. Typical trade union organisation structure

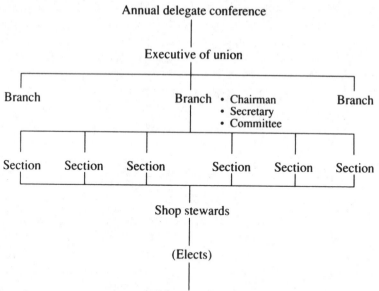

General membership in the organisation (or section of organisation)

Irish Congress of Trade Unions (ICTU)[17]

The ICTU is the central coordinating body for the Irish trade union movement with over 90 per cent of trade unionists in membership of unions affiliated to Congress (sixty-seven of the eighty unions in 1983). While Congress acts as representative of the collective interests of the Irish trade union movement, individual unions retain a large degree of autonomy and the ICTU relies on the co-operation of affiliated unions in promoting its overall goals. Ultimate decision-making power within Congress is vested in the Annual Delegate Conference. Here delegates from affiliated unions consider various resolutions presented by union delegates and those adopted become ICTU policy. The executive is responsible for policy execution as well as general administration. Congress plays an extremely important role at national level, representing and articulating union views to government and other institutions. It has representatives on several national bodies (such as the Employer Labour Conference) and provides union nominees for the conciliation and arbitration services.

Various committees operate under the auspices of the ICTU. These include the Disputes Committee which deals with inter-union disputes concerning membership, the Demarcation Tribunal which deals with inter-union disputes in relation to work boundaries and the Industrial Relations Committee, which has the particularly important responsibility of granting an all-out picket in disputes. Such a picket obliges all union members employed in the organ-isation engaged in the dispute not to pass the picket. Individual unions can, however, sanction a 'one union picket', whereby only members of the union in dispute are obliged not to pass. In practice, employees have been reluctant to pass pickets, whether directly involved in the dispute or not.[18]

Trades Councils

These are voluntary groupings of unions on a regional or local basis. They are made up of officials and members of local unions who meet regularly to consider matters of regional and, sometimes, national significance. They can be extremely influential in determining union policy and are often perceived to relate more closely to membership needs than Congress. Trades councils may become particularly active in relation to certain political issues and were very much to the fore in the PAYE protests of the early 1980s. Forty-two trades councils were affiliated to Congress in 1988 (twenty-nine in the Republic).

Perceived Problems with Irish Trade Unions

Several criticisms have been made of the Irish trade union movement and it is useful to highlight some of these and consider their current validity.

a) Union multiplicity: probably the most common criticism is that there are too many unions relative to total membership. It has been suggested that this causes problems for management who have to deal with a number of unions, and also leads to inter-union rivalry and conflict as they compete with each other for membership. Ireland does have a large number of unions for a relatively small membership base. The data discussed above showed some eighty unions catering for a total membership of approximately 470,000. While initially these figures would seem to indicate a problem with multiplicity, a closer examination shows a somewhat different picture. It emerges that a small number of quite large unions cater for the majority of members, while a large number of small unions cater for a very small percentage of total union membership. The four unions with over 20,000 members (ITGWU, FWUI, MSF and ATGWU) cater for well over half the total union membership. At the opposite end of the scale over forty unions cater for less than 7 per cent of the membership.

While management may recognise several unions at workplace level these will often represent different categories of employees (such as general, craft and white-collar workers). Even where a greater degree of multi-unionism exists, trade unions may choose to form a union group and negotiate as a unit, thereby reducing the problem of multiple negotiations. Thus, while the issue of multiplicity and potential of inter-union rivalry may cause concern in some areas, it does not seem to be a major problem.[19]

b) Non-Congress Unions: approximately 90 per cent of all trade union members are in unions affiliated to the ICTU. Although this still means that a minority of unions are not affiliated to Congress, most of these are small, with only four having a membership of over 2,500: the Marine Port and General Workers Union, the Irish Nurses Union, the Irish Bank Officials Association and the National Busmen's Union. On most issues of national significance Congress acts as the *de facto* voice of the Irish trade union movement, and while it would clearly like to have all unions affiliated, the non-Congress issue does not seem to be a major cause of concern at the present time.

c) British and Irish unions: in 1983 fifteen of the eighty trade unions operating in the Republic had their head offices in Britain. These included major unions such as the ATGWU and AUEW. Because unions rely primarily on current income from membership subscriptions, these unions are often in a strong financial position due to their higher levels of overall membership (both in the UK and Ireland), with the result that they may be in a strong position to resource and service their Irish membership adequately. On the other hand, policy decisions within such unions may be taken in the UK and there has sometimes been debate on the priority accorded to the concerns of Irish membership.[20] Roche and Larragy note the declining trend in the share of union members catered for by British unions, but attribute this to changes in the structural composition of the workforce rather than any factors deriving from their national base.[21]

d) Trade union democracy: another common criticism of trade unions is that they fail to exercise adequate control over their membership or that militant minorities exercise undue influence over union affairs. These often refer to situations where it is alleged that a particular group of trade union members pursues a course of action which is at odds with the wishes of either the majority of the membership or the union officialdom. An implication of this line of thought is that unions can exert a type of autocratic control over the membership. This fails to appreciate the internal structure and operation of trade unions within our voluntary tradition. The very existence of trade unions is centred on meeting the needs of the membership. If they fail to do this then their very *raison d'être* diminishes.

Trade union discipline and control is based on a moral set of acceptable practices and the union hierarchy will be keen to ensure these are upheld through persuasion rather than compulsion in order to retain membership confidence.[22] While it is true that unions do have power to decide on issues it seems that control works in both directions.[23] A union can exert a certain degree of control over its members in deciding on an appropriate line of action and it also has a disciplinary role in certain circumstances. However, the membership also has the right to decide on policy, and they can exert control over the union to get it to serve their needs as perceived by that membership (by withholding subscriptions or threatening to join another union, for example). In a multi-union environment, a trade union must be very circumspect in meeting those needs lest it experience an exodus of membership.

e) Union recognition: despite the relatively high level of unionisation in Ireland, no specific statutory provisions exist to govern the process of collective bargaining and particularly trade union recognition. The constitutional guarantee of freedom of association embodied in article 40.6.1. of the Constitution confers the right on workers to form or join associations or unions.

The implications of this provision were demonstrated in a Supreme Court case of 1961 involving industrial action by a section of a company's workforce to enforce a 'closed shop' (compulsory union membership for all employees). In this case it was held that while the Constitution conferred on employees the right to joint trade unions it also included an implied right not to join and on this basis found against the union and its actions.[24] This finding renders suspect many post-entry closed shop agreements although pre-entry closed shop (where union membership is a condition of the job offer) would seem to be in line with the provisions of the Constitution.[25]

While the Constitution supports the freedom of workers to organise, there does not seem to be any obligation placed upon employers to recognise or bargain with such unions.[26] Neither is there any specific provision for recognition in the Trade Union Acts of 1941 and 1971. These acts stipulate that, apart from certain bodies, only 'authorised' trade unions holding negotiating licences are permitted to carry on negotiations in relation to pay and employment conditions, and specify conditions which a union must fulfil before it will be issued with such a licence. There are no statutory guidelines existing on the circumstances which should apply when an authorised trade union holding a negotiation licence seeks recognition from an individual employer.

In spite of the lack of any statutory mechanism for securing trade union recognition, the issue does not seem to cause any great difficulties for the majority of organisations or employees. Indeed, many employers seem happy to recognise and conclude collective agreements with trade unions. This may be a result of our tradition of dealing with employee relations through collective bargaining with unions.[27] However, with the declining membership and power of Irish trade unions the issue of recognition has again become contentious, with some evidence of increased opposition to unionisation in recent years, particularly among some multinational organisations and indigenous small firms.[28]

f) Declining membership: possibly the most worrying factor for the Irish trade union movement is the serious decline in membership experienced since 1980. This decline has its origins in the large-scale unemployment and emigration experienced in recent years. However, a number of other contributory factors have been identified, notably structural changes in employment with decline and stagnation occurring in traditionally highly unionised sectors (older traditional manufacturing organisations, public and semi-state sector), and any growth emanating from areas more difficult for union penetration (high-technology manufacturing, less-unionised service sector).[29] Such developments possibly represent the greatest challenge faced by trade unions in recent times. In an era of financial constraint, more and more organisations are evaluating their approach to employee relations, paying particular attention to the role of trade unions.

ROLE OF THE STATE

As we have seen, the primary responsibility for the conduct of employee relations rests with management and employees with a strong emphasis on collective bargaining—an approach which has proved satisfactory for large numbers of organisations. Within this framework the role of the State has been largely restricted to the establishment of legislative ground rules and the provision of mediation and arbitration machinery. Statutory interference in the conduct of collective bargaining is kept to a minimum, leaving employers and unions free to develop work rules and procedures to suit particular organisational or industrial contexts. Occasionally the State will become actively involved by establishing commissions of enquiry, encouraging various reforms to the system or as a party to national-level negotiations. Similarly, it will have a direct influence as a major employer. More generally, however, the State's role is restricted to that of legislator and provider of dispute resolution agencies.

Conciliation and Mediation

In the area of mediation the State provides four specific institutions: the Labour Court, Rights Commissioners, the Employment Appeals Tribunal and Equality Officers.

a) The Labour Court: while the Labour Court fulfils several functions within the Irish employee relations scene, a key one is investigating and making recommendations on cases referred to it by the parties in dispute. These are normally issues where the parties have failed to reach agreement or compromise at local level. The usual way in which a dispute comes before the Labour Court is outlined in figure 9.2.

At the first stage the parties in dispute are obliged to go through conciliation. This stage involves an Industrial Relations Officer (IRO) presiding over a meeting of the conflicting parties. Having listened to both parties, the IRO may hold separate meetings with both to get a better idea of the basis

Fig.9.2. Labour Court referral

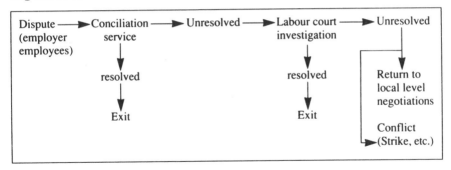

for the dispute and what is required to resolve the issue. The IRO can then guide the parties towards an acceptable solution. Conciliation is essentially voluntary, with the IRO acting as a facilitator in the search for a solution. Success rates in resolving issues at conciliation has fluctuated over the years, and there have been frequent criticisms that both employers and unions abuse the system through their unwillingness to settle at conciliation. Conciliation had an average success rate of 50 per cent for much of the 1980s but recently this has increased to over 60 per cent, possibly reflecting less accommodation by IROs of unions or management wishing to use the service as a stepping stone to full Labour Court investigations.[30]

Should an issue still remain unresolved despite conciliation, it may then be referred for a full investigation by the Court. This requires the certification by the IRO that a solution could not be reached at conciliation. A Division of the Labour Court normally consists of an independent chairman, and an employer and a union representative. Hearings are generally held in private, involve written and oral submissions by the parties, and some element of cross-examination. When the Court feels it has adequately investigated the case it will conclude the hearing and set about issuing a recommendation which is not legally binding. The Court has had a very satisfactory record with over three-quarters of its recommendations accepted by both parties. Even where Labour Court recommendations are rejected their terms may often form the basis for a solution on return to local level negotiations.

In addition to its investigative role, the Labour Court also plays a significant regulatory role in certain industries or sectors of industry. Of particular importance is the Court's role in the operation of Joint Industrial Councils and Joint Labour Committees. Joint Labour Committees are statutory bodies comprised of employer and trade union representatives and independent members which regulate wages and conditions of employment in areas where collective bargaining is poorly established (such as hair-dressing, agricultural labourers).[31] Joint Industrial Councils are permanent voluntary negotiating bodies to facilitate collective bargaining at industry level in certain sectors (for example, the construction industry).

b) Rights Commissioners are appointed by the Minister of Labour under the auspices of the Industrial Relations Act 1969. They operate outside the scope of the Labour Court and are available to parties in dispute provided both agree to such a hearing. They are not permitted to investigate issues involving rates of pay, hours of work or holidays relating to a body of workers or disputes where the Labour Court has already issued a recommendation. In practice, they mainly investigate disputes concerning individual employees (discipline, demarcation, transfer).

More recently their role has been extended to dealing with cases under the Unfair Dismissals Act 1977 and the Maternity (Protection of Employees) Act 1981. Hearings are held in private with Rights Commissioners examining each case on its merits and issuing a written recommendation which is not legally binding. A great advantage of this service is its flexibility and accessibility, providing a quick and efficient mechanism for dealing with problems which have proved intractable at local level. In 1985 some 2,200 cases were referred to Rights Commissioners and Kelly comments on the 'quite remarkable performance' of the service over the years.[32]

c) Employment Appeals Tribunal: The Employment Appeals Tribunal (EAT) operates within somewhat narrower terms of reference dealing with issues which arise under the terms of specific legislation, viz., The Redundancy Payments Acts 1967-1979, Minimum Notice and Terms of Employment Act 1973, Maternity (Protection of Employees) Act 1981, Protection of Employees (Insolvency) Act 1984 and most notably the Unfair Dismissals Act 1977. It has exclusive jurisdiction under the Redundancy Payments Acts, Minimum Notice and Terms of Employment Act, and the Maternity (Protection of Employees) Act. However, the situation in relation to dismissals is more complex. In this area, aggrieved employees can take a claim of wrongful dismissal at common law to the Civil Courts. Alternatively, if dismissal was in relation to the Employment Equality legislation, an aggrieved employee could take the case to an Equality Officer and later, an appeal, to the Labour Court. However, employees wishing to proceed under the Unfair Dismissals Act 1977 may follow the procedure outlined in figure 9.3.

A claim under the Unfair Dismissals Act may be handled directly by a Rights Commissioner but if either party objects to this route then it will proceed directly to the EAT. Most claims under the Unfair Dismissals Act are referred directly to the EAT. The EAT usually sits in a Division of three, comprised of an independent chairman (who is legally qualified), and an employer and a union representative. Hearings are held at various regional locations and are normally in public, although the Tribunal may hear a case in private if requested to do so.

Fig. 9.3. Claim under the Unfair Dismissals Act 1977

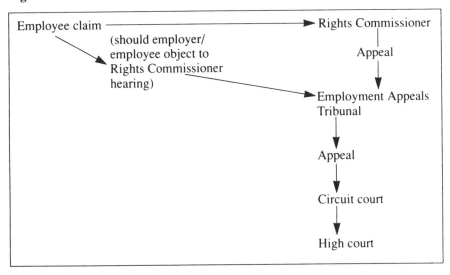

Although the procedure for EAT hearings is established by law, the Tribunal is free to set its own ground rules. In practice, the Tribunal attempts to promote informality and flexibility, although this is not always achieved. The Tribunal normally takes evidence under oath. Any party has a choice of representing his/her own case, using an employer organisation (such as an FUE [FIE] official) or engaging legal counsel. After hearing a case, the Tribunal concludes its deliberations and issues a decision some time later. The Tribunal makes a straight majority decision on cases. Decisions in the area of redundancy, minimum notice and maternity rights are final and binding and may only be appealed to the High Court on a point of law. For Unfair Dismissals cases the Tribunal issues a determination which can be appealed to the Circuit Court within six weeks. Should an employer fail to carry out the terms of an EAT determination, proceedings may be issued by the Minister for Labour to ensure compliance.

d) Equality Officers: these deal with issues relating to discrimination on the grounds of sex or marital status arising under the Anti-Discrimination (Pay) Act 1974 and the Employment Equality Act 1977. The Anti-Discrimination Act entitles women to equal pay for like work while the Employment Equality Act prohibits discrimination against women on the grounds of sex or marital status in non-pay areas like recruitment, training, promotion and working conditions.

Employers are obliged to abide by the terms of both acts. Should a dispute arise, either party can refer it to an Equality Officer. Equality Officers operate within the scope of the Labour Court. When a dispute is referred to an Equality Officer, they carry out an investigation and issue a recommendation based on the merits of the case. If either party is dissatisfied with this recommendation, they may appeal to the Labour Court within forty-two days. The Court's determination in such circumstances is final and legally binding on the parties.

Legislation

Legislation in Irish employee relations falls into two broad categories: collective labour legislation and individual employment law. While a comprehensive treatment of these diverse legal areas is beyond the scope of this text, a summary overview of both areas is given below.[33]

a) Collective labour legislation: such legislation deals with the relationship between employer(s) and collectivities of employees (normally trade unions) and is based on earlier British legislation. Article 50 of the Irish Constitution of 1937 provides that, subject to its provisions, the laws in force prior to 1937 should continue unless they are repealed or found to be repugnant to the Constitution. Consequently, Irish trade union and trade disputes law remains broadly similar to that which applied in 1922 in Britain and Ireland. With some minor amendments, the Trade Union Acts of 1871, 1876 and 1913, the Conspiracy and Protection of Property Act, 1875 and, most notably, the Trade Disputes Act 1906—as amended by the Trade Disputes (Amendment) Act 1982—still apply in Ireland and provide the legislative framework for the evaluation of trade union activity, industrial action and picketing.

Some of the personal fundamental rights of the citizen are outlined in Article 40 of the Constitution, and include the right of citizens to express their opinions and convictions freely, and to form associations and unions. The citizen's right to form associations and unions is qualified by the State's right to enact laws in the public interest governing its exercise. The citizen's right includes that of not being forced into joining or leaving a union, or being dismissed because of trade union membership. The Unfair Dismissals Act 1977 additionally provides that the dismissal of an employee because of trade union membership or activity shall be deemed unfair. The Constitutional guarantee does not preclude employers and employees (or their trade unions) from making agreements specifying which union, or one of a number of unions, workers in the particular employment will join. However, the constitutionality of some such closed shop arrangements remains open to question.

b) Employment legislation: the contract of employment through its common law provisions constitutes the legal basis of the employer-employee relationship. More recently, legislation has had a significant impact on this relationship, with the passing of a number of acts affecting individual employee rights at work. Since the 1970s several important acts have been passed and a large number of regulations and statutory instruments introduced under existing employment legislation. Much of this change has been in the area of dismissals and sex discrimination. These are categorised in table 9.4.

Table 9.4. Summary of employment legislation in Ireland

(1) Terms & conditions of employment	*Main provisions & scope of application:*
Conditions of Employment Acts 1936 &1944	Hours of work, overtime shift-work, breaks
Holidays (Employees) Act 1973	Minimum annual leave; public holidays
Protection of Young Persons (Employment) Act 1977	Conditions for employing young persons
Minimum Notice & Terms of Employment Act 1973	Minimum employment details which must be given to employees
Payment of Wages Act 1979	Payment by cheque
(2) Employment equality	
Anti-Discrimination (Pay) Act 1974	Equal pay for 'like work'
Employment Equality Act 1977	Equality in working conditions, recruitment, training & promotion
Maternity (Protection of Employees) Act 1981	Maternity pay and job security
(3) Dismissals	
Unfair Dismissals Act 1977	Protection against unfair dismissal
Redundancy Payment Acts 1967-84	Lump-sum payment on redundancy
Protection of Employment Act 1977	Consultation prior to group redundancies
(4) Health, safety and welfare	
Safety in Industry Acts 1955–80	Minimum health & safety standards; establishment of safety committees
Safety, Health and Welfare at Work Act 1988	Duties of employers and employees
Office Premises Act 1958	Minimum health & safety standards
Dangerous Substances Act 1972	Safety in handling certain substances

The Public Sector

Apart from its legislative and facilitatory functions, the State plays a significant role as the country's major employer. It accounts for about one-third of
all employees in a range of areas principally composed of the Civil Service
proper, education, local authorities and health boards, security forces, and
State-sponsored bodies, most of whose employees are organised into trade
unions or staff associations.[34]

In some public sector areas, distinctive employee relations features have
developed but, as Cox and Hughes note, it would be inappropriate to view
public sector employee relations as inherently different from that pertaining
in the private sector.[35] Indeed, the report of the Commission on Industrial
Relations (1981) suggests that personnel problems in both the public and
private sectors are similar although differences tend to occur in the procedural
responses made.[36]

In relation to the negotiation of pay and conditions of employment, a
notable distinction may be drawn between those public sector areas subject
to agreed Conciliation and Arbitration (C & A) schemes and those which
come within the scope of the Labour Court.[37] Conciliation and Arbitration
schemes date from the 1950s and currently different schemes operate for
categories such as the (non-industrial) Civil Service, teachers, gardai, local
authorities and health boards and the VECs. A unique feature of the Civil
Service scheme is the network of staff panels who evaluate any claims from
recognised unions or staff associations before these are forwarded to
conciliation.[38] Conciliation consists of joint councils of management and
employee representatives which consider claims before them and issue an
agreed report. The composition and specific role of conciliation councils
differ between schemes, and only specific issues may be referred to
conciliation. These generally include pay, allowances, working hours,
overtime, grading, and policies on recruitment, promotion, discipline,
pensions and sick pay. Most schemes exclude issues relating to individual
employees. The vast majority of issues are resolved at conciliation, but
those which are not may proceed to arbitration provided they are arbitrable
under the appropriate scheme.[39] An Arbitration Board normally consists of
an agreed chairman (often legally qualified) and two representatives from
both the management and staff side. Detailed written submissions are made
by both sides and these are supplemented by oral submissions and witnesses
as appropriate. The finding of the Board is sent to the Minister of Finance
and the other appropriate Minister who have one month to approve the
report or submit it to the government. The government has the option of
accepting the report or moving a Dail motion to reject or amend it—a
course of action which is normally seen as exceptional. The local authority
and health board scheme differs from the above format in that the

management or staff side have the option of rejecting the decision of Arbitration.

In addition to specific grades in the public sector discussed above, employees in most State-sponsored bodies have access to the Labour Court. Exceptions are An Post and Telecom Eireann who have a separate C & A scheme.

A notable characteristic of public sector employee relations is the role of the Department of Finance (previously this role was executed by the Department of the Public Service). It acts as the government's advisor on matters relating to public sector pay and employment-related matters. It will critically review pay claims, lay down appropriate policy guidelines and oversee their implementation through direct and indirect involvement in negotiations. The Department represents the State as employer at the Employer Labour Conference and is involved in many of the Conciliation and Arbitration hearings.

Another important factor on the management side in the public sector is the Local Government Staff Negotiations Board (LGSNB) whose role is to assist local authorities and health boards in employee relations. Representatives of the board act on behalf of management on the appropriate Conciliation and Arbitration scheme and in major negotiations with non-officer grades.

EMPLOYER ORGANISATIONS

As with worker organisations, employers are equally likely to combine for purposes associated with employment and labour matters.[40] It is important to distinguish between employer organisations, which were established to deal with labour matters, from those which were established for trade and commercial reasons and which are normally referred to as trade associations.

In their early attempts to grapple with organised labour and employment matters, employers soon found it opportune to combine on either a temporary or more permanent basis. The reasons behind the formation of such organisations were largely functional. Most of the early business enterprises were owner-managed and it has been suggested that such entrepreneurs have a weaker spirit of association than other social groupings and therefore any attempts at combination would need to have a solid rationale.[41] Consequently, many of the early employer organisations were forums for exchanging views and opinions and this role later developed into one of joint strategy formulation. Such organisations operated on a regional or industry basis with the creation of central umbrella organisations following as a later development.

Structure

Employer organisations in Ireland are classified into two categories—employer associations and trade associations—both of whom must register with the Registrar of Friendly Societies. Employer associations are involved in employee relations and must hold a negotiating licence under the Trade Union Act 1941. This distinguishes them from trade associations who are not required to hold such a licence. Employer associations are in effect trade unions of employers and fall within the same legal definition as a trade union. While this may not initially seem significant it can have important implications for the role and membership of employer associations. In particular, it suggests an approach to employee relations which emphasises the role of collectivities or combinations as opposed to individuals.

In 1987 sixteen employer associations as defined above were registered with the Department of Labour:[42]

Table 9.5. Employer associations in Ireland, 1987

Name of association	Number of members in the State	Year to which membership relates
1. Construction Industry Federation	2,064	1987
2. Cork Master Butchers Association	54	1986
3. Dublin Master Victuallers' Association	212	1987
4. Federated Union of Employers*	3,188	1987
5. Irish Commercial Horticultural Association	220	1985
6. Irish Flour Millers Union	8	1987
7. Irish Hotels Federation	439	1985
8. Irish Master Printers Association	63	1985
9. Irish Pharmaceutical Union	1,303	1987
10. Irish Printing Federation	52	1987
11. Licensed Vintners Association	571	1985
12. Limerick Employers Association	28	1987
13. Petroleum Employers Association	11	1987
14. Retail Grocery Dairy & Allied Trades Association	2,200	1986
15. Society of Dublin Coal Importers	11	1984
16. Society of the Irish Motor Industry	1,103	1985

Source: Department of Labour 1988.   * now the Federation of Irish Employers.

While the number of employer associations is less than their trade union counterparts, there is considerable diversity in membership composition. One can find within this listing examples of traditional masters' associations, industry-based associations and a general association which is national in scope.

By far the largest employer association in Ireland is the Federation of Irish Employers (FIE) with over 3,000 members. Total employment in member firms is around 250,000 or more than 50 per cent of the country's labour force excluding agriculture, the public service and the self-employed. Unlike most other employer associations, the FIE's role is confined solely to labour relations, and its major functions involve providing employee relations advice and assistance to members. The provision of such advice and assistance may involve direct FIE participation in negotiations with trade unions and would also cover research and specialist advisory services, as well as assistance with the preparation of employment agreements, consultation on particular personnel issues and the provision of premises and facilities for consultation and negotiation. Particularly important among these services is the FIE's role in representing member firms at mediation, conciliation and arbitration hearings. While the FIE is not extensively involved in employee relations training, it undertakes such training in response to membership needs. This may take the form of short workshops or briefings as well as longer training programmes (often in association with a training institution like the Irish Management Institute). It has become involved in providing training material in the form of videos and other published material. A major role of the FIE is the representation of employer interests to government and the public at large. It also maintains employer representation on various national and international bodies.

The Construction Industry Federation is the second largest employer association and is an excellent example of an industry-based association dealing with both trade or commercial matters and employee relations. Its affiliated membership totals just over 2,000, representing over 46 per cent of all firms in the construction industry, and these firms are estimated to employ around 50,000 workers or 75 per cent of all workers in privately owned construction firms. In the area of employee relations, the main role of the CIF involves monitoring and handling industrial relations on all large sites, dealing with any matters referred to it by member organisations, negotiation of national registered agreements, representing members at conciliation and arbitration, and providing information and advice to affiliates.[43]

Most of the other employer associations are primarily concerned with trade and commercial issues, although some are quite involved in employee relations. The labour relations role of the Irish Hotels Federation is largely confined to representing employer interests on the Hotel Joint Labour Committee and providing general employee relations advice to members. It does not involve itself in local bargaining. Similarly, the Society of the Irish Motor Industry is mostly concerned with trade and commercial issues but does provide a personnel and industrial relations advisory and assistance service. The Licensed Vintners Association provides a range of services to Dublin publicans, one of which involves labour relations. It conducts negotiations on pay and working conditions with the Irish National Union for Vintners and Allied Trades Assistants and also provides affiliated members with a personnel advisory service covering areas like personnel policy, discipline and dismissal and redundancies.

The involvement of the remaining employer associations in employee relations is limited. However, an interesting association is the Limerick Employers Federation, which is a rare example of a regional association involved in labour relations. It is largely representative of retail and distribution organisations in the greater Limerick area, and in addition to its trade and commercial role it provides advice and assistance, and acts as a forum for the exchange of views on employee relations and personnel matters generally.

Irish Employers Confederation: the Irish Employers Confederation (IEC) was set up in 1969 just prior to the advent of centralised pay bargaining and at a period of considerable industrial unrest. One of its purposes was the desire to present a united employer front on labour relations issues and to rationalise multi-unionism on the employer side. This latter issue was particularly noteworthy at the time as employers had frequently criticised Irish trade unions for their multiplicity. At the time of its foundation there were twenty-one employer associations holding negotiation licences under the trade union acts. While this was considerably less than the ninety-odd trade unions operating in the State, it was still a cause for concern that there was no central employer body. The initial membership comprised of seven major employer associations including the FUE (FIE), Federation of Builders, Contractors, and Allied Employers (now the CIF), and the Limerick Employers Association, but the major driving force seemed to be the FUE.

During the period of centralised bargaining (1970-81) the IEC played an important role in representing employer interests at the Employer Labour Conference. While the Employer Labour Conference was initially established as a bipartite forum for discussion of pay, prices and general employee relations matters, it became most widely known as the mechanism for the negotiation of successive national wage agreements. The employer side of the conference was represented by the IEC, together with representatives of State-owned enterprises and government (in its role as an employer).

Since the end of centralised pay bargaining the role of the IEC has become increasingly ambiguous. Its membership consists of eleven affiliates, only four of which are employer associations with the remainder mostly semi-state organisations. Its current role seems totally overshadowed by the FIE which seems the *de facto* voice of Irish employers on employee relations issues. Thus, while the IEC played a significant role in centralised pay bargaining, it never really reached the status of a federation for all employers associations and today seems even further from that role, and the most significant employer association in Irish employee relations remains the FIE.

Objectives

A particular and traditional reason why employers have formed representative associations is to prevent harmful economic competition with each other, particularly in relation to pay, and to counter the power of trade unions. Another reason has been the increasingly complex nature of collective bargaining and employment legislation, in addition to providing a forum for the exchange of views among employers.

Employer objectives in employee relations are discussed later and include support for the private enterprise system, achievement of satisfactory returns for the owners, effective utilisation of manpower, maintenance of management prerogative in decision-making and ensuring good employer-employee relations. Most employers would subscribe, with varying degrees of commitment, to these general objectives, and many have found that through combination they can portray a common front and more effectively achieve employer goals at both the micro and macro level.

Windmuller believes it inappropriate to refer to the views and approaches of employer organisations as constituting a specific ideology, and suggests that employer organisations, unlike trade unions, do not subscribe to some ideal economic and social system and are not part of a quasi-political movement.[44] While it may be valid to say that employer organisations do not affiliate to a particular political party, many do have broad economic, social and political objectives. Similarly, at organisation level they will seek to provide members with a range of services to help them manage employee relations more effectively. A summary classification of broad employer association objectives is outlined in box 9.1.

Box 9.1. Objectives of employer associations

Political: to represent effectively employer views to government, the general public & other appropriate bodies so as to preserve and develop a political, economic & social climate within which business objectives can be achieved;

Economic: to create an economic environment which supports the free enterprise system & ensures that the managerial prerogative in decision-making is protected;

Social: to ensure that any social or legal changes best represent the interests of affiliated employers;

Employee relations: to ensure a legislative and procedural environment which supports free collective bargaining & to coordinate employer views & approaches on employee relations matters & provide assistance to affiliated employers.

In a political era where lobby groups are becoming increasingly important, employer associations have assumed a significant role in representing employer interests on national issues. They provide a mechanism through which governments can solicit employer views on areas like labour legislation and are important vehicles for influencing public opinion on more general political issues. This political role of employer associations is most clearly associated with their desire to influence broad economic decision-making. Employer organisations will generally support what could be termed conservative economic policies which serve to protect the interests of capital and ensure freedom from an excess of State intervention in business. In the area of social policy the approach of employer organisations will be largely pragmatic. On the one hand they will generally attempt to prevent, or at least lessen, the effects of protective labour or social legislation, such as legal moves towards extending industrial democracy or information disclosure. On the other, they will accept some degree of social and legislative reform, provided their perceived effects on the interest of capital are not adverse. An outline summary of the FIE's general objectives is given in box 9.2.

Box 9.2. Objectives of the Federation of Irish Employers

Legislation: to encourage legislation which supports employer interests & to oppose any legislation which mitigates management prerogative or rights;
Individual Freedom/Private Enterprise: to promote & support policies & legislation which seeks to protect the interests of private enterprise & freedom of the individual;
Industrial Relations Policy: to promote, coordinate & support industrial relations policies conducive to employer interests & business efficiency;
Collective Bargaining: to assist & represent individual members in the conduct of collective bargaining & related industrial relations matters; to provide members with advisory and negotiation services in pay issues, discipline, grievances, etc; to represent employers before third party institutions; to provide facilities to support the above;
Advisory, Research and Consultancy: to provide basic information on issues like pay rates, working conditions & procedures to members; to undertake & make available research data on the labour market, economic trends, etc.; to help member firms in specific tasks (e.g. job evaluation, employment agreements, technological change);
Training and Publications: to assist in the provision of labour relations training for members through courses, workshops, publications & audio-visual material;
Representation: to represent employer views on labour relations issues to government, trade unions, national & international organisations & any other interested parties;
Public Relations: to communicate employer views on legislation, disputes & general industrial relations issues to the public at large through the media & internal publications & communications;
Legal Services: to provide advice & assistance to members on all aspects of labour relations legislation.

Internal Governing Structures

Most employer associations are organised so that ultimate decision-making power resides with the affiliated membership. Windmuller suggests that the governing structures of employer associations will be composed of between three to four levels: assembly or general meetings; general or executive council; executive board or management committee; and presiding officer.[45] This structure attempts to cater for membership participation while allowing day-to-day management to be carried out by full-time staff.

General assemblies are largely a vehicle through which the membership influence and communicate with the central administration, help to decide general policy and elect various committees. The less cumbersome executive or general council will be responsible for monitoring the work of the various committees and the general running of the association. Possibly the most important layer in the governing structure is the management or executive committee. Its membership will consist of representatives elected on a regional basis, from the various branch or industrial divisions, or major enterprises in addition to some office-holders. It will exert considerable influence on association policies, and together with the association president and senior staff will be primarily responsible for policy formulation and execution. For many associations the position of chairman or general secretary remains a part-time position held by a senior manager from an affiliated enterprise. However, with the increasing demands of association work this often creates a dilemma for the incumbent as this job requires considerable time away from his company. Depending on the demands of the position, the relationship between the president and full-time senior manager of the association (director general or managing director) will be crucial. Generally the director general will be expected to administer the association's affairs according to the policy guidelines laid down by the general assembly, the general council and/or the executive committee. He will be expected to work closely with the association president and take his advice on general policy matters. A primary role for the director general will be to manage the professional staff.

Within the organisation structure of the FIE, the role of the general membership is to elect a National General Council comprising 250 representatives who then determine general policy and appoint the National Executive Council. The Council itself comprises of office-holders and nominees from the various regions and branches totalling fifty in all. It is primarily responsible for overseeing policy formulation and implementation, appointing the key specialist committees and the permanent secretariat in conjunction with the director general and federation secretary. The director general and the full-time staff are responsible for carrying out the primary activities and services of the Federation.

Fig. 9.4. Structure of the FIE

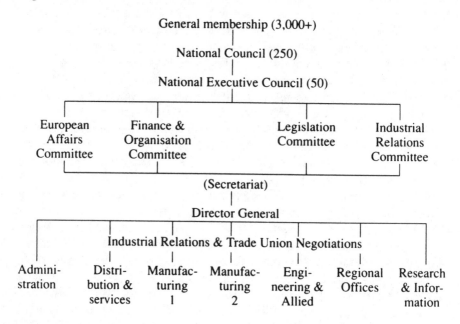

General membership (3,000+)

National Council (250)

National Executive Council (50)

| European Affairs Committee | Finance & Organisation Committee | Legislation Committee | Industrial Relations Committee |

(Secretariat)

Director General

Industrial Relations & Trade Union Negotiations

| Admini-stration | Distri-bution & services | Manufac-turing 1 | Manufac-turing 2 | Engi-neering & Allied | Regional Offices | Research & Infor-mation |

Membership

Employer associations are comprised of a regionally, industrially and structurally diverse membership. Some regional and industrial variations have their roots in the traditional masters' associations, which were particularly common in the building and butchering trades and whose objectives were confined to local trade- and employment-related matters. While some of these associations still exist today, many have amalgamated with larger national associations. Thomason argues that the change in composition of association membership from entrepreneur owner-managers to corporate business forms run by professional managements partly explains the differing roles of employer associations.[46] There are some tentative indications that foreign ownership influences employer association membership.[47] This may be related to the corporate approach to trade unions and collective bargaining. Where this involves a preference for non-union status, such organisations may be reluctant to join an employers' association.[48] The issue of public sector organisations becoming members of an employer association is a more recent phenomenon. While initially it might seem incompatible for public sector organisations to join an employers' association (traditionally a bastion of free enterprise), many have adopted a pragmatic approach by utilising employer association services in certain areas.[49] The Department of Finance and the Local Government Staff Negotiations Board fulfils the key advisory and assistance role for management in many parts of the public sector. However, in some areas, particularly among the semi-states, considerable use may be made of employer organisations.

A specific factor influencing employer association membership is organisation size. It has been suggested that small firms have more to gain by joining employer associations because of cost and expertise consider-ations.[50] When a small organisation reaches the stage where it becomes involved in formalised collective bargaining it may be particularly attractive to join an employers' association. Such firms may not be in a position to employ personnel specialists, and the owner or manager may not have the necessary time or expertise to handle such matters effectively. Since the cost of joining employer associations is normally related to organisation size it may be relatively inexpensive for small firms to join. Despite the apparent validity of this argument there is no conclusive evidence to support the view that small firms are more likely to join employers' associations.[51] In fact, some British surveys suggest that employer associations are not more frequently used by smaller organisations and indicate that the key influential factors are ownership, trade union recognition and the presence of a specialist personnel function.[52] Other important variables influencing membership are the industry, market position, collective bargaining struc-tures and corporate personnel philosophy. It is up to the individual enterprise to evaluate critically its own position and decide if membership is advantageous in the context of the organisation's corporate philosophy and business goals.

The next section reviews the services provided by employer associations which correlate closely with the advantages of employer association mem-bership. Below, some of the reasons why organisations may choose not to join an employer association are considered.

One of the disadvantages of employer association membership is a potential reduction of *autonomy* in decision-making for the individual organisation. Employer associations will be keen that members maintain a standard line in negotiations on pay and conditions of employment through the development of agreed policy guidelines (for example, organisations may be expected to keep pay increases in a period below 3 per cent). These guidelines will reflect the needs of a diverse membership (in terms of organisation size, profitability, etc.). The individual organisation must decide if such norms are appropriate to its particular needs. For example, an organisation may wish to negotiate a pay increase which breaches the common strategy of the employer association.

Comparability is also an important factor. By virtue of association membership an organisation's pay and conditions will be closely reviewed in relation to other member firms. Trade unions will use the terms of collective agreements struck with some member firms as 'leverage' to secure similar terms with other organisations.

These issues reflect the difficulties employer associations face in developing common policies for a diverse membership. They also highlight the difficulties they face in enforcing policy guidelines and raises the issue of control over affiliates.

Breaches of agreed policy guidelines by individual member organisations detrimentally affect the credibility of such guidelines and may incur the wrath of sections of the affiliated membership. This has occasionally resulted in firms withdrawing from membership or being disaffiliated by the association. Such breaches of discipline are almost inescapable in associations where membership is voluntary and general policies are laid down for a diverse membership. Like trade unions, employer associations will strive to ensure maximum organisation of its potential members and in practice exercise a more informal authority over members, relying on persuasion and peer pressure to secure adherence to common policies. Employer associations are generally reluctant to punish non-conforming members and particularly so when expulsion is considered. Should a large number of enterprises, or even a few significant employers, not join an employer association its representativeness is clearly called into question.

Sisson notes some important British organisations which have either withdrawn from membership or never joined employer associations (Esso, Daily Mirror, British Leyland and Ford).[53] In Ireland too, there is some evidence of notable enterprises not in association membership. These are often major employers and exert considerable influence on local pay trends and general employee relations (such as Waterford Glass in Waterford, Howmedica Inc. in Limerick). An important factor in such decisions seems to be related to the degree of influence such organisations believe they might have on association policy and the restrictions that membership would place on their flexibility of manoeuvre.

A recent development in relation to this issue has been the creation of special status membership categories which allow such affiliates to maintain flexibility in decision-making while retaining association membership and engaging in less formal policy coordination.

It is also important to evaluate how association membership fits in with the *corporate personnel philosophy*. Employer associations are in effect trade unions of employers, and generally prefer to deal with their employee counterparts through collective bargaining. However, some firms have a clear preference for the non-union route. In recent years Ireland has seen considerable growth in the 'high technology' sector. This has largely been the result of foreign firms (particularly US-based) establishing manufacturing plants here. Non-union US companies such as Digital, Wang, Amdahl and

Verbatim are now an integral part of the manufacturing scene. Some of these firms have brought with them a particular corporate approach to employee relations which places an emphasis on dealing with employees on an individual basis rather than through trade unions. For such firms membership of an employers' association (being a trade union of employers) would be totally incompatible with a management approach based on direct contact with the individual.

A more pragmatic reason for non-membership is related to *cost*. An important issue here may be that firms pay the full cost of membership regardless of services used. By contrast, an organisation which uses consultants simply pays for services rendered. Most association subscriptions are related to size of firm (number of employees) and costs can be substantial for larger organisations.[54] Related to this may be the feeling among firms with a developed personnel function that they do not need association services and that, as Reynaud suggests, employer associations become '. . . an organisation of services for the small undertakings paid for by the big ones'.[55] Experience does not support this view and it seems that large firms use employer associations as much, and often more than small ones.[56]

It would be inappropriate to conclude a discussion on employer organisations without reference to the fact that employers may come together in less formal groupings to exchange views and coordinate approaches on labour relations issues. Such groupings have the advantage of informality and cohesiveness with none of the obligations or costs attached to formal association membership. Such associations may be formed on a regional (the Limerick/Shannon Personnel Managers Group) or industrial basis (the electronics sector) and may meet on either a semipermanent basis or only when a significant issue arises.

Employee Relations Services
In relation to utilisation of association services, some British studies have suggested that employer associations are most relevant in the private sector and that membership is positively related to trade union recognition, increased company size and the presence of a specialist personnel function.[57] Indeed, trade union recognition appears to be a key factor. Formalised collective bargaining arrangements, procedural agreements, a developed shop steward system (all characteristics of an 'industrial relations' approach) make for a situation where membership of an employers' association and extensive utilisation of its services are probable. Even in the smaller organisation the prospect of employer association membership may become increasingly attractive when such firms reach a stage of development where trade union recognition has been granted and there is a move towards formalising the company's approach to employee relations management.[58]

Sisson suggests that the employee relations functions of employer associations may be classified under four main headings: negotiation of pay and conditions of employment; operation of disputes procedures; advisory and consultancy services; and representation.[59] The applicability of this classification in Ireland is considered below.

a) Negotiation of pay and conditions of employment: unlike Britain, multi-employer bargaining at industry level never dominated employee relations in Ireland. In the post-war period collective bargaining has been characterised initially by the wage round system and later by a series of national agreements. Between 1946 and 1970 we had twelve wage rounds, five of which were negotiated centrally between employer representatives and trade unions, giving a prominent role to employer associations. The remainder were characterised by periods of intensive collective bargaining at either industry or enterprise level, with wage increases permeating through to most organised employees.

In the 1970-82 period employer associations, largely through the Irish Employers Confederation, played a major role in the negotiation of a series of centralised pay agreements. When this system ended in 1982 there was a return to so-called 'free' collective bargaining on an enterprise basis. This significantly changed the role of employer associations from being the key employer actor in pay negotiations to a more supportive role in providing advice and assistance to individual enterprises and coordinating approaches to pay negotiations. The current arrangement (1989), negotiated by the major social partners in the 1987 National Programme for Economic Recovery, whilst restoring the FIE to its pivotal position in national pay bargaining also provides for plant level bargaining, thereby maintaining a potential role for employer associations in the conduct of establishment-level employee relations.

The supportive and coordinating role at establishment level is an important one from an employer viewpoint. By giving advice on pay trends and related issues, employer associations provide the basic information with which the individual organisation enters the bargaining process. By coordinating employer approaches, it establishes a framework for the conduct of such negotiations and by providing negotiating personnel it may either conduct the negotiations or advise and assist management in such negotiations. Thus, while the role of employer associations has changed significantly in recent years, its new role is equally important from the organisation's perspective.

b) Operation of disputes procedures: unlike Britain, the operation of external disputes procedures by employer associations never played a significant role in the Irish employee relations framework. Here disputes procedures are normally negotiated at organisation level. The role of the employer associations is primarily to assist and advise members on the formulation and operation of such procedures.

c) Advisory and consultancy services: the Warwick study in Britain concluded that the provision of advisory services may now be the most significant role for employer associations.[60] This seems indicative of the increasing importance of the provision of advisory services by employer associations. Increased employment legislation and greater complexity in pay bargaining has made many employers rely heavily on their employers association for advice.

Consultancy services covering a wide range of areas such as job evaluation, bonus schemes and employment equality are also becoming increasingly important. In an Irish pilot study Butler found that advisory and consultancy services are seen by members as the most useful function of employer associations and found that those dealing with legislation, pay and redundancy were most widely utilised;[61] see table 9.6.

Table 9.6. Utilisation of advisory and consultancy services

Services	Percentage of companies utilising services
Recruitment	7.7%
Education & Training	32.5%
Labour Legislation	100%
Work study, bonus schemes	15.4%
Job evaluation	0%
Redundancy Policy	77%
Local pay levels	100%
National pay levels	84.5%
Incomes policy	38.5%
Others	7.7%

These trends would suggest that employer associations are becoming increasingly important as a resource centre for specialist advice and assistance.

d) Representation: the representational role of employer associations involves both a political dimension and third party representation. Representing employer views to government, State institutions, trade unions, the general public and other interested parties is a key role of employer associations. In executing this role a clear distinction is made between representation on trade and commercial issues and on employee relations matters. The Confederation of Irish Industry is the national organisation representing employers in matters of trade, economics, finance, taxation, planning and development but does not involve itself in labour relations. This latter role is primarily executed by the FIE which is consulted by, and makes representations to, government on labour and social issues. It represents employers on various international committees and institutions (such as the EC, OECD, ILO). It also represents employer interests on various national committees and institutions, as well as providing employer representation on various mediation and arbitration bodies such as the Labour Court and the Employment Appeals Tribunal. Apart from the FIE, industry-based associations also carry out representative functions related to their own sector.

It would appear that representation at Labour Court, Employment Appeals Tribunal and other third party hearings is a valued and important service of employer associations.[62] Affiliated firms will generally use the services of their employer association if involved in third party proceedings, although such utilisation may be only obtaining advice and direction. At Labour Court hearings in particular it is common for the employer case to be presented by an employer association official. This may also occur at EAT hearings, although there is a tendency for employers to opt for legal representation.

Table 9.7. FUE (FIE) involvement in mediation, arbitration and negotiations

	(Cases per year)				
	1984	1985	1986	1987	1988
Labour court investigation	458	420	538	488	386
Labour court conciliation	1,176	963	1,470	1,146	874
Employment appeals tribunal	241	302	396	190	n/a
Rights commissioner	439	312	586	429	n/a
Equality officer	16	16	28	35	n/a
Consultation with members	7,203	8,155	6,400	6,919	6,726
Trade union negotiations	3,590	2,664	2,928	2,842	2,702

Source: FUE (FIE) Annual Reports 1984-88.

EMPLOYER OBJECTIVES, ORGANISATION AND APPROACHES

The primary concern for organisations operating in a competitive environment will be to maximise organisational effectiveness and generate satisfactory returns for the owners or stakeholders. Such returns are often expressed in terms of cost effectiveness and, for the commercial organisation, profitability. Management's primary role is to organise the factors of production, including labour, to achieve these objectives. Consequently, it must make decisions in a variety of areas to facilitate the achievement of corporate goals. Employee relations is one such area where management must decide on optimal structures and practices.

EMPLOYER OBJECTIVES

It is difficult to assess the degree to which employers have specific employee relations objectives or adopt related workplace strategies. Organisations vary so greatly in terms of structure and philosophy that it would be impractical to suggest a comprehensive set of employee relations objectives. It also misses the key point that an organisation's employee relations objectives derive from its overall business goals which will differ considerably between organisations. Nevertheless, it is worthwhile considering some general beliefs common among employers.[63] Such beliefs might include:

a) Preservation and consolidation of the private enterprise system:[64] this has larger political overtones and relates to the concerns of employers to preserve an environment conducive to achieving business objectives at enterprise level. They will be particularly concerned that principles such as private ownership, the profit motive and preservation of authority and control are maintained.

b) Achievement of satisfactory returns for the owners: this relates directly to the organisation's primary business goals. For commercial organisations to survive in the long term, satisfactory profit levels must be achieved and managerial approaches and strategies will always be influenced by this primary concern. Non-profit-making organisations will be equally concerned with cost-effectiveness and the quality of their product or service.

c) Effective utilisation of manpower resources: manpower is a key management resource and its effective utilisation is central to the management process.

d) Maintenance of control and authority in decision-making: employers will strive to ensure effective control and authority in executing its management role, particularly in strategic decision-making.

e) Good management-employee relations: employers will also strive to maintain good working relations with employees but this must be achieved within the operational constraints of the organisation. The scope to agree attractive remuneration levels and conditions of employment, etc., will vary according to the organisation's market position and profitability as well as its personnel philosophy. Good employee relations will be a priority since they are an important ingredient in ensuring that the organisation achieves its primary business goals as well as being laudable in itself.

MANAGEMENT ORGANISATION

The diversity of bargaining arrangements used by employers is a distinctive characteristic of the 'voluntarist' model of employee relations. These varying arrangements are often distinguished by the locus of decision-making power on strategic employee relations matters. This refers to the degree of strategic decision-making power retained by the top management, and the amount of discretion afforded to the management of operational units. Thomason has suggested that employers have four main options in the selection of bargaining arrangements, which vary from a centrally organised corporate structure where power is retained at the centre to a looser federal-type structure where considerable power is given to operational units;[65] see table 9.8.

Role of the Specialist Personnel Function
Purcell and Sisson have suggested that increases in the size and multidivisional pattern of organisations have contributed to greater specialisation of personnel and employee relations management.[66] It has also been facilitated by greater government intervention, particularly through legislation, which has increased the demand for employee relations expertise and the search for competitive advantage through better workforce management, which in turn has increased the significance of employee relations issues at senior management level. Daniel and Millward also found substantial growth in the personnel function.[67] Throughout the 1970s personnel specialists were increasingly employed to look after personnel management at workplace level in British organisations. Daniel and Millward argue that this was positively related to the growth in formality in employee relations. However, they also noted that many organisations did not employ personnel or employee relations specialists, and even for those who did, the practitioners were poorly qualified for the task.

Irish research evidence suggests that the personnel function here has achieved greater significance in strategic matters within larger organisations and multinationals in particular, placing considerable emphasis on a highly developed and powerful personnel function. In many other organisations personnel and employee relations issues may continue to be handled by non-specialists without any formal training or qualifications. Wallace's study of industrial relations in Limerick city and its environs found that less than one-third of the firms surveyed had a personnel department and that foreign firms were more likely to have a personnel department than indigenous ones.[68] As in Britain, the most influential factor was size of organisation. Wallace also found that specialists who were employed generally lacked formal qualifications and training. So while the role of the specialist personnel function in the management of employee relations must be closely considered, its very existence and role are dependent on factors such as organisation size, structure and ownership.

MANAGEMENT APPROACHES
A key responsibility for employee relations management at organisation level lies with line management. How they approach and handle employee relations issues will be a major factor in determining the nature of shopfloor

Table 9.8. Collective bargaining arrangements: centralisation v. decentralisation

	1 Centralised	2 Coordinated decentralisation	3 Constrained decentralisation	4 Autonomous unit
Central decision-making authority e.g. corporate management, main board of directors	Retain power to decide on all strategy/policy matters	Decide on overall corporate policy guidelines	Sets overall budget	Acts as service/advisory function
Local management e.g. senior plant management in multi-plant organisation; department or division in single plant company	Implement policy, handle non-strategic local issues	Discretion to decide on how to implement corporate policy within broad parameters laid down by the corporate management	Decide on their own arrangements but within budget guidelines	Total responsibility to make own arrangements

employee relations. Line managers represent management in the day-to-day affairs of the organisation, dealing with issues like grievances, discipline and communications. Some of the factors influencing line management approaches to employee relations are considered below. Later, corporate employee relations approaches or styles are discussed.

Attitudes, Perception and Behaviour

Because line managers play such a key role in shopfloor-employee relations it is worth considering why individual managers may approach broadly similar issues in different ways and react differently in certain situations. It is equally important that line managers be aware of their own attitudes, approaches and behaviour in dealing with employee relations.

Attitudes held by a person are basically a set of beliefs about a situation or issue which influences that person to act in a particular way. For example, a particular manager might hold a belief that 'shop stewards are troublemakers'. As a result the manager is likely to behave in a largely antagonistic way in dealing with shop stewards. Attitudes determine how people act in given situations and may be based upon experience, knowledge, values, loyalties, etc. They will be developed through, amongst other factors, the influence of parents, social class and education.

While attitudes influence how people approach and act in different situations, *perception* refers to the process through which we experience and interpret situations and events. It helps to explain why people see things differently. Management may see a union as being obstinate in opposing the introduction of new technology, thus 'deliberately hindering the company's progress'. Union representatives may see management as being 'bloody-minded' in putting jobs at risk and unilaterally changing established working practices. Both parties perceive the situation differently and this influences their approaches and behaviour. People tend to interpret what they see in a selective fashion according to their particular attitudes, experiences, expectations and needs. This particularly applies to our dealings with other people. Managers who perceive trade unions as a rival source of authority will generally adopt an adversarial attitude towards employee representatives and any issues articulated through the trade union.

This process of observing and drawing conclusions is done in a largely unconscious fashion. People do not always realise their own predispositions and biases. Habits, past experiences, values, attitudes, etc. influence how events and people are perceived and this, in turn, influences reactions and behaviour.[69] Because experiences, values, etc. differ it is inevitable that people will perceive events differently and will consequently behave in different ways (see figure 9.5). The values and beliefs held by management act as a lens through which actions are justified, filtered and strategies formulated.

Fig. 9.5. Factors influencing perception and behaviour

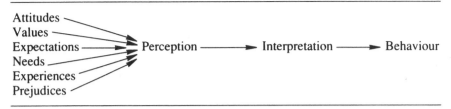

The relationship between perception and behaviour is particularly important for line managers in handling employee relations. They must be able to evaluate critically their own approach to employee relations and to workforce management generally. Perceptions will differ, so that a particular approach which may seem perfectly logical to one person may be totally unacceptable to another. For example, unionisation may be very attractive to a group of employees with several grievances, but be totally unacceptable to the company manager who views unionisation as an unnecessary and unwanted challenge to his/her personal authority. Managers must be prepared to examine their approach to employee relations and to appreciate that one's perception of the situation is not necessarily absolute.

Line Management Approaches

A useful starting point in examining management approaches to employee relations is to examine the frame of reference adopted by managers.

Fox argues that the approach adopted by an individual manager to employee relations will be largely influenced by the frame of reference adopted.[70] A frame of reference embodies 'the main selective influences at work as the perceiver supplements, omits and structures what he notices'.[71] Fox suggests that a manager's frame of reference is important because *a)* it determines how we expect people to behave and how we think they should behave; *b)* it determines our reactions to people's actual behaviour; *c)* it shapes the method we choose when we want to change their behaviour. He identified two alternative frames of reference which highlight the potentially extreme variations in management approaches to employee relations: the *unitarist* and *pluralist* perspective. The key features of both frames of reference are summarised in table 9.9.

In practice, most managers will not rigidly adhere to any single approach. However, they represent dominant orientations which may be present in particular managerial approaches and offer a useful framework which managers can use to analyse their own approach to employee relations. In this context it is useful to consider how management approaches might differ depending on the frames of reference adopted. Marchington suggests that the unitarist and pluralist frames of reference differ in three basic

Table 9.9. Unitarist and pluralist frames of reference

Unitarist	Pluralist
Emphasises the dominance of common interests; everyone—management and employees—should strive to achieve the organisation's primary business goals since everyone will then benefit	The organisation is viewed as composed of a variety of interest groups & coalitions possessing different aims & objectives, but linked together instrumentally by their common association with the same organisation
There is only one source of authority (management) and it must command full loyalty	Management's role is to achieve some equilibrium level by satisfying the interests & objectives of the various interest groups, thus helping to achieve the organisation's goals
Anyone who does not share these common interests and does not accept managerial authority is viewed as a dissenter/agitator	A certain amount of conflict is inevitable since the interests/objectives of the parties will clash on occasion
Since dissenters endanger organisational success they must either fall into line, appreciate the overriding importance of corporate goals and accept managerial authority or risk elimination from the organisation	Management must expect & plan for conflict, in order that it can be handled successfully & to avoid endangering the achievement of the organisation's primary objectives
	Management should not seek to suppress conflicting interests but rather aim to reconcile them in the organisation's interests

respects: management approaches to *a)* the role of trade unions; *b)* managerial prerogative; and *c)* industrial conflict.[72] According to Marchington, managers who hold a unitarist perspective would see no role for *trade unions*. They would be seen as 'encroaching on management's territory', making unreasonable demands, preventing change, flexibility, and therefore competitiveness. This approach is personified in attitudes like 'trade unions were necessary years ago, but there's no need for them now', or 'there is a need for a union in some companies but not here'. Unions are viewed as an externally imposed body which introduces conflict into the organisation and prohibits the development of good employee relations. Employees associated with the introduction of trade unionism are seen as disloyal agitators. On the other hand, managers who hold a pluralist perspective would see a legitimate role for trade unions in representing and articulating employee needs. Unions are not seen as being in competition for employee loyalty but rather as a useful mechanism for handling employee relations issues in a logical and acceptable fashion.

Management prerogative refers to areas of decision-making where management see themselves as the sole authority. With the growth of organised labour, employers have had to share some of their decision-making power and come to terms with other forms of authority within the organisation—particularly trade unions. Marchington suggests that the two frames of reference contrast in their approach to the reduction of management prerogative by trade unions. Managers holding a unitary view would be less likely to accept a curbing of management prerogative as a result of trade union organisation. Management is seen as the legitimate decision-making authority and it is their job to take decisions in the best interests of both the organisation and its employees, deciding which issues to discuss with employees and those where management alone should decide. Those veering towards the pluralist view would appreciate other sources of leadership and loyalty in the organisation and that management should share some of its decision-making authority with other legitimate interest groups, particularly trade unions. Such a management approach would hold firm views on the specific role the trade union should play and would not wish to see it veer beyond this or interfere with other aspects of management decision-making. In effect the pluralist approach, while accepting certain limits on managerial prerogative (areas of collective interest such as wages, hours of work etc.) would strive to retain authority in areas where it does not see a legitimate role for trade unions (in corporate decisions like investment). This approach is often manifested in company-union agreements which outline the status and rights of both management and trade unions.

Depending on the frame of reference adopted, attitudes and approaches to industrial conflict may vary considerably. Managers holding a unitarist perspective would see their firm very much in the team or family mould, with everyone working together to achieve company objectives. Within this model the prospect of conflict arising would be unlikely but should industrial conflict arise such managers would tend to believe that the causes must be as result of something going wrong—misunderstanding or poor communications—or else the work of agitators or troublemakers. Conflict is not seen as inherent in workplace employee relations but rather a symptom of either a breakdown in the employee relations framework within the firm or introduced by people who do not have the company's interests at heart. Managers holding a pluralist perspective would see a certain degree of conflict as inevitable, due to the differing objectives held by the various groups in the organisation. They will not tend to look for immediate causes such as bad communications or 'troublemakers', but will examine the sources and nature of such conflict and try to find mutually acceptable solutions with the aid of the other party. Such managers, because they see employer and employee interest as inevitably coming into conflict, will seek to plan for such occurrences and create procedures, rules and institutional arrangements to ensure such conflict is handled in a reasonable fashion and does not have a detrimental impact on the overall employee relations fabric.

CORPORATE MANAGEMENT AND EMPLOYEE RELATIONS

An organisation's corporate style and related strategies in employee relations will significantly impact on workplace employee relations. This highlights the important relationship between business goals, corporate culture and employee relations styles and strategies.

A central issue in examining corporate approaches to employee relations is the degree to which organisations have different corporate styles or cultures and their resultant impact on employee relations. Much of the recent work in management research has concentrated on identifying different corporate cultures and highlighting the characteristics of corporate cultures of successful (and less successful) organisations. While this task is difficult, there seems little doubt that some of the more successful organisations have distinctive cultures which are the foundations of corporate success. Corporate culture may be loosely looked upon as deeply held beliefs within an organisation concerning how decisions should be made, work organised and people managed. Variations in culture may arise because of various factors in the organisation's development and environment and will influence the structure and ethos of the organisation, including its approach to employee relations.

Corporate Approaches

An important influence on workplace employee relations will be the structure and approach of the organisation in which people work. With the ownership of industry primarily vested in the hands of private enterprise, profitability remains the major yardstick of corporate success, and management objectives are consequently primarily identified with owner interest. But management must also be responsible to other interest groups. One such group are the organisation's employees, often represented by trade unions. In such circumstances collective bargaining is the main vehicle for the management of employee relations which thus incorporates political as well as economic considerations. In this political relationship management play the role of decision-makers by virtue of their mandate from the owners and construct complex organisational and authority structures to achieve their various objectives. Consequently, management possess considerable power and influence, making decisions on investment, location, recruitment, technology, etc. While such decisions are made within certain constraints, they are indicative of the immense influence management can exercise on the operating environment of employee relations.

Strategic decisions are taken by senior management to help achieve corporate objectives. These will stem from the organisation's primary business goals and determine the nature and direction of the organisation. Strategic business decisions involve a range of areas including production, finance, marketing, etc. Often their influence on employee relations will be indirect. For example, an organisation may decide to terminate a particular product line because of financial and market considerations. However, it might mean redundancies and might, as a result, detrimentally affect morale and ultimately employee relations.

Management may also take strategic business decisions which directly influence employee relations. Whether senior management actually do take strategic employee relations decisions is a matter for debate. A traditional feeling has been that senior management concentrate their strategic decision-making on 'primary' business areas such as investment, product or technology, and any attention devoted to employee relations was secondary and somewhat incidental to the main thrust of such strategic decision-making. On the other hand, it is evident that many organisations adopt a particular corporate personnel style or approach and take well thought out strategic decisions to establish and further this approach. Indeed, practice would seem to vary widely from a general approach of 'incidentalism', characterised by little or no strategic decision-making in employee relations, to a planned approach involving a series of key strategic decisions taken and pursued to achieve a particular approach which may often involve a significant role for the specialist personnel function (see figure 9.6).

Fig. 9.6. Employee relations and strategic decision-making

'Incidentalism'	Planned employee relations approach
Strategic decision-making pays no attention to employee relations	Key strategic decisions taken to achieve/ advance a particular approach

On this continuum organisations may adopt a variety of positions and it is difficult to ascertain the exact status of employee relations in strategic decision-making. It is, however, possible to identify areas where management may take strategic decisions which directly or indirectly impact upon employee relations (see figure 9.11). In a 'greenfield' situation a new organisation may achieve non-union status through its decisions on location, recruitment and personnel policies. Equally, a large unionised organisation could dramatically alter employee relations by shifting the locus of collective bargaining from corporate (multi-plant) to establishment level, thereby delegating greater responsibilities to local plant management.

Table 9.10. Strategic decision-making in employee relations (some examples)

Decisions	Impact on employee relations (ER)
Location of plant	Influences the composition of organisation's workforce and related issues (e.g. likelihood of unionisation) indirectly influencing ER
Size of plant	Influences span of managerial control, communications, management style; indirectly impacting upon ER
Employee development	Manpower training and development allows employers the opportunity to influence both management and employee approaches and attitudes to ER
Unionisation	In a 'greenfield' situation corporate management may have the opportunity to decide on unionisation or non-unionisation; obviously affecting the nature of, and approaches to, ER
Level of bargaining	In a unionised framework management can influence the nature of ER and particularly the role of trade unions by determining the bargaining level
Procedural formalisation	The degree to which ER procedures are adopted and implemented will influence workplace ER

Management Styles

Organisations clearly differ in their approach to employee relations, Varying attempts have been made to identify differing management styles and classify them according to specific criteria. One such classification, developed by Purcell and Sisson, is based on differing approaches to trade unions, collective bargaining, consultation and communications and is summarised in Table 9.11.[73]

Despite the inherent difficulty in using such classifications this approach provides us with a valuable analytical framework to evaluate corporate approaches to employee relations. While acknowledging, therefore, the shortcomings of this approach the following variation is proposed as being appropriate in the Irish context (see figure 9.7).

Table 9.11. Management styles in employee relations

Management style	Characteristics
1. Traditionalist	'Orthodox unitarism': oppose role for unions; little attention to employee needs
2. Sophisticated paternalist	Emphasise employee needs (training, pay, conditions, etc); discourage unionisation; demand employee loyalty and commitment
3. Sophisticated modern	Accept trade union's role in specific areas; emphasise procedures & consultative mechanisms: two variations *a)* constitutionalists: emphasise codification of management/union relations through collective agreements *b)* consultors: collective bargaining established but management emphasise personal contact and problem-solving, playing down formal union role at workplace level
4. Standard modern	Pragmatic approach; union's role accepted but no overall philosophy or strategy developed—'fire-fighting' approach

(adopted from Purcell & Sisson 1983)

This classification highlights four major management styles with differences dependent on attitudes and emphasis on trade union recognition, employee welfare, job satisfaction, career development and the role and sophistication of the personnel function. This categorisation is seen as indicative of the predominant styles that might be adopted by organisations. There will obviously be grey areas where the management approach will have characteristics common to two or more styles and categories. This is acknowledged by highlighting the fact that certain characteristics may be common between different styles—see shaded areas, figure 9.7. These varying styles are discussed below:

a) Anti-union: such firms would reject any role for trade unions and would have characteristics similar to Purcell and Sissons' 'traditionalists'. Top management would pay little or no attention to personnel or employee relations except where absolutely necessary. There would be no developed personnel function and a marked absence of any procedures or mechanisms for communicating or consulting with employees. Management practice would veer very much towards Theory X principles, with autocracy being the order of the day. Such an approach would be common among many owner-managed small firms but would also be found among some traditional manufacturing firms and in the service sector.

Fig. 9.7. Management styles in employee relations

Note: shaded areas indicate characteristics of management styles which are common to two styles.

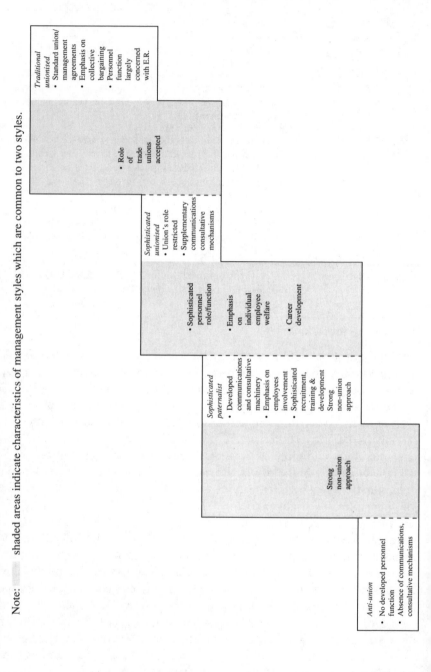

b) Sophisticated paternalist: while sophisticated paternalist firms bear the same dislike of trade unions as the anti-union category, this is where the similarity ends. The hallmark of firms in this category is a heavy emphasis on individual employee welfare and wellbeing. This approach emanates from the very top of the organisation (often the founder) and is followed right down the line. It is initially manifested in the organisation's recruitment and training policies. Where possible, young and ambitious people are recruited, and they are given good opportunities to develop and grow within the organisation. A remuneration policy based—at least partially—on merit is often a characteristic. While such firms may not claim to be overtly 'anti-union' they would take careful steps to ensure that a need for unionisation does not arise by, for example, extensive line management training in employee relations, prompt handling of employee grievances, good terms and conditions of employment, attractive fringe benefits and, sometimes, they are relatively lax in approaches to supervision. Such firms would also emphasise the role of various consultative and communications machinery such as quality circles, briefing groups and joint consultative committees. Techniques like job evaluation and performance appraisal might also be common. There would be a conscious effort throughout the organisation to prevent unionisation by removing the basic role of unions—articulating employee claims and grievances—and such firms would not be members of employer associations. A key component in this overall approach is a well-staffed and developed personnel function which has a major input into corporate policy.

This approach seems to stem from some of the large Japanese corporations who place a heavy emphasis on employee needs and loyalty, and whose welfare policies are very comprehensive, down to the guarantee of lifetime employment. In Ireland a variation of this approach is most visible among the so-called high-technology firms of foreign—often US—origin, and their apparent success may encourage a greater number of Irish organisations to experiment in this direction. The introduction of profit-sharing schemes, 'single status' arrangements and upgrading of training and development may be symptoms of such change in management policy. However, it must be remembered that such policies can be costly both in terms of money and manpower, and it may be difficult for firms operating in a highly competitive environment, where labour costs represent a major proportion of total costs, to afford all the trimmings of the sophisticated paternalist approach. Irish examples include Digital and Wang.

c) Sophisticated unionised: firms in this category are characterised by an acceptance of the trade union's role but supplemented by an emphasis on employee welfare which is designed to eliminate a need for trade union activity at shop floor level. They would differ from sophisticated paternalists on the union issue but otherwise would pursue similar policies. Union recognition would generally be formalised in a procedural agreement specifying management and union rights and collective bargaining arrangements (possibly incorporating closed shop). At shop-floor level management would seek to keep formality to a minimum. Emphasis will be placed on adopting a 'caring' approach to employees. Again, this will be manifested through careful selection and good training and development opportunities. Employees will be encouraged to deal directly with management on any issues that concern them. Line management staff will be well trained in employee relations and backed up by a developed personnel department which will, on the one hand, coordinate collective bargaining with the trade unions and, on the other, oversee the organisation's various employee-oriented policies.

Such organisations will often be members of an employer association but will tend to use them for advice rather than direct assistance in managing employee relations. Various other types of consultative machinery may be used, and again techniques like quality circles, briefing groups and joint consultative committees will be popular. Management will be keen to ensure that communication with employees is not done solely through the trade union. Collective bargaining is seen as having an important but restricted role to play, and beyond this management attempt to move away from 'distributive bargaining' to a greater emphasis on 'integrative bargaining' and joint problem solving.[74] Various types of organisations would fall into this category. Many of the multinational companies who have recognised trade unions follow this approach (Abbots, Analog) as well as some established indigenous firms (Guinness, Superquinn) and more recently some semi-states such as the IDA.

An interesting development within this category is the increased interest in 'new-style collective agreements'. Originating in the UK, these agreements involve a comprehensive re-evaluation of traditional collective bargaining arrangements and the development of new-style agreements involving single union recognition, industrial peace clauses, work flexibility, harmonised working conditions, consultative mechanisms and pendulum arbitration.[75] As yet the extent and operation of such agreements here is limited and it would be premature to draw any conclusions. However, British trends indicate that variations of such agreements are becoming more common, while in Ireland there seems to be increased interest in the area, with some organisations such as Packard and ECCO already experimenting with such agreements.[76]

d) Traditional unionised: the Irish employee relations system has long centred around the principle of free collective bargaining, ensuring that at organisation level employer-employee relations has focused on negotiations between management and trade unions. This emphasis on collective bargaining, often termed the 'adversarial' model of employee relations, has formed the basis for traditional approaches to 'industrial' relations management.

The traditional unionised approach is characterised by union recognition and extensive reliance on collective bargaining. Trade union officials play a key role in dealing with major issues such as pay, and will often have built up strong personal relations with company management. Shop stewards are actively involved at workplace level, dealing with claims and grievances and shopfloor negotiations. The management-union relationship may be formalised in a procedural agreement which regulates relations between the parties and covers issues like union recognition (including closed shop), disciplinary, grievance and disputes procedures.[77] However, some organisational arrangements have never been formalised in a comprehensive written agreement and are largely a product of custom and practice. The majority of these organisations will have a specialist personnel function whose primary role will be to coordinate collective bargaining and deal with trade union representatives and shop stewards. They will work under the direction of top management on all major employee relations issues. Membership of an employer's association will be common, and the association's officials may be extensively used for advice and assistance in management-union negotiations.

This approach is widespread in Ireland, particularly in medium and large indigenous organisations in both the manufacturing and service sector, some of the older multinationals and much of the public sector including many of the semi-states. More recently some organisations would seem to have shifted away from this approach to the more sophisticated unionised variant, and the line between these two styles may become increasingly clouded—a good example being Waterford Glass.

In reflecting upon the Irish situation, the most striking feature of the above classification of management styles relates to the middle two groupings (sophisticated paternalists and sophisticated unionised). These two categories are significant because they indicate a coordinated and centrally planned approach to employee relations management. The other two styles (anti-union and traditional unionised) are more representative of the 'incidentalist' approach, where no one coordinated style is adopted by senior management.

The widespread adoption of more strategic approaches to employee relations would herald a significant change in Irish employee relations. It involves corporate management analysing optional approaches to employee relations and adopting an appropriate style to suit their organisational needs. An important catalyst in any such development is the difficult trading conditions which many organisations experienced in the 1980s. Organisations have been forced to review their operations critically and make appropriate changes. New models of workforce management were developed which incorporated changing approaches to employee relations.

An added factor has been the weak position of trade unions which facilitated change, particularly the adoption of corporate styles which reduced or eliminated the union role. Although it is debatable if this trend will continue with the advent of economic recovery, there is undoubtedly a greater interest in more strategic approaches to employee relations management, often integrated into a broader corporate approach to workforce management. It is likely that this trend will continue in the foreseeable future.

Explaining the factors which influence the choice of corporate employee relations styles is more difficult. A number of influential contextual factors may be identified. These include technology, workforce composition, market position, capital and labour cost ratio, size, location and the historical development of employee relations itself. Recent changes in the product market, technology and economic environment have acted to create a climate where organisations have been forced to review their approaches to employee relations.

Apart form these general factors, the influence of individual personalities should not be overlooked. For example, corporate personnel management and employee relations approaches of many prominent organisations may be traced to particular beliefs about workforce management held by the organisation's founders. This would seem to be particularly true of some multinational organisations in the high-technology area. The initially high growth rate of these firms meant that they became large corporations while their founders were still at the helm and whose philosophies on workforce management permeate approaches to employee relations. Digital, Wang and Hewlett Packard are prominent multinational examples. The influence of entrepreneurial founders is also prominent among indigenous firms, and the styles adopted by organisations like Guinness Peat Aviation or Superquinn can to a large extent be traced back to their respective chief executives.

Chapter 10

Employee Relations Activities

INTRODUCTION
Employee relations has been identified as the single most significant activity area within personnel management. Shivanath concluded that employee relations was the 'most crucial area' of the personnel practitioner's role, with most organisations operating a range of employee relations policies and procedures.[1]

Table 10.1. Employee relations activities within organisations

Activity	% of organisations	Personnel None	Department Joint	Involvement (Total)
Major ER negotiations	88.7%	9.5%	36.5%	54.0%
Operate participation schemes	39.4%	42.9%	35.7%	31.4%
Handle grievances, discipline, disputes	90.1%	6.3%	53.1%	40.6%
Advice on labour law	85.9%	4.9%	18.0%	77.0%
Prepare conciliation/ arbitration cases	83.1%	6.8%	33.9%	59.3%
Present conciliation/ arbitration cases	81.7%	6.9%	27.6%	65.5%

Source: Adapted from Shivanath, G. 'Personnel Practitioners 1986: Their role and status in Irish Industry'. Unpublished MBS Thesis NIHE Limerick 1987.

While the relative emphasis on different employee relations activities will vary between organisations, this chapter considers some key activities common in Irish organisations.

COLLECTIVE BARGAINING AND THE NEGOTIATING PROCESS
Collective bargaining refers to the process through which agreement on pay, working conditions, procedures and other negotiable issues are reached between organised employees and management representatives.

In Ireland the scope of collective bargaining is extensive, and the terms of collective agreements negotiated become implied terms of the individual employee's contract of employment. Collective bargaining may cover both procedural and substantive issues. Procedural matters refer to methods of formally handling specific issues that might arise, such as trade union recognition, disciplinary issues or dispute resolution. On the other hand, substantive matters refer to the detailed outcomes of negotiations, such as a percentage pay increase or an extra day's annual holiday.

The conduct of collective bargaining may vary considerably between organisations but remains essentially voluntary in nature, relying on the moral commitment of the participants. It represents a mechanism by which divergent interests in organisations are reconciled through an orderly process involving negotiation and compromise.

Level of Collective Bargaining

For unionised organisations an important influence on employee relations practice is the level at which collective bargaining is conducted (figure 10.1).

Fig. 10.1. Levels of collective bargaining

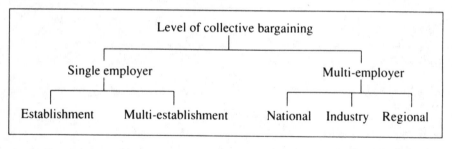

Collective bargaining may take place at multi-employer or single employer level. In Ireland the traditional focus of collective bargaining on major issues has been on multi-employer bargaining with supplementary work-place bargaining at establishment level. Within this approach employer views on major employee relations issues, particularly pay, are represented through the appropriate employer association. This approach has numerous advantages for employers. It relieves them of the need to deal with annual wage negotiations, and its reliance on standard rates of pay and working conditions avoids pay competition between organisations. At a more strategic level multi-employer bargaining concentrates union attention at trans-company level, separating the locus of management decision-making (corporate management) from the locus of collective bargaining, effectively denying unions access to key management decision makers at organisation level.

For many organisations in comfortable trading positions multi-employer bargaining is a relatively painless way of dealing with employee relations. From the end of the Second World War to the early 1980s employee relations in Ireland were dominated by a series of wage rounds and centralised collective agreements maintaining the locus of collective bargaining at multi-employer level.

Despite the advantages of multi-employer bargaining it has not fully survived the test of time in Ireland or the UK. Workplace (single-employer) bargaining became established in Ireland in the 1960s.[2] With the advent of highly centralised bargaining arrangements in 1970 a clear differentiation was created between issues for negotiation at national level and at establishment level. General pay increases were negotiated at national level, while the emphasis at local level was on dealing with anomalies, productivity and working conditions via workplace bargaining between shop stewards and company management.[3]

The last two decades have seen a marked increase in informal workplace bargaining. The concentration of collective bargaining at multi-employer level created a serious vacuum at workplace level. With the attention of trade union officialdom focused on multi-employer bargaining, shop stewards assumed an increasingly important workplace role in handling shop floor issues such as grievances, disciplinary issues and minor claims. Informal bargaining became an important component of workplace employee relations, and employers had to assume greater responsibility for managing their own employee relations.

From the managerial perspective an important factor facilitating the growth of workplace bargaining was the desire to improve productivity and competitiveness through the negotiation of unique arrangements between management and unions to suit local needs. This has also been facilitated under the Programme for National Recovery (1987) which provides for the agreement of centralised pay guidelines while allowing management and employees to negotiate on other issues at establishment level.

For multi-establishment organisations the issue of whether to bargain at corporate (multi-establishment) or establishment (individual enterprise) level remains. Kinnie suggests that competitive pressures brought about by the recession led to two possible employer responses.[4] On the one hand, corporate management sought to exert central control over costs and work practices through greater centralisation in employee relations management. At the same time many employers wished to decentralise control to create individual cost centres and delegate responsibility for increased efficiency.

Kinnie argues that, while the trend in managerial control is for greater centralisation, this does not necessarily involve a move away from establishment-level bargaining, suggesting that organisations are trying to strike a balance between pressures for centralisation and decentralisation.

The growth of supplementary bargaining in conjunction with the recent recessionary pressures has increased the need to coordinate strategic decision-making at corporate level while allowing greater operational discretion at local level. An important reason for such change lies in attempts by some employers to curtail the power of trade unions and reduce their impact on collective bargaining. By separating the locus of strategic decision-making (corporate level) from the locus of collective bargaining (establishment level) trade unions are effectively prevented from influencing strategic employee relations decisions on issues such as investment, technology and overall corporate strategy. On the other hand, the difficult trading conditions experienced here highlighted the need to give plant management greater discretion to manage their own affairs by making operational decisions affecting work practices, flexibility and general employee relations. In this way corporate managements have sought to restore management prerogative while at the same time giving local management greater scope to decide on plant-level issues.[5] These changes have not gone unnoticed by unions but their weak position and traditional difficulties in coordinating collective bargaining on a multi-employer level renders their ability to oppose such changes questionable. While these factors have undoubtedly led to a degree of opportunism by employers it would be unfair to suggest that such changes are merely a symptom of 'macho-management'. They may also be indicative of a greater strategic awareness of the role of employee relations among senior management.

Employee Relations Negotiations
The cornerstone of collective bargaining is the negotiations process. Employee relations negotiations involve discussions and interactions over some divisive issue(s) with the objective of reaching agreement.[6] For the unionised organisation, management-union negotiations represent the major vehicle for reaching agreement over a broad range of employee relations issues such as pay and conditions of employment. Such negotiations are normally termed 'distributive bargaining', since they involve bargaining or haggling over issues where a favourable settlement for one party means an element of loss for the other.[7] This 'win-lose' approach represents an adversarial model of collective bargaining where each party pursues its own specific objectives and strives to concede minimal concessions to the other party. It is most obvious in pay negotiations where concessions by management inevitably represent both a quantifiable cost and a reduction in profits and dividends. On the other hand, negotiations can have a more joint problem solving approach, sometimes referred to as 'integrative' or 'co-operative' bargaining, where both parties are concerned with finding a jointly acceptable solution, resulting in benefits for both sides (often

referred to as a 'win-win' approach).[8] Inevitably workplace negotiations will involve a combination of both approaches with the mix being influenced by the extent of trust and openness between the parties.

The Negotiations Process: possibly the most striking aspect of employee relations negotiations is their ritualistic nature, resembling an elaborate game between competing teams.[9] At the formal level it involves one party making claims on the other, meeting and discussing issues in a specific context, bargaining and haggling over the divisive issues and reporting back to their respective constituents. It may conclude either by reaching a mutually acceptable agreement or by entering a deadlock situation which may be resolved through further discussion, mediation and arbitration or use of sanctions.

The outcome of the negotiating process will depend on the willingness to compromise, the persuasive abilities and bargaining skills of both sides, and, ultimately, the power balance between the parties.[10] In this context it is important to note that negotiating is an ongoing process which is not limited to one particular issue or time. Consequently, the maintenance and development of a stable long-term relationship between the parties may often take precedence over achieving 'victory' on a particular issue.

Negotiations also take place at a more informal level, involving line management and employees and/or their representatives. Such negotiations will cover more individual-type issues such as grievances, disciplinary action, minor claims. The mechanism for handling claims, grievances or disputes are often outlined in a formal procedure agreement.[11]

The basic stages in the negotiating process are outlined in table 10.2 and discussed below.

Table 10.2 The negotiating process

Stage	Activities	
1. Pre-negotiation	•Preparation •Research	•Agree objectives •Team composition
2. Negotiation	•Bargaining •Expectation structuring	•Discover positions •Compromise & movement
3. Post-Negotiation	•Document agreement •Agree action plans •Implement	•Clarify •Communicate •Review

1. Pre-Negotiation

a) Preparation: careful preparation is a prerequisite for success in negotiations. Effective negotiators will be familiar with the details of the case, have specified their objectives, clarified their mandate and negotiating range, obtained all relevant information on the other side's position and agreed strategy and tactics with the members of their negotiating team. Effective preparation involves gathering all relevant information and retaining this for use at the bargaining table and ensuring that any agreement and procedures are adhered to.[12]

It also involves ensuring that appropriate administrative arrangements are made in relation to the location, timing, administrative and physical facilities. Most negotiations will take place within the organisation. However, there may be occasions when it is appropriate to move 'off-site' to provide a more neutral atmosphere, avoid on-the-job interruptions or leaks from the negotiations. Administrative arrangements include ensuring that all parties are aware of the issues and the timing of the negotiations. It also involves the provision of adequate physical facilities including the venue (spacious, free from interruptions, convenient), seating and adjournment arrangements (non-intimidating, caucus rooms) and back-up facilities (phone, fax, typing, etc.).

b) Research: adequate back-up research ensures that management's case is well substantiated. This helps to focus negotiations on facts rather than discussing opinions or value judgments. In researching management's case, all available sources both within and outside the organisation should be utilised. Of particular relevance are indices and trends of pay increases and working conditions, comparable settlements and agreements in other organisations, information on trade union claims and policies. It should also incorporate an evaluation of the repercussions of likely settlement options. Employer associations can be particularly useful in providing back-up research. Informal contacts with other firms or surveys of pay and conditions may be utilised, as can other sources of published material.

c) Negotiating team: an important role for personnel practitioners involves representing management in negotiations. The role will vary depending on the issue and level of negotiations. Personnel will not be directly involved on relatively minor issues, although they may provide advice and guidance to line management. On more serious issues the senior personnel practitioner will often lead the management team, acting as chief negotiator. Alternatively this role may be carried out by the chief executive, with the personnel practitioner acting as key advisor.

A common issue in undertaking negotiations is deciding on the size and composition of the management team. This decision will be largely determined by the nature of the issue, the organisational context and the time and resources available. Nierenberg feels that using a single negotiator ensures clarification of responsibility, speedy decision-making and prevents differences of opinion.[13] He also suggests that increasing the number of representatives ensures greater technical knowledge, improved planning and judgment.

It is generally advisable that the management negotiating team be comprised of a minimum of two people. This facilitates the allocation of responsibilities in presenting the case, analysis of verbal and non-verbal responses, record keeping, and adequate consideration of the consequences of various settlement options and management responses. It also increases objectivity, provides a witness to the event and facilitates conclusion of the final agreement.

Management representatives should have a sound knowledge of the organisation and the issue at hand. They need to be flexible and articulate in presenting arguments, good listeners and possess the analytical ability, self-discipline, patience and stamina necessary for employee relations negotiations. A spread of interests and roles facilitates the development of strategy and tactics within the team. It provides a useful source of information and allows for different negotiating styles which may incorporate a 'devil's advocate'. Canning identifies three main tasks which need to be provided for within the management negotiating team.[14]

Spokesman/Team Leader: the role of the chief management representative is to present arguments, control tactics, and take major on-the-spot decisions. This role is often the responsibility of the senior personnel practitioner.

Observer: here the role is to evaluate progress relative to objectives, spot key reactions, identify changes in approach and advise the chief negotiator.

Recorder: this involves recording key points in negotiations and documenting the final agreement.

d) Agree objectives: management should have a clear idea of what they want to achieve from the collective bargaining process in general and each particular set of negotiations. General goals might include the maintenance of a good working relations with employees and their representatives, maintaining managerial prerogative in certain areas and the avoidance of industrial conflict. Particular objectives may vary according to the issue at hand and should involve specific targets, trade-off options and resistance points. Flexible objectives are generally more appropriate than rigid ones, since information may be uncovered during negotiations which can alter the substance of the management case. It is important that management's objectives are approved by top management so that the negotiating team has a clear mandate; and objectives should be agreed and communicated within the negotiating team to ensure commitment to their achievement.

A central issue in agreeing negotiating objectives is deciding upon the bargaining range and, consequently, the limits or parameters within which agreement can be achieved. Negotiating inevitably means compromise and movement. The degree to which this is possible, and consequently the scope for reaching agreement, depends on the bargaining range of both parties and the degree to which these overlap.

At preparation stage, management should establish its ideal settlement point and also its resistance point beyond which the organisation is not prepared to reach agreement.[15] If the employee or union team carry out a similar exercise the overall bargaining range and area of settlement will be circumscribed (see figure 10.2).

Fig. 10.2. Setting negotiating parameters

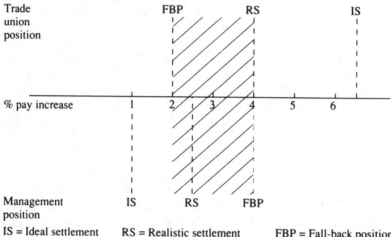

IS = Ideal settlement   RS = Realistic settlement   FBP = Fall-back position

From the managerial perspective this process facilitates the identification of bargaining objectives, deciding on trade-offs and concessions, and provides a benchmark against which to evaluate progress. In the above example agreement is only possible where resistance points (fall-back positions) overlap, in the 2 percent to 4 percent pay range. A settlement is not possible outside this range unless one of the parties alters its position. Alternatively a dispute situation may arise.

e) Assess bargaining power: bargaining power may be interpreted as the degree to which one party can achieve its negotiating goals despite the opposition of the other side.[16] It will significantly influence the outcome of negotiations, since the balance of settlement will normally favour the party with the greatest bargaining power.

Bargaining power is multi-faceted and depends on factors both external and internal to the negotiations process. The general economic and business environment will have a major impact. For example, a full order book will favour a union claim for bonus payments, as management will be keen to meet production targets. On the other hand, cutbacks in production will make a favourable annual wage increase unlikely. Bargaining power will also be influenced by the relative skill and ability of the negotiators and the degree to which they have prepared their case.

An important step in assessing the other side's bargaining power is to identify accurately the resistance points of the other side and their commitment to achieving their stated objectives. Much of the negotiations process involves rhetorical arguments indicating the level of feeling on a particular issue. Much of this bluff and rhetoric is aimed at convincing the other side that one's resistance (fall-back position) is higher than it actually is, to encourage the other party to make concessions. An accurate perception of actual fall-back positions indicates how far management can go without risking breakdown in negotiations. It also helps if management weigh up the advantages and disadvantages of varying concession levels.

f) Develop strategy and tactics: previous steps in the pre-negotiations phase will indicate management's overall approach to the negotiations. This will influence the tactics adopted in the course of the negotiations.

Negotiating strategy refers to the overall approach to be adopted in negotiations, while tactics refer to the various techniques which are implemented to achieve this strategy. To use a sporting analogy, a football team may decide to adopt a defensive strategy in a particular game. The resulting tactics may involve selecting extra defenders in the team and adopting a close marking system. In negotiations numerous tactics may be adopted. Some of these are discussed below.

Agenda and timing: at the very outset the structuring of the agenda may allow one side an advantage. For example, management can create a conciliatory atmosphere by placing simple non-contentious issues first and making concessions on these. When a major issue then comes up they may throw down the gauntlet claiming how reasonable they have been and asking the other side to make 'similar' concessions. On the other hand, a crucial issue may be placed first, with a stipulation that agreement must be reached here first before moving on. This can pressurise the other side which may be more concerned with subsequent matters on the agenda. The structure of the agenda may also be used to put time pressures on the other party by placing issues crucial to them at the bottom, giving limited time for their discussion and possibly ensuring their deferral. Lastly, it is important to note that management-union negotiations are generally expected to be tough, drawn-out affairs and concessions should not be made too early or easily, leading the other party to infer that even better settlement levels can be obtained.

Probe and question: if management have adequately prepared their case, they are in a strong position to probe and question the factual basis of the union's position. The validity of comparisons or reliability of data used may be questioned. If the other party's case is shown to be factually weak they may be forced to reconsider. Such probing should be done sensitively so that the other party does not lose too much face or is 'backed into a corner' from which they react aggressively. As mentioned earlier, the longer-term relationship must be considered, and in such situations adjournments become useful to allow for changes in position and to provide an escape route for the less fortunate party.

Hard and soft: a popular tactic employed by some negotiators is to alternatively adopt an extremely aggressive and then more conciliatory approach. These roles may often be divided up between members of the negotiating team, with one giving no quarter while the other infers that there may be room for compromise. The basic idea is to make the concessions offered by the softer partner appear more attractive than they otherwise would.

Bottom line: here management try to convince the other party of the seriousness of their stance by outlining the implications of the union claim on factors like costs, competitiveness, survival, etc. This may be achieved by using financial information to demonstrate relative ability to pay or by bringing the chief executive into the negotiations to demonstrate the strength of feeling on the issue.

Split the opposition: should there be some hint of differences in the opposing team, management may try to exploit this. Probing questions may be used to uncover these differences. In such circumstances the other party may be forced to withdraw, regroup its forces and reconsider its position.

Fait accompli: here management take a particular initiative on an issue which is subject to negotiation and await reactions from the employee side. For example, management may introduce new technology while this is still subject to negotiation. This represents a calculated risk, the implications of which must be carefully evaluated by management in advance.

2. Negotiation

The bargaining process: actual bargaining interactions often pass through a number of identifiable phases as follows:

  i) establishing or discovering positions;
  ii) structuring expectations;
  iii) offer and movement;
  iv) agreement or breakdown;
  v) close.

At the outset it is management's responsibility to ensure that appropriate arrangements are made so that negotiations go ahead in a businesslike manner. The bargaining process often begins with both parties outlining their respective positions. This may involve management referring to the subject matter for negotiation, the details of any claim served upon them and their position on such issues. Alternatively, they may ask the union team to clarify or substantiate their position. Either way, the approach and tone adopted by management will influence the subsequent bargaining climate. After this stage both parties will have established each other's positions and evaluated the degree to which movement and concession is possible.

At this point the real bargaining can begin. Both parties may attempt to expound their commitment to their respective positions and, possibly, try to highlight the weaknesses in each other's case. They will try to structure or influence the other party's expectations and try to convince them to accept whatever concessions are offered. For example, the management team in pay negotiations may emphasise factors like the poor economic outlook, need to retain competitiveness, danger of redundancies, etc. In so doing they attempt to shape the union's expectations by painting a bleak picture of the organisation's operating conditions, thus increasing the likelihood of their accepting a lower level of increase.

The next step is for some initial offers or concessions to be made. Timing is crucial, and major concessions should not be made too early. Any movement should take account of all aspects of the issue at hand so that further claims or issues cannot be raised subsequently. Each offer and concession should be carefully weighed up in terms of its implications for the organisation. At this stage adjournments may be useful by allowing for a consideration of progress. After some time it will become clear if agreement is possible, whether the parties will have to refer back to their respective constituents, or if a breakdown is imminent. Either way the details of the issues discussed, offers and concessions made, agreement reached or reasons for breakdown should be carefully recorded.

In the event of breakdown, channels of communication should be kept open. Negotiations should not break down in disarray with one party walking out, since the issue of who initiates subsequent communications may become a matter of principle, needlessly prohibiting further progress. Again it is important to remember that negotiating is an on-going process and stability in the long-term relationship is a primary objective. For this reason the parties should be keen to avoid damaging conflict and be prepared to compromise on certain issues for the benefit of that longer-term perspective. .

The closing stages in negotiations will often be self-evident. It will involve finalising the agreement, issues for further negotiation or details of breakdown. Adequate time should always be available for this stage. Both parties should be clear on interpretation and their various commitments. Details for implementation or further meetings should be specified.

3. Post-negotiation

At the end of negotiations the management team will have to report back on the outcome. The implementation process should be agreed upon and the implications thoroughly discussed in relation to the overall employee relations context and the nature of future negotiations. The mode of communication of the agreement to employees should be agreed upon and any administrative obligations carried out. All aspects should be carefully documented for further reference and communicated to all relevant personnel, particularly line management. Details of implementation should be worked out and responsibilities allocated. Lastly, the total negotiations experience should be reviewed to gain maximum benefit and assess how the lessons learned can be used for maximum benefit in the future.

Towards Successful Negotiations

Since the negotiations process involves interactions between people of varying personality in different organisational contexts, their outcome and conduct are impossible to predict. Persistent problems in negotiations may arise for numerous reasons, such as inflexibility and unwillingness to compromise, abrasive style and language, or poor preparation and knowledge. Some of these problems may be tackled by improving negotiating skills through careful team selection, training and experience.

However, some writers have suggested that other drawbacks in negotiations are inherent in the way they have been traditionally conducted and that the process itself needs re-evaluation. A general criticism has been the perceived dominance of distributive bargaining with its emphasis on dividing limited resources. It is sometimes felt that this approach encourages both parties to develop adversarial positions, believing that any gains can only be made by inflicting losses on the other party. Distributive bargaining reflects the very essence of traditional approaches in 'industrial' relations management: claims, offers, bluff, threats, compromise, movement, agreement or conflict. Approaches based on a more integrative and co-operative bargaining or joint problem-solving attitude are often seen as a more attractive alternative, with their emphasis on a joint approach exploring common ground and seeking solutions of mutual benefit to both parties.

Undoubtedly both approaches are appropriate in differing contexts and it is doubtful if traditional bargaining will disappear, given the structure of organisations with their inherent potential for conflict of interests. Fisher and Ury's work on developing an alternative approach to negotiations has been one of the most influential in critically evaluating the negotiations process.[17] They suggest that traditional haggling forces the parties to take opposing positions and adopt bargaining stances designed to justify and achieve that position. They feel that such 'positional bargaining' produces unwise agreements, is inefficient and endangers the ongoing relationship. Alternatively, Fisher and Ury prefer a 'principled' approach to negotiations, based on the merits of the case.

Other writers have emphasised the importance of negotiating skills as a means of achieving success in negotiations.[18] A major influence on the negotiating approach will be the organisational context and the issue at hand. A move away from positional bargaining will help to reduce traditional barriers to agreement and bring both parties close to the joint solution seeking approach. However, distributive bargaining will continue to play a key role, maintaining the personnel practitioner's key role in preparing the management brief, leading negotiations, and ultimately, concluding a successful agreement.

INDUSTRIAL CONFLICT

It is inevitable that some difficulties will arise between employers and their workforce. Such conflicts are not necessarily harmful and need not give rise to industrial action.

Explanations of industrial conflict vary. In the previous chapter it was suggested that managers adopting a pluralist frame of reference accept that conflict will occur because the needs and objectives of various interest groups will clash on occasion.[19] Allen suggests that the structure of the employment relationship, which emphasises management's need for productivity, cost-effectiveness and change, is often at odds with employee needs for security and attractive rewards, thus causing inevitable conflicts of interest.[20] The Marxist explanation goes further, suggesting that alienation caused by the organisation of work within the capitalist framework, involving divisions along labour, ownership and hierarchical lines, makes conflict between labour and management endemic to industrial organisations.[21] On the other hand, the more unitarist 'teamwork' approach suggests that management and employees have the same interest, and conflict only occurs as a result of misunderstandings or the efforts of troublemakers.[22] Regardless of the explanation adopted, some degree of conflict is inherent to workplace employee relations. Although such conflict may not become manifest, it is a source of ongoing concern to management and employees alike. Consequently, much of the management focus in employee relations will be concerned with eliminating or reducing sources of conflict and creating mechanisms through which issues can be resolved amicably without resort to sanctions.

Forms of Industrial Conflict

It is possible to classify industrial conflict into two broad categories: that which is explicit and organised, and reactions which are unorganised and more implicit.[23] The latter category includes absenteeism, labour turnover, high accident levels and poor performance, and may often reflect low levels of employee satisfaction and morale. Overt forms of conflict include strikes, go-slows, works-to rule, withdrawal of co-operation and overtime bans. These represent organised and systematic responses by employees.

The strike weapon is the most visible form of industrial action. Withdrawal of labour, or the threat of withdrawal, by employees is a powerful tool through which trade unions have sought and secured improvements in terms and conditions of employment.[24] Strikes may take different forms and arise for a variety of reasons. Official strikes are those which have been approved by the union executive. Such strikes normally take place after a series of negotiations and meetings have failed to resolve the issue and it has exhausted all stages in a dispute procedure. Such strikes, once approved, may involve large numbers of workers and last for a prolonged period. On the other hand, unofficial strikes lack official union approval and are often sparked off by a particular event or incident at workplace level. Unless subsequently granted official approval by the trade union, unofficial strikes normally last for a shorter time and involve fewer workers.[25]

A decision to take strike action will be based on a combination of factors. Particularly significant will be the issue at hand and the commitment of employees to using the strike weapon to achieve their particular goals. Related factors include the perceived chances of success and the power balance between the parties. Decisions on strike action will be significantly influenced by contextual factors such the business cycle, unemployment levels and inflation.

It should be noted that a decision to take strike action may involve considerable hardship for strikers through lost income and the risk of job loss. Consequently, such action is rarely taken lightly. For the union too, strike action represents a major dilemma: the prospects of success or failure must be weighed up together with implications for union membership, status and finances. Lastly, it is important to note that, despite their headline grabbing status, strikes are relatively rare and many organisations never experience strike action.

An Overview of Irish Strike Patterns

The three key indices used in analysing strike activity are strike frequency (number of strikes occurring in a particular time period), workers involved (number of workers participating in strikes) and mandays lost (number of working days lost due to strike activity). Irish strike figures for the period 1922–86 are given in table 10.3 and the trend according to each key index is represented graphically in figures 10.3A, 10.3B and 10.3C.[26]

These figures indicate an upward movement in strike activity in the 1960s and 1970s with some decline in the 1980s. However, there is a need for caution in interpreting these trends. The level and pattern of strike activity will be influenced by the levels of economic activity (business cycle factors), employment levels (tightness or looseness of the labour market), industrial development, inflation and unionisation. It will also be influenced by sectoral changes in employment (shifts in the employment share of agriculture, industry and services) and the nature and level of collective bargaining (particularly the existence of centrally agreed incomes policies).

Table 10.3. 5-yearly statements of numbers of strikes, workers involved and mandays lost, 1922–86

Period	Number of strikes (A)	Workers involved (B)	Mandays lost (C)
1922–6	471	79,128	2,594,218
1927–31	301	17,876	607,325
1932–6	463	41,520	896,058
1937–41	541	59,750	2,299,418
1942–6	426	35,112	609,196
1947–51	786	91,993	1,742,393
1952–6	401	46,550	962,282
1957–61	299	58,709	800,275
1962–6	418	141,664	2,219,011
1967–71	606	194,100	2,805,715
1972–6	817	168,899	2,038,178
1977–81	712	174,968	3,424,294
1982–6	686	306,388	1,951,079

Source: Teresa Brannick, Aidan Kelly, University College, Dublin.

Fig. 10.3A. Mandays lost 1922–88

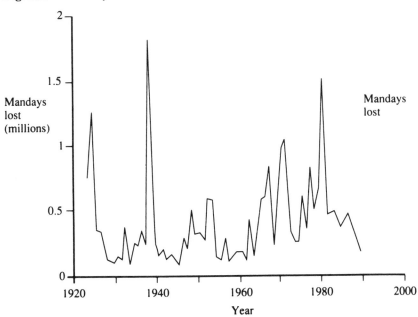

Fig. 10.3B. Workers involved 1922–87

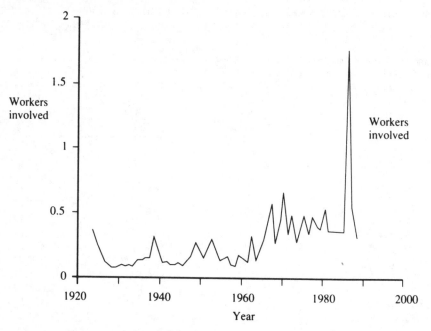

Fig. 10.3C. Strike Frequency 1922–88

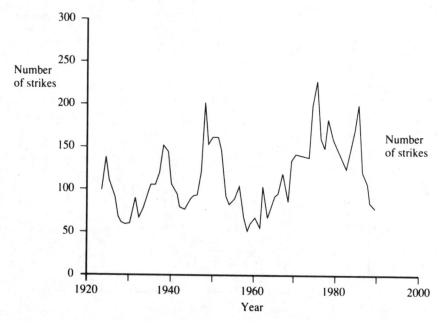

Source: Teresa Brannick, Aidan Kelly, University College, Dublin.

In analysing these trends in Irish strike patterns Kelly and Brannick highlight two important factors: the disproportionate effect of a few large strikes and the varying strike patterns in the public and private sectors.[27]

On the impact of large strikes (which Kelly and Brannick define as strikes resulting in the loss of 30,000 or more days) over the twenty-year period 1960–79, they state:

> Forty three such strikes took place during the past twenty years . . . while these strikes represent only 2 percent of the total for the period they involved a loss of over 5.7 million mandays or 57 percent of all days lost due to strikes over this time. Clearly, the Irish strike pattern is extremely sensitive to this comparatively small number of large strikes and it has been an enduring feature over the twenty-year period. Indeed, should these be removed from the Irish strike quantum the result would be a record which would show a comparatively strike-free nation in terms of workers involved and total mandays lost.[28]

Looking at strike trends in the public and private sectors over this period, Kelly and Brannick find that the private sector has been the source of most strike activity in the 1960–86 period. However, the proportion of strike activity accounted for by the private sector was greatest during the 1960s and has been falling since with a marked increase in the proportion of strike activity accounted for by the public sector over the period (see table 10.4).

Table 10.4. Public and private strike activity as a percentage of total strikes 1960–86

	Strike frequency (%)		Workers involved (%)		Mandays lost (%)	
	Private Sector	Public Sector	Private Sector	Public Sector	Private Sector	Public Sector
1960–69	82.1	17.9	63.5	36.5	75.8	24.2
1970–79	81.7	18.3	67.4	22.6	62.1	37.9
1980–86	72.8	27.2	31.2	68.8	64.1	35.9
1960–86	79.4	20.6	59.3	40.7	67.5	32.5

Source: Kelly, A. & Brannick, T. 'The Changing Contours of Irish Industrial Conflict' UCD 1989 (Unpublished).

In the private sector Kelly and Brannick found that manufacturing was by far the most strike-prone sector.[29] Within this sector they identified significant changes in strike activity which reflected structural changes in Irish industry. Certain industrial sectors, particularly printing and paper and metal and engineering, became increasingly strike prone while others, notably textiles and furniture and woodwork, experienced less strike activity.

The importance of structural and business cycle factors was also evident in Kelly and Brannick's analyses of strike activity among indigenous and foreign-owned organisations.[30] Over the period 1960–86 levels of strike activity in indigenous organisations have fallen significantly. In the same period strike activity in multi-national organisations has increased considerably. Kelly and Brannick found that British-owned organisations were most strike prone.[31] They attribute this to trading difficulties experienced by British companies which resulted in a loss of competitiveness, cost-cutting and lay-offs which ultimately affected employee relations.

In the public sector Kelly and Brannick found that much of the strike activity has been concentrated among a relatively small number of organisations.[32] They identified nine organisations who accounted for 62 percent of all strikes, 85 percent of workers involved and 86 percent of mandays lost in the public sector during the 1960–84 period.

A final issue relating to strike action is the relative impact of official and unofficial strikes. In their study of unofficial strikes in Ireland (1987) Wallace and O'Shea found that there has been a dramatic reduction in unofficial strikes since the mid-1970s (see figure 10.4A).[33] Since 1982 approximately 40 percent of strikes have been unofficial (29 percent in 1987) comparing with an average of 66 percent in the mid 1970s. Since unofficial strikes are normally of shorter duration and involve less employees this has meant that unofficial strikes now account for a very small proportion of mandays lost due to strike activity. In the years 1985 and 1986 the figure was 10 percent and 6 percent respectively (see figure 10.4B).[34]

Other Forms of Overt Industrial Action
Other forms of overt action, though less dramatic, can be equally successful while not involving the hardships of strike action. Go-slows, overtime bans and withdrawal of co-operation may place considerable pressure on management to move towards resolution while protecting employee income and not jeopardising their job security to as great a degree in undertaking strike action. Again, the effectiveness of such measures depends on the organisational context (for instance, an overtime ban is unlikely to meet with much success when order books are empty and production requirements are low). A lock-out by management involves preventing the workforce from attending at work. It represents the equivalent of strike action by employers and should only be contemplated in the most extreme of circumstances.

Conflict Resolution
From the managerial perspective it is important that any conflict which does arise is kept within acceptable limits and is not allowed to damage the employee relations fabric with detrimental consequences for organisational performance.

Fig. 10.4A. Total number of strikes 1976–87

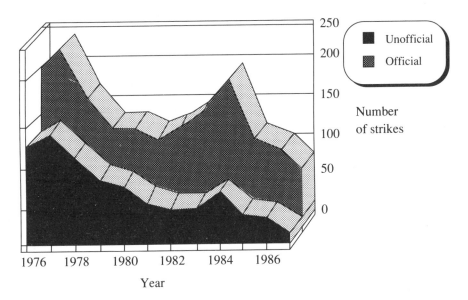

Fig. 10.4B. Working days lost 1976–87

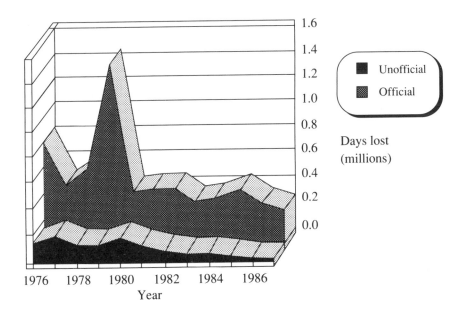

Source: Wallace, J. 'Unofficial Strikes in Ireland', *Industrial Relations News*, nos. 8 & 9 1988.

All levels of management have an important role to play in conflict handling and resolution. An integral part of the line management task is to effectively handle disputes and grievances which arise at shopfloor level. Top management are responsible for the establishment of an organisational climate which fosters and values good employee relations. It should develop effective policies and procedures to handle conflict issues which arise. The specialist personnel function will be responsible for advising top management on optimal employee relations strategies and developing appropriate procedures and practices. It may also provide training, advice and guidance to line management in handling workplace issues. Should a case be referred for mediation or arbitration, the personnel function will generally be responsible for preparing and presenting the management case.

Industrial conflict can have certain positive effects. It allows employees to highlight issues of concern and facilitates change and development in the employment relationship. Possibly the most widespread response to conflict has been the development of joint mechanisms to discuss and resolve differences. Such institutionalisation of conflict involves the development of agreed practices and procedures for handling issues and is most clearly manifested in the significance of collective bargaining and trade union organisation.[35]

The institutionalisation of conflict through the development of appropriate procedures reflects a tacit acceptance that issues of conflict will arise. It strives to create a framework through which the parties can interact, argue, disagree and agree while allowing for the ongoing operation of the business. Employee relations procedures of various kinds have over the last two decades become a permanent feature of workplace employee relations in Ireland. These may vary between organisations but will generally provide for the orderly resolution of grievances, disputes, and disciplinary issues and provide an operating framework for management-union negotiations.

Handling Grievances and Disputes

The bulk of workplace grievances and disputes will be handled at shopfloor level by line management. However, it is important that organisations have a formal procedure outlining the stages through which grievances and disputes should be processed. Such procedures often form part of a procedural agreement and reflect management and union commitment to the peaceful, orderly and speedy resolution of any issues raised by employees.

Differing terminology is often used to describe disputes and grievance procedures with 'grievance procedures' referring to issues raised by individual employees and 'disputes procedures' covering more broadly-based claims by all or a substantial section of the workforce. In practice, both terms are used interchangeably with any differences only applying to the level at which an issue enters the procedure.[36]

Trigger issues: grievances or disputes may arise from issues involving either an individual employee or a group of employees. Humphrey suggests that an individual employee's problems at work fall into two categories, personal and work-related.[37]

Personal problems may only concern the organisation where they influence work performance. For example, a domestic problem might detrimentally affect that employee's performance or attendance. In such situations the organisation should be both supportive and concerned.

All employees will, at some time, have issues which cause them concern at work. Should employees have problems which they wish to raise with management these should be handled as expeditiously as possible. Line managers must be aware of the importance of this task and be prepared to listen to and act on employee grievances. The non-handling of grievances gives rise to frustration which can permeate through to other employees and promote an uneasy working environment in which disputes and poor employee relations can arise.

Disputes normally refer to collective issues raised by a group of employees (often through their trade union) which warrant the attention of management.

It would be unreasonable to expect an organisation to anticipate all potential disputes and grievances; the number which can arise is infinite (for example, overtime allocation, unsafe conditions, inadequate canteen facilities or holiday rostering). However, it is possible for management to take measures which facilitate the effective handling of such issues. In this regard a number of key guidelines are suggested as follows:

a) management should make every effort to understand the nature of, and the reasons for, disputes and grievances;

b) management should establish a policy which sets out an orderly and effective framework for handling disputes and grievances;

c) all levels of management should be aware of the key influence which grievance handling has on employee relations and company performance generally;

d) line management, particularly first-level supervision, must be aware of their key role in effective grievance handling.

An initial step is for management to try and understand the nature of disputes and grievances. This facilitates an appreciation of the wide variety of issues which can cause disputes and grievances and highlights the importance of prevention. A useful approach is to analyse the conditions which are most likely to give rise to serious disputes and grievances. These might include poor working conditions, unsafe work practices, discrimination, job insecurity, inadequate wages and unrealistic rules and regulations. Of course, the list is endless and is particular to the organisation concerned. However, the prime concern of management should be to develop policies and procedures which eliminate the conditions leading to disputes or grievances.

Grievance/Dispute Procedures: developing formal procedures in any area of employee relations involves establishing a framework for handling particular issues and inevitably involves some potential drawbacks. However, a degree of procedural formalisation is necessary if key employee relations issues are to be effectively and consistently handled.[38] Hawkins highlights a number of benefits of procedural formality such as increased clarity, prevention of misunderstandings and arguments over interpretation, ease of communication, and increased fairness and consistency in application.[39]

Management approaches to handling grievances and disputes will be influenced by the overall corporate approach to workforce management. Differences in approach will result in varying organisational policies and practices. A example of one company's policy is outlined in box 10.1.

Box 10.1. Sample company policy on disputes/grievances
(pharmaceutical company)

The company recognises that employees have a legitimate interest in the affairs of the enterprise and thus have a right to be concerned and informed about issues which affect them.

Employees have a right to bring matters which concern them to the attention of management.

Management and employee opinions may be at variance on occasion. In such instances management will strive to understand the employee(s) viewpoint, explain the management position and seek a mutually acceptable solution.

Management will give consideration to matters brought to their attention by employees and action these matters in an appropriate, effective and equitable manner.

Most problems or complaints raised by employees should be handled by the immediate supervisor without recourse to a formal disputes and grievance procedure. However, issues will inevitably arise which warrant more thorough consideration. These may be handled through a more formal written and agreed procedure. A grievance and disputes procedure will normally be in writing. It should be simple and easy to operate and aim to handle disputes and grievances fairly and consistently.

Such procedures are often hierarchical in nature. This allows employees to process their grievance through progressively higher levels of management and, ultimately, to external conciliation or arbitration. A sample grievance and disputes procedure in a unionised organisation is given in box 10.2. The same principles would apply in non-union organisations. Indeed, it is possibly more important that non-unionised firms have effective grievance and disputes procedures since employees in these organisations may have less support in processing issues. Many of the larger non-unionised companies place considerable emphasis on the prompt and effective handling of employee grievances.

Box 10.2. Sample grievance and disputes procedure (engineering company)			
Stage	Nature of grievance/claim	Procedural level	
		Management	Employees/ trade union
1.	Grievance concerning local work rules or employment conditions affecting an individual or small work group	Immediate superior	Employee(s) concerned
2.	(a) Any issue which has remained unresolved at stage 1 (b) Grievance or claim where the issue has direct implications for a group of workers on a departmental or section basis	Department section manager	Employee(s) concerned & shop steward
3.	(a) Any issue which has gone though the appropriate lower stages unresolved (b) Grievance or claim with company-wide implications	Personnel manager & line management	Employee(s) concerned or/and employee representatives including union official
4.	An unresolved issue which has been through the appropriate lower stages	Third party investigation: rights commissioner/labour court conciliation	
5.	Any issue which remains unresolved after stage 4	Full labour court investigation/ employment appeals tribunal	

In operating such procedures it is generally agreed that grievance and dispute issues are best handled as near their source as possible, with the major responsibility resting with line management. Grievances and disputes should also be resolved as speedily as possible. Delays in handling issues can become an additional source of agitation. Consequently, it may be advisable to operate time limits which are both realistic (allowing reasonable time and opportunity to handle the issues adequately) and fair (avoiding unnecessary delay and frustration).

Role of management: both management and employees (including trade unions) should be fully committed to the procedure and know how to operate and enforce it. The specialist personnel function has an important role to play in establishing effective procedures, monitoring their operation, dealing with more serious issues and helping line management to handle issues in their area. This involves ensuring that line managers have adequate skills and knowledge to carry out their role effectively.

The vast majority of grievances and disputes issues arise at employee-supervisor level. Management must ensure that most of these issues are solved at this level. It is also important that senior management delegate adequate authority so that supervisors can handle issues raised at their level. Equally, supervisors must be willing and able to take action on issues at this level, thus preventing their further progression in the procedure. When an issue is raised at the appropriate managerial level, the first task is to listen carefully and understand. Responding impulsively or pre-judging the issue without having the full facts should be avoided. Although managers may not attach as much importance to the issue as the employee(s) concerned, they should appreciate that if employees feel strongly enough to raise issues in the first place then they equally merit that management listen, understand and take appropriate action as necessary.

Unless the issue is very straightforward, the manager concerned should take time to consider the issue, consult other people as necessary and respond to the employee within a reasonable time period. Responses to employee grievances should take account of the implications of other employees, the extent to which a precedent is being created and consistency with company policy. The manager involved should ensure that any responses are correct in the circumstances and explain these to employees. If the response is negative the further stages in the procedure should be outlined.

Informality is an inherent part of workplace employee relations and will continue to play a key role even where adequate procedures are established. Procedures help management and employees to deal with contentious issues in an orderly fashion. On occasion issues may arise which need a different approach from that set down by procedure. For example, an employee may be reluctant to raise a personal problem with his supervisor. Should an issue merit action by a more senior manager or the personnel function this should be done. Procedures should not prohibit these informal but useful inter-actions. However, such departures from procedure should be an exception and the role of the supervisor should be maintained in handling the great majority of workplace issues.

Adequate record keeping is another important aspect in the effective handling of disputes and grievances. Some written records need to be maintained which progress above the first stage in a procedure. Some organisations require that issues entering the procedure above the first stage must be served in writing with details of the issue and the employee(s) concerned. This helps to clarify the exact nature of the claim or grievance and helps to avoid misunderstandings. Such records also provide management with useful information on trends and the effectiveness of procedures. However, management should avoid unnecessary red tape.

External referral: where the parties fail to find a solution at organisation level, the issue may be referred to a third party for resolution. The various third party institutions were considered earlier. Conciliation normally refers to the introduction of a third party who tries to guide the parties towards a solution but does not make a final decision. Arbitration involves referral to a third party who makes a final decision on the merits of the case.[40]

In Ireland most arbitration decisions are non-binding, though there are exceptions (for example, certain Labour Court decisions such as an equality officer's decision, and in areas of the public sector). Arbitration involves the evaluation of both parties' positions and the issuing of a decision based on their respective merits. More recently there seems to be some interest in pendulum-type arbitrations, which involves choosing either of the final positions of the parties. This approach is based on the rationale that traditional arbitration does not encourage the conflicting parties to compromise prior to third party referral, whereas the pendulum variety encourages them to take more reasonable positions which give the greatest chance of winning the arbitrator's approval.

It has been accepted practice that organisations refer cases externally only when all internal efforts have been unsuccessful. However, John Horgan, a former Chairman of the Labour Court, feels that increases in the number of cases being referred externally (particularly to the Labour Court) reflects a greater reluctance on behalf of managements and unions to compromise at local level. He feels this has resulted in an over-reliance on third parties which, he suggests, is bad for industrial relations.[41]

Grievance and disputes procedures normally contain a provision that no form of industrial action be taken by either party until all stages of the procedure have been exhausted, and that even then a period of notice be given before such action is initiated. Effectively operated, this ensures that both parties have ample opportunity of settling issues either through direct discussion or third party referral. Such terms should not be used to delay unreasonably the processing of claims and grievances as this may give rise to employee frustration, resulting in breaches of procedure and, possibly, unofficial action.[42] Lastly, it should be noted that workplace procedures are merely a facilitator of good employee relations and will be of little use where the basic employee relations climate is poor.[43]

DISCIPLINE ADMINISTRATION

As with disputes and grievances, the issue of disciplinary procedures and their administration is an inherent aspect of workplace employee relations. Organisations will seek to establish and maintain acceptable standards or norms in areas like employee performance, conduct, etc. When employees breach such standards management will, ultimately, seek to take some form of disciplinary action. However, discipline should not just be looked upon in the narrow punitive context of the need to discipline transgressors. The wider organisational and legal context should also be taken into account.

Legal Context

The law places various constraints on how discipline should be administered in organisations. The fundamental principles of natural justice constrain the behaviour of management in instigating discipline. These fundamental principles require that:

 i) there should be a basic understanding of what constitutes a transgression; therefore company rules and standards should be clearly outlined and communicated;

 ii) the consequences of breaching such rules and standards should be clear;

 iii) employees not achieving the required standards should be so informed and given the opportunity to improve where possible;

 iv) employees who are alleged to have breached discipline are entitled to fair and consistent treatment, including the opportunity to state their case, access to representation and a right to appeal to a higher authority.

Apart from the above principles, changes in employment law have substantially altered the area of discipline administration. Along with the extension of collective bargaining, the legal framework now ensures that employees and trade unions play an important role in discipline administration at work.[44] In relation to legislative change the Unfair Dismissals Act 1977 has been the major influencing factor. It requires that employers have a formal disciplinary procedure, lays down guidelines as to what constitutes fair and unfair dismissal, and provides a mechanism for dealing with claims of unfair dismissal and deciding upon redress for those found to be unfairly dismissed.

Disciplinary Procedures

Case law on unfair dismissal has indicated that for a particular dismissal to be held as fair it must normally be preceded by the application of an acceptable disciplinary procedure, particularly where the offence was one which would not warrant instant or summary dismissal. The principles of natural justice allied to legislative change require that organisations must have some formal disciplinary procedure in operation, ensure employees are familiar with its contents and apply this procedure in a reasonable way.

In developing a disciplinary procedure the first area of concern to the organisation is outlining company rules and standards. The Advisory Conciliation and Arbitration Service (ACAS) Code of Practice (UK) suggests that workplace rules are necessary to ensure consistency in the treatment of employees and to help the firm to operate effectively.[45] Their major contribution is in establishing standards of conduct at work which employees are expected to adhere to and in helping to ensure equity in dealing with employees who fail to achieve these standards. The central responsibility for discipline administration lies with management. It is their task to establish workplace rules and standards. Employees and their representative organisations should be consulted in this process.

It is difficult to specify how far the organisation can go in outlining rules and standards. The primary consideration must be the nature of the enterprise. It would be impossible to cover all the possible transgressions that might occur so that stated rules and standards can only outline general areas or deal with specific common transgressions. This is clearly acceptable, as very often rules can only be indicative of the type of offences which will lead to discipline. However, management should be as precise as possible—as the ACAS code states, 'rules should not be so general as to be meaningless'.[46]

A preliminary step is to spell out those rules and standards where breaches may lead to dismissal in the first instance.[47] Again, every possible offence cannot be forecast, but examples might include theft, violence, interference with clock cards or criminal offences. Offences which might warrant summary dismissal in a particular organisation but might not do so elsewhere should be clearly highlighted, such as hygiene rules in a food processing firm, or confidentiality where research and development is carried on. Case law indicates that instant dismissal (without a hearing or investigation) is extremely difficult to initiate fairly. Where a serious offence occurs, it is generally recommended that the employee be suspended pending a thorough investigation and hearing. After this investigation appropriate disciplinary action may be initiated.

Secondly, management should outline those rules and standards where breaches would lead to the operation of a standard disciplinary procedure (such as lateness, absenteeism, inadequate work performance). The details of such procedures should be given to all employees. Apart from serious misconduct, most breaches of discipline will lead to the application of a standard disciplinary procedure, an example of which is given in box 10.3.

Box 10.3. Sample disciplinary procedure

Preamble: the following disciplinary procedure will be used to deal with all breaches of company rules and standards except where the offences or transgression constitute gross misconduct.

The primary aim of this procedure is to help employees whose conduct or performance falls below company requirements to achieve the necessary improvements. It is desirable both in contributing to company success and the fair treatment of employees. It is company policy to apply this procedure as reasonably as possible and to ensure consistency and order in its application. It will apply to all breaches of company rules or standards not constituting gross misconduct which may typically include, but are not limited to, the following:

i) Bad time-keeping	*ii)* Unauthorised absence
iii) Lack of co-operation	*iv)* Unacceptable work performance
v) Poor attendance	*vi)* Breaches of safety regulations

Procedure:

a) in the first instance the individual will be asked to attend a Counselling Interview by his supervisor where the employee's transgression will be made clear, the standard of performance required outlined and the employee verbally reprimanded.

b) in the second instance the employee will receive a Verbal Warning at a formal meeting with his supervisor and department manager, where details of the misdemeanor and the consequences of further offences will be outlined.

c) in the third instance the employee will receive a final written warning from the personnel manager at a meeting with the personnel manager, the department manager and, if appropriate, the supervisor, where the employee will be informed of the details of the offence, future performance standards required and that further offences will lead to suspension or dismissal.

d) in the last instance the employee will either be suspended without pay or dismissed (depending on the offence), notice of which will be given to the employee at a meeting with the General Manager where the offence will be outlined both verbally and in writing and the employee advised of his right of appeal.

Gross misconduct: gross misconduct is conduct of such a serious nature that the company could not tolerate keeping the employee in employment and it is hoped that such instances will not occur. However, for the mutual protection of the company and its workforce, any employee found guilty of gross misconduct may be dismissed summarily. Examples of gross misconduct include:

i) Violation of a criminal law	*ii)* Consumption or possession of alcohol or illegal drugs
iii) Threats or acts of physical violence	*iv)* Theft from another employee or from the company
v) Malicious damage to company property	*vi)* Falsifying company records (including clock cards)

Before any action is taken the company will thoroughly investigate the case, during which time the employee will be suspended. After such investigation the employee will attend a meeting with company management where she/he will have an opportunity to state his case and be advised of his right of appeal. Should the company still feel the employee was guilty of gross misconduct he will be dismissed and given a letter outlining the nature of the offence and reasons for dismissal.

Disciplinary procedures should be: (1) agreed, (2) fair, (3) understood, and (4) applied consistently. These and other operational aspects of discipline administration are discussed below.

Warnings: managers will engage in the ongoing coaching and counselling of employees as part of their daily supervisory role. This may occasionally involve verbally reprimanding employees. However, where the facts point to the need for more formal disciplinary action management should adhere to the disciplinary procedure and adopt the prescribed practice of giving a disciplinary warning. Such warnings should outline the offence, explain how the employee can effect improvement in a reasonable timescale and clearly outline the consequences of further transgressions. Management should take any reasonable measures which might facilitate improvement. Warnings should normally be in writing and be given to the employee and their representative (if appropriate).

The length of time warnings should remain on an employee's record will depend on the nature of the offence and company rules and practice. Minor warnings will have a shorter timescale than those for more serious issues, but defining specific guidelines poses difficulties. The ACAS code of practice suggests that warnings should be 'disregarded after a specific period of satisfactory conduct' but does not indicate any guidelines.[48] Hawkins is more specific suggesting that verbal warnings remain on an employee's record for six months, written warnings for twelve months and for very serious offences a period of two years or more.[49] Many organisations do not specify limits but, in practice, allow warnings to lapse after a reasonable period of satisfactory performance.

Representation: a basic ingredient of procedural fairness and equity in discipline administration is the employee's right to adequate representation (either a fellow-employee or trade union representative as appropriate). Management should also be aware of the need for independence in discipline administration. Where issues reach a serious stage at least two management representatives should be present to ensure correct and consistent application of rules and procedures. The personnel practitioner can play an important role here.

Record keeping: accurate records should be kept of all disciplinary issues. At counselling interview stage a brief note of the issue, the individual concerned, the date and the nature of the discussion would suffice. At verbal, written, and all subsequent stages records should be more elaborate. This is particularly important at and above final warning stage, where it should be clearly documented that the employee was informed of the seriousness of the issue and the fact that future offences may lead to dismissal.

At each stage a written record of the nature of the issue, the date, the action taken and the reasons should be given to the employee for his retention. A copy which has been signed by the employee (as evidence that he received and understood the letter) should be placed on his personal file. A copy should also be given to the employee's representative, the trade union (if appropriate) and to the manager(s) involved.

Much of this work will be the responsibility of the specialist personnel function. The importance of accurate record keeping in the administration of discipline cannot be over-emphasised. Since the Unfair Dismissals Act 1977 places the burden of proof primarily on the employer, companies must be able to back up reasons for discipline with substantial documentary evidence.

Appeal: one of the basic principles of natural justice is that employees subject to discipline have the right of appeal to somebody not directly involved.[50] The major obligation on management is to thoroughly investigate the case and make a fair decision based on the facts. If the employee is not satisfied with such a decision he should have the right of appeal to a higher level of management or external arbitration. Indeed management should remind employees of their right of appeal during disciplinary meetings and the appropriate procedures for lodging such an appeal.

Handling disciplinary meetings: when a disciplinary matter arises management should thoroughly investigate the circumstances and establish the facts of the incident. This may involve talking to the employee(s) involved and any witnesses, examining relevant records, reviewing the employee's file, etc. Impulsive action should be avoided. However, if, after a thorough investigation, management decide that disciplinary action is merited, a meeting should be arranged with the employee(s) concerned.

The purpose of a disciplinary interview is to assess culpability, decide on appropriate action and attempt to effect the desired change in employee behaviour. It allows employees to present their point of view which helps give a comprehensive picture of the case and to facilitate constructive discussion of the issue. In conducting disciplinary interviews the following factors merit careful consideration:

a) *Who?* Management should decided who carries out the interview (supervisor at initial levels; senior management involvement later) and consider the role of employee representatives.

b) *Where?* Interviews should generally be conducted away from the shopfloor, at an appropriate time with sufficient notice.

c) *What?* The person responsible for conducting the interview should ensure that management have established the relevant facts before the interview and have available any information pertinent to the case. Such information might include details of the employee's job and the incident, information on the employee(s) concerned (background, records etc.).

Conducting the interview: the disciplinary interview should be treated as a problem solving exercise with objective of positively influencing employee behaviour. Management representatives have the primary responsibility for effectively conducting the interview. This involves stating management's position and attitude to the issue; advising employees of their rights; encouraging them to fully outline their views; facilitating discussion through open-ended questions; probing any grey areas and remaining calm and unemotional at all stages. Disciplinary interviews should be approached with an open mind. Only after establishing the facts and discussing the issue with the employee(s) are management in a position to decide on appropriate action. The employee's perspective may throw new light on the incident and management may need to get additional information or call for an adjournment.

Should the meeting point towards disciplinary action, management's position should be explained to the employee who should be made fully aware of his shortcomings and management's concern. The nature of improvement and the means for its achievement should be outlined, as should the consequences of future transgressions. Management must ensure that the employee fully understands the discipline imposed and the right of appeal.

After the interview, the details should be recorded accurately and a copy given to the employee(s) concerned (and their representative as necessary). Any commitments entered into should be carried out promptly. In the longer term the total process should be monitored from a number of viewpoints (impact on employee behaviour, trends in disciplinary incidents, effectiveness of various forms of discipline).

Management Approaches

Management should approach the area of discipline administration in a positive vein with the overall objective being to change employee behaviour. The personnel function has an important role to play in establishing disciplinary policy and related procedures and in monitoring their application throughout the organisation. Two key factors which need to be kept in mind are the need for reasonableness and consistency. In his study of unofficial strikes, Wallace notes that employees often expect management to act leniently in disciplinary matters so that the introduction of a more strict managerial approach often causes problems.[51] This highlights the need to take consistently similar approaches in disciplinary matters so that accusations of favouritism or purges cannot be forwarded with any justification. Equally, employers should act reasonably in the circumstances. This infers that every disciplinary situation be carefully evaluated, taking account of any special considerations or mitigating circumstances. Every issue is different; an employee may have developed a bad time-keeping record for a very legitimate reason (such as difficult family circumstances) and managerial decisions should reflect such considerations.

In general, it seems that the impact of unfair dismissals legislation on employers has been largely favourable. There has been a fall-off in levels of strike activity resulting from dismissals since the introduction of the 1977 Act.[52] It would also seem to have encouraged management to adopt appropriate disciplinary procedures and practices. O'Connor found that managements were now exercising greater care when recruiting, evaluating employee performance more closely and generally adopting a more systematic approach to handling discipline.[53] This 'learning effect' may be partially reflected in the increased number of Employment Appeals Tribunal decisions favouring employees.

Another factor is the continued significance of collective bargaining as a mechanism for processing dismissal matters.[54] This is particularly so where the union case is strong and might infer that cases allowed to proceed to the Tribunal are often weak from the union standpoint or deal with non-unionised employees (many professional and managerial grades, for example).[55] Indeed, it would seem that the legislation has not greatly increased the job security of employees since reinstatement or re-engagement is awarded in only a minority of cases.[56]

HEALTH, SAFETY AND WELFARE

Irish industry experiences a number of fatal accidents and several thousand reported accidents annually.[57] Employers are responsible for the wellbeing of their employees and should be aware of the need to develop policies and practices which help to protect workers against employment-related hazards.[58] In particular, emphasis should be concentrated on preventing potential health and safety problems by identifying hazards, taking effective safety precautions and, where accidents, occur, taking effective remedial action.

Table 10.5. Industrial deaths/accidents 1982–7

Year	Deaths	Notifiable accidents
1982	16	4671
1983	14	3874
1984	15	3825
1985	18	3580
1986	12	3310
1987	12	3048

Source: Department of Labour 1988.

The Legal Context

Health, safety and welfare at work is a very complex legal area comprising various components including common law, statute law and related statutory instruments, and custom and practice. Particularly significant are the obligations imposed on employers at common law. One of the major common law obligations on employers is that they must exercise 'reasonable care' towards employees and guard against any reasonably forseeable injury or disease. This common law duty of 'reasonable care' involves a duty on employers to provide the following:

 i) Safe system of work: including layout, work practices, etc;
 ii) Safe place of work: safe, well-maintained premises;
 iii) Safe plant & machinery: equipment, tools, etc;
 iv) Safe/competent workforce: i.e. employees;
 v) Adequate supervision: including enforcement of safety rules.

These common law obligations form part of the contract of employment. Should an employer fail to fulfil any of these common law duties and as a result an employee is injured (or becomes ill) that employer may be sued for compensation arising out of their negligence.[59] Since it is sometimes difficult for employers to defend such cases successfully, prevention through progressive safety policies is by far the best option.

While common law provisions extend to all contracts of employment, statute law in the area of health and safety is primarily concerned with manufacturing industry, although particular acts may concentrate on other areas of employment (such as offices or mines). Factory workers enjoy the greatest protection, with the principal act being the Factories Act of 1955, amended by the Safety in Industry Act 1980 (read jointly as Safety in Industry Acts 1955 and 1980).

Much statute law is essentially enabling legislation, giving the Minister power to subsequently introduce statutory instruments detailing various health, safety and welfare provisions. This is especially important under the Safety in Industry Acts 1955 and 1980, with statutory instruments covering areas like drinking water and washing facilities (SI No.33, 1959) and lighting (SI 96, 1959). These Acts constitute by far the most comprehensive pieces of legislation dealing with health, safety and welfare at work in this country. This legislation contains numerous provisions for implementation in industrial-type employments.

These include an obligation on employers to exhibit an abstract (or summary) of the legislation and to report immediately all 'notifiable accidents' (that is, any accident which causes loss of life or disables workers for more than three days from performing their normal job) to the Minister for Labour. Employers are required to maintain a 'general register' which is a type of official log book where details of the number of employees aged less than eighteen, records of regular cleaning and maintenance, and all notifiable accidents are recorded. The legislation specifies that employers must bear the cost of statutory safety precautions and not make deduction from wages.

In relation to employees, the legislation requires that workers take reasonable care of their own and others' safety and co-operate with the employer in complying with any legal regulations. They must not intentionally interfere with or misuse anything provided for their health, safety or welfare and must use any clothing, appliance, etc. provided.

Safety Committees and Representatives

A major change introduced by the Safety in Industry Act 1980 was the obligation on organisations to have safety committees or representatives. Despite an energetic campaign by the National Industrial Safety Organisation (NISO), the voluntary system of safety committees encouraged by the 1955 Factories Act never really took off. The 1980 Act made mandatory the use of a safety representative or a safety committee, with the emphasis on a more consultative approach, giving committees an opportunity to assist management in establishing safety policy.

Organisations employing more than twenty employees must appoint a safety committee comprised of management and employee representatives, whilst smaller organisations may have a safety committee or a safety representative. There are guidelines on the frequency and duration of meetings, membership criteria, quorum and facilities required, and the maintenance of written records.

The main objectives of safety committees and representatives are to facilitate workplace co-operation and communication on health, safety and welfare matters, and to agree on the content and application of the organisation's safety statement. The safety statement is a general policy statement setting out the means by which health and safety are to be secured. It should be prepared in all organisations employing more than ten persons and include any arrangements for safeguarding health and safety, the co-operation required from employees, duties of any safety officers, details of safety training programmes or facilities and the measures to be taken in relation to specific hazards and dangers.

Responsibility for the enforcement of health and safety legislation primarily rests with the Industrial Inspectorate, whose representatives regularly visit companies to inspect and advise on health and safety matters. Inspectors are empowered to enter, inspect and examine factories and there are penalties for obstruction or delay. Firms should ensure they have regular visits from their factory inspector, particularly at start-up stage. Inspectors are empowered to prosecute organisations not fulfilling their statutory obligations and, exceptionally, the Minister may prohibit all activities in an organisation pending the removal of a particularly serious health or safety hazard.

More radical changes in Irish health and safety legislation are proposed in the Health, Safety and Welfare at Work Bill 1988.[60] In addition to the present safety legislation which applies mainly to industrial workers, this new Bill proposes to extend cover to practically all categories of employees including shops, hospitals, transport, farmers and other self-employed persons. It also proposes a new National Authority for Occupational Safety and Health with a board consisting of trade union, employer and government representatives.[61]

Role of Management[62]
The primary responsibility for the prevention of accidents, health risks and the enforcement of relevant regulations rests first and foremost with management. Particular emphasis should be placed on identifying causes of accidents and the conditions under which they are most likely to occur. A breakdown of the causes of notifiable accidents (1983–4) as recorded by the Department of Labour is outlined in figure 10.5:

Fig. 10.5. Causes of accidents 1983–4

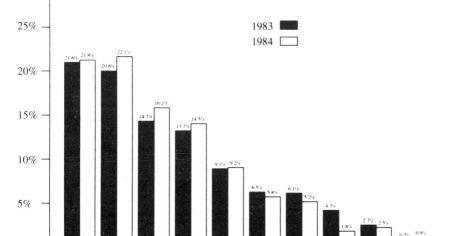

Source: Labour Inspection Report 1983–4, Government Publications Office

Ideally, health and safety considerations should be incorporated into management decision-making with account taken of health and safety factors at design stage. It is management's responsibility to carry out regular inspections and take appropriate action to eliminate health and safety risks. Accidents should be investigated and appropriate measures taken to prevent their recurrence. The maintenance of adequate records and statistics helps to identify problem areas. Management also need to conduct a continuous programme of education and training on safe working practices and generally provide a healthy and safe environment, including the design of safety equipment and provision of protective equipment. Arnscott and Armstrong identify a number of basic procedures that management can use

---

Box 10.4. Procedures for improved safety management

1.	Procedure for approval of new machines, processes & materials
2.	Rules for handling/using/storing substances
3.	Training arrangements for new employees/transferees
4.	Informing employees, contractors, visitors, etc. of safety rules
5.	Licensing of drivers of internal factory vehicles
6.	Action to be taken in the event of accident or emergency
7.	Arrangements for medical examinations
8.	Procedures for safety inspections and checks
9.	First Aid and medical arrangements available on site
10.	Maintenance of accident records and statistics
11.	Accident and incident reporting procedure
12.	Rules on the use of personal safety equipment
13.	Regular maintenance of plant and machinery
14.	Implementation of an effective housekeeping plan
15.	System of permits to work in specified areas

---

as summarised in box 10.4:[63]

Another useful mechanism in ensuring more effective health and safety management is to develop a system for monitoring health and safety hazards so that action can be taken before accidents occur. It is unrealistic to assume that all hazards can be predicted; some may arise due to lack of technical knowledge or maybe the circumstances causing hazards are not accurately recognised. More often, hazards may result simply from people not considering the implications of their actions. In some cases, certain hazard levels become socially acceptable, such as motor car accidents. To prevent hazards creating accidents it is necessary to carry out regular inspections which may comprise some or all of the following:

a) Safety audits: preparation of checklists and a programme designed to check these out at regular intervals;

b) Spot checks: random checks to cover special problems such as poor use of protective clothing or safety equipment;

c) Daily checks: often conducted by supervisors to check safety points in the areas under their control;

d) Regular inspections: may relate to specific areas, such as boilers, pressure vessels, pipelines, dangerous processes, lifts, etc.

There is a danger that involving direct supervision in all inspections may result in their developing a 'perceptional blindness' to hazards in their area. Here a system of checklists can be helpful. It may also be useful to use members of the safety committee to conduct some of the different inspection methods. Involvement of employees in safety inspections may help increase employee interest in and awareness of safety matters. A good working environment is possibly the single most significant factor in promoting health and safety at work. Bad working conditions (noise, light, dirt, etc.), although not necessarily causing accidents, can lead to tension and frustration resulting in accidents. Related factors contributing to higher levels of accidents include speed of production, age (extreme ends of working life), fatigue and boredom. Walsh and Russell's study of accidents in the UK revealed a small group of causes and concluded that three key factors contributed to such accidents: ignorance, lack of discipline and poor communications.[64]

Employee Involvement

Since health and safety is a major consideration for employees they should be afforded every opportunity to participate in the construction and implementation of relevant policies and practices. Safety committees provide an important mechanism for such joint involvement. A major advantage of safety committees is in facilitating a dialogue with employees on safety, health and welfare issues. An effective safety committee can help to harness the support and co-operation of employees, both in forming and implementing the safety policy and in ensuring regular consultation on safety matters. Its primary role should be to advise on the development of sound working practices.

However, management are primarily responsible for maintaining a safe place of work and this responsibility cannot be passed to the safety committee. The activities of the safety committee must not replace, or be seen to replace, normal management channels. Safety is a key part of a manager's job and reporting of hazardous conditions or practices should be dealt with on the spot with the immediate supervisor and never 'stored up' for safety committee meetings. Safety committees should concentrate on detecting hazards before the event or through trends revealed by the accumulated records, rather than duplicating the investigation of individual accidents at the expense of a more long-term view. It is the prevention of future accidents rather than apportioning the blame for past accidents which is the main objective.

EMPLOYEE PARTICIPATION

It has been suggested earlier that structure of industrial organisations, with the support of our legal and business system, has traditionally placed decision-making power in the hands of employers. Since the foundation of this system, various initiatives have been taken to increase employee involvement in managerial decision-making. Such involvement may range from the relatively superficial level of management informing employees of decisions which affect them, to consultation with employees on certain decisions or joint participation in the actual decision-making process.

These participative initiatives may result in a variety of institutional arrangements to facilitate employee participation at workplace level, such as suggestion schemes, joint consultative committees, works councils, quality circles and board level participation. Employee participation can also be facilitated through the collective bargaining process when attempts to lessen the sphere of managerial prerogative and make more issues subject to joint negotiation and agreement are made.

Employee participation may be broadly interpreted as incorporating any mechanisms designed to increase employee input into managerial decision-making. It is based on the concept that those who are involved in an organisation are entitled to share in decisions which affect them. It is sometimes seen as the political democratisation of the workplace in so far as it facilitates the redistribution of decision-making power within organisations.[65]

The movement for increased employee participation has its roots in early attempts to achieve worker control dating from the industrial revolution period in the UK.[66] These initiatives were based on a rejection of a new economic order based on capitalism and wage labour (which from the Marxist perspective created worker alienation and frustration as a result of divisions of labour, the removal of discretion and responsibility from the individual worker and the creation of hostile social classes). The movement for workers' control and self-management highlights an important element in the worker participation debate: whether it should aim at achieving a new economic order through re-drawing the decision-making mechanisms within organisations or try to bring about greater employee participation within the current structure of industrial organisations. It now seems that most developments in employee participation are along the latter route.[67]

Developments in employee participation have taken varying directions and proceeded at different paces in different countries. With the demise of the early movements for workers' control, participation achieved its most concrete form through the extension of collective bargaining as evidenced, for example, by the establishment of joint councils for collective bargaining and consultation in Britain after the First World War. More extensive developments took place in the post-Second World War era with various institutional arrangements developed to further employee participation in a number of European countries. Mulvey distinguishes between those countries where such arrangements were given statutory support (West Germany, Yugoslavia) and those where they were based on collective agreements (Norway, Sweden, Denmark).[68]

Most of the recent focus of the employee participation debate has taken place at European Community (EC) level, where various policy documents have concentrated on board-level participation and disclosure of financial information. Initial proposals through the first draft of the European Company Statute proposed a two-tier board system along West German lines, with the senior supervisory board having one-third employee representatives. It also dealt with the role of works councils and information disclosure. The Draft Fifth Directive also favoured the two-tier board system, with employee participation on the supervisory board. The EC Green Paper on Employee Participation and Company Structure represented a more flexible approach, and reflected widespread opposition to the imposition of structures deemed contrary to some traditional national systems. It suggested that the worker director route was only one option in extending employee participation and, while believing that the two-tier approach of the Fifth Directive represented the optimal solution, proposed flexibility in developing transitional arrangements. At the same time the Vredling Directive on employee rights to information disclosure recommended that multi-national companies must consult and inform employees in subsidiaries of their plans and decisions. Additionally, other proposals have demanded the provision of financial information through consolidated accounts. While many of these proposals remain at a fairly tentative stage they have immense implications for management structures and employee relations generally, and represent some major departures from traditional arrangements in Irish organisations.

The employee participation debate really only took off in Ireland after our entry into the European Community. This resulted in much discussion and activity throughout the 1970s and early 1980s. This surge of interest was most clearly manifested in the passing of the Worker Participation (State Enterprises) Act 1977 which introduced board-level participation to seven semi-state companies. This Act was extended to a number of other State organisations under the terms of the Worker Participation (State Enterprises) Act 1988.

Options in Participation

The variety of institutional arrangements adopted in different countries and by different organisations reflect different philosophies and approaches to employee participation. Variations may stem from a variety of reasons such as the structure and development of collective bargaining, the attitude of management and trade unions or the political philosophy of government. Participation may be supported by the law or may be established through collective agreements and may be minimal or extensive. It is possible to identify three differing types of participation, each varying in both the level and nature of participation.

a) Representative participation: this form of participation has been the focus of most attention and applies to institutionalised arrangements which give employees an input into management decision-making, sometimes with statutory support. The most obvious example is provision for the election of worker directors to the board of management. It also applies to lower-level participation such as joint consultative committees and works councils. Many of these initiatives stem from EC proposals on employee participation and are based on favourable continental experiences with worker directors and works councils.

Board-level representation in Ireland has been largely restricted to the initial seven (now nine) semi-state bodies nominated in the Worker Participation (State Enterprises) Act, 1977. In evaluating the operation of worker directors under the terms of the 1977 Act, Kelly suggests that the experience has been 'broadly successful'.[69] Using the findings of some preliminary research on board-level participation, he concludes that employees have positive attitudes to board-level participation and management, though harbouring some reservations about the role and contribution of worker directors, and have now largely accepted their role in the senior decision-making process.[70] On the issues of conflict with traditional collective bargaining and trade union structures, Kelly found this was a non-runner. He found that trade unions had largely dominated the participatory process in the organisations concerned. Consequently, the likelihood of an alternative representative mechanism to the trade union developing 'dissolved into insignificance'.[71]

Apart from these developments in the State sector, the prospects for the extension of board-level participation in other areas seem dim in the absence of statutory compulsion. Neither trade unions nor employers have shown any great enthusiasm for the concept. Employer bodies have generally favoured the extension of participation at sub-board level, particularly through works councils, and have advocated flexibility in allowing organisations to develop their own participative arrangements. The Institute of Personnel Management adopts a similar approach suggesting that 'Participation may be attained through a wide variety of means depending on the characteristics of the organisation and the nature of its activities, structure, technology and history.'[72]

Morrissey notes some renewed interest in extending participative arrangements at sub-board level while acknowledging that the 'absence of a sustained commitment' from employers and trade unions has been a major stumbling block to more extensive developments.[73] He notes the difficulties which mechanisms such as works councils pose for trade unions and the reluctance of both parties to move from the 'tried and trusted' ground of collective bargaining. A number of other writers have warned against the blanket adoption of European models. In particular, Kelly suggests that the 'European format' may not suit our collective bargaining or trade union structures and that initiatives in expanding worker participation here should be focused at shopfloor level.[74]

b) Equity participation: mechanisms through which employees can gain an equity stake in their organisations through various profit sharing and share-ownership schemes were discussed earlier. Most of these schemes have the broad-based objective of increasing employee loyalty, commitment and morale through the closer identification of employee interests with those of the organisation. Such schemes may often be accompanied by some form of consultative or participative machinery which allows for greater employee participation in certain management decisions. However, equity participation by itself will not normally allow for a substantial increase in employee influence, as employees will generally represent a minority of the share-holders.

c) Job/work participation: ever since some of the less attractive aspects of industrial work became evident, various initiatives have been undertaken to increase employee satisfaction and motivation by designing jobs in a way which offers employees greater opportunities for expression, responsibility and achievement. Many of the initiatives involve devolving greater discretion to employees in deciding how jobs should be carried out and giving them a greater decision-making role in their immediate work environment. Increased employee participation in workplace decision-making requires effective, high-trust, two-way communications between management and employees, where workers feel they have a valuable input to make and where that input is recognised and valued by the organisation's management. It demands a more flexible and open approach to the management process with less emphasis on direction and supervision and more on coordination and communication.

Job or work participation is a most practical type of employee participation but can be difficult to effect successfully. It involves an element of role reversal, with superiors listening to employee comments, discussing these with top management and consulting employees on decisions. Such approaches may take a variety of forms ranging from some type of Management by Objectives (MBO), to job enlargement, autonomous work-groups, quality circles, suggestion schemes and consultative meetings. An important facilitator of increased job or work participation is a high level of informality, trust and openness in the manager-employee relationship, and the adoption of a managerial style which makes employees feel that their participation is both valued and worthwhile.

A broader development relying on various forms of direct job partici-pation is the Quality of Working Life Movement (QWL) which attempts to encourage an organisational culture that promotes employee feelings of control, responsibility and involvement.[75]

Trade unions have traditionally been suspicious of such managerial initiatives, believing them to stem from attempts to undermine the union's role, particularly the predominance of collective bargaining. Such suspicions are undoubtedly fuelled by the extensive use of such techniques by non-union firms.[76]

d) Participation through collective bargaining: despite some success with the above options, many would argue that the most notable improvements in extending employee participation have been achieved through collective bargaining and that it should remain the major vehicle for further develop-ments. The growth of workplace bargaining in Ireland has greatly facilitated this process, with trade unions being the key mechanism for representing and extending employee rights at workplace level. While there may be evidence of a demise in trade union influence and consequent reliance on the collective bargaining process, it still seems that union representations through collective bargaining offer a most pragmatic route to greater employee participation.

The trade union role is a crucial one. Despite occasional pronouncements, the union movement has not seemed particularly committed to representative participation through worker directors or works councils. Reactions to participation through equity participation have been mixed, and no discernible trend is evident. Indeed, apart from support for greater disclosure of information, the trade union approach to employee participation has been marked by a considerable degree of apathy. Such apathy has its origins in the doubts many trade unionists harbour about the implications of rep-resentative participation for the union's role in collective bargaining.

While some models have suggested that representative participative mechanisms would operate concurrently but separate from established collective bargaining arrangements, it is difficult to see how such approaches would operate effectively in practice. It is equally difficult to imagine trade unions allowing an alternative method of employee representation to be established at workplace level. In countries where worker directors and works councils are extensively used (such as West Germany) the trade union's role primarily involves industry-level negotiations. At workplace level issues are handled through the works council. In Ireland the trade unions play a key role in workplace bargaining and would therefore be keen to retain a significant role in any representative participative mechanisms.

However, although collective bargaining has been a successful mechanism for extending employee participation, it has limitations. Firstly, collective bargaining depends on employee organisation and a degree of power balance between the parties. These ingredients may not be present in a large number of organisations and thus collective bargaining is not a viable option. Secondly, collective bargaining operates best at workplace level. Where the locus of management decision making is removed to a higher level, such as in many multinational organisations, the effectiveness of collective bargaining in achieving employee participation may be severely limited.

Achieving Participation

From differing perspectives, all parties involved in employee relations can benefit from increased employee participation. Organisations need a flexible and committed workforce who will respond to change and perform at high levels of productivity with minimum levels of supervision. For employees, achieving an input into decisions which affect their working lives is a very legitimate goal, allowing them greater control and discretion in their jobs. At the macro level, the State and the community at large can benefit from positive workplace relations based on trust, open communications and employee satisfaction.

However, the achievement of real participation within organisations remains problematic. Business confidence and discretion in decision-making must be maintained to encourage investment and expansion. At the same time, barriers to worker involvement must be removed and employees given a worthwhile say in decision-making. The four types of participation described above should be viewed as options in a participative mix, any combination of which may suit a particular organisational context. Imposed models may not be acceptable, and it is important that any legislative measures allow for flexibility in the modes of participation to be adopted. As much as anything, effective participation requires a high level of commitment and positive attitudes from both management and employees. Trust is a key factor facilitating good communications, information disclosure and exchange, and positive management-employee relations. If a high level of trust and commitment is present then the mechanisms for worker participation will be largely incidental. Whether works councils, briefing groups or joint consultative committees are used they will be successful vehicles for facilitating participation because the appropriate climate has been created.

Significantly, however, an ESRI report, which suggests that the prospects for success in worker participation depends on a high degree of trust in the worker-management relationship, noted the 'strikingly low levels of trust' which employees had of management in Irish organisations, and concluded that progress in achieving employee participation had been disappointing.[77] The study also suggested that the traditional approaches of trade unions and management in collective bargaining resulted in their adopting adversarial positions which militated against employee participation. Effective participation requires a reappraisal of this attitude, and would involve management and unions reviewing traditional approaches to employee relations and altering these to suit a more participative style of management.[78] In a climate of improving business prospects, organisations have an opportunity to develop a positive approach to workforce management and with the commitment of its employees should strive to establish the necessary conditions for effective participation. Employment security, codified in a statement of intent by the organisation, is a potentially powerful tool for developing the high trust required to facilitate real participation within an organisation.

The personnel practitioner's role in employee participation is primarily that of catalyst. Effective participation should take place at the locus of management-employee interactions and remain a major responsibility of line management. Personnel can help to provide an organisational environment conducive to greater employee participation, oversee the implementation of legislative requirements, help to design and monitor the operation of the various mechanisms used to effect participation and conduct necessary training and development.[79] However, the decision on whether to adopt a positive approach to participation and what mechanisms to develop rests with top management, with the personnel practitioner providing specialist advice and direction.

Chapter 11

Trends and Developments Affecting Personnel Management Practice

INTRODUCTION

The objective of this chapter is to identify factors in the international and Irish business environment which are likely to have a significant impact upon the personnel practitioner in the future. Many of the trends discussed are in fact currently visible, and in that sense the shape of future developments is already with us.

These trends include the emergence of the flexible firm associated with the development of 'atypical' employment forms, widespread introduction of new technology, 'total quality' initiatives associated with attempts to achieve competitive advantage in both service and manufacturing environments, the emergence of large non-union companies, alterations in strike contours, and the emergence of 'human resource management' (HRM). While the emergence of HRM as a distinctive approach to workforce management is perhaps currently the most widespread debate within the personnel management profession, it is not considered in any depth until the final chapter of the text. Double digit unemployment and particularly the high levels of youth unemployment, by creating what is often described as an employer's market, has set the context for many of the developments identified, for example, the emergence of the flexible firm and the development of new two-tier payment systems. The chapter is divided into six sections, each devoted to an analysis of the factors outlined. Whenever possible, each trend is documented by reference to research or secondary source data available on the Irish labour market. Speculation, however, is inevitable, particularly when the implications of certain trends for the practice and future development of the personnel function and its associated departmental organisation are considered.

'ATYPICAL' EMPLOYMENT FORMS OF
THE INSTITUTE OF MANPOWER STUDIES (IMS)

Before examining the growth in 'atypical' employment forms it is necessary to clarify exactly what is meant by the term. Any form of employment which deviates from the full-time, permanent and often pensionable job with a single employer is deemed to be 'atypical'. Atypical employment therefore includes the following: self-employment (with or without employees), temporary work, part-time employment (casual or regular), home working (self-employed or on contract) and clandestine or black economy work.[1] Rigorous data on the extent of the informal or black economy is however unavailable, and therefore will not be considered here.

International studies of new forms and areas of employment growth in countries such as Ireland, the United Kingdom, Germany, France, Spain, Belgium, Italy and the Netherlands all indicate that some growth in atypical employment has occurred in the last decade.[2] This growth has been associated with shifts in the sectoral composition of employment away from industry and towards the service sector economy akin to the developments in the Irish economy. In addition, the rise in female labour force participation rates, increased unemployment and the preference of some employers to avoid the restrictions and responsibilities placed upon them by providing full-time employment have all contributed to the growth in atypical employment. In certain instances, the preferences of married females for part-time employment has also contributed to this growth pattern. Box 11.1 outlines the main features of each employment form concentrating on the most widely accepted definitions of atypical employment: part-time, temporary and self-employment.

The Emergence of New Employment Patterns

The aggregate changes in the growth and nature of atypical employment are shown in tables 11.1–3. It can be seen that part-time and temporary employment have grown during the 1979-87 period, while self-employment has declined overall. The increase in part-time employment is associated with both demand and supply side characteristics. On the supply side, the increases in female participation rates rose from 14.5 per cent of the labour force in 1975 to 20.2 per cent in 1985.[3] Some female categories, particularly married women, voluntarily opt for part-time employment as it is easier to accommodate with the domestic responsibilities of looking after children. In 1987, 72 per cent of women voluntarily opted for part-time work compared to 17 per cent of men.[4] Of course, it should be remembered that in many cases such women are forced to seek work in order to supplement family income and might also avail of full-time job opportunities if they were available. Married women account for 52 per cent of all part-time

---

Box 11.1. Typical and atypical employment forms

Typical/standard employment
Full-time employee:
This is the traditional standard form of employment and usually refers to a 35–40 hour week although in certain instances a lower limit of 30 hours applies. Overtime payments are typically payable for hours worked in excess of whichever standard hours applies.

Atypical/non-standard employment
Part-time employee:
This normally refers to situations where less than 30 hours per week are worked.

Temporary employee:
In this employment relationship there is little expectation that the job or work involved will last other than for a specified period of time. A variant on this form of employer-employee relationship is that of the agency worker such as office 'temps' and secretaries where the supplying agency pays the employee's wages, insurance etc. with the employer paying a fee to the agency in return for supplying the 'temp'. The agency's profit is the difference between the wages, insurance contribution, etc. which it pays to the 'temp' and the fee the agency receives from the employer. This is sometimes referred to as a 'triangular' employment relationship.

Self-employed worker
The self-employed may or may not employ others. The contractual relationship with the employer is that of a contract *for* services rather than a contract *of* service with an employer. The self-employed typically attend to their own tax, insurance and pension affairs. The self-employed category includes employers and own account workers but excludes unpaid family workers and employees.[5] Some but not all 'homeworkers' (those who work from home) are self-employed.

---

employment, and part-time employment is most pronounced in the service sector (clerical, commercial, service and professional workers). On the demand side, particular business patterns (such as those experienced in the hotel and catering sector) generate a fluctuating demand for manpower which has facilitated the growth in part-time employment. Firms typically pay less to part-time employees in terms of wages and fringe benefits and are unconstrained by protective social legislation in situations where employees work less than eighteen hours per week.

Temporary employment is roughly similar in scale to part-time employment when taken as a percentage of total employment. About one half of temporary employment is accounted for by males. Temporary employment is concentrated among the under-25s; in 1985, approximately 60 per cent of temporary employees were under twenty-five. This concentration can be explained largely by the large proportion of young persons on AnCO and CERT Training Schemes (44, 651 in 1985) and work schemes for the long term unemployed.[6] Temporary employment is essentially a demand side phenomenon: 55 per cent of those in such employment are there because they could not find work.

While overall, self-employment fell during the 1979-87 period, considerable growth took place within the non-agricultural sector. In a detailed sectoral analysis of this period, it was found that there was strong growth in particular sectors. Self-employment in the 'other production industries' sector grew by 34 per cent, professional services by 20 per cent and transport, communication and storage by 14 per cent. In the non-agricultural sector, almost 14 per cent of self-employment is located within the commerce, insurance, finance and business sectors.[7] The strong presence of such business services has allowed small and medium-sized enterprises to 'contract in' training, recruitment, advertising and marketing services.[8]

Table 11.1. Changes in Part-time employment in Ireland by job type

	1979	1987
	'000's	'000's
Regular part-time	35.5	65.6
Occasional part-time	22.1	12.8
All part-time	57.6	78.4
Part-time as % of total employment	5.4%	7.1%

Table 11.2. Changes in temporary employment, 1983-87

	Males	Females	Total	%*
	'000's	'000's	'000's	
1983	25.5	26.4	51.9	6.0
1987	32.8	38.9	71.8	8.5

*Temporary/total employment

Table 11.3. Self-employment as a proportion of total employment by broad sectors: Ireland, 1979 and 1987

	1979		1987		% Change
	'000's	%*	'000's	%*	1979–1987
Agriculture	160.7	72.5	123.4	75.2	-23.2
Non-agriculture	94.9	10.2	110.9	12.0	+16.9
Total	255.6	22.2	234.3	21.5	-8.3

Sources: Labour Force Survey 1979 and 1987.   * % of total employed in sector

IMPLICATIONS OF TRENDS IN 'ATYPICAL EMPLOYMENT' FOR PERSONNEL MANAGEMENT PRACTICE

Having documented in some detail the extent to which atypical employment forms have developed in recent years, we are now in a better position to answer the key question of what these trends imply for the practice of personnel management, both now and in the future. It is essential, therefore, that we consider in some detail the 'flexible firm' hypothesis developed by John Atkinson.[9] Many critical commentators have pointed out that the empirical evidence in favour of the supposed spread of the flexible firm is often forgotten or ignored by commentators addressing the question.[10] Having examined the trends in atypical employment using the best available sources (the Labour Force Surveys), it is hoped that the pitfall of confounding enthusiasm with evidence will be avoided. Indeed, the argument which is advanced here is that atypical employment forms do not imply so much a flexible firm scenario as a segmented labour market at industry sector level. Nonetheless, the development of atypical employment forms offers a wider range of alternative strategies to employers in relation to manpower planning.

THE FLEXIBLE FIRM SCENARIO OF THE INSTITUTE OF MANPOWER STUDIES (IMS)

John Atkinson of the Institute of Manpower Studies at the University of Sussex has been the most influential writer on the notion of the flexible firm. Atkinson argues that firms faced with considerable market uncertainty due to the recession are reluctant to take on additional full-time permanent staff. Instead, he argues, they prefer the alternative strategy of taking on part-time and temporary employees who can be recruited and shed quickly, thus allowing a greater flexible response on the part of the organisation. He argues that, as a result, two distinct categories of employees will develop within many organisations: a core or primary labour market group of full-time employees, and a periphery or secondary labour market group. His model is set out in figure 11.1.[11]

The data on which Atkinson based his argument is detailed in two surveys which were carried out in 1982-3 of seventy-two and thirty-one firms respectively, employing in excess of 600,000 employees in food and drink, manufacturing, engineering, retailing and financial services. Neither study was a statistically representative sample and, as Innes points out, the thirty-one firms in the second study were chosen because they were known to have introduced reasons to promote greater flexibility.[12] It can be seen therefore that this fact qualifies the extent to which the flexible firm may be emerging as flexible firms were over-represented in the sample. Three types of flexibility were identified within the IMS studies:

Fig. 11.1. Categories of peripheral employees

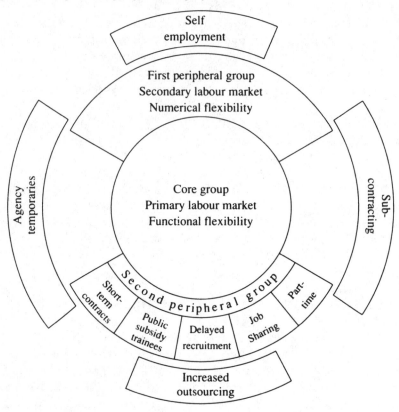

Source: Flexible Manning: the way ahead, Brighton, IMS/Manpower Ltd 1984.

a) Functional flexibility: here core employees are trained to be multi-skilled, which is usually accompanied by a relaxation of traditional craft demarcation lines. Examples here would include operators carrying out routine maintenance work on machines previously carried out by craftsmen (fitters, electricians, technicians) and the retraining of professional and managerial grades to allow them to carry out a broader range of tasks.

b) Numerical flexibility: here peripheral workers (temporary, subcontractors and part-time staff) are drafted in to cope with short-term changes in demand for the firm's product or service. These employees are then let go when demand drops. Examples in this category would include clerical workers in insurance and banking drafted in to cope with peak loads in claims processing, temporary manual employees drafted in to assist in meeting increased customer orders in manufacturing, seasonally induced demand in retailing (pre-Christmas shopping) etc.

c) Financial flexibility: Here the firm attempts to develop payment systems which support and reinforce the organisation's requirements for flexibility. This would include attempts to relate pay to the state of the labour market rather than to traditional reference groups, and attempts to use pay as a mechanism to encourage employees to become flexible. An example of the first category would be the recently well-publicised case of Bank of Ireland's introduction of a new grade of banking assistant.[13] Skill-based pay, where employees are paid at the highest rate of skill which they acquire, would be an example of the second. In addition the recent popularity of 'pay for performance' systems using bonus and merit pay administered via a performance appraisal system would also be an example where the rewards system is designed to encourage and reinforce flexibility.

The IMS study argues that organisations are moving away from traditional employment practices towards a core-periphery model. The core group of employees receives the greatest investment in terms of training (particularly directed towards achieving functional flexibility), receives good pay and conditions and has better promotion opportunities than peripheral workers who have tenuous linkages with the organisation. The pay system is also used to encourage these core workers to acquire extra skills, reinforcing the training oriented to the encouragement of functional flexibility. In return for greater flexibility, core employees receive enhanced guarantees of job security. Indeed, the use of peripheral temporary employees may be presented as a strategy to protect the job security of core employees. Xidex, UK Ltd refers to their use of temporary and part-time workers as rings of defence for their core workers.[14] Peripheral workers bear in effect the insecurities on behalf of the core workforce. It is worth pointing out that this policy has the effect of pitting core employees against temporary employees and can also have the effect of reducing union penetration as peripheral employees are less likely to be unionised.

The Composition of the Peripheral Workforce

Peripheral workers constitute two sub-groups, one considered more marginal than the other. The first group consists of full-time employees with skills which are readily available in the labour market, such as clerical, secretarial and unskilled manual work. These categories have less promotion and training opportunities than core workers. The second peripheral group consists of part-time workers, 'temps', subcontractors, work experience trainees, job sharers, etc. These categories have virtually no guarantees of job security. The IMS study reported that almost 70 per cent of the firms studied had increased their use of temporary workers in the five years prior to the survey and a similar proportion had increased their use of subcontractors, while 20 per cent had increased their use of self-employed workers.

To what extent has the Flexible Firm developed in Ireland?

The data on the growth in atypical employment which was documented earlier at an aggregate level is broadly supportive of the development of 'flexibilisation', particularly in certain sectors, such as services. However, such practices in the services sector are by no means novel, having been practised traditionally in this sector.

A number of qualifications must be made. Under the Atkinson scenario, organisations facing the greatest uncertainty would be most likely to utilise or develop a core-periphery workforce. On this basis we would expect that non-core *manufacturing* employment would have risen sharply during the recession. However, we saw earlier that apart from transport and communications, finance, insurance and commerce and other services, part-time employment actually dropped in all other industrial sectors. Nor was there a massive explosion of temporary working outside of the services sector. Thus, the prediction of the model, certainly as it relates to numerical flexibility, is dependent upon the sector under analysis. It would seem more likely that manufacturing firms would aim towards achieving greater functional flexibility. For example, multi-skilling which (while crossing demarcation lines in certain instances) would be perhaps more acceptable to unions organising in manufacturing than the widespread usage of temporary and part-time workers. Indeed, the extensive introduction of new technology—information technology, computer numerically controlled (CNC) machinery, computer assisted design (CAD), materials requirement planning (MRP) etc.—places a premium, in the manufacturing environment, on a committed and highly skilled workforce; this is another factor which encourages moves towards functional flexibility while not necessarily encouraging the development of numerical flexibility. Furthermore, firms who wish to protect their core workforce could shed sub-contractors (in catering, security, etc.) and utilise core employees to carry out these tasks. In this situation sub-contracting might actually fall rather than increase in a recession.

Suttle, using the weekly Industrial Relations News Bulletin (IRN) as a data source, carried out an exploratory analysis of the development of the three forms of flexibility already mentioned in the 1980-88 period.[15] (The study acknowledges that this method ignores cases not reported by IRN and may underestimate non-union flexibility deals which typically are not reported, as 'non-union companies are more likely to be able to introduce more radical changes without facing opposition from the workforce'.) A total of ninety-six companies were found to have introduced some form of flexibility in the eight-year period—with a total of 115 instances of flexibility occurring (due to the fact that some companies were reported more than once in the IRN bulletin). The sectoral breakdown of these cases is reported in table 11.4.

Table 11.4. Sectoral breakdown of flexibility cases, 1980-88

Public sector	Total	%
Local authorities	9	7.9
Health service	5	4.3
Government departments	2	1.7
Civil service	1	0.9
State-sponsored companies		
Manufacturing	5	4.3
Service	17	14.8
Total	39	33.9
Private sector		
Manufacturing	52	45.2
Service	21	18.3
Construction and mining	3	2.6
Total	76	66.1
Overall total	115	100.0

Source: Suttle (1988)

Suttle points out that one method of assessing whether flexible firms were emerging would be to see how many have introduced more than one form of flexibility. Of the ninety-six companies which he identified 'none attempted to combine all three forms of flexibility and only ten combined two—numerical and functional' (Irish Distillers, Irish Press, New Dublin Gas, Aer Lingus, Irish Cement, Packard Electric, B & I, Arthur Guinness, Memorex Media Products and Irish Biscuits). As Suttle points out, while flexibility may have increased, the flexible firm would appear not to have emerged yet. Table 11.5 reports the data in this study when broken down by type.

Numerical flexibility is the category which predominates, with the use of contractors being very important within this category. Functional flexibility is reported by Suttle as being most frequently found in the private manufacturing sector (accounting for 65 per cent of the 40 cases of functional flexibility reported). Numerical flexibility was less frequently found in private manufacturing (accounting for 40 per cent of the eighty-five cases found). As Suttle concludes, 'this exploratory research shows that while instances of flexibility have increased over recent years, the emergence of a "flexible firm" as outlined by Atkinson does not seem to have occurred. Rather, those firms introducing flexibility only introduce it in certain areas and the notion of dividing workers into two distinct

Table 11.5. Type of flexibility, 1980-88

Numerical	Total	%
Contractors	51	40.0
Temporary staff	13	10.0
Part-time staff	8	6.5
Self-employment	5	4.0
Casual labour	5	4.0
Freelance labour	2	1.5
Flexible staffing	1	1.0
Total	85	67.0
Functional		
Flexibility deal		
Function	16	12.5
Interchangeability	7	5.5
Removal of demarcation	7	5.5
Flexibility in job category	6	5.0
Flexible work practices	4	3.0
Total	40	31.5
Financial		
Two-tier wages	2	1.5
	127	100.0

groups—a core and a periphery—does not seem to be uppermost'. It would appear that, on the basis of both the aggregate data cited earlier and this study by Suttle, while part-time and temporary employment are frequently used by firms, this is more appropriately explained by the nature of the business at industry sector level rather than being attributable to the planned development of the flexible firm *per se*. Nonetheless, even if the flexible firm has not yet emerged as predicted, the notion of core-periphery employees is extremely relevant to the service sector. Furthermore, as the service sector is the area which can be expected to grow in the future, the core-periphery dichotomy will become an increasing factor affecting personnel management practice there.

Handy however, argues that firms in all industry sectors will increasingly develop manpower strategies utilising a core-periphery model.[16] Should this trend develop it would predicate a move away from single status organisations and harmonisation of pay and benefits, which has been a very popular strategy aimed at improving employee relations throughout the late 1970s and 1980s. For example, single status arrangements (common health, welfare and benefit packages, job security, canteen facilities etc.) would increasingly become the prerogative of a shrinking number of core employees which (in view of the trends in automation of production processes) would include a small proportion of unskilled manual and greater proportions of 'knowledge' workers. The fact that peripheral workers are frequently poorly paid, do not possess any guarantees of job security, training or promotion prospects, suggests that firms utilising large proportions of such employees may well not achieve the productive efficiency levels of full-time employees whose commitment and motivation can be expected to be higher. In fact, peripheral workers are likely to have a higher propensity to turnover, produce lower quality goods or services and require more supervision than full-time employees.[17] Their usage, therefore, may well be limited to low-skill areas within organisations.

Handy argues that, when part-time and temporary employment exceeds 20 per cent of total employment, governments under pressure from the unions (who have only recently begun to view part-time and temporary workers as relevant recruitment domains) will begin to legislate minimum standards and rights for such categories of employees.[18] Recent Department of Labour proposals suggest that the rights accorded to full-time employees under the Unfair Dismissal legislation, redundancy legislation etc. may soon be extended to include employees who work less than eighteen hours per week.[19]

Firms who utilise high numbers of peripheral employees may increasingly experience dual patterns of industrial conflict: low levels amongst their well-paid core employees and high levels of conflict amongst their regular but peripheral employees.

The strike of contract cleaners averted in January 1989 may well be a demonstration of an upsurge in industrial unrest amongst a previously poorly organised sector.[20] (The fall-out in industrial employment and the shift towards the service sector has caused the unions to view penetration of that sector as essential to their future survival as organisational entities.) Whether trade unions in Ireland attempt to create linkages between core and periphery employees remains to be seen. The T & GWU in Britain has launched a 'link-up' campaign which seeks to link the bargaining strength and interests of core employees with peripheral workers.[21] In Great Britain it has been estimated by Handy that by the year 2000, as much as 50 per cent of civilian employees may work in the peripheral sector of the economy. Even though the data presented earlier does not offer strong support to the emergence of an integrated flexible firm (one combining all three forms of flexibility), it would be unwise to suggest that firms are unlikely to continue to utilise increasing numbers of peripheral employees (due to the cost-efficiencies involved and market uncertainty) unless these categories develop a militancy which has not been evident to date. If the trend does develop, it marks the end of the single status organisation which, as Kenny points out, must be very disappointing for personnel practitioners:

> even seasoned veterans of the occupation had seemed to believe that history was on the personnel manager's side and that sooner or later everywhere, the personnel director of the new post-industrial society would look out from the boardroom to a flat, single status organisation. Within it, there would be few industrial relations problems and improved employee attitudes where the growing armoury of personnel techniques could be deployed and traditional personnel values incorporated. To contemplate a radical split between a core group, to whom the traditional aspirations of personnel managers would apply, and a peripheral group with little security, career prospects and training is found painful.[22]

If the trend is not a cyclical one, then increasingly the personnel manager may be faced with managing diverse cultures within the one organisation. At the core will be the managers, professionals, research and development technologists, skilled craftsmen etc.

Increasingly, these categories will be dealing with special project work as routine, and standardised work will be offloaded onto periphery employees. Core employees will have shorter careers within firms according to Handy, perhaps twenty years or less, after which they will become self employed or act as consultants to the firm which previously employed them. (As a result, systematic human resource policies will need to be designed to attract, maintain and develop core employees.)

Increasingly, organisations may find themselves designing 'tenure tracks' for their most skilled categories (akin to the American university system) with rapid 'fast track' promotion and development for 'leading edge' staff, such as research and development specialists, electronic engineers, information technologists. These groups will demand greater voice and participation within the organisation, reflecting both high expectations of what constitutes a good quality of working life (QWL) and the knowledge that they possess considerable bargaining advantage as their skills will be in short supply. Flat organisation systems with enriched task environments may well become the norm for these categories. Administrative work will be pushed out on to peripheral employees in order to free development staff to engage in creating future-oriented products and services. Increasingly, these core employees will have the status of self-managing professionals akin to the university lecturer analogy—freed from supervision and 'clock in' arrangements as long as they continue to produce high-quality services.

The management of a 'high performance' culture (including features of both task and person cultures)[23] will pose considerable challenges for the personnel manager dealing with core employees, but the personnel activities in relation to peripheral employees will be considerably less elaborate.

While cyclical recruitment of peripheral staff will become an increasingly frequent event for the personnel manager in the core-periphery organisation (unless, of course, agencies are used), training and development activities for this category will be almost non-existent. However, motivational problems associated with expected low commitment of employees—who see little reason to work hard for an organisation which has no commitment to them—may demand tight supervision, using up the valuable time of core employees. When regular part-timers are used, they can be expected to join unions who will attempt to improve their wages and conditions. In view of the fact that the organisation uses peripheral staff *because* of their low cost these wage demands will not be readily conceded to. As a result, the personnel manager will perhaps find him/herself reverting to the 'contracts manager' mode identified by Tyson and Fell, albeit only in relation to part-time staff.[24]

The 'procedural' approach to industrial relations can be expected to dominate the organisation-part-time employee relationship, with full-time officers of unions playing a major role in negotiations on behalf of these categories. Peripheral employees can be expected to seek trade union membership because of poor working conditions, low pay and lack of voice within the firm. The contrary may occur for core employees, where trade union influence may in fact decline as it is effectively eroded when a personnel strategy designed to build a strong organisation culture for core employees is implemented.[25] While some authors would predict the disappearance of the traditional industrial relations model, the rationale of the core-periphery organisation suggests that personnel professionals will continue to include negotiation and grievance-handling activities as an integral part of their work. Devolution of the personnel function to line staff, currently a very popular strategy, will not eliminate the personnel department, as the demands of peripheral employees will become more strident for improved conditions and the need to retain core employees will increasingly demand sophisticated and innovative approaches (similar to the approaches outlines in Foulkes' study of large non-union companies) on the part of the personnel department.[26]

Financial Flexibility and the Emergence of New Recruitment Grades

The question of financial flexibility is in many ways a more complex one than whether or not numerical or functional flexibility has developed during the recession. Financial flexibility includes both attempts by organisations to link pay to market factors (such as the supply of labour) and also to develop pay structures which include a large variable pay element (bonus, profit-sharing, etc.). The recent development of new 'two-tier' pay systems in Aer Lingus and the Bank of Ireland reflect elements of the first approach—linking pay to market supply of labour—while trends towards profit-sharing in companies such as GPA, Guinness and Analog reflect a markedly different approach. It is to the Aer Lingus and Bank of Ireland arrangements that we now turn. Both of these organisations have introduced a new entry grade: junior bank assistant in the case of Bank of Ireland, hospitality assistant in case of Aer Lingus. Bank of Ireland, in introducing their new grade of junior bank assistant, argued that existing bank officials were carrying out routine work which was more appropriate to a clerical assistant type grade. They claimed that 30 per cent of a typical bank official's workload involved these routine activities. In addition, it was argued that with the advent of 1992 their labour costs would place them at a serious competitive disadvantage with their foreign EC competitors. On referral of the issue to the Labour Court for recommendation, the court found largely in favour of Bank of Ireland, although some minor changes to the basic starting pay were recommended.[27] The new grade was accepted by a majority in a subsequent ballot of IBOA members. Starting salary for this grade is £6,500 per annum with a ten-point scale rising to a maximum of £10,200 per annum. Recruits to this grade will have the opportunity to compete for promotion to higher grades, but the extent to which this will allow upward movement can only be judged over the next 4-5 year period. Viewed on the basis of comparable work (in solicitors' offices, clerical workers in insurance etc.), starting pay would appear to be justifiable in view of the deskilled nature of the job. However, it represents a significant trend towards a wage flexibility hitherto unknown in the Irish labour market and is undoubtedly linked to the high levels of youth unemployment (15-24-year-olds) in the Irish labour market which ensures that there is considerable demand for such positions despite the low entry wage paid. Various reports have estimated between 10,000-24,000 applicants for the initial 800 jobs offered at this level.[28] Aer Lingus also have a low entry wage grade for their new hospitality assistants and clerical grades. The base wage is £5,481 per annum with a 31-point pay spine rising to £13,000. Periodic lay-offs for up to six months are also incorporated into the terms and conditions of these new recruits, although full integration into existing pay and conditions is allowed for. Grafton argues that this is a preferable arrangement to the possible creation of a permanent underclass in the Bank of Ireland case where no *automatic* integration will take place.[29] It would appear that the trend is developing. Dublin Bus is expected to introduce a lower-paid junior grade of driver for its Tallaght and outer-city routes:[30]

The bus company will employ 50 junior drivers aged between 25 and 35 to operate the smaller (25-9) seat buses operating on the 'local link' routes in Tallaght and around Finglas, Blanchardstown, Clondalkin and Crumlin . . . the new grade will serve as a recruitment grade and new recruits will be paid at less than the current rate of pay. Drivers of the large one-person buses currently receive an allowance of one third of their basic pay.

Allied Irish Bank are also expected to introduce a new recruitment grade of bank assistant although the starting pay levels will be higher than the Bank of Ireland case. Should this trend develop it will again present personnel practitioners with the difficult task of managing two cultures within the same organisation, a 'core' culture of existing full-timers and a 'regularised' periphery of junior recruits carrying out work which is not greatly dissimilar in skill content. The possibilities for comparability disputes and re-grading claims would appear to be considerable, again reinforcing the arguments presented earlier in relation to the re-emergence of the 'contracts manager' role of the personnel practitioner in the future.

Another approach to financial flexibility is the increasing tendency of organisations to build a variable pay element into the remuneration package. This typically includes some bonus or profit-sharing element. The European Foundation study of payment systems in Ireland identified five general wage payment systems: flat rate only, flat rate plus individual, group or plant-wide bonus and piecework.[31] They point out that:

> the first system, which is the least complicated to administer, pre-dominates among both direct and indirect production-line manual employees. The incidence of the other systems, where payments are in whole or in part directly related to performance, is increasing. It is estimated that by 1990, over one-third of the manufacturing establishments in Ireland will be operating bonus schemes of some sort with regard to their direct manual employees.

The key factors identified (in the case of direct manual employees) which have a bearing on the payment system utilised include:

a) nationality of head office—UK and continental European companies (when compared with US companies) tend to utilise individual bonus schemes more frequently;

b) size of establishment—companies employing less than fifty employees typically utilise a flat-rate system;

c) technological process—most Irish establishments in manufacturing tend to use large batch production techniques, and the use of payment by performance is more common in such establishments than in firms using small batch or continuous process systems;

d) capital intensity—as capital intensity increases, the use of flat rate and plant-wide bonus schemes is more frequently reported. In labour intensive schemes, individual and group bonus schemes predominate.

Nor is the increasing tendency to include an inbuilt variable pay element confined to the private sector. At the 1988 FIE Conference on Industrial Relations, Dermot Gleeson presented a paper entitled 'Developing Systems of Pay for Performance in the Irish Public Sector' which reported a review body's recommendations on the subject. The review body recommended performance-related pay to be introduced for key executives of state-sponsored bodies in Category 1 and for assistant secretaries in the Civil Service. Category 1 bodies would be mainly commercial bodies which are closest in nature to private sector companies and which compete in the market place for their business (for example, Aer Lingus, Irish Life). If such schemes are adopted (and performance appraisal would be the main mechanism used in implementing these arrangements) it could be expected that the schemes would eventually be extended to cover middle management type grades in the public sector (such as Higher Executive Officer grades in the Civil Service).

Another interesting development is the increasing spread of share-ownership schemes in the Irish Republic due to favourable tax provisions under the 1986 Finance Act. Arguments in favour of increasing employee share ownership derive from two sources: economists and organisational psychologists. An outstanding contributor to the economic debate in favour of share ownership has been Martin Weitzman of the Massachusetts Institute of Technology (MIT). Weitzman recommends a switch in the remuneration system away from a wage payment system to a share system (pure revenue sharing).[32] This he believes will sustain a drive towards full employment and yet curb central inflationary pressures. Weitzman argues that when firms pay via a share system which is based on profitability this will encourage them to hire additional employees.

Behavioural arguments in favour of extending employee share ownership have been advanced by Bradley and Gelb.[33] Bradley and Gelb argue that when employees are working for themselves it has the effect of both internalising motivation and increasing democracy at workplace level, in that individuals have an increased economic stake in the enterprise. They also argue that increasing employee share ownership prevents further State encroachment and, in the case of privatisation, has the effect of 'rolling back' the public sector when flotations of public sector shares result in a nationalised enterprise returning to private ownership. The results of studies of employee share ownership on motivation, commitment, organisational attachment and industrial relations have been quite mixed. The studies by Conte and Tannenbaum found that managers perceive employee ownership as having a substantially positive effect on employee attitudes.[34] Bell and Hanson found similar effects in relation to job attitudes, in that employees take a greater interest in profits and financial results. By contrast, studies by Kruse on a small number of US companies found that few employees viewed employee share ownership as having a positive effect on company identification.[35] Nor did Long find any strong effects on motivation in his study of a Canadian electronics company.[36]

It would appear that the critical element in improving motivation, commitment and industrial relations is whether the introduction of share ownership is linked to the introduction of further organisational changes in management style, increased communications both upwards and downwards, innovations in eliciting employee contributions (such as quality circles), etc. If share ownership is seen as a panacea to motivational problems and is simply introduced as a single measure, its behavioural benefits would seem unlikely to be realised. A study of thirty-four Irish companies offering share-ownership schemes in Ireland found that a range of reasons for their introduction was frequently cited by respondents.[37] The most frequently cited reasons were to give employees a sense of identification with the company and to encourage involvement and co-operation. The actual spread of the schemes would seem to be taxation led, in that many of the companies introduced their schemes following favourable tax provisions under the Finance Acts, 1978, 1982, 1984 and 1986. Certain political spokespersons have recommended the use of employee share ownership to 'privatise' the employment relationship, and organisations such as the Irish Planned Sharing Association and the Irish Productivity Centre provide advice to companies wishing to introduce such schemes. Companies such as Carroll Industries, Analog Devices B.V. and Guinness Ireland operate share-ownership schemes. Should the government proceed with privatisation of semi-state companies in the future, the debate on employee share-ownership can be expected to assume renewed vigour and importance.

NEW TECHNOLOGY: SCOPE, DIFFUSION AND IMPLICATIONS

To understand fully the impact of new technology on employment practices it is important to consider what is meant by the term 'new technology', the reasons for its introduction and its effects upon the social and technical organisation of production. Personnel managers play a key role in terms of informing general management about the human implications of introducing new technology, the choices which can be made in terms of enskilling or deskilling work operations and the management of change itself which develops with the introduction of new technology. Many individuals believe that we are entering a new industrial era—the age of information technology—which will radically alter the shape of organisations as we know it. Academic futurologists such as Charles Handy argue that we are already leaving the post-industrial society phase of economic development and entering the information age where 'knowledge workers' will replace unskilled- and semi-skilled-based industries. The term new technology is used in its broadest sense to include office-based technologies, such as word processing and information retrieval systems, and manufacturing-based technologies, which include computer-assisted design (CAD) and manufacture (CAM) systems, computer numerically controlled machinery (CNC) and robotics. It also includes service-based technologies such as electronic point of sale systems in retailing, where barcoded products are priced by an electronic sensor, cash dispensers (automatic teller machines or ATM) and electronic funds transfer in banking. Research into microelectronic technology has resulted in the development of smaller and more compact microprocessor 'chips' which replace valves, transistors and printed circuits. Their newness lies in the degree of cheapness, speed, reliability and breadth of application which is being achieved. Future applications can be expected to determine both the quantity and quality of employment available, in that computer-based technology allows both partial and full automation of processes previously carried out by hand. Applications have permeated all industrial sectors: industrial, service and agricultural. The major reasons for its widespread application lie in its relative cheapness, versatility, labour-saving nature and contribution to productive efficiency. Nor is the impact of new technology necessarily uni-directional: the application of new technology does not always displace employment, deskill work content, concentrate control within management etc. Studies at the Harvard Business School by Richard Walton point out that these effects are variable and indeed often unplanned. He points out that:

1) Applications of new technology sometimes narrow the scope of job, and sometimes broaden them.
2) They may emphasise the individual nature of task performance or promote the interdependent nature of the work of groups of employees.
3) They may change the locus of decision making toward centralisation or decentralisation, with implications for the steepness of the hierarchy.
4) They may create performance-measurement systems that emphasise learning and self control or surveillance and hierarchical control.
5) They may transfer certain work functions from the unionised work force to supervisory or professional groups or they may provide developmental opportunities for workers.
6) They can increase the flexibility of work schedules to accommodate human preferences, or they can decrease flexibility and introduce shift work.

7) They often contribute to social isolation, but sometimes have the opposite effect.[38]

Walton found that when new technology is used to increase employee discretion, autonomy and responsibility, to decrease centralisation of authority and to emphasise learning, its effect is to increase employee commitment to the organisation and results in greater utilisation of the technical capability and economic performance of the technology. By contrast however, he found that, when new technology is used to make work more routine and controlled, requiring less skill and knowledge, the typical reaction was to respond negatively to its utilisation which undermines the technical capability and economic performance of the technology.

The effects of new technology include effects on employment, relocation, health and safety, bargaining units, skill and income, job qualifications and job advancement, job control, work intensity and job satisfaction.[39] The employment effects are difficult to gauge with any precision. Watson quotes a UK study by the Policy Studies Institute which suggested that only 5 per cent of the job losses occurring in UK manufacturing could be attributed to technical changes.[40] However, in 1982, microprocessor technology was relatively undiffused in British manufacturing. In Ireland, manufacturing employment has steadily declined since 1975. However, it could be argued that this is as much a lack of technical change and innovation as a side-effect of its introduction. New technology may also involve relocation effects: employees may be able to work at home via teleworking arrangements or alternatively may have to move to a completely new centralised location.

Health and safety effects may develop in relation to, for example, the widespread usage of visual display units, while tasks may be transferred outside of certain bargaining units (such as production departments) away from operatives to supervisors or vice versa. New technology can also deskill work operations (where automation or partial automation is pursued) or alternatively result in enhanced skill acquisition when employees carry out their own quality control and process inspection. When new technology is used to deskill operations, pressure develops to reduce associated pay levels while 'pay for knowledge' systems encourage operators to acquire new skills. Job qualification effects may result when employees are unable to acquire the skills required in, for example, CNC working in manufacturing. New technology can result in eliminating certain positions which may distort the creation of career ladders and 'job families' which results in job advancement effects. Job control can be increased, particularly when a strategy of creating 'ownership of the process' is followed, such as in manufacturing. Many firms are now attempting to develop systems whereby operatives carry out their own quality control and process inspection, using statistical process control. However, job control also can be diminished, particularly when new technology subjects workers to more frequent monitoring of their performance and job-related behaviour. An interesting example of the latter was reported in *Industrial Relations News* in 1988 concerning the introduction of the industrial engineering technique of MOST (Manyard Operation Sequence Technique) in Thermo King.[41] MOST is a technique which uses video equipment to record work activity—such systems are frequently viewed as a form of 'surveillance' by workers and considerable friction developed in relation to its introduction, resulting in a dispute which was eventually settled following intervention by the Labour Court. Similarly, job satisfaction can be affected, depending on whether the application of the new technology results in jobs which are more or less routinised and involve lesser or greater degrees of discretion.

Union responses to the introduction of new technology are typically to slow down its rate of introduction (unless guarantees of job security are granted), seek retraining for members who are likely to be dislocated, influence staffing plans and avoid deskilling of operations whenever possible.[42] Both Clegg and Walton provide interesting examples of the extent to which management strategies in relation to work organisation using new technology derive from critical assumptions concerning the nature of human resources.[43] The findings of these authors suggest that where management assume that employees tend to be antagonistic or apathetic towards work, they develop work technology which replaces or deskills labour and monitors employees. As a result, adversarial industrial relations are promoted and employee attitudes and apathy are reinforced. Where management assume that employees are resourceful humans, employees are involved in the change process as much as possible, and they are encouraged to develop new skills and suggest possibie alterations to work organisation (to facilitate social interaction via 'cell group' or autonomous group-working). Job security guarantees are critical to such an approach, as innovativeness and flexibility will not be forthcoming when employees fear that their jobs may be lost as a result of the introduction of new technology. Many large non-union companies in electronics, such as Digital and Verbatim, offer an implicit (if not legally binding) guarantee of job security, which is viewed as a critical factor in facilitating frequent change in work organisation.

New technology, of course, has even more direct implications for personnel management activities, with the wide availability of computer-based personnel records systems. These remove much of the mundane record-keeping role involved in personnel administration, and facilitate a pro-active diagnostic approach to personnel management. For example, computerised records systems allow personnel managers to retrieve information speedily on absenteeism trends by department, age, sex, etc. within minutes, when previously it might take several hours to generate the analysis required.[44]

THE 'JAPANISATION' OF PRODUCTION SYSTEMS AND QUALITY MANAGEMENT INITIATIVES

One of the most interesting examples of the far-reaching implications of alterations in the social and technical organisation of production is outlined by Owen in relation to the introduction of 'just in time' systems of manufacture.[45] He contrasts 'just in time' with the traditional large-scale organisation of production described as 'just in case' approaches. 'Just in case' has a number of common characteristics: the pursuit of high-volume production runs in order to ensure low unit costs, the holding of inventory (raw material inputs, work in progress and final product) in anticipation of future demand which leads to high expenditure on warehousing. The social-technical organisation of 'just in case' systems of production is typified by a fragmented deskilled labour process with employees carrying out a small number of tasks. One of the end results of this system, according to Owen, is that employees develop rigidities, refusing to transfer between tasks or job stations and this can lead to

> an absence on the part of operatives of a perspective on the workplace as an integrated totality. This can lead to an indifference to matters such as quality control and render the continuity of the system liable to disruption where there is strong worker organisation. This possibility requires the attention of a hierarchy of controls and supervision, which in turn can generate tensions within the labour management relationship, leading to a wide range of worker responses such as: rigid adherence to rules or systematic soldiering, as well as sabotage, absenteeism, strikes etc.

The system of production associated with car manufacture until recently typified the approach outlined above, and its negative consequences in terms of employee relations are well documented in Huw Benyon's 'Working for Ford' study.[46] 'Just in time' (JIT) is an approach which differs significantly from the rationality expressed in the 'just in case' scenario. It is perhaps best described as a total philosophy of production which has the objectives of reducing set up time, reducing buffer stocks to the lowest practical level, building in of quality control and process inspection to employees' job routine, pursuit of high-quality production, greater use of subcontractors and increased coupling between suppliers and customers. A recent article in *Management* magazine outlined the principles of the JIT approach operating in Digital Equipment Corporation's (DEC) European

Software Distribution Centre in Mervue (Galway) and its manufacturing establishment in Ballybrit, Galway.[47] The company's main business is to manage and coordinate the supply of software-related products to the European market and to develop software products for the European market. This software is often used in machines which can cost several million pounds and the slightest flaw in the software can result in massive damage and costs. As a result, the quality of software is a major strategic objective within DEC and dedication to quality is an essential part of the Digital corporate culture. This manifests itself in the company's investment in training and learning programmes, to make employees aware of and contribute to the goal of high-quality production and to make its suppliers aware of its requirements in terms of quality-assured materials. Deciding to install JIT and 'total quality control' systems of production meant that suppliers of materials to DEC had to upgrade their quality control systems in order that a 'ship-to-stock' policy could be pursued. DEC have in fact trained their suppliers in quality control techniques in order to facilitate this ship-to-stock policy. Ship-to-stock means that any goods supplied are already checked for quality by the supplier and can be entered directly into stock or into the production process by the purchaser. As a result, buffer stocks can be reduced, with consequent savings in terms of warehouse space, labour costs and capital tied up in stock. It also eliminates order checking by the purchaser and administration associated with returning unsatisfactory materials to suppliers, etc.

However, quality assurance of materials supplied is only one aspect of the Total Quality Control (TQC) approach. The next element is to ensure that the conversion process utilising these assured inputs operates within specified quality limits or 'tolerances'. Traditionally, companies have set up specialist quality control departments for this purpose. Increasingly, companies, influenced by the powerful figure of Edward Deming,[48] are rejecting this approach in favour of one which allows operators to carry out their own quality control on output from a process and to check that the process is operating within specified tolerances. It has the advantage of creating a sense of 'ownership of the process' in the mind of the operator, which results in increased attention to quality. If the process seems to be operating outside specified tolerances (which are recorded on standard mean and range charts) then operators have the authority to stop the process before the poor-quality product continues on to the next stage of the process. Operatives have to receive extensive training before they can execute their own quality control but overall costs are reduced. This results from the fact that improved quality results in less rework, fewer delays, better utilisation of machine time and materials, which in turn increases productivity which allows firms to increase their market share by offering better quality products at lower prices than their competitors. SPC (Statistical Process Control) is carried out by operatives in all of DEC's Irish operations. The implementation of JIT depends upon close co-operation and integration of all stages of the production cycle and is facilitated when a positive working relationship exists between workers and management. In fact, JIT is totally dependent for its success on the willingness of operators to pay close attention to quality of material, usage, output and process inspection. In the absence of such attention JIT can become a system prone to malfunction and breakdown. Because JIT is so dependent upon the responsiveness of workers it drives a whole sequence of management initiatives to involve and train workers in all aspects of the production process. No longer is it sufficient for workers to understand their role alone in the production cycle; they also need to understand the complete flow of the production cycle from raw material to point of sale. As a result, extensive briefing needs to take place in informing employees of the objective of the company in introducing the JIT system and outlining their role in its implementation. One of the end results of the full implementation of JIT is shrinking inventory levels—which can be profoundly disturbing to employees who have been accustomed to a 'just in case' approach to production. The existence of large stock holdings in certain cases acts as a psychological security buffer—their elimination or persistent reduction can trigger fear and anxiety in the minds of employees who may fear that the company is reducing its stock prior to closure. Indeed, there has been one case where a small non-union company in electronics components manufacture became unionised due to inadequate explanation by management of the reasons for stock elimination prior to JIT implementation. Total involvement of employees is necessary to install JIT successfully and this sometimes implies a total shift of emphasis within management in their relations with employees. Indeed, as implementation of JIT frequently demands solution of production and quality-related problems, workers have frequently to be involved in their solution. This is one reason why quality circles have been revived in many manufacturing companies during recent years. Quality circles (QC) are a technique which combines theories of group dynamics with a statistical approach to quality control. A quality circle is a group of people, typically between six and ten in number, who meet regularly to discuss and solve production and quality-related problems. The circle meets under the guidance of a circle leader, typically a supervisor or superior, to identify problems and generate possible solutions to the problem using brainstorming techniques. Members of the QC are trained in techniques of statistical analysis, including 'cause and effect' analysis and 'pareto analysis' (so called after the Italian economist, Alfred Pareto, who demonstrated the 'pareto principle' or 80:20 rule, for example, 80 per cent of typical inventory value is accounted for by 20 per cent of the inventory maintained, etc.). When potential solutions are generated, the circle works to identify which solution is most appropriate and likely to succeed, costs of implementation are established and the circle's findings are presented to an evaluation team of top management who may decide to accept or reject the possible solutions presented. Introducing quality circles is a long, intensive process both in terms of assuring unions that established collective bargaining mechanisms will remain undisturbed and convincing supervisors and management that their utility will not be eroded. In many cases, supervisors need to be trained to lead quality circles and also to view their subordinates as potential repositories of useful ideas and solutions to production-related problems, which many supervisors trained to 'control' their subordinates find difficult to adjust to. Hill, commenting on the results of an investigation into quality circles in Northern Ireland, points out that while

> it is possible for quality circles to survive and achieve in Ireland . . . the QC technique is not a panacea; nor is it appropriate for all industrial organisations. For example it is unlikely to operate successfully in a firm where industrial relations are poor or where the future in terms of jobs is uncertain. Where the environment does appear suitable, it would also be inadvisable to expect too much too quickly . . . an output of two or three major project completions per circle per year would appear to be a reasonable expectation.[49]

He goes on to point out that the establishment of quality circles often results in an improved working relationship between management and employees, greater awareness of the importance of quality and possibly some improvement in the quality of output or service and cost reduction, increased involvement of employees which improves job satisfaction and wider sharing of responsibility for organisational performance amongst employees.

Other conditions necessary for successful implementation of JIT according to Owen include a highly flexible multi-skilled workforce and a simplified pay structure. 'Multi-skilling' of operatives is often necessary to ensure that operatives can detect and solve problems in the process as they arise in order to ensure continuity of workflow through the production process. Again, this often means a blurring of demarcation lines between employees, particularly between maintenance craftsmen and semi-skilled employees. The pay system consequently has to be simplified and in some cases a 'pay for knowledge acquired' or 'skill-based pay' approach is used, where employees are encouraged to become multi-functional and are paid at the top level of skill acquired. (Some interesting training programmes designed to increase speed of skill acquisition have been used in Krups Engineering Ltd, where computer-based training was utilised.)

Redesign of work organisation, away from flow line principles toward 'cell group' working (autonomous and semi-autonomous team working), is frequently another by-product of implementing a JIT system. It can be seen therefore that new approaches to production such as JIT may fundamentally alter approaches to workforce management and work organisation. The personnel department plays a major role in the management of this change process, both in terms of establishing teams to solve production problems, engaging consultants to advise on quality circle operations, redesign of pay systems, re-evaluation of jobs altered by new technology and advising on the choices which can be made in relation to the type of technology installed (in terms of their skill, motivation and commitment implications). 'Quality management' initiatives have not been confined to the private sector alone. Major quality initiatives using the Scandinavian Airline System 'putting people first' programmes have been implemented in Aer Lingus and Aer Rianta. The purpose of these programmes is to highlight the importance of customer satisfaction (dependent upon perceptions of quality of service provided in many cases) in purchasing decisions and the importance of viewing fellow-employees as 'clients' of one's own service.

The 'just in time' system has been described by many authors as typifying the approach to production within many Japanese enterprises. Its diffusion and emulation by Western competitors has led various authors to describe it as the virtual 'Japanisation' of Western industry. These authors argue that Japanese employment strategies often follow in the wake of these production methods. Many large Japanese corporations, for example, utilise a core-periphery employment strategy with perhaps 30 per cent of employees representing the core workforce. Indeed JIT production systems within car manufacture in Japan allow widespread sub-contracting of work to suppliers and utilisation of part-time and temporary workers during peak production periods. If the reader perceives shades of the flexible firm emerging, then the reader is correct. Perhaps new technology will further accentuate 'Japanese drift' in employment strategies of the type identified in the earlier section of this chapter.

THE 'NEW INDUSTRIAL RELATIONS' AND THE 'NON-UNION' PHENOMENA

It would be remiss to conclude this chapter without some consideration of the extent to which certain trends indicate the emergence of 'new' industrial relations. These trends include the steep drop in union density during the recession, the decline in official and unofficial strikes, the limited emergence of 'new style' agreements and a hardening of attitudes towards union recognition, as witnessed by the increased number of recognition disputes being processed by the Labour Court in recent years, and the sustained ability of certain companies to maintain a non-union status despite recently increased recruitment drives by the unions. As Wood points out, there is considerable dispute (arising from similar trends in the US and UK) as to both the novelty, performance and extent of the new industrial relations.[50] Indeed Owen commenting on the Irish situation argues that 'notions of a new realism, of a new industrial relations, constitute not merely a conceit, but a calculated one'.[51] The purpose of this final section is to examine the factors outlined above and to speculate as to whether a permanent shift in emphasis has in fact occurred in the collective bargaining sphere. There is no disputing the fact that trade unions have suffered as a result of the recession. Roche points out that trade unions lost 51,000 members during the 1980-85 period.[52] This decline emanated from the interaction of three major factors: the business cycle, alterations in the structural composition of employment and institutional factors (the employment practices of firms). Low inflation since the mid 1980s, the decline in employment and rapid rise in unemployment since 1980 represent the business cycle factors contributing to this decline. The structural shift in employment away from industry and towards the service sector (away from the sector where unions have been strongest and towards the sector—excluding insurance and banking—where unions have been weakest in organisation) has also acted against the union's favour. Similarly, the 'institutional' factor *vis à vis* the practice of 'human resource management' has in certain companies eroded the perceived requirements for trade union membership. Some would argue that this trend is a secular one which will eventually result in the disappearance of the unions from the industrial scene: the 'dinosaur theory'.[53] But certain factors could militate against this scenario developing:

a) trade unions are still strong within the employed categories of the labour force, accounting for 60 per cent of all of those in employment;

b) the public sector, while unlikely to grow, would also seem unlikely to be dismantled. The Fianna Fail party has abandoned earlier flirtations with the notion of privatisation in favour of a 'neo-corporatist' approach to economic development and wage restraint in the public sector via the 1987 Programme for National Economic Recovery;

c) the unions are likely to play an increased role in relation to peripheral or marginalised workers, particularly the low-paid, temporary and part-time workers. While these categories are difficult to organise, they are also the category which has most to gain from unionisation. Furthermore, trade union membership is prone to fluctuations in the business cycle and could conceivably begin to increase if the economic climate improves. Of course, a critical factor here is whether employees in the 'knowledge' growth industries of financial services, high technology, pharmaceuticals etc. will join trade unions if their employing organisations pursue a progressive employee relations strategy (see the following chapter for a full discussion of this point).

At first glance, the aggregate decline in official and unofficial strikes (discussed in chapter 10) would support the view that a 'new realism' in industrial relations is emerging. However, it would be unwise to suggest that an upturn in industrial conflict is unlikely to occur if economic conditions improve, as many studies of strikes (Kelly and Brannick, 1988, Wallace and O'Shea, 1987) highlight the importance of the business cycle factor.[54] Both strike frequency and mandays lost attributable to strikes were at their highest levels in Ireland during the 1970s when GNP growth was at its highest. The business cycle plays a critical role in structuring expectations about the likely success and consequences of taking industrial action; when unemployment is high and jobs may be at risk, individuals are less likely to take industrial action unless there is an overwhelming importance attached to the issue in dispute.

Nonetheless, the work of Kelly and Brannick points out some significant alterations in strike activity rates in the private sector.[55] As they point out:

> In the twenty-seven year period, 1960-86, 79 per cent of strikes in Ireland took place in private sector companies; these strikes accounted for 59 per cent of total workers involved and 68 per cent of total mandays lost. These proportions for the private sector were highest during the 1960s and have been on the decline throughout the 1970s and 1980s, thus the private sector is very much less dominant in the overall strike picture, with a noticeable shift in the overall volume of strike activity towards the public sector.

It could be argued that this shift downward in private sector strike activity will be maintained, as many organisations have revived consultation procedures and improved their control of the industrial relations process during the recession. If this is the case, and the Programme for National Recovery is successful in securing industrial peace in the public sector, then there may well be a long lasting downward shift in strike activity. Wage concession bargaining, apart from the well-publicised (and exceptional) case of the B & I shipping line in 1987 has not been evident during recent years although it might be argued that the recruitment grade wage structures in the banks and Aer Lingus are concessionary in nature and evidence of a reduction in union power. New-style agreements of a *comprehensive* nature (single union negotiating rights, peace clauses and pendulum arbitration) would not seem to have developed in Ireland to any great extent although features of these have been reported (for example, the contentious Packard

Electric 'no strike' clause) from time to time. However, there is nothing essentially 'new' about any of these features and it could be argued that many organisations have sought to incorporate these into their agreements in the past. There would, however, appear to be strong evidence to suggest an increasing opposition to unionisation in the 1980s, particularly within indigenous Irish companies. McGovern (1988) points out that in the 1980s the total number of recommendations issued in general and on union recognition by the Labour Court reached their highest ever level.[56]

John Horgan has also spoken of the increasing tendency of employers to make concessions via the Labour Court rather than offer these concessions themselves.[57] Many of these cases have involved small companies ranging from courier services to high-tech companies in pharmaceuticals, which McGovern points out does not augur well for union recruitment in these 'growth' industries.[58] He also identifies an upturn in the frequency, size and duration of union recognition strikes in the 1980-85 period. When one combines these findings with the emergence of large non-union establishments in manufacturing during the 1970s (see chapter 10 for further details) there would indeed seem to be considerable increases in the nature of the challenges posed to the unions in the 1980s.While the 'new realism' may well be a feature of a cyclical downturn in the economy's fortunes, the extent to which the unions overcome these challenges will determine the nature of the terrain on which collective bargaining is played out in the 1990s.

To conclude, several major trends have been identified in this chapter which are likely to impinge upon personnel management practice:

a) the growth in atypical employment which has allowed firms to experiment with a wider range of manpower-planning strategies, including core-periphery organisational models;

b) widespread introduction of new technology, which has involved personnel practitioners in the challenging tasks of both managing change and influencing strategic decisions made in relation to the motivational and employee commitment implications of alterations in work organisation associated with the introduction of new technology;

c) quality management initiatives associated with Japanese-style quests for 'perfection in production' and the introduction of 'just in time' approaches to the social and technical organisation of production;

d) the emergence of increased opposition to unionisation as indicated by the increase in the numbers of large non-union companies existing in Ireland during the 1980s and the recent upsurge in union recognition strikes. The next chapter explores the link between human resource management, non-union management strategies and the implications for the unions in greater detail.

Chapter 12

Human Resource Management: Promise, Possibilities and Limitations

INTRODUCTION

'Human Resource Management' or HRM for short, has emerged as one of the 'buzzwords' of the late 1980s in relation to workforce management. The very use of the term HRM evokes an extremely mixed reaction amongst academics, management practitioners and trade unionists alike. Many academics, and indeed practitioners, who believe in a collective industrial relations tradition look upon the practice of 'human resource management' as a clinical calculated approach to reducing the power of trade unions. Others point to the tremendous possibilities inherent in what is seen as a new proactive and strategic approach to workforce management. Some personnel practitioners view the term with a jaundiced eye and consider it as a simple re-titling of personnel management or as a new 'fad' approach, which will follow the usual path to oblivion of 'flavour of the month' approaches to workforce management. Other personnel practitioners, particularly those from high-technology and advanced manufacturing plants, react enthusiastically to concepts such as 'control versus commitment' approaches to workforce management, and identify with personnel practices designed to elicit the loyalty and commitment of employees. In the practitioners' case, the argument often turns on whether they come from workplaces where unions are recognised or not. Certainly it is our experience that personnel specialists from high-technology, large non-union manufacturing plants immediately identify with the approaches lauded in prescriptive texts such as the 'Managing Human Assets' textbook produced by the Harvard Business School group.[1] Trade unionists (particularly officers and lay representatives) share many of the aforementioned divisions. Some see HRM as a calculated approach to avoid unionisation and as a technique to create a unitarist culture within the organisation which sees no necessary or obvious role for trade union representation. Others see it as providing what their union membership have always wanted:

consultation before major organisational changes, regular briefings on the operating success or decline of the business, good pay and conditions, including advanced welfare facilities, the opportunity to train and develop with the aid of company-assisted tuition refund policies, recognition of individual merit and performance which is monitored by performance appraisal, etc.

It can be seen therefore, that considerable conceptual and empirical confusion exists in relation to the topic. The purpose of this chapter is to attempt to identify the environmental changes which have promoted this new approach to workforce management, to identify the range of alternative approaches described as HRM, to present a case for a distinctive view of HRM and propose an associated model, and finally to examine the evidence in support of such a view. The key issue of whether or not the practice of human resource management is compatible with collective trade union representation is also examined.

THE EMERGENCE OF A STRATEGIC PERSPECTIVE ON WORKFORCE MANAGEMENT

In order to understand the HRM phenomenon, we need to understand the factors which have popularly promoted it as the new way forward for workforce management. Various authors have enumerated these as including: the quest for competitive advantage linked to total quality initiatives in production; financial market preferences for decentralised organisational models; shifting employment patterns and declining trade union power; the influential 'excellence' literature on corporate culture; the supposed failure of traditional approaches to personnel management; and the availability of new models of workforce management. One can add to this list the rise to senior management of business graduates influenced by the humanistic psychology of Argyris, McGregor and Alderfer. It is worth examining each of these factors in turn.

The Search for Competitive Advantage

Competitive advantage can be described as any factor(s) which allow one organisation to differentiate its product or service from another competitor in order to increase the organisation's existing or potential market share of a consumer product market.

Two obvious factors by which organisations differentiate their products or service are price and quality. In the case of manufactured goods (watches, transistors, aircraft components, jeans, etc.) either or both of these factors will affect the purchasing decision of potential consumers. Similarly, services (education, financial services, airline passage, advertising, retailing, etc.) are differentiated amongst competitors on the basis of price and quality. In situations where organisations are producing similar goods or services for a particular market segment then *perceived* costs and quality of the goods or service will be the major differentiating factor. In certain cases, price cannot be lowered beyond a certain point if breakeven is to be achieved. In this situation, quality of the goods or service is the factor which allows one organisation to gain advantage over the other. Airline services are a frequently cited example of a business where competition (while undoubtedly dependent on pricing decisions) is often on the basis of level of customer service offered. Feigenbaum points out that increasingly the purchasing decision of both goods and services is being made less on the basis of price and more often on the basis of quality.[2] The Irish data on PIMS (Profit Impact of Market Strategy) collected by Charles Carroll would support that viewpoint.[3] Quality itself is an elusive concept and most individuals include aspects such as durability, reliability and 'classiness' if asked to explain the concept. Robson defines it as 'meeting the (stated) requirements of the customer both now and in the future'.[4] If organisations wish to achieve dominance or superiority then increasingly they must focus on achieving the definition of quality outlined above. This implies that activities within organisations must be aligned with each other to achieve this goal; for example, each sub-unit (department, section, etc.) must view itself as both a client of a service provided to it (by other departments, sections, etc.) and a producer of a service to other departments until external customer satisfaction is achieved. Put another way, in servicing external customer requirements, sub-units within the organisation must view themselves as elements in a quality chain oriented towards meeting these requirements. This is described by Robson as 'the internal and external customer orientation'.

Achievement of quality thus defined becomes synonymous with the care and attention to each step of the production process given by every employee involved. For an organisation to achieve competitive advantage it needs to orient and utilise its human resources towards the achievement of this goal. Beer *et al* (1985) argue that human resources are often under-utilised within organisations by comparison with the attention paid to resource utilisation in the finance and technology areas.[5] They also argue that by virtue of this under-utilisation, organisations which have a coherent strategy to utilise their human resources will often achieve an 'edge' on competitors which do not maximise their utilisation of employees' potentialities. Similarly, if an organisation aims to compete largely on price the extent to which employees contribute to cost control of raw materials, avoidance of wastage etc. will again have major bearing on the competitive position of an organisation. It can be seen therefore, that an organisation's competitive advantage can only be achieved via maximum utilisation of all its resources: human, financial and technical.

Shifting Employment Patterns and Declining Trade Union Power
The decline in trade union density, itself a major indicator of trade union power, has been described elsewhere.[6] Nonetheless, a few points are worth noting again. The decline in trade union density has been largely associated with the decline in absolute terms of the numbers employed in the Irish Republic and the shift away from industrial employment to service employment. Additionally, the substantive employment practices of firms, particularly the practices of large non-union companies, have acted to reduce union penetration, particularly in the high-technology sectors of the economy. This decline in union power has facilitated a switch away from traditional collective adversarial industrial relations towards more individual co-operation centred employee relations of the human resource management type.

The Excellence Literature on Corporate Culture
The best-selling works of Kanter and Peters and Waterman have had a major effect in popularising the notion that a strong organisational culture can contribute significantly to an organisation's innovativeness, flexibility, responsiveness and ultimately success.[7] All of these studies highlight the importance of a firm's employment practices in establishing a strong organisation culture. Organisational culture is itself an elusive concept, but generally refers to a system of shared beliefs, norms and attitudes within an organisation as to the legitimacy or otherwise of its objectives and practices pursued in their achievement. When an organisation's members do not share a common set of beliefs or adhere to a common set of norms it can be described as a weak culture, usually composed of sub-cultures which often compete with each other. Toner in his seminal work on non-union companies in Ireland identifies a range of employment practices designed to emphasise the 'mutuality' or shared interests of employees and management in achieving certain organisational goals.[8] These goals include firm profitability and growth, high-quality production and high performance. A range of employment practices to support the achievement of these goals is identified by Toner and includes lifelong employment, single status, merit pay, regular communications, gain sharing, internal promotion and continuous development of employees. The effect of these employment practices is to create a tangible awareness amongst employees of the shared interdependency between their contribution to productive efficiency and the achievement of corporate objectives.

The 'Failure' of Traditional Approaches to Personnel Management and the Availability of New Organisational Models
When judged in terms of its impact upon strategic decision-taking in relation to employment practices, it could be argued that personnel

management has failed to promote a strategic awareness at board level of the importance of an organisation's human resources contribution to corporate success. Indeed it is noteworthy that HRM is a generalist perspective which places a strong emphasis upon devolving the practice of personnel management to first line supervisory management. Indeed, Beer *et al* argue that policy decisions in relation to human resource issues are too important to be left to personnel specialists and need to be incorporated into mainstream management activities.[9]

Furthermore, new 'models' of workforce management have emerged (see later) from the business schools, which blend aspects of the scientific management approach and the humanistic growth psychology perspective of Argyris and McGregor. As Guest points out, the business schools can act as influential gatekeepers for new developments in business practice.[10] Courses in HRM are now part of the prescribed MBA curriculum at business centres such as Harvard, Berkeley and MIT.

EMPIRICAL AND CONCEPTUAL DERIVATIONS OF HRM
Much of the confusion surrounding HRM stems from the fact that it can be derived either from practice (empirical derivation) or from theory (conceptual derivation). If the concept is empirically derived then practices *described* as HRM by definition *become* HRM. Thus, if one describes the workforce management strategies of large non-union companies as HRM, the term becomes synonymous with the employment practices of large non-union companies. HRM thus risks the danger of becoming a catch-all phrase devoid of any meaning. An alternative approach is to develop a sound theoretical basis for a model of HRM using concepts derived from organisational behaviour. This allows one to develop propositions about the likely impact of personnel policies in terms of employee responses and behaviour. In an effort to make sense out of the various definitions and descriptions of HRM, David Guest at the London School of Economics (LSE) developed the framework[11] shown in figure 12.1.

Dimension 1 is a 'soft-hard' dimension depending on whether the emphasis is on the human resource viewpoint associated with McGregor's Theory Y (that is, that employees are creative, responsible, goal-oriented individuals who respond to enriched task environments, discretion, autonomy and reward systems which are trust-based) or on management with its implications of strategy and quantification. Dimension 2 is a loose-tight dimension depending on how tightly defined the term HRM is.

In its loosest form, HRM simply is a re-titling of personnel management. This is sometimes a method by which a personnel department attempts to revive a jaded image and is likely to be the least durable and effective approach unless there are significant changes in approach accompanying the

Fig. 12.1. Definitions of human resource management

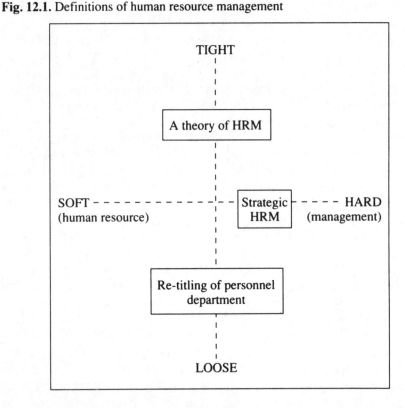

change of title. In its strongest form, HRM is carefully defined to reflect a particular approach to workforce management and has an explicit theoretical basis. Furthermore, it should emphasise a strategic approach—it should be goal oriented—and ensure that the various sub-elements of personnel activities (recruitment, selection, appraisal, training and development) are *coherent* (one activity does not undermine the other) and *mutually reinforcing* (each activity supports the other) in order to achieve these goals and objectives. If one is to argue that HRM is distinctive it is necessary to do three things:

a) utilising a comparator, show how it differs from accepted practice;

b) develop an explicit theoretical model;

c) compare empirical evidence with the predictions of the model in relation to specified outcomes.

Comparisons between HRM and Traditional Personnel Management

The most developed framework to date has been developed by Guest at the LSE, where he contrasts stereotypes of HRM and personnel management.[12] This framework is outlined in table 12.1.

Table 12.1 Personnel Management and HRM compared

	Personnel Management	HRM
Input into corporate planning	Issue specific	Integrated
Time & planning perspective	• Short-term • Reactive, ad-hoc • Marginal	• Long-term • Proactive • Strategic
Psychological contract	• Compliance	• Commitment
Employee relations perspective	• Pluralist • Collective • Low-trust • Adversarial	• Unitarist • Individual • High-trust • Mutuality
Preferred structures/ systems	• Bureaucratic/mechanistic • Centralised • Formal defined roles	• Organic • Devolved • Flexible roles
Roles	Specialist/professional	• Largely integrated into line management • Change agent
Evaluation criteria	Cost minimisation	• Maximum utilisation of human resource (Human asset accounting)
Employment assurance	nil	• Implicit guarantees

adapted from Walton 1985, Guest, 1987.

It can be seen that on these criteria HRM is indeed different from personnel management, although there is some merit in the argument that when personnel management and HRM are compared at the normative level ('this is how the practice should be') there is little difference. Guest wisely offers the caveat that one should not assume that HRM is necessarily better than personnel management. He argues that, in certain contexts (such as public service bureaucracies, organisations with adversarial industrial relations, traditions etc.), personnel management in the traditional mode may be the most appropriate course of action to adopt. It begs the question however, of how one might *move* away from such a traditional mode and *towards* a HRM-type approach of the type identified in table 12.1. This is a critical issue, that is, how does one move away from a control-oriented strategy towards a commitment-oriented strategy, and it is considered in some detail at the end of the chapter.

When HRM is contrasted with more traditional personnel management, as in table 12.1, a number of key differences emerge. Firstly, human resource considerations are fully integrated into the corporate planning process in the HRM model, whereas within the traditional approach to personnel management such inputs are ad hoc and more issue-specific in nature. Secondly, HRM is viewed as being more long term in its orientation, more proactive and strategic than personnel management. Thirdly, HRM effects the management process by inculcating loyalty and commitment to the organisation amongst employees while personnel management effects this process via supervisory control. Fourthly, HRM is unitarist in nature (seeing no obvious or necessary areas of conflict between employer and employee) and as a result there is a greater focus upon individual employee relations with a greater emphasis on high-trust relations. HRM emphasises the 'mutuality' of interest between employee and organisation, for example, the need for high performance to achieve profitability which allows the organisation to provide job security to employees. Personnel management, by contrast, is more pluralist in orientation, seeing the organisation as legitimately composed of various interest groups. An a result it is more comfortable with the collective representation of employees by trade unions and it is characterised by low-trust relations and an adversarial (counter-campaigning) stance in industrial relations.

The fifth major difference highlighted is related to preferred operating structures and systems. HRM is characterised as operating in an organic or fluid organisation structure with devolved responsibilities and flexible roles, whereas personnel management is characterised as a bureaucratic role-dominant approach with formal defined roles (often effected through rigid job classification systems).

The sixth major difference is in relation to the role of the personnel department. In the HRM approach, considerable authority and responsibility for motivating and managing employees is devolved to first line and supervisory management with the personnel specialist adopting an 'architect' or change-agent role in relation to the achievement of corporate-wide organisation change and corporate culture transformation.

Evaluation criteria is the seventh major difference in approach. Traditional personnel management is characterised as subservient to the dominant organisational philosophy of management accounting, with its emphasis on cost control of overheads (including human resources in this instance). HRM is oriented towards maximum utilisation of employee potentialities, and in certain cases a system of human asset accounting underpins this.

Finally, HRM is characterised by Walton as providing implicit guarantees of job security while traditional personnel management approaches rarely, if ever, provide such guarantees.[13] Torrington adds to the distinctions outlined in table 12.1 by arguing that HRM represents a shift in emphasis from workforce centredness to resource centredness, from a traditional 'man in the middle' role to a total identification with management interests, and from a unified organisation-wide personnel strategy to a core-periphery approach.[14] Torrington argues that:

> we have a major shift of approach to the employment of people; moving away from the traditional orientation of personnel management towards conciliation, propitiation and motivation of employees as a potential uncooperative cost. Those who do the work of the organisation are instead to be seen as an asset, in which to invest, needing less supervision and more scope and autonomy. A less apparent feature of HRM is that some of those who do the organisation's work are regarded as less committed to their organisation through being located at the periphery rather than in the core. The starting point becomes the resource required rather than the workforce to be deployed, with overtones of human capital theory.

As defined by Mackay and Torrington, HRM is 'directed mainly towards management needs for human resources (not only employees) to be provided and deployed.[15] There is greater emphasis on planning, monitoring and control, rather than on problem solving and meditation. It is totally identified with management interest and it is relatively distant from the workforce as a whole.' One can detect a certain critical tone in Mackay and Torrington's definition and it would appear that their view of HRM is that it is a colder, more clinical and calculative approach than traditional personnel management practices.

There are some dangers here for the credibility and effectiveness of personnel specialists. For the personnel specialist to be effective, s/he must have some identification and loyalty to the workforce. If s/he is totally identified with managerial interests then the ability to articulate the position of other interest groups may be lost, with potential consequential undermining of effectiveness and credibility. One could also point out that many of the role models of HRM emerge from the US where unionisation rates are much lower and the pluralist tradition in industrial relations is weaker.

Armstrong, acknowledging this fact, advances a revised concept of HRM which is based on four major principles:[16]

a) human resources are the most important assets an organisation has, and their effective management is the key to its success;

b) this success is most likely to be achieved if the personnel policies and procedures of the enterprise are closely linked with, and make a major contribution to, the achievement of corporate objectives and strategic plans; *c)* the corporate culture and the values, organisational climate and managerial behaviour that emanate from that culture will exert a major influence on the achievement of excellence. This culture needs to be managed, which means that organisational values may need to be changed or reinforced, and continuous effort, starting from the top, may be required to get them accepted and acted upon;

d) integration, in the sense of getting the members of the organisation working together with a sense of common purpose, is an important aim of HRM, but this must take account of the fact that all organisations are pluralist societies in which people have differing interest and concerns which they may well feel need to be defended collectively.

The principles enunciated above include aspects of both the 'hard' and 'soft' versions of HRM. The quantitative and business strategy aspects of controlling headcount (the 'hard' view) is blended with an emphasis on human resource utilisation, communication, motivation and transmission of organisational values. As an approach to industrial relations and workforce management, it is markedly different from the proceduralised, rule administration emphasis so commonly found in texts on industrial relations.

There is considerably less emphasis on joint regulation, negotiation, custom and practice, etc. Instead, the management of organisational culture is emphasised and, one assumes, is expected to replace the traditional framework of industrial relations outlined above. If this is the case, and if collective bargaining structures continue to remain strongly embedded in unionised environments, it may mean that HRM approaches of the type enunciated by Armstrong may only work in union-free or weakly unionised (or organised) establishments. Of course, it is conceivable that an evolutionary approach to the introduction of HRM into such environments might progressively erode collective bargaining activities.

SOME MODELS OF HUMAN RESOURCE MANAGEMENT

There has been little development, with the exception of Guest's contribution, of an explicit theory of HRM. However, there have been some models developed. One of the most impressive of these has been the model developed by Beer *et al,* the Harvard Business School (HBS) model which presents a broad casual map of the determinants and consequences of HRM policies (see figure 12.2).[17] It is not a theory as Guest points out because the 'range of stakeholder interests and situational factors emphasise policy choices rather than clear prescriptions'.[18] The HBS model is outlined in figure 12.2.

Fig. 12.2. Map of the HRM territory

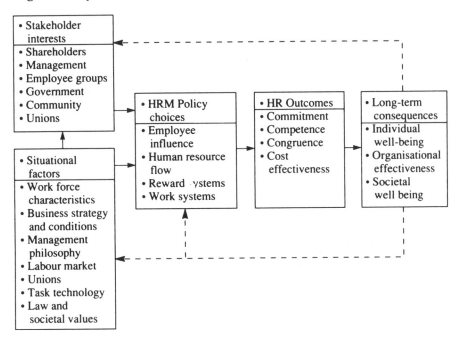

Beer *et al* define HRM very broadly as 'involving all management decisions and actions that affect the nature of the relationship between the organisation and its employees—its human resources'. This definition highlights three aspects of HRM:

a) that the majority of decisions impact upon employees irrespective of whether that decision is concerned with plant location decisions, diversification or office layout;

b) that the nature of the relationship between employee and organisation is affected by such decisions (it may act to strengthen or dilute the linkages which bind individuals to the organisation);

c) the fact that HRM is the responsibility of all those who manage and supervise within the organisation.

In the HBS model, HRM seeks to achieve long-term objectives for the organisation while taking account of the various stakeholders within the organisation and their various interest positions. The desired HR outcomes are *commitment* (strong acceptance of and belief in the organisation's goals and values, willingness to exert effort on behalf of the organisation, and a strong desire to maintain membership of the organisation); *competence* (skills, knowledge and experience necessary for job performance); *cost effectiveness* (in terms of cost stability of wages and benefits, industrial peace, absenteeism, etc.); and *congruence* (mutuality of interest between organisation and individual employee). These HR outcomes are affected by the policy choices made in four key areas: the reward system, human resource flow, work system and employee influence. The HR outcomes further impact upon (see figure 12.2) the long-term consequences for the wellbeing of the individual, organisational effectiveness and societal wellbeing.

The reward system area includes both financial and non-financial rewards. The human resource flow policy area includes inflow policies (recruitment, selection, socialisation and organisational norms); internal flow policies (evaluation of potential, career development, internal placement, etc.); and outflow policies (termination, retirement, redundancy). The work system policy area includes the combined interaction between job tasks, technology, skills, management style and personnel policies and practices, while employee influence refers to the extent to which employees are involved and their preferences taken account of in making decisions which affect employees' working lives. In the HBS model, employee influence is considered as a key indicator of the organisation's corporate philosophy towards employees. All of these policy areas are viewed in the HBS model as areas of strategic choice which will dramatically affect employee behaviour and attitude towards the organisation. The policy choices made are constrained by two additional factors: situational constraints (including workforce characteristics, business strategy, management philosophy, the labour market, unions, task technology, laws and societal values) and stakeholder interests (including shareholders, management, employee groups, government, community and union expectations).

In the HBS model the general manager or chief executive assumes a key role in aligning the corporate and personnel strategies to be pursued. Indeed, it is the view of the HBS researchers that only when this activity is carried out by the chief executive can it be expected that coherence between personnel and business strategy will be achieved. It should be noted however, that, while chief executive involvement should be welcomed, not all chief executives will have the breadth of vision, experience or expertise to carry out this activity on their own. The personnel specialist should continue to have a key advisory role, even more so in view of the fact that policy choices must be delivered on at the operational level via the routine personnel activities of line and supervisory management.

The HBS model however, is not a prescriptive theory. Nonetheless, it has had a powerful impact upon the thinking of senior managers within the US as their approach is widely taught in many top business schools as an essential integrative element of the MBA curriculum.

Guest, while acknowledging the importance of the HBS approach in emphasising the strategic nature of HRM policy areas, argues that 'HRM only becomes more interesting to academics and practitioners, if it can be presented as a novel and distinctive approach to management'.[19] He proceeds to elaborate a theory of HRM which has its roots in three developments: the industrial application of 'humanistic/growth' psychology, the utilisation of a range of psychological techniques and the use of strategy.

The first of these factors concerns the revived interest in the ideas of Alderfer, McGregor and Argyris.[20] These theorists have emphasised the need for organisations to focus on the intrinsic and extrinsic needs of individuals and subsequently to develop employment practices which strengthen behavioural and affective (attitudinal) linkages between employees and the organisation in order to achieve organisational goals. Richard Walton is one of the most influential of the current exponents of this view and he argues that if organisations develop policies and practices which emphasise 'mutuality' of interest between employer and employee (such as gainsharing, employment assurance) then employees will become committed to organisational goals and targets provided in return they are given sufficient autonomy, discretion, resources (financial, time, material) and rewards to sustain motivation.[21]

The second factor concerns the application of psychological techniques to the recruitment, socialisation and performance management of employees.

Fig. 12.3. An integrated model of the application of psychological techniques to workforce management

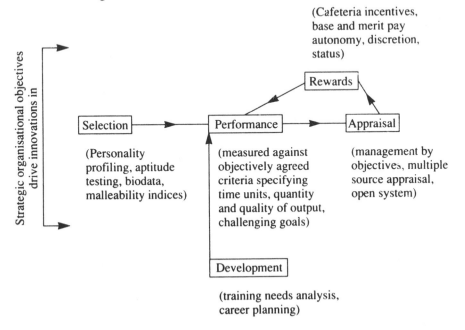

An integrated model of the application of such methods is shown in figure 12.3.While only a small number of organisations (in the UK and Irish context) would seem to use an integrated approach to the above, research at Warwick University and the University of Limerick suggests an upsurge of interest in many organisations of at least one of the above psychological applications. More recently the Government Task Force Report on Management Development has suggested that there is much to be gained from such applications (for example, open learning using programmed instructional aids which are cognitively based). Guest points out that US industry is much more receptive to experimentation, with ideas derived from organisational behaviour due to the fact that (on a per capita basis) there are more organisational psychologists working in US industry than in the UK.[22] In the Irish context this is also true, but it is likely that the type of emphasis in teaching at many of the biggest Irish business schools on organisational psychology since the 1960s will probably allow greater diffusion of these techniques in the near future.

The third factor, the use of strategy, according to Guest is the distinguishing feature of HRM when compared with previous false dawns (the organisation design and quality of work life movements). The factors promoting a concern with achieving competitive advantage were discussed earlier. Greater human resource utilisation is often a key element of the drive to achieve and sustain competitive advantage. As shown in figure 12.3, personnel practices need to reinforce each other and the careful application of psychological techniques to recruitment, selection, appraisal, rewards and development can provide thematic unity to this process.

The theory of HRM proposed by Guest (1988) has two central propositions.[23] His *first proposition* is that organisations will be more successful (in terms of organisational outcome criteria specified in figure 12.4) if they pursue the following HRM goals: strategic integration, employee commitment, flexibility and quality.

His *second proposition* is that these HRM outcomes can be achieved through the consistent application of a set of policy levers (see the left-hand side of figure 12.4).

Strategic integration infers that *a)* HRM is integrated into strategic planning; *b)* HRM policies are integrated so that they complement each other across policy issues and across hierarchical levels of application; *c)* that the importance of HRM must be accepted and internalised by line managers at all levels so that it informs their day-to-day management practice; and *d)* that all employees are integrated into the organisation. Employee commitment includes both affective or attitudinal commitment and behavioural commitment to high performance. Attitudinal commitment to the organisation would encompass a strong belief in and acceptance of the organisation's goals and values, a willingness to exert considerable effort on behalf of the organisation and a strong desire to maintain membership in the organisation.

Fig. 12.4. A theory of HRM

HRM policies	Human resource outcomes	Organisational outcomes
Organisation/job design		High job performance
Management of change	Strategic integration	High • Problem-solving • Change • Innovation

Recruitment
  selection
  socialisation
	Commitment	

Appraisal, training
  development
	Flexibility/
	  adaptability
		High cost-
		  effectiveness

Reward systems		
Communication	Quality	Low • Turnover • Absence • Grievances

Leadership/culture/strategy

Flexibility in Guest's model includes structural mechanisms to ensure that organisations are responsive to external and internal pressures to change. This implies that jobs be designed 'on the assumption of high trust and competence to ensure that variances can be handled close to the source of error or uncertainty'. Thus jobs are to be designed to maximise the autonomy and self-control of employees. Interestingly, flexibility according to Guest should encompass functional (multi-skilling) flexibility and numerical flexibility, including the use of subcontracting and external consultants. Guest's model therefore implicitly builds in the core-periphery organisational model into the theory of HRM, a point overlooked by many academic commentators.

In order to achieve the strategic goal of quality or 'perfection in production', employee competencies (knowledge, skills, experience and attitude) must be attuned and management policies and practices must encourage, lead and reward the pursuit of total quality.

His second proposition is that HRM outcomes can be achieved by the consistent application of a set of policy levers (organisation and job design; management of change; recruitment, selection and socialisation; appraisal, training and development; reward systems and communication).

As Guest acknowledges, this may be construed as nothing more than sophisticated personnel management. However, he argues that its distinctive quality is the focus on the HRM policy goals as the basis for policy choice; it is therefore necessary to select for commitment, to emphasise socialisation into a specific culture with its expectations of high performance standards, to use communication as feedback to reinforce quality standards, etc.

The final element of Guest's model emphasises the role of top management in the organisation in leading, managing and embedding an appropriate organisational culture. Leadership by example, particularly in transmitting the organisation's philosophy (in terms of 'what we aim for, why we value it' and explicating a code of practice as to 'how we achieve it') is therefore emphasised in this model.

One of the most interesting and challenging aspects of Guest's model is its essentially unitarist philosophy and its individualistic orientation. Its values are unitarist, in that there would seem to be no obvious acceptance of a fundamental interest difference between employer or management and employees. This, for practitioners and academics who believe in a collective industrial relations tradition, is very hard to accept and one could argue that Guest's model therefore, by definition, excludes its application to unionised environments. In addition, the value emphasis on commitment and individualism is one which most shopfloor workers are unfamiliar with, although many managers are familiar with such an organisational approach. The type of HRM policies pursued by the large non-union and some unionised companies in Irish electronics are consistent with such approaches and are applied at both shop floor, supervisory and managerial levels. HRM poses many challenges to the collective pluralist tradition of industrial relations and trade union representation. Nonetheless, HRM by itself is not necessarily anti-union. However, by eroding the usual basis for unionisation it poses serious challenges for the trade unions' normal adversarial *modus operandi* and basis for organisation. A fundamental issue is whether in unionised environments HRM is integrated into the existing collective bargaining structures or whether unions are by-passed and HRM promoted via direct consultation and communication with the workforce, using management-controlled channels such as briefing groups, 'special deals' with individual workers, etc. In addition, if management practices in relation to promotion, development, grievance handling, etc. are perceived to be equitable by employees their perceived need for defensive-type representation by the unions may be diminished.

Fig. 12.5. A model of HRM outcomes

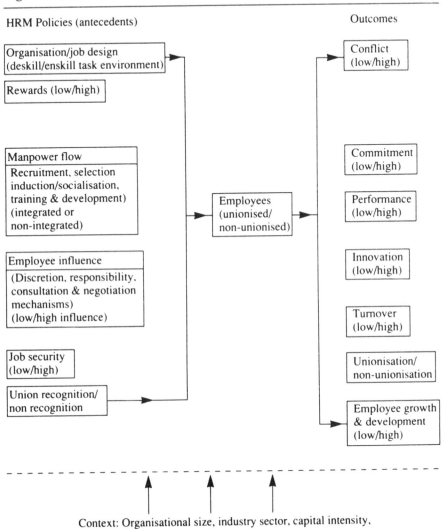

HRM Policies (antecedents)   Outcomes

Organisation/job design
(deskill/enskill task environment)

Rewards (low/high)

Conflict (low/high)

Manpower flow
Recruitment, selection
induction/socialisation,
training & development)
(integrated or
non-integrated)

Employee influence
(Discretion, responsibility,
consultation & negotiation
mechanisms)
(low/high influence)

Job security
(low/high)

Union recognition/
non recognition

Employees
(unionised/
non-unionised)

Commitment (low/high)

Performance (low/high)

Innovation (low/high)

Turnover (low/high)

Unionisation/
non-unionisation

Employee growth & development (low/high)

Context: Organisational size, industry sector, capital intensity,
legislation, government initiatives & leadership

Guest argues that while there may be competitive advantages in HRM, it is not always the most sensible policy to pursue. Five conditions are necessary in Guest's view for HRM type approaches to have any success: corporate leadership (for the values inherent in HRM to succeed); strategic vision (that HRM is a key component of the corporate strategy); technological or production feasibility (where heavy investment has not taken place to install a short-cycle, repetitive production assembly line, as this mitigates against job design principles and autonomous teamworking); employee or industrial relations feasibility (multi-union status, low-trust relations and a strong industrial relations orientation mitigate against HRM); and the ability of personnel specialists to put HRM policies into place with the assistance of top, middle and line management.

A variant on Guest's theory of HRM has been advanced by researchers at the University of Limerick[24] and is shown in figure 12.5.

This model has the advantage of specifying a range of likely outcomes associated with HRM policies, and includes non-unionisation as a potential outcome. Like Guest's theory it argues that advanced HRM policies will lead to a range of desirable organisational outcomes and assumes a strong theoretical formulation. However, it also encompasses the situation where HRM policies are not coherent or are not sophisticated in their application. Thus high conflict, low performance, etc. is seen to derive from the application of HRM policies which are not fully developed or carefully applied.

EVIDENCE TO SUPPORT THE MODEL OF HRM

While it has been argued that HRM is significantly different when compared with stereotypical personnel management and a theoretical core for HRM has been identified, it still remains for researchers to fully test the model. However, it is possible, drawing from a range of sources of evidence, to speculate upon the likely impact of HRM in terms of some of the outcomes listed in figure 12.5.

The evidence comes, in the Irish context, from studies of non-union companies by Bill Toner at the College of Industrial Relations and some exploratory research by Aidan Kelly and Teresa Brannick at University College, Dublin on the HRM strategies of companies operating in the Irish Republic which are recognised as leaders in their field.[25] In addition, research upon the impact of HRM policies upon organisational commitment has been carried out at the University of Limerick using a sample of union and non-union companies.[26] In the wider context, evidence about the impact of HRM upon industrial relations and trade unions is available from studies at the University of Warwick and in the United States.

Toner's study of a sample of union and non-union companies in Irish manufacturing shows that when companies pursue sufficiently attractive personnel policies and build an organisational culture which strengthens employee-organisational linkages (see figure 12.6) the workforce are unlikely to unionise.[27]

Fig. 12.6. Model of strong culture in large non-union company

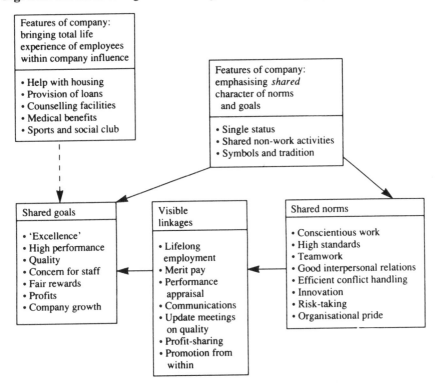

Source: B. Toner (1987) Union or non union: Employee Relations Strategies in the Irish Republic, PhD Thesis, L.S.E.

Toner compared perceptions of personnel policies and practices among a sample of 244 workers drawn from three non-union and four unionised plants. Each plant was located within the high-tech electronics sector and had been set up in the late 1960s or 1970s. On fourteen of the nineteen items which examined perceptions of personnel policies, the attitudes of non-union employees were more positive. The impact of HRM in this context has been to keep the unions out. Kelly and Brannick's study highlights the following facets of HRM practices in their sample of 'best practice' companies: careful recruitment and selection, socialisation into company norms via induction, devolution of authority for the implementation of personnel policies to line management who are held accountable for their implementation, strong value commitment to human resource development, extensive communication mechanisms and explicit statements of their human resource philosophy. An example of this from Kelly and Brannick's study is shown in box 12.1.

Box 12.1

Examples are
(i) 'XYZ company has a policy of open management and genuine respect for each individual employee. The company believes that it is in achieving your own goals and objectives that you will best help the Company obtain its goals. To this end, the Company is ready to help its employees achieve greater job satisfaction and improve the quality of worklife. The Company encourages and appreciates effort and creativity while recognising that a reasonable level of mistakes is inevitable in a learning environment';
(ii) 'the foundation of our success has been the clever and innovative ideas that all our employees have applied to solving our business problems';
(iii) 'product quality is the hallmark of our success';
(iv) 'ours is a culture that stresses the value of the human resource'. These philosophy and value statements are not treated lightly; they represent the core ethical statement of the companies' relationships with their employees and external constituencies.

In an explicit attempt to assess the impact of HRM policies, Dillon carried out a survey of employee attitudes and levels of organisational attachment in a sample of union and non-union companies who are recognised as leaders in their personnel practices.[28] It was found that general HRM policies had no impact upon the organisational commitment levels of employees, but the extent to which the task environment promoted autonomy, responsibility and feedback had a major impact upon levels of organisational commitment. Interestingly, no significant differences in organisational commitment were found between union and non-union plants. This would suggest that the nature of the work carried out in conjunction with the HRM policies pursued is a more important factor in eliciting employee loyalties than the mere presence or absence of a union.

Studies at the University of Warwick by John Storey upon the impact of HRM when it is introduced into a unionised environment suggest two likely scenarios.[29] One is where unions are given a relatively marginal role and collective bargaining structures are bypassed using direct workforce consultation mechanisms or joint consultation arrangements which are not union based. The role of the trade union loses its significance and their influence over work organisation is diminished because there are now two mechanisms for solving problems: collective bargaining and joint consultation. The research by Storey shows that in most instances trade unions have effectively been bypassed.

The consequences of this have sometimes been negative, with the continuing arms-length bargaining relationship leading to dualism in management's approach to the workforce. This is counterproductive in the long term, according to Storey.

The second scenario here is where unions are integrated into HRM activities via such mechanisms as participative councils and negotiation at plant level. This, it must be stated, would be most likely the exception rather than the rule. Examples of this in the UK would include the strategies adopted by EEPTU to gain recognition with Toshiba. In return for sole representation rights, the union is committed to flexibility, industrial peace during the lifetime of the agreement and pendulum arbitration for any disputes which arise during its application.

Based on the foregoing analysis the following predictions could be made: *a)* large companies establishing in greenfield sites, particularly high-tech companies, will continue to choose the non-union alternative; furthermore, there would appear to be strong evidence to suggest an increasing opposition to unionisation in the 1980s, particularly in indigenous Irish companies;
b) in establishments which have a strong union tradition, HRM-type initiatives will most likely be introduced in a piecemeal fashion in an evolutionary manner and avoid disturbing collective bargaining structures;
c) the long-term impact of these policies is more difficult to gauge, but we would expect that if they are successful and if the unions demonstrate a willingness to compromise they may become increasingly incorporated into company decision-making. It is essential that middle management are committed to a philosophy of total involvement of employees if such initiatives are to demonstrate a long-term pay-off. Within the public sector, HRM initiatives will probably be modelled on extending the worker director mechanisms to sub-board level via consultation mechanisms. Dualism (where consultation parallels collective bargaining structures) is a likely scenario in the established unionised environment. It is probable, however, that such a dualism is ultimately counterproductive.

Trade unions, particularly in the current environment, are likely to embrace any initiatives which give them a greater voice and influence in corporate decision-making. Therefore, it is probably the best opportunity for introducing involvement initiatives. To gain full trust, commitment and employee involvement, the evidence would suggest that guarantees of job security are an essential factor in achieving long-term success.

This brings us to a final consideration, how companies can move from a traditional control-oriented workforce strategy to a commitment-oriented HRM-based strategy. The answer would seem to lie in the careful application and use of HRM policy levers to *gradually* move away from a control-oriented strategy. This suggests that transition phases have to be mapped out in relation to reward structures, job design practices, employee influence, etc.

Job security (employment assurance) guarantees are an essential element in generating the high-trust relations so necessary to move in this direction. Very few organisations are willing to even consider such guarantees and are constrained in their HRM strategies as a result. 'Guarantees' as Peters points out, can become an elastic term to include use of temporary employees to protect 'core' workers, limited period guarantees, etc.[30] Nonetheless, organisations must experiment with the concept of employment assurance if they are to successfully elicit the maximum involvement of employees. The more restrictive the definition of employment assurance the less trust it is likely to engender. Indeed, the rapid ageing of the European workforce, including the anticipated fall in the number of 15-24 year olds in the Irish Republic post-2010, may well spur on innovations in employment assurance when such workers are in short supply. Organisations will then be competing for young workers and innovative approaches in this area may then become a competitive weapon to attract the best and the brightest.

The future directions in workforce management cannot be predicted with any certainty. However the 'non-union system' of which HRM is a key element can be expected to challenge many of the existing approaches to collective bargaining and personnel management practice in the future.

Notes

NB Since many of these books and papers were written, the NIHE Limerick has become the University of Limerick and the FUE the FIE. The bibliographical reference uses the former names as they were correct at that time.

Chapter 1 (pp. 5 – 25)

1. Fowler, A., *Personnel Management in Local Government*, IPM 1975.
2. Institute of Personnel Management, 'Statement on Personnel Management and Personnel Policies', *Personnel Management*, March 1963.
3. Thomason, G., *A Textbook of Personnel Management*, IPM 1978.
4. Miller, K., 'Psychological Testing', Gower 1975 (as quoted in Thomason, G.) *op. cit.*
5. Legge, K., *Power, Innovation and Problem-solving in Personnel Management*, McGraw-Hill 1978.
6. Thomason, G., *op. cit.*
7. Armstrong, M., *A Handbook of Personnel Management Practice*, Kogan Page 1988.
8. See, for example, Gunnigle, P. and Brady, T., 'The Management of Industrial Relations in the Small Firm' in *Employee Relations*, Vol. 6, no. 5, 1984; Gunnigle, P., 'Management approaches to industrial relations in the small firm' in *Industrial Relations in Ireland: Contemporary Issues and Developments*, UCD 1987.
9. For an outline of personnel department activities in Irish organisations see Keating, M., 'Personnel Management in Ireland' in *Industrial Relations in Ireland: Contemporary Issues and Developments, op. cit.*
10. Armstrong, M., *op. cit.*
11. See, for example, Miner, J.B. & Miner, M.G., *Personnel management and industrial relations: A managerial approach*, Macmillan 1977.
12. Tyson, S., 'The Management of the personnel function', *Journal of Management Studies* Sept. 1987; also see Tyson, S. & Fell, A., *Evaluating the personnel function*, Hutchinson 1986; Tyson, S., 'Is this the very model of the modern personnel manager', *Personnel Management*, May 1985.
13. Shivanath, G., 'Personnel Practitioners 1986: Their Role and Status in Irish Industry', unpublished MBS thesis, NIHE Limerick 1987; for further information on personnel management practice in Irish organisations readers might also refer to the work of Murray, S., *Employee Relations in Irish Private*

Sector Manufacturing Industry, IDA 1984, or Keating, M., *Survey of Personnel Practitioners in Ireland*, Dept of Industrial Relations, UCD, forthcoming.

14. Shivanath, G. , *op. cit.*
15. Institute of Personnel Management , *Annual Report*, 1988.
16. Tyson, S. & Fell, A., *op. cit.*; also see Daniel, W.W. & Millward, N., *Workplace Industrial Relations in Britain*, DE/PSI/SSRC Survey, Heinemann 1983; Clegg, H., *The changing system of industrial relations in Great Britain*, Blackwell 1979.
17. Institute of Personnel Management, *Report of the Working Party on the future of the IPM in the Republic of Ireland*, IPM 1981.
18. Shivanath, G., *op. cit.*

Chapter 2 (pp. 26 – 39)

1. It is noteworthy that the origins of our current Joint Labour Committee (JLC) system lie in concerns over the use of 'sweated labour' at the turn of the century, resulting in the establishment of Trade Boards to enforce minimum pay rates in certain occupations; see, for example, McMahon, G.V., 'The Joint Labour Committee System' in *Industrial Relations in Ireland: Contemporary Issues and Developments*, UCD 1987; Blackwell, J. & McMahon, G.V. , 'Labour Market Characteristics of Low Pay in Ireland: The Policy Options', *Administration* (forthcoming, 1990).
2. See, for example, Niven, M., *Personnel Management 1913-1963*, IPM 1967; Byrne, T.P., 'IPM in Ireland 1937-1987', *IPM News* vol. 3, no. 2, 1988.
3. 'Industrial Health and Safety', *Final Report of the Health of Munition Workers Committee*, HMSO 1918.
4. Farnham, D., *Personnel in Context*, IPM 1984.
5. Taylor, F.W., *Scientific Management*, Harper & Row 1947.
6. The most detailed account of the Hawthorne Studies are to be found in Roethlisberger, F.J. & Dickson, W.J., *Management and the Worker*, Harvard UP 1939; for a later critique of the Hawthorne Studies see, for example, Carey, A., 'The Hawthorne Studies: A Radical Criticism', *American Sociological Review*, June 1967.
7. For a useful review of the development of trade unions in Ireland see McNamara, G., Williams, K. & West, D., *Understanding Trade Unions: Yesterday and Today*, O'Brien Educational Press 1988.
8. Nevin, E., *Wages in Ireland*, Economic and Social Research Institute 1963.
9. For a detailed review of the wage round system and pay bargaining in Ireland up to the early 1970s see McCarthy, W.E.J., O'Brien, J.F. & Dowd, V.D., *Wage Inflation and Wage Leadership*, Economic and Social Research Institute 1975; also O'Brien, J.F., 'Pay Determination in Ireland' in *Industrial Relations in Ireland: Contemporary Issues and Developments*, *op. cit.*
10. O'Mahony, D., *Industrial Relations in Ireland*, Economic Research Institute 1958.
11. For a breakdown of collective bargaining arrangements in the public sector see Cox, B. & Hughes, J., 'Industrial Relations in the Public Sector' in *Industrial Relations in Ireland: Contemporary Issues and Developments*, *op. cit.*; also see Gaffney, S., 'Industrial Relations in the Public Sector', *Administration* vol. 27, no. 3, 1979.

12. See O'Brien, J.F., *A Study of National Wage Agreements in Ireland*, ESRI Paper no. 104, 1981.
13. *Ibid.*; McCarthy, C., 'A Review of the objectives of the National Pay Agreements 1970-1977', *Administration* vol. 25, no.1, 1977.
14. Browne, M.H., 'Industrial Labour and Incomes Policy in the Republic of Ireland', *British Journal of Industrial Relations*, March 1965.
15. For a detailed account of this period see McCarthy, C., *The Decade of Upheaval: Irish Trade Unions in the Nineteen Sixties*, IPA 1973.
16. For an excellent review of Irish government strategies in industrial relations see Roche, B., 'State Strategies and the Politics of Industrial Relations in Ireland' in *Industrial Relations in Ireland: Contemporary Issues and Developments*, UCD 1987.
17. For an indication of the impact of the Unfair Dismissals Act 1977 on management practice see O'Connor, K., 'The impact of the Unfair Dismissals Act 1977 on Personnel Management and Industrial Relations', *Journal of Irish Business and Administrative Research* vol. 5, no.2, 1983.
18. Several writers have noted the personnel management emphasis of multinational organisations; see, for example, Murray, S., *Employee Relations in Irish Private Sector Manufacturing Industry*, IDA 1984; McCrohan, J. *et al.*, *Top Management attitudes to Personnel in Ireland—Survey Results*, Jim McCrohan Associates, Federation House, Dublin 1987; Kelly, A. & Brannick, T., 'The management of human resources: New trends and the challenge to trade unions', *Arena*, Aug. 1988; McMahon, G., Neary, C. & O'Connor, K., 'Multinationals in Ireland—Three Decades On', *Industrial Relations News* no. 6, 1988.
19. For a review of employee relations approaches of MNCs see Kelly, A. & Brannick, T., 'Industrial relations practices of multinational companies in Ireland', *Journal of Irish Business and Administrative Research* vol. 7, no. 1, 1985; Enderwick, P., 'Multinationals and labour relations: The case of Ireland', *Journal of Irish Business and Administrative Research* vol. 8, no. 2, 1986; Also see Murray, S., *op. cit.*
20. Murray, S., *ibid.*
21. Van Ham, J., 'Personnel management in changed environment', *Personnel Review* 15 March 1986.
22. For a more detailed review of non-union approaches see McGovern, P., 'Increasing Opposition to Unionisation in the 1980s', *Industrial Relations News* no. 45, 24 Nov. 1988; 'Trade Union Recognition – Five Case Studies', *Industrial Relations News* no. 6, 6 Feb. 1989; also see Flood, P. & Garavan, T.N., 'HRM, Industrial Relations and the Implications for Unions', *Industrial Relations News* no. 12, 23 March 1989.
23. See, for example, Beer M. *et al.*, *Human Resource Management: A General Manager's Perspective*, The Free Press/Macmillan 1985; Armstrong, M., *A Handbook of Personnel Management Practice*, Kogan Page 1988; Guest, D., 'Human Resource Management and Industrial Relations', *Journal of Management Studies* vol. 24, no. 5, 1987.
24. Kelly, A. & Brannick, T., *Op. cit.*

Chapter 3 (pp. 40 – 63)

1. See, for example, Peters T. & Waterman, R. H., *In Search of Excellence*, Harper & Row 1982; Goldsmith, W. & Clutterbuck, D., *The Winning Streak*, Weidenfeld & Nicholson 1984.
2. Cascio, W.F., *Managing Human Resources: Productivity, Quality of Work, Life, Profits*, McGraw-Hill 1986.
3. *Ibid.*
4. Bowey, A.M., *A Guide to Manpower Planning*, Macmillan 1974; also see Bell, D.J., *Planning Corporate Manpower*, Longman 1974.
5. Bramham, J., *Practical Manpower Planning*, IPM 1988.
6. Federated Union of Employers, *Absenteeism Control: A Practical Handbook for Management Action*, FUE 1980.
7. See, for example, Readmond, G., 'Absenteeism—A Cure for Lost Days', *Management*, Feb. 1989.
8. Bramham, J., *op. cit.*
9. The Federated Union of Employers has frequently pointed out the serious effects of absenteeism on Irish industry and indicated measures to control it in the workplace: FUE, *op. cit.* Also see O'Muircheartaigh, C., *Absenteeism in Irish Industry*, Irish Productivity Centre 1975; Readmond, G., *op. cit.*; Murphy, T. & Hanley, J., 'Absenteeism in Irish Industry: A case of Restored Management Control?', *Working Paper no. 9*, Dept of Industrial Relations, UCD 1984; O'Kelly, K.P., 'Attendance at work: A Review of the Problem', *Industrial Relations News* no. 14, 1988; Turner, T., 'Absenteeism in Ireland: Getting the Figures Right', *Industrial Relations News* no. 21, 1988.
10. Blennerhassett, E. & Gorman, P., *Absenteeism in the Public Service: Information Systems and Control Strategies*, Institute of Public Administration 1986.
11. Mondy, R.W. & Noe, R. M., *Personnel: The Management of Human Resources*, Allyn & Bacon 1984.
12. Dineen, D.A., 'Employment development in the Irish Economy since 1979'; Paper presented to the International Conference on 'The Changing Nature of Employment: New Forms and New Areas', BIPE Paris 1987.
13. For an evaluation of job creation initiatives, see Laffan, B., 'The Youth Employment Scheme in Ireland', Strathclyde Paper, 1984.
14. Fox. R. & O'Reilly, A.P., *Corporate Manpower Planning in Ireland*, AnCO 1979.
15. Shivanath, G., 'Personnel Practitioners 1986: Their Role and Status in Irish Industry', Unpublished MBS thesis, NIHE Limerick 1987; Cairns, N.W. & Thompson, J.E., 'Manpower Planning in Northern Ireland', *Journal of Irish Business and Administrative Research (IBAR)* vol. 9, 1988.
16. Cairns, N.W. & Thompson, J.E., *Ibid.*
17. Downes, D., 'Manpower planning in Ireland: A survey of current practice in the Mid-West region', Unpublished BBS project, NIHE Limerick 1986.
18. Shivanath, G., *op. cit.*
19. An excellent outline of the respective roles of corporate, personnel and line management in manpower planning is given in the IPM's *Statement on Human Resource Planning*, IPM 1986.

Chapter 4 (pp. 64 – 95)
1. Lewis, C., *Employee selection*, Hutchinson 1985.
2. Plumbley, P., *Recruitment and Selection*, IPM 1985.
3. Ungerson, B., *How to Write a Job Description*, IPM 1983.
4. McMahon notes the impact of Employment Equality Legislation on the recruitment process pointing to a number of important Labour Court and Equality Officer decisions; McMahon, G.V., 'Rush the Recruitment—Rue the Results', *Management*, Feb. 1988.
5. Institute of Personnel Management, *The IPM Recruitment Code*, IPM London.
6. Garavan, T.N. & O'Dwyer, D., *Management consultants: Their use by personnel departments*, IRN 1 Oct. 1987; also see Mackay, L. & Torrington, D., *The changing nature of personnel management* IPM 1986.
7. McMahon, G.V., *op. cit.*
8. A 1975 IMI survey found the interview to be far the most widely used selection technique: Gorman, L., Moynihan, T., McConnell, J. & Hynes, G., *Irish Industry – How it's managed*, Irish Management Institute 1975. This finding has been confirmed by more recent studies at the College of Commerce, Rathmines and NIHE, Limerick; McMahon, G.V., 'Personnel selection in Ireland: Scientific prediction or crystal-ball gazing', *IPM News* vol. 3, no. 3, Oct. 1988; Shivanath, G., 'Personnel Practitioners 1986: Their Role and Status in Irish Industry', unpublished MBS thesis, NIHE Limerick 1987.
9. Lewis, C., *op. cit.*; Herriot, P. & Rochwell, C., 'Expectations and impressions in the graduate selection interview', *Journal of Occupational Psychology* no. 56, 1983.
10. See, for example, Hollingworth, H.L., *Vocational Psychology and Character Analysis*, Appleton, NY 1929; Kelley, E.L. & Fiske, O.W., *The prediction of performance in Clinical Psychology*, University of Michigan Press 1951; Ulrich, L. & Trumbo, D., 'The Selection interview since 1949', *Psychological Bulletin* no. 63, 1965; Arvey, R.D. & Campion, J.E., 'The employment interview: A summary and review of recent literature', *Personnel Psychology* vol. 35, no. 2, 1982; Makin, P. & Robertson, I., 'Selecting the best selection techniques', *Personnel Management* November 1986.
11. Plumbley, P., *op. cit.*
12. Higham, M., *The ABC of interviewing*, IPM 1979.
13. Makin, P. & Robertson, I., *op. cit.*
14. Latham, G.P. *et al.*, 'The situational interview', *Journal of Applied Psychology* vol. 65, no. 4, August 1980.
15. See, for example, Locke A.E. & Bryan J.F., 'Performance Goals as Determinants of Level of Performance and Boredom', *Journal of Applied Psychology* April 1967; Ghiselli, E.E., *The validity of occupational aptitude tests*, Wiley 1966.
16. See, for example, Torrington, D. & Hall, L., *Personnel Management: A New Approach*, Prentice-Hall 1987.
17. Munro-Fraser, J., *Employment Interviewing*, MacDonald and Evans London 1966; Rodger, A., *The Seven Point Plan*, 3rd ed., National Institute of Industrial Psychology, 1970; For a useful discussion on both frameworks and the interview in general see 'The Effective Manager', Book 6, *Choosing and Developing your team*, Open University 1983.
18. Lewis, C., *op. cit.*

19. McMahon, G.V., 'Rush the Recruitment—Rue the Results', *op. cit.*
20. Shivanath, G., *op. cit.* Makin, P. J. & Robertson, I., *op. cit.*
21. Lewis, C., *op. cit.*
22. Tyson, S. & York, A., *Personnel management made simple*, Heinemann 1982.
23. For an excellent outline on the application of selection tests see the Institute of Personnel Management's Code of Practice on Occupational Testing.
24. McMahon, G.V., 'Personnel selection in Ireland: Scientific prediction or crystal-ball gazing', *op. cit.*
25. Shivanath, G., *op. cit.*
26. McMahon, G.V., 'Personnel selection in Ireland: Scientific selection or crystal-ball gazing', *op. cit.*; Robertson, I. & Makin, P.J., 'Management selection in Britain: A survey and critique', *Journal of Occupational Psychology* 1986.
27. McMahon, G.V., *ibid.*
28. Makin, P.J. & Robertson, I., 'Selecting the best selection techniques', *op. cit.*
29. For further information on these selection devices see Mackenzie, Davey and Harris, M., *Judging People*, McGraw-Hill 1982; a critique of graphology as an aid to selection may be found in Klimoski, R.J. & Rafeli, A., 'Inferring personal qualities through handwriting analysis' *Journal of Occupational Psychology* 1983; Lynch, B., 'Graphology: Towards a hand-picked workforce', *Personnel Management* March 1985.
30. Shamoon, S., 'Read between the lines', *Observer* 3rd November 1985; Courtis, J., *Cost Effective Recruitment*, IPM 1985.
31. Roberston, I. & Makin, P.J., 'Management selection in Britain: A survey and critique', *op. cit.*
32. McMahon, G.V., 'Personnel selection in Ireland: Scientific prediction or crystal-ball gazing', *op. cit.*
33. Lewis, C., 'What's new in selection?', *Personnel Management* Jan. 1984; Makin, P.J. & Robertson, I., 'Selecting the best selection techniques', *op. cit.*; See also, Bridges, A., 'Assessment centres: Their uses in industry in Great Britain', unpublished MSc dissertation, University of Manchester Institute of Science and Technology 1984.
34. Smith, M., 'Selection: Where are the best prophets?', *Personnel Management* Dec. 1986; Also see Smith, M. & Robertson, I., *The theory and practice of systematic staff selection*, Macmillan 1986.
35. McMahon, G.V., 'Personnel selection in Ireland: Scientific prediction or crystal-ball gazing', *op. cit.*
36. Makin, P.J. & Robertson. I., 'Selecting the best selection techniques', *op. cit.*; Smith, M., *op. cit.* also see Owens, W.A. & Schoenfelt, L.F., 'Towards a classification of persons', *Journal of Applied Psychology* 1979.
37. McMahon, G.V., 'Personnel selection in Ireland: Scientific prediction or crystal-ball gazing', *op. cit.*

Chapter 5 (pp. 96 – 113)

1. Maslow, A., 'A Theory of Human Motivation', *Psychological Review* vol. 50, no.4, 1943.
2. *Ibid.*
3. Hall D. and Nougaim, K., 'An examination of Maslow's need hierarchy in the organisational setting', *Organisational Behaviour and Human Performance*,

vol. 3, no.1, 1968; Porter, L., 'Job attitudes in management: II: Perceived importance of needs as a function of job level', *Journal of Applied Psychology* April 1963.

4. Alderfer, C.P., 'An empirical test of a new theory of human needs', *Organisational Behaviour and Human Performance*, vol. 4, 1969; *Existence, Relatedness and Growth*, The Free Press NY 1972.

5. See McClelland, D.C., *The achieving society*, Van Nostrand NY 1961; 'Business, drive and achievement', *Harvard Business Review* July/August 1962.

6. McClelland, D, & Boyatzis, R., 'Leadership motive pattern and long term success in management', *Journal of Applied Psychology* vol. 67, 1982.

7. McGregor, D., *The Human Side of Enterprise*, McGraw-Hill 1960.

8. Herzberg, F., Mausner, B. & Synderman, B., *The Motivation to Work*, Wiley 1967; Herzberg, F., 'One more time: How do you motivate employees', *Harvard Business Review* Jan/Feb. 1968.

9. Vroom, V., *Work and motivation*, Wiley 1964; Mitchell, T.R., 'Expectancy models of job satisfaction, occupational preference and effort; a theoretical, methodological and empirical appraisal', *Psychological Bulletin* vol. 81, 1974; Wahba, M.A. & House, R.J., 'Expectancy theory in work and motivation: Some logical and methodological issues', *Human Relations* vol 27, Jan. 1974; Connolly, T. & Mitchell, T.R., 'Expectancy-value models in organizational psychology' in Feather, N. (ed.), *Expectancy, incentive and action*, Erblaum and Associates NY 1980.

10. Vroom V., *op. cit.*

11. Nadler, D. & Lawler, E., 'Motivation: A diagnostic approach', in Steers, R. and Porter, L. (eds), *Motivation and Work Behaviour*, McGraw-Hill 1979.

12. Porter, L. & Lawler, E., *Managerial Attitudes and Performance*, Irwin 1968.

13. Blennerhassett, E., *Work Motivation and Personnel Practices: A Study of Civil Service Executive Staff*, Institute of Public Administration 1983.

14. See, for example Steers, R.M. & Rhodes, S.R., 'Major Influences on Employee Attendance: A Process Model'; Steers, R.M. & Mowday, R.T., 'Employee Turnover in Organisations', both in Steers, R.M. & Porter, L.W., *Motivation and Work Behaviour*, McGraw-Hill 1987; also Mowday, R.T., Porter, L.W. & Steers, R.M., *Employee-Organization Linkages: The Psychology of Commitment, Absenteeism and Turnover*, Academic Press 1982.

15. Hackman, J.R. & Oldham, G.R., *Work Redesign*, Addison-Wesley NY 1980.

16. Blennerhasset, E., *op. cit.*

17. See, for example, Peters, T.J. & Waterman, R.H., *In Search of Excellence*, Harper and Row 1982; Beer, M. *et al. Human Resource Management: A General Manager's Perspective*, The Free Press/Macmillan 1985; Daft, R.L. *Organisation Theory and Design*, West Publishing Co. 1986.

18. See, for example, Vaziri, M.T., Won Lee, J. & Krieger, L., 'Onda Moku: The true Pioneer of Management through Respect for Humanity', *Leadership and Organisation Development Journal* vol. 9.1, 1988.

19. Ouchi, W., *Theory Z*, Addison-Wesley 1981.

20. Ouchi, W. & Jaeger, A. M., 'Type Z Organisations: Stability in the Midst of Mobility', *Academy of Management Review* no. 3, 1978.

Chapter 6 (pp. 114 – 35)

1. Beer, M. *et al.*, *Human Resource Management: A General Manager's Perspective*, The Free Press/Macmillan 1985.
2. See Lawler, E.E., 'Reward Systems' in Hackman, J.R. & Suttle, J.L. (eds), *Improving Life at Work: Behavioural Science Approaches to Organisational Change*, Goodyear 1977.
3. Blennerhassett, E., *Work Motivation and Personnel Practices: A Study of Civil Service Executive Staff*, Institute of Public Administration 1983.
4. For a useful discussion of the motivational impact of financial incentives see Biddle, D. & Evenden, R., *Human aspects of management*, IPM 1989.
5. See, for example, Adams, J.S., 'Toward an understanding of inequity', *Journal of Abnormal and Social Psychology* vol. 67, 1963; 'Inequity and social exchange' in Berkowitz, L. (ed.), *Advances in experimental social psychology* vol. 2, NY Academic Press 1965.
6. See, for example, Skinner, B.F., *Walden Two*, Macmillan 1948; *Science and human behaviour*, Macmillan 1953; *Contingencies of reinforcement*, Appleton-Century-Crofts 1969; *About Behaviourism*, Knopf NY 1974; Luthans, E. & Kreitner, R., *Organizational Behaviour Modification*, Scott Forsman 1975; Davis, T. & Luthans, F., 'A social learning approach to organisational behaviour' *Academy of Management Review* vol. 5, 1980; O'Brien, R., Dickenson, A., & Rosow M. (eds.), *Industrial behaviour modification: a learning-based approach to industrial organisational problems*, Pergamon 1982.
7. Robertson, I. and Smith M., *Motivation and Job Design: Theory Research and Practice*, IPM 1985.
8. For fuller review of payment systems see Advisory Conciliation and Arbitration Service, 'Introduction to Payment Systems' *Advisory Booklet no. 2*, ACAS 1982; for a useful review of payment systems in Ireland see Mooney, P., *An Inquiry into Wage Payment Systems in Ireland*, Economic and Social Research Institute/European Foundation for the Improvement of Living and Working Conditions, Dublin 1980; also *Working Paper EF/WP/87/41/EN* 'Wage Payment Systems: Case Studies – Ireland', European Foundation for the Improvement of Living and Working Conditions 1987. *Profit Sharing for Ireland?*, Economic and Social Research Institute/Social and Statistical Inquiry Society of Ireland, Dublin 1982; Irish Productivity Centre, *A Guide to employee Shareholding through Profit Sharing*, IPC 1986. For current information on pay levels and fringe benefits see, for example, *Executive Salaries and Fringe Benefits*, Inbucon (Irl) Ltd 1988; Carroll, B., *Executive Salaries in Ireland 1988* IMI 1988; (The FUE also provides information on pay and conditions to affiliates.)
9. Bowey, A.M. & Thorpe, R., *Payment Systems and Productivity*, Macmillan 1986.
10. Mooney, P., *op. cit.*
11. See, for example, Clarke, P., *Payment by Results Schemes – A Review of Trends*, IRN no. 8, 23 Feb. 1989; *Gainsharing: Why it should prove so popular in Ireland*, IRN no. 13, 6 April 1989.
12. Long, P., 'A Review of Approved Profit Sharing (Trust) Schemes in Ireland and the UK', unpublished dissertation, College of Commerce, Dublin Institute of Technology 1988.

13. Fowler, A., 'New Directions in Performance Pay', *Personnel Management* Nov. 1988; see also *Paying for Performance,* Income Data Services 1988; and White, M., 'What's New in Pay', *Personnel Management* Feb. 1985.
14. See, for example, Beattie, D., 'Managing for performance: Relating management performance to pay in the private sector' and Gleeson, D., 'Developing systems of pay for performance in the Irish Public Sector': Papers presented to Federated Union of Employers Conference on Industrial Relations, Dublin 1988; McDonough, D., 'Merit Pay – A Real Reward in the Public Service or a Token of Appreciation', *Public Service* vol. 6, no. 4, 1985.
15. Bowey, A. M. & Thorpe, R., *op. cit.*
16. Incomes Data Service/Institute of Personnel Management, 'The Merit Factor— Rewarding Individual Performance', *Joint IDS/IPM Report* 1985.
17. Grafton, D., 'Performance Related Pay: Securing Employee Trust', *Industrial Relations News* no. 44, 17 Nov. 1988.
18. Blennerhassett, E., *op. cit.*
19. For a fuller discussion of the aims of job evaluation see Armstrong, M., *A Handbook of Personnel Management Practice*, Kogan Page 1988.
20. Gorman, L. *et al., Irish Industry: How it's Managed*, Irish Management Institute 1975.
21. Institute of Personnel Management (Irish Branch), *Report on Job Evaluation in Ireland*, IPM (Dublin) 1980.
22. For a useful discussion of job evaluation methods see Burke, J., *Personnel Management*, Irish Management Institute 1985.
23. See, for example, Advisory Conciliation and Arbitration Service 'Job Evaluation', *Booklet no 1* ACAS 1982.
24. For a trade union perspective on job evaluation see *Job Evaluation: Information and advice on methods and procedures involved in job evaluation*, Irish Congress of Trade Unions, undated.
25. Institute of Personnel Management (Irish Branch), *Job Evaluation Survey*, IPM (Dublin) 1976.
26. Institute of Personnel Management, (Irish Branch) (1980) *op. cit.*
27. Armstrong, M., *op. cit.*

Chapter 7 (pp. 136 – 53)

1. Gorman, L. *et al., Irish Industry – How it's managed*, IMI 1975; Shivanath, G., 'Personnel Practitioners 1986 – Their Role and Status in Irish Industry', unpublished MBS thesis, NIHE, Limerick 1987.
2. Gill, D., Ungerson, B., & Thakur, M., *Performance appraisal in perspective: A survey of current practice*, IPM 1973; Gill, D., *Appraising performance: Present trends and the next decade*, IPM 1977; Long, P., *Performance appraisal revisited*, IPM 1986.
3. Gorman, L. *et al., op. cit.*
4. Fletcher, C., 'Performance appraisal' in Guest, D. & Kenny, T., *A textbook of techniques and strategies in Personnel Management*, IPM 1983.
5. For a more detailed discussion on Behaviourally Anchored Rating Scales (BARS) see Dessler, G., *Personnel Management*, Prentice-Hall 1984; Fogli, L., Hulin, C. & Blood, M., 'Development of first level behavioural job criteria', *Journal of Applied Psychology* vol. 55, 1971.

6. Drucker, P., *The practice of management*, Heinemann 1955.
7. Long, P., *op. cit.*
8. Fletcher, C., *op. cit.*
9. Wellins, R., *A wider role for assessment centres – The US experience*, IPM National Conference Harrogate 1984.
10. See, for example, Bridges, A., 'Assessment centres: Their uses in industry in Great Britain', unpublished M.Sc. dissertation, UMIST 1984; Fletcher, C. & Williams, R., *Performance appraisal and career development*, Hutchinson 1985.
11. McMahon, G., 'Personnel Selection in Ireland: Scientific prediction or crystal-ball gazing' *IPM News* vol. 3, no.3, Oct. 1988.
12. Gorman *et al., op. cit.*
13. Blennerhassett, E., *Work Motivation and Personnel Practices: A Study of Civil Service Executive Staff*, IPA 1983.
14. See, for example, Mc Gregor, D., 'An Uneasy Look at Performance Appraisal', *Harvard Business Review* no. 35, 1957; Rowe, K., 'An appraisal of appraisals' *Journal of Management Studies* no. 1, 1964; Pym, D., 'The politics and rituals of appraisals', *Occupational Psychology* vol. 47, no. 4, 1973.
15. Meyer, N., *The appraisal interview*, University Associates, La Jolla, California 1976.
16. See, for example, Lee, M. & Zimerman, W., 'Designing a motivating and team building employee appraisal system', *Personnel Journal* July 1976; Fombrum, C.J. and Land, R.L., 'Strategic issues in performance appraisal theory and practice', *Personnel* Nov./Dec. 1983; Bureau of National Affairs, *Performance appraisal programs*, BNC Washington DC 1983; Eichel, E. & Bender, H., *Performance appraisal: a study of current techniques*, American Management Association NY 1984; Lacho, K., Stearns, G. & Villere, M., 'A study of employee appraisal systems of major cities in the United States', *Public Personnel Management* vol. 8, no.2, March/April 1979.
17. Income Data Services/Institute of Personnel Management, *The merit factor: Rewarding individual performance*, IDS 1985.
18. Grafton, D., 'Performance-related Pay: Securing Employee Trust', *Industrial Relations News* no. 44, 17 Nov. 1988.
19. Meyer, H., Kaye, E. & French, J., 'Split roles in performance appraisal', *Harvard Business Review* no. 43, 1965.
20. IPM Surveys on Performance Appraisal 1973, 1977, & 1985; *op. cit.*
21. Meyer, H., 'Self-appraisal of job performance', *Personnel Psychology* no. 33, 1980.
22. Clarke, P., 'Performance by Results Schemes – A Review of Trends', *Industrial Relations News* no. 8, 23 Feb. 1989.
23. Long, P., *op. cit.*

Chapter 8 (pp. 154 – 79)
1. See, for example, Manpower Services Commission, *Adult training in Britain*, IFF Research Ltd, Report, Sheffield, MSC 1985; Beer, M. *et al., Human Resource Management: A General Manager's Perspective*, The Free Press/Macmillan 1985.

2. Advisory Committee on Management Training, *Managers for Ireland: The Case for the Development of Irish Managers*, Government Publications Office 1988.
3. See, for example, Owens, D., 'Systematic Training', *IITD News* May 1986.
4. Garavan, T.N., 'Promoting natural learning activities within the organisation', *Journal of European Industrial Training* vol. 11, no. 7, 1987.
5. See, for example, Bass, B.M. & Vaughan, J.A., *Training in industry; the management of learning*, Tavistock Publications, London, 1966; Jenkins, D., 'Designing and Resourcing training' in Guest, D. and Kenny, T. (eds.), *A textbook of techniques and strategies in Personnel Management*, IPM 1983.
6. See, for example, Flanaghan, V., 'Analysing Training Needs', *IITD News* August 1986.
7. Walters, B., 'Identifying training needs' in Guest, D. and Kenny, T., *op. cit.*
8. See, for example, Armstrong, M., *A Handbook of Personnel Management Practice*, Kogan Page 1988.
9. Patrick, P., 'What's new in training' *Personnel Management* Sept. 1984.
10. Mager, R., *Preparing instructional objectives*, Fearon, San Francisco 1984.
11. Jenkins, D., *op. cit.*
12. *Ibid.*
13. See, for example, Kirkpatrick, D.L., 'Techniques for evaluating programmes', *Journal of the American Society of Training Directors* vol. 13, 1959; Whitelaw, M., *The evaluation of management training - a review*, IPM 1972; Warr, P., Bird, M. & Rackman, N., *Evaluation of management training*, Gower 1970; Hamblin, A.C., *Evaluation and control of training*, McGraw-Hill 1974.
14. Kenny, J. & Reid, M., *Training interventions*, IPM 1986.
15. *Ibid.*
16. *Ibid.*, for a useful review of possible structures and role of the training function.
17. Leigh Doyle, S. & McGennis, B., *Role of Training Managers in Irish Industry*, AnCO 1983.
18. Shivanath, G., 'Personnel Practitioners 1986: Their Role and Status in Irish Industry', unpublished MBS thesis, NIHE Limerick 1987.
19. Armstrong, M., *op. cit.*
20. Rowlandson, P., 'The oddity of OD', *Management Today* 1984.
21. McLean, A., 'Organisation Development: A Case of the Emperor's New Clothes', *Personnel Review* vol. IV, no. 1, 1981.
22. Leach, J., 'The notion and nature of careers', *Personnel Administration* Sept. 1977.
23. See, for example, Keenay, G.A., 'The Camel Model: a model for career planning in a hierarchy', *Personnel Review* vol. 6, no. 4, Autumn 1977; Fletcher, C., *Performance appraisal and career development*, Hutchinson 1985; Schien, E.H., *Career development: Theoretical and practical issues for organisations*, ILO Management Development Series no. 12, 1985.
24. For greater detail see Beach, D.S., *Personnel: The Management of people at work*, Macmillan 1980; Walker, J.W., 'Does career planning rock the boat?' *Human Resource Management* Spring 1978.
25. See, for example, Walker, J.W., *ibid.*; Super, D.E., *The Psychology of Careers: An Introduction to Vocational Development*, Harper and Bros 1957.

26. Garavan, T.N. & Gurren, P., *Career Development Practices in Irish Industry*, Industrial and Commercial Training International (Forthcoming).
27. For an indication of how organisations can best facilitate learning/development see Garavan, T.N., 'The organisation as a learning environment: Its nature and implications', *Arena* 1987. For a review of the factors which influence an organisation's approach to training and development see Pettigrew, A., Sparrow, P. & Hendry, C., 'The Forces That Trigger Training', *Personnel Management* December 1988.
28. Kenny, J. & Reid, M., *op. cit.*
29. Dillon, A., 'Managerial Obsolesence', unpublished BBS thesis, NIHE Limerick 1986.
30. Institute of Personnel Management, *The IPM Code on Continuous Development*, IPM 1984.
31. Advisory Committee on Management Training, *op. cit.*

Chapter 9 (pp. 180 – 226)
1. *Report of the Commission of Inquiry of Industrial Relations*, Government Publications Office, Dublin 1981.
2. See for example, Shivanath, G., 'Personnel Practitioners 1986: Their Role and Status in Irish Industry', unpublised MBS thesis, NIHE Limerick 1987; Keating, M., 'Personnel Management in Ireland' in *Industrial Relations in Ireland: Contemporary Issues and Developments*, UCD 1987; Mackay, L. & Torrington, D., *The Changing Nature of Personnel Management*, IPM 1986.
3. Brannick, T. & Kelly, A., 'Voluntarism and order in Trade Unions: Union officials' attitudes to unofficial strike action' in *Industrial Relations in Ireland: Contemporary Issues and Developments*, *op. cit.*
4. Roche, B., 'Social Partnership and Political Control: State Strategy and Industrial Relations in Ireland' in Kelly, M. *et al.* (eds), *Power, Conflict and Inequality*, Turoe Press 1982; 'State Strategies and the Politics of Industrial Relations in Ireland since 1945' in *Industrial Relations in Ireland: Contemporary Issues and Developments, op. cit.*
5. Hillery, B., 'Legislation: Has it a useful role to play' in *Industrial Relations in Ireland: Contemporary Issues and Developments, op. cit.*
6. Roche, B., *op. cit.*
7. See, for example, McCarthy, C., *The decade of Upheaval; Irish Trade Unions in the Nineteen Sixties*, IPA 1973; *Trade Unions in Ireland 1894-1960* IPA 1977; Roche, B., *op. cit.*
8. For a comprehensive review of Irish Trade Union law see Kerr, A. & Whyte, G., *Irish Trade Union Law*, Professional Books 1985 or, for a more concise overview, Kerr, T., 'Trade Unions and the law' in *Industrial Relations in Ireland: Contemporary Issues and Developments, op. cit.*
9. See Armstrong, M., *A Handbook of Personnel Management Practice*, Kogan Page 1988.
10. The classification of Irish trade unions into different types must be utilised carefully as few unions can now be seen as falling purely into one classification. Some craft unions will accept certain semi-skilled workers into membership. General unions will have craft and white collar members. Therefore, the classification should be seen as indicative of ideal union classifications. See

Hyman, R., *Industrial Relations: A Marxist Introduction*, Macmillan London 1975.

11. Kelly, A. & Bourke, P., *Management Labour and Consumer*, Gill and Macmillan 1979.
12. Roche, B. & Larragy, J., 'The trend of unionisation in the Irish Republic' in *Industrial Relations in Ireland: Contemporary Issues and Developments, op. cit.*
13. *Ibid.*
14. Roche, B., 'Ireland: Trade Unions in Ireland in the 1980s', *European Industrial Relations Review* no. 176, Sept. 1988.
15. *Ibid.*
16. For a more detailed account of trade union activities at workplace level see Murphy, T., 'The Union Committee at the Workplace' in *Industrial Relations in Ireland: Contemporary Issues and Developments, op. cit.*
17. For a detailed outline of the structure and operation of the ICTU see Hillery, B., 'The Irish Congress of Trade Unions' and Cassells, P., 'The Organisation of Trade Union in Ireland', both in *Industrial Relations in Ireland: Contemporary Issues and Developments, op. cit.*
18. See Schregle, J., *Restructuring the Irish Trade Union Movement*, ICTU 1975.
19. Wallace, J. & O'Shea, F., *A Study of Unofficial Strikes in Ireland*, Government Publications Office 1987.
20. McCarthy, C., *Trade Unions In Ireland 1894-1960, op.cit.*
21. Roche, B. & Larragy, J., *op. cit.*
22. Brannick, T. & Kelly, A., *op. cit.*
23. Marchington, M., *Managing Industrial Relations*, McGraw-Hill 1982; a study by Flood, P., 'Trade Union Government and Membership Participation in the Irish Transport and General Workers' Union', Ph.D thesis (unpublished), London School of Economics, 1988, argues that unions are more accurately described in terms of polyarchic control structures rather than pure democracies or oligarchies.
24. *Educational Company of Ireland V. Fitzpatrick and others*, IR 345 1961; Von Prondzynski, F., 'Collective Labour Law' in *Industrial Relations in Ireland: Contemporary Issues and Developments, op. cit.*
25. Abbott and Whelan V. Southern Health Board, Unreported 1981.
26. *Report of the Commission of Inquiry on Industrial Relations*, Government Publications Office 1981.
27. Roche, B., 'Ireland: Trade Unions in the 1980s', *op. cit.*
28. See, for example, Mc Govern, P., 'Increasing Opposition to Unionisation in the 1980s' *Industrial Relations News* no. 45, 24 Nov. 1988; 'Trade Union Recognition: Five Case Studies' *Industrial Relations News* no. 6, 9 Feb. 1989.
29. For a comprehensive review of the Rights Commissioner service see Connaughton, M., 'A study of the Rights Commissioner service in the Republic of Ireland', Unpublished MBS dissertation, UCD 1982.
30. Labour Court Annual Reports.
31. For a useful review of the operation of Joint Labour Committees see McMahon, G.V., 'The Joint Labour Committee System' in *Industrial Relations in Ireland: Contemporary Issues and Developments, op. cit.*
32. Kelly, A., 'The Rights Commissioner: Conciliator, Mediator, or Arbitrator?' in *Industrial Relations in Ireland: Contemporary Issues and Developments, op. cit.*

33. Readers are referred to Von Prondzynski, F. & McCarthy, C., *Employment Law*, Sweet and Maxwell 1984; Redmond, M. *Redmonds Guide to Irish Labour Law*, Blackfoot Press 1984; Kerr, A. & Whyte, G., *op. cit.*

34. Department of the Public Service Estimates 1987.

35. Cox, B. & Hughes, J., 'Industrial Relations in the Public Sector' in *Industrial Relations in Ireland: Contemporary Issues and Developments, op. cit.*

36. Report of the Committee on Inquiry on Industrial Relations, *op. cit.*

37. For a useful classification of appropriate adjudication bodies for different categories of public sector employees see Cox, B. & Hughes, J., *op. cit.*

38. For a useful commentary on the operation of the Civil Service Scheme see Gaffney, S., 'Industrial Relations in the Public Sector', Paper presented at the National Conference on Industrial Relations, Galway Regional Technical College Oct. 1979.

39. For an outline of the success of conciliation in the Civil Service Scheme see Dowling, J., 'The structure of Civil Service Staff Relations 1922-1983' Unpublished research dissertation, TCD 1985.

40. Smith, A., *The Wealth of Nations*, Pelican 1970.

41. Oechslin, J., 'Employers' organisations' in Blanpain, R. (ed) *Labour Law and Industrial Relations*, Kluwer 1985.

42. Department of Labour, 1987.

43. Pollock, H. & O'Dwyer L., *We can work it out: Relationships in the workplace*, O'Brien Press 1985.

44. Windmuller, J.P., 'Employers Associations in Comparative Perspective; Organisation, Structure and Administration' in Windmuller, J.P. & Gladstone, A., *Employer Associations and Industrial Relations*, Clarendon, Oxford 1984.

45. *Ibid.*

46. Thomason, G., *A Textbook of Industrial Relations Practice*, IPM 1984.

47. Brown, W, *et al.*, *The Changing Contours of British Industrial Relations*, Blackwell, Oxford 1981.

48. Purcell, J. & Sisson, K., 'Strategies and Practice in the Management of Industrial Relations' in Bain, G. (ed), *Industrial Relations in Britain*, Blackwell, Oxford 1983.

49. See, for example, Oechslin, J., *op. cit.*

50. See, for example, *Collective Bargaining in Industrialised Market Economies*, ILO 1975.

51. Government Social Survey (UK), Workplace Industrial Relations, HMSO 1968.

52. Brown, W. *et al., op. cit.*; Daniel, W.W. & Millwards, N., *Workplace Industrial Relations in Britain*, Heinemann 1983.

53. Sisson, K., 'Employer Organisations' in Bain, G. (ed), *Industrial Relations in Britain, op. cit.*

54. Ridgely, P., 'How relevant is the FUE' *Irish Business* Feb. 1988.

55. Reynaud, J.P. *et al.*, 'Problems and prospects for collective bargaining in the EEC member states', Commission of the European Community *Document no. V/394/78-EN* Brussels 1978.

56. Brown, W. *et al., op. cit.*; Daniel, W.W. & Millward, N., *op. cit.*

57. Brown, W. *et al., op.cit.*; Daniel, W.W. & Millwards, N., *op.cit.*

58. Gunnigle, P., 'Management Approaches to Industrial Relations in Small Firms' in *Industrial Relations in Ireland: Contemporary Issues and Developments, op. cit.*

59. Sisson, K., *op. cit.*
60. Brown, W. *et al., op. cit.*
61. Butler, P., 'Employer Organisations: A Study', unpublished BBS project, NIHE Limerick 1985.
62. FUE Annual Reports 1980-1985; CIF Annual Reports 1980-1984; Labour Court Annual Reports 1980-1985.
63. For a useful review of employer objectives in employee relations see Thomason, G., *op. cit.*
64. *Ibid.*
65. *Ibid.*
66. Purcell, J. & Sisson, K., 'Strategies and Practice in the Management of Industrial Relations' in Bain, G. (ed.), *op. cit.*
67. Daniel, W.W. & Millward, N., *op. cit.*
68. Wallace, J., *Industrial Relations in Limerick City and its Environs*, NIHE Limerick 1982.
69. Warr, P., *The Psychology of Collective Bargaining*, Hutchinson 1973; Buchanan, D.A. & Huczynski, A.A., *Organisational Behaviour: An Introductory Text*, Prentice-Hall 1985.
70. Fox, A., *Industrial Sociology and Industrial Relations*, Research Paper no. 3 to the Royal Commission on Trade Unions and Employers' Associations HMSO 1966.
71. Thelen, H. & Withall J., 'Human Relations' (1949) quoted by Fox, A., *op. cit.*
72. Marchington, M., *op.cit.*
73. Purcell, J. & Sisson, K., *op. cit.*; for further analysis of this approach see Deaton, D., 'Management Style and Large Scale Survey Evidence', *Industrial Relations Journal* vol. 16, no. 2, Summer 1985.
74. Walton, R. & McKersie R., *A Behavioural Theory of Labour Negotiations*, McGraw-Hill 1965.
75. See, for example, Burrows, G., *No-strike agreements and pendulum arbitration*, IPM 1984; Bassett, P., *Strike Free; New Industrial Relations in Britain*, Macmillan 1986.
76. For a review of developments in Ireland see Hannaway, C., *New style collective agreements — an Irish approach*, IRN Report no. 13, 26 March 1987; Sheehan, B., *New style collective agreements — IMI Seminar*, IRN Report no. 14, 2 April 1987.
77. Wallace, J., 'Procedure Agreements and their Place in Workplace Industrial Relations' in *Industrial Relations in Ireland: Contemporary Issues and Developments, op. cit.*

Chapter 10 (pp. 227 – 70)
1. Shivanath, G., 'Personnel Practitioners 1986: Their Role and Status in Irish Industry', unpublished MBS thesis, NIHE Limerick 1987; also see Keating, M., 'Personnel Management in Ireland' in *Industrial Relations in Ireland; Contemporary Issues and Developments*, UCD 1987; Mackay, L. & Torrington, D., *The Changing Nature of Personnel Management*, IPM 1986.
2. McCarthy, C., *The Decade of Upheaval*, IPA 1975.
3. O'Brien, J.F., 'Pay Determination in Ireland' in *Industrial Relations in Ireland: Contemporary Issues and Developments, op. cit.*

4. Kinnie, N.J., 'Changing Management Strategies in Industrial Relations', *Industrial Relations Journal* vol. 16, no. 4, 1985: 'Single Employer Bargaining; Structures & Strategies', *Industrial Relations Journal vol.* 14, no. 3, 1983; 'Patterns of Industrial Relations Management', *Employee Relations*, vol. 8, no. 2, 1986.

5. See, for example, Roche, B., 'Ireland: Trade Unions in the 1980s', *European Industrial Relations Review 176*, Sept. 1988.

6. See, for example, Atkinson, G., *The Effective Negotiator*, Quest Research Publications 1977; Hawkins, K., *A Handbook of Industrial Relations Practice*, Kogan Page 1979; Sisson, K., *Negotiating in Practice*, IPM 1977; Warr, P., *Psychology and Collective Bargaining*, Hutchinson 1973; Scott, B., *The Skills of Negotiating*, Gower 1981; Fisher, R. & Ury, W., *Getting to Yes*, Hutchinson 1981.

7. Walton, R.E. & McKersie, R.B., *A Behavioural Theory of Labour Negotiations*, McGraw-Hill 1965.

8. *Ibid*; also see Chamberlain, N.W. & Kuhn, J.W., *Collective Bargaining*, McGraw-Hill 1965.

9. Sisson, K., *op. cit.*

10. Hawkins, K., *op.cit.*

11. For a useful discussion of procedure agreements see Wallace, J., 'Procedure Agreements and their Place in Workplace Industrial Relations' in *Industrial Relations in Ireland: Contemporary Issues and Developments, op. cit.*

12. Nierenberg, G.I., *The Art of Negotiating*, Cornerstone NY 1968.

13. *Ibid.*

14. Canning, L., 'Negotiating in Industrial Relations', unpublished, IMI 1979.

15. Hawkins, K., *op. cit.*

16. Cole, G.A., *Personnel Management: Theory and Practice*, DPP Publications 1986.

17. Fisher, R. and Ury, W., *op. cit.*

18. Scott, B., *op. cit*; Nierenberg, G.I., *op. cit.*; Atkinson, G., *op. cit.*

19. Fox, A., 'Industrial Sociology and Industrial Relations' *Research Paper no. 3 to the Donovan Report*, HMSO 1966; *Man-Management* Hutchinson 1974.

20. Allen, V., *The Sociology of Industrial Relations*, Longman 1971.

21. See, for example, Hyman, R., *Industrial Relations: A Marxist Introduction*, Macmillan 1976.

22. For a review of explanations of industrial conflict see Worsley, P. (ed), *Introducing Sociology*, Penguin 1977.

23. Bean, R., 'Industrial Reactions' in Cohen, E. & Studdard, G., *The Bargaining Context*, Arrow 1976.

24. For an in depth analysis of strike action see Hyman, R., *Strikes*, Fontana 1972 or Crouch, C., *Trade Unions: The logic of collective action*, Fontana 1982.

25. For an excellent outline of different forms of strike action and discussion of unofficial strikes in Ireland see Wallace, J. & O'Shea, F., *A Study of Unofficial Strikes in Ireland*, Government Publications Office 1987; also Wallace, J., 'Unofficial Strikes in Ireland', *Industrial Relations News*, nos. 8 and 9, 25 February and 3 March 1988.

26. For a comprehensive overview of Irish strike patterns see Kelly, A. & Brannick, T., 'The Changing Contours of Irish Industrial Conflict' Unpublished Paper

presented to the International Polish/Irish Conference, University of Warsaw 1989; Also see Kelly, A. & Brannick, T., 'Strikes in Ireland: Measurement, Indices and Trends' in *Industrial Relations in Ireland: Contemporary Issues and Developments, op. cit.*

27. Kelly, A. & Brannick, T., 'The Pattern of Strike Activity in Ireland, 1960-1979: Some Preliminary Observations', *Irish Journal of Adminsitrative and Business Research (IBAR)* vol. 5, no. 1, April 1983.
28. *Ibid.*
29. Kelly, A. & Brannick, T., 'The Changing Contours of Irish Industrial Conflict', *op. cit.*
30. *Ibid.*
31. Kelly, A. & Brannick, T., 'Explaining the strike-proneness of British companies in Ireland', *British Journal of Industrial Relations* vol. 26, no. 1, March 1988.
32. Kelly, A. & Brannick, T., 'The Changing Contours of Irish Industrial Conflict', *op. cit.*
33. Wallace, J. & O'Shea, F., *op. cit.*
34. *Ibid.*
35. Jackson, M., *Industrial Relations: A Textbook*, Kogan Page 1982.
36. Wallace, J., 'Procedure Agreements and their Place in Workplace Industrial Relations' *op. cit.*
37. Humphrey, P., *How to be your own personnel manager,* IPM 1979.
38. See, for example, Wallace, J., *op. cit.*
39. Hawkins, K., *op. cit.*
40. For a useful discussion on the interpretation and operation of conciliation, mediation and arbitration in the Republic of Ireland see Kelly, A., 'The Rights Commissioner: Conciliator, Mediator or Arbitrator' in *Industrial Relations in Ireland: Contemporary Issues and Developments, op. cit.*
41. Horgan, J., 'The Future of Collective Bargaining', Paper presented to the Annual Conference of the IPM in Ireland, Galway 1985.
42. See, for example, Wallace, J., 'Workplace aspects of unofficial strikes', *Industrial Relations News* no. 9, 3 March 1988; 'Procedure Agreements and their Place in Workplace Industrial Relations' *op. cit.*
43. *Ibid.*
44. See for example, Von Prondzynski, F., 'Operating a disciplinary procedure—The essential requirements', *Industrial Relations News Report* (IRN Report) no. 45, 26 November 1982.
45. Advisory Conciliation Arbitration Service (ACAS) 'Disciplinary Practices and Procedures in Employment', *Code of Practice no.1, Employment,* HMSO 1977.
46. *Ibid.*
47. Summary dismissal means dismissal in the first instance of an offence. It will normally take place after a thorough investigation of facts where the employee has been given a chance to state his case and access to representation.
48. ACAS, *op. cit.*
49. Hawkins, K., *op. cit.*
50. National Engineering and Electrical Trade Union (NEETU) V. Mc Connell, ILRM 422 1983.

51. Wallace, J. & O'Shea, F., *op. cit.*; for a further discussion of employee's 'leniency' or 'indulgency' expectation of management behaviour see Gouldner, A.W., *Wildcat Strike*, Harper NY 1954.
52. Murphy, T., 'The Dismissal Issue in Industrial Relations: Employers and Trade Unions show improved performances since 1977', *IRN* no. 29, 24 July 1986; 'The Impact of the Unfair Dismissals Act, 1977 on Workplace Industrial Relations' in *Industrial Relations in Ireland: Contemporary Issues and Developments, op. cit.*
53. O'Connor, K., 'The impact of the Unfair Dismissals Act, 1977 on Personnel Management and Industrial Relations', *Journal of Irish Business and Administrative Research* vol. 5, no. 2, 1982.
54. Murphy, T., *op. cit.*; Lennon, P., 'The Unfair Dismissals Act 1977 – A Critical Evaluation', *IRN* no. 21, 1983.
55. Meenan, F., 'A Survey of Unfair Dismissal Cases 1977-1984', *FUE Bulletin Supplement* June 1985.
56. Lennon, P., *op. cit.*
57. Department of Labour, 1988.
58. Armstrong, M., *A Handbook of Personnel Management Practice*, Kogan Page 1988.
59. Von Prondzynski, F. & Mc Carthy, C. *Employment Law*, Sweet and Maxwell 1984; this text also contains a comprehensive overview of Health, Safety and Welfare law in Ireland.
60. Safety, Health and Welfare at Work Bill 1988, Government Publications Office 1988.
61. Department of Labour, *Note on the Health, Safety and Welfare at Work Bill 1988*, Government Information Services 1988.
62. A series of useful guidelines on the effective management of health and safety at work have been published by the National Industrial and Safety Organisation (NISO).
63. Arnscott, P. & Armstrong, M., *An Employer's Guide to Health and Safety Management*, Kogan Page 1977.
64. Walsh, W. & Russell, L., *ABC of Industrial Safety*, Pitman 1974.
65. See, for example, Chamberlain, N.W., *The Union Challenge to Management Control*, Harper 1948; Schregle, J., 'Labour Relations in Western Europe: Some Topical Issues', *International Labour Review* Jan. June 1974.
66. Coates, K. & Topham, A. (eds), *Industrial Democracy in Great Britain*, McGibbon and Kee 1968.
67. See, for example, the definition of employee participation adopted by the Advisory Committee on Worker Participation in their Report to the Minister for Labour, Government Stationery Office, 1986 or the aims of employee participation as outlined in the Code of Practice on Employee Participation published jointly by the Industrial Participation Association and the Institute of Personnel Management, *Employee Involvement and Participation: Principles and Standards of Practice*, IPM/IPA 1983.
68. Mulvey, C., *Industrial Democracy: A Report by the Federated Union of Employers and the Confederation of Irish Industry*, FUE/C11 Dublin, undated.
69. Kelly, A., 'The Worker Director in Irish Industrial Relations' in *Industrial Relations in Ireland: Contemporary Issues and Developments, op. cit.*

70. Kelly draws on the findings of two studies on Board Level Participation in Ireland: Murphy, T. & Walsh, D., *The Worker Director and his impact on the enterprise: Expectations, Experience and Effectiveness in Seven Irish Companies*, IPC 1980 and an unpublished survey undertaken by the Department of Industrial Relations UCD; See also, Galvin, D., 'Worker Participation Survey', dissertation, NIHE Limerick 1980.
71. Kelly, A., *op. cit.*
72. IPM/IPA Code of Practice, *op. cit.*
73. Morrissey, T.J., 'Employee Participation at Sub-Board Level' in *Industrial Relations in Ireland: Contemporary Issues and Developments, op. cit.*
74. Kelly, A., 'The Nature of Worker Participation in Ireland: The incongruity of European and Irish industrial relations structures', Paper presented at the National Conference on Industrial Relations, Galway Regional Technical College, 1979.
75. For a useful review of the Quality of Working Life Movement see Schuler, R.S., *Personnel and Human Resource Management*, West Publishing Company 1987.
76. Morrissey, T.J., *op. cit.*
77. Whelan, C., 'Worker Priorities, Trust in Management and Prospects for Worker Participation', *Paper 111*, Economic and Social Research Institute 1982.
78. *Ibid.*
79. Brewer, R., 'Personnel's role in participation', *Personnel Management* Sept. 1978.

Chapter 11 (pp. 271 – 98)
1. Cordova, E., 'From Full-time Wage Employment to Atypical Employment: A Major Shift in the Evolution of Labour Relations', *International Labour Review* vol. 125, no. 6, Nov. Dec. 1989; Dineen, D., *Changing Employment Patterns in Ireland: Recent Trends and Future Prospects*, Final Report for the Irish National Pensions Board, 1989;
2. See Conference Papers, International Conference on 'The Changing Nature of Employment: New Forms and New Areas', BIPE Paris 1987.
3. Dineen, D., *op.cit.*
4. *Ibid.*
5. *Ibid.*
6. Government White Paper on Manpower Policy, Stationery Office, Dublin, 1985.
7. Dineen, D., *op. cit.*
8. Garavan, T. & O'Dwyer, D., 'Management consultants: Their Use by Personnel Departments' *Industrial Relations News* no. 37, Oct. 1987.
9. Atkinson, J.S., 'Flexibility: Planning for an Uncertain Future', *Manpower Policy and Practice* vol. 1 Summer.
10. Innes, J., 'The Question of Flexibility', Personnel Review 17 March 1988.
11. Atkinson, J., *Flexible Manning: The Way Ahead*, Brighton, IMS/Manpower Ltd, 1984.
12. Innes, J., *op. cit.*
13. See *Industrial Relations News* no. 41. 27 Oct. 1988.
14. Evans & Walker in Curtin, C. (eds), *Flexible Patterns of Work*, IPM 1986.
15. Suttle, S., 'Labour Market Flexibility' *Industrial Relations News* 38, 6 October 1988.

16. Handy. C., *The Future of Work – A Guide to a Changing Society*, Blackwell, 1984.
17. Hunter, L., 'Some Aspects of Flexible Decisions', International Conference on 'The Changing Nature of Employment: New Forms and New Areas', *op. cit.*
18. Handy, C., *op.cit.*
19. Department of Labour, 'Unfair Dismissals, Employment Equality, Payment of Wages', *Discussion Document,* Dept. of Labour 1987.
20. See *Industrial Relations News* no. 2, 12 Jan. 1989.
21. Keenan, & Thom, 'The Future Through the Keyhole', *Personnel Review* vol 17, no.1, 1988.
22. Kenny, T., 'New Roles for the Personnel Manager' in Fowler, S. (ed.), *The Personnel Management Handbook*, London 1987.
23. Handy, C., *Understanding Organisations*, Penguin, 1987.
24. Tyson, S. & Fell, A., *Evaluating the Personnel Function*, Hutchinson, 1986.
25. Toner, B., 'Union or Non-Union—Employee Relations Strategies in the Republic of Ireland', unpublished PhD thesis, London School of Economics and Political Science, 1987.
26. Foulkes, F., *Personnel Policies in Large Non-Union Companies*, Prenctice Hall 1980.
27. See, for example 'Bank of Ireland – New Recruit Projections', *Industrial Relations News* no. 3, 19 Jan. 1989.
28. *Ibid.*
29. Grafton, D., 'Current Trends in Employee Relations', Paper presented to MBA Class, University of Limerick, 1989.
30. *Sunday Tribune*, 15 January 1989.
31. 'Payment Systems in Ireland', *Report of the European Foundation for the Improvement of Living and Working Conditions,* Dublin, 1986.
32. Weitzman, M., *The Share Economy* MIT Press, Massachussets, 1984.
33. Bradley, K. & Gelb, A., *Shareownership for Employees*, Public Policy Centre, London, 1986.
34. Conte, M. & Tannenbaum, A., 'Employee owned companies: Is the difference measurable', *Monthly Labour Review* July 1978.
35. Kruse, D., *Employee Ownership and Employee Attitudes: Two Case Studies,* Norwood 1984
36. Long, R., 'Worker Ownership and Job Attitudes: A Field Study', *Industrial Relations* 21 Feb. 1982.
37. Murtagh, S., 'Employee Share Ownership in Ireland: Panacea or Pitfall', Unpublished B.P.A. dissertation, University of Limerick, 1988; a study by Flood, P., 'Employee Shareownership and the Search for Competitive Advantage' in *Banking Ireland,* Winter 1989 states that as of September 1989, seventy-one companies had introduced share schemes while one hundred and seventeen companies had introduced share option schemes.
38. Walton, R., 'Challenges in the Management of Technology and Labour Relations' in Walton, R. and Lawrence, P. (eds.), *HRM: Trends and Challenges*, Harvard Business School, 1985.
39. Walton, R., *ibid.*
40. Watson, T., *Management, Organisation and Employment Strategy: New Directions in Theory and Practice*, Routledge & Kegan Paul 1986.

41. *Industrial Relations News* no.15, 21 April 1989.
42. Walton, R., *op. cit.*
43. Clegg, C., 'Information Technology—Personnel Where are you?' *Personnel Review* 15 Jan. 1986; Walton, R., *op. cit.*
44. Bramham, J. & Cox, D., *Personnel Administration Made Simple: Forms, Cards & Computers*, IPM 1984.
45. Owen, G., 'The "Japanisation" Thesis: Some Considerations', *Industrial Relations News* 5, 29 Jan. 1987.
46. Benyon, H., *Working for Ford*, Penguin, 1973.
47. Corr, F., 'Quality Management', *Management* vol. 35, no 9, 1988.
48. Deming, E., *Quality Productivity and Competitive Position*, MIT Centre for Advanced Engineering Study, 1982.
49. Hill, F.,'A Study of Quality Circles in Northern Ireland Manufacturing Industry' *Journal of Irish Business and Administrative Research*, vol. 8, Feb. 1989.
50. Wood, S., 'Researching the New Industrial Relations', *Employee Relations*, vol. 8, May 1986.
51. Owen, G., 'The New Realism and Collective Bargaining – An Alternative View', *Industrial Relations News* 20, 21 May 1987.
52. Roche, B., 'Trade Unions in Ireland in the 1980s' *European Industrial Relations Review* no. 176, Sept. 1988.
53. Handy, C., *op. cit.*
54. Kelly, A. & Brannick, T., 'The Changing Contours of Irish Industrial Conflict', Paper presented to the International Polish/Irish Conference, University of Warsaw 1989; Wallace, J. & O'Shea, F., *A Study of Unofficial Strikes in Ireland*, Government Publications Office 1987.
55. Kelly, A. & Brannick, T., 'Strike Trends in the Irish Private Sector', *Journal of Irish Business and Administrative Research* vol 9, 1988.
56. McGovern, P., 'Trade Union Recognition – Five Case Studies', *Industrial Relations News* no. 6, Feb 1989; also 'Increasing Opposition to Unionisation in the 1980s', *Industrial Relations News* no 45, Nov. 1988.
57. Horgan, J., 'The Future of Collective Bargaining', Paper presented to the annual conference of the IPM in Ireland, Galway 1985.
58. McGovern, P. *op. cit.*

Chapter 12 (pp. 299 – 320)
1. Beer, M. *et al.*, *Human Resource Management: A General Manager's Perspective*, The Free Press/Macmillan 1985.
2. Feigenbaum, A., *Total Quality Control*, McGraw-Hill 1983.
3. Carroll, C., *Building Ireland's Business; Perspectives from PIMS*, Irish Management Institute 1985.
4. Robson, M., *The Journey to Excellence*, Wiley 1986.
5. Beer, M., *et al.*, *op. cit.*
6. Roche, B., 'The Trend of Unionisation in the Irish Republic' in *Industrial Relations in Ireland: Contemporary Issues and Developments*, UCD 1987.
7. Peters, T. & Waterman, R.H., *In Search of Excellence*, Harper & Row 1982; Kanter, R., *The Change Masters*, Counterpoint London 1984.
8. Toner, B., 'The Unionisation and Productivity Debate: An Employee Opinion Survey in Ireland', *British Journal of Industrial Relations* 22 Feb. 1985;

'Union or Non-Union—Employee Relations Strategies in the Republic of Ireland', unpublished Ph.D thesis, London School of Economics 1987.

9. Beer *et al., op. cit.*

10. Guest, D., 'Human Resource Management and Industrial Relations', *Journal of Management Studies* 24 May 1987.

11. Guest, D., 'Personnel and HRM: Can You Tell the Difference?' *Personnel Management* January 1989.

12. Guest, D., 'Human Resource Management; A New Opportunity for Psychologists or Another Passing Fad?, *The Occupational Psychologist* Feb. 1988.

13. Walton, R., 'Towards A Strategy of Eliciting Employee Commitment Based on Policies of Mutuality', in Walton, R. & Lawrence, P., *HRM: Trends and Challenges*, HBS Press 1985.

14. Torrington, D., 'How Does Human Resource Management Change the Personnel Function', *Personnel Review* 17 June 1988.

15. Mackay, L. & Torrington D., *The Changing Nature of Personnel Management*, London IPM, 1986.

16. Armstrong, M., 'Human Resource Management: A Case of the Emperor's New Clothes', *Personnel Management* August 1987.

17. Beer, M., *et al., op. cit.*

18. Guest, D., 'Human Resource Management and Industrial Relations,' *op. cit.*

19. *Ibid.*

20. See earlier chapter on motivation theory.

21. Walton, R., *op. cit.*

22. Guest, D., 'Human Resource Management: A New Opportunity for Psychologists or Just a Passing Fad', *op. cit.*

23. Guest, D., 'Human Resource Management and Industrial Relations, *op. cit.*

24. Flood, P. & Garavan, T., 'HRM, Industrial Relations and the Implications for Unions', *Industrial Relations News* 12 March 1989.

25. Toner, B., 'Union or Non-Union: Employee Relations Strategies in the Republic of Ireland',unpublished PhD thesis London School of Economics 1987; Kelly, A. & Brannick, T. 'Trends in the Management of Human Resources', *Arena* August 1988.

26. Dillon, A., 'Organisational Commitment: A Human Resource Management Perspective', unpublished MBS thesis University of Limerick 1988.

27. Toner, B., 'Union or Non-Union: Employee Relations Strategies in the Republic of Ireland', *op. cit.*

28. Dillon, A., *op. cit.*

29. Storey, J., 'Developments in the Management of Human Resources: An Interim Report', *Warwick Papers in Industrial Relations* 17, 1987.

30. Peters, T., *Thriving on Chaos*, Pan, London 1987.

Index

Numbers in italics refer to figures or tables.

Industrial Development Authority (IDA), 224
Industrial Inspectorate, 260-61
industrial relations
    effect of HRM, 316-20
    new industrial relations, 295-8
    traditional, 180
Industrial Relations Act, 1946, 31
Industrial Relations Act, 1969, 192
Industrial Relations News, 278-9, 290
Industrial Relations Officer, 190-91
industrial revolution, 26-8
industrial sector, 57
industrial unions, 183-4
information technology, 278, 287-8
Innes, J., 275
Institute of Industrial Welfare Workers, 28
Institute of Labour Management, 23, 31
Institute of Manpower Studies
    'atypical' employment forms, 272-4
    flexible firm scenario, 275-87
Institute of Manpower Studies (IMS), 277
Institute of Personnel Management, 7-9, 23, 31, 35, 134
    appraisal interview survey, 148
    appraisal techniques survey, 144-5
    Code on Continuous Development, 177
    codes of practice, 23-5
    employee participation, 266-7
    membership, 24
    recruitment code of practice, 71
Institute of Public Administration, 177
intelligence tests, 90-91
internal constraints, 54
internal equity, 116
internal labour market, 42-3, 55
    drawbacks of, 73
    source of recruitment, 72-4
    workforce profiles, 42
international labour markets, 43
International Labour Organisation, 210
interview conduct, 84-7
    control, 86
    encounter and opening, 85
    listening and note-taking, 87
    number of interviewers, 87-9
    physical setting, 84
    questioning, 86
    structure, 84-5
interviews
    appraisal interview, 148-50
    common errors in, 89

disciplinary, 256-7
interpreting, 89-90
objectives, 82
preparation for, 81-2
types of, 82-4
    biographical, 82-3
    problem-solving/situational, 83-4
    stress, 83
intrinsic motivation, 30, 104-5, 114
Irish Bank Officials Association (IBOA), 184, 188, 284
Irish Biscuits, 279
Irish Cement, 279
Irish Congress of Trade Unions, 186-7
    non-Congress unions, 188
Irish Constitution, 1937, 180, 181, 189, 194
Irish Distillers, 279
Irish Employers Confederation, 200-201, 208
Irish Hotels Federation, 199
Irish Institute of Training and Development, 177
Irish Life, 286
Irish Management Institute, 45, 177, 199
Irish National Teachers Organisation, 183
Irish National Union for Vintners and Allied Trades Assistants, 200
Irish Nurses Union, 188
Irish-owned firms, 22, 212
Irish Planned Sharing Association, 287
Irish Press, 279
Irish Productivity Centre, 287
Irish Shoe and Leather Workers Union, 184
Irish Transport and General Workers Union (ITGWU), 30, 183, 187
Italy, 272

Jacobs, 27
Japanese corporations, 223
    work organisation, 110-12
Japanisation, 291-5, 298
job analysis, 52, 66-7
    and employee development, 160
    and payment structure, 128
job classification, 129, 130-31, 134, 135
job control, 289-90
job description, 67-8
job design, 29
    and job analysis, 66
    and work organisation, 105-13
job enrichment, 107-9

Wood, S., 296
work-groups, 29
work organisation, 29, 105-13
    choice for organisations, 113
    employee influence, 109-10
    job redesign, 107-9, 295
    Theory Z, 111-12
    traditional model, 106-7
work study, 53, 116
worker directors, 266, 268-9
Worker Participation (State Enterprises)
    Acts, 165, 265

workforce management
    competitive advantage, 300-301
    corporate culture, 302
    new organisational models, 302-3
    psychological techniques, 311-12
    strategic perspective, 300-303
    and trade unions, 180, 302
workplace bargaining, 229
works councils, 269
works-to-rule, 239

Xidex, UK Ltd, 277

Yugoslavia, 265